POLITICS, PLANNING, AND THE PUBLIC INTEREST

The Case of Public Housing in Chicago

BY MARTIN MEYERSON

AND EDWARD C. BANFIELD

THE FREE PRESS OF GLENCOE
COLLIER-MACMILLAN LIMITED, LONDON

Printed in the United States of America

FIRST FREE PRESS PAPERBACK EDITION 1964

For information, address:
The Free Press of Glencoe
A Division of The Macmillan Company
The Crowell-Collier Publishing Company
60 Fifth Avenue, New York, N. Y., 10011

Collier-Macmillan Canada, Ltd., Toronto, Ontario

DESIGNED BY SIDNEY SOLOMON

Library of Congress Catalog Card Number: 55-7335

CONTENTS

PREFACE *11*

1. BACKGROUND TO THE CASE STUDY *17*
2. THE ORGANIZATION AND ITS TASKS *29*
3. THE POLITICIANS *61*
4. THE CLIMATE OF NEIGHBORHOOD OPINION *91*
5. THE DEVELOPMENT OF POLICY *121*
6. THE STRUGGLE BEGINS *153*
7. CLIMAX *189*
8. SETTLEMENT *225*
9. POLITICS *253*
10. PLANNING *269*
11. THE PUBLIC INTEREST *285*

SUPPLEMENT: NOTE ON CONCEPTUAL SCHEME *303*

MAP APPENDIX *331*

ACKNOWLEDGMENTS AND REFERENCE NOTES *338*

INDEX TO PARTICULAR CONCEPTS *346*

GENERAL INDEX *348*

PREFACE

Housing is, in fact, one of the great universal tests in this difficult and dangerous postwar world: a test of ideals, ideas, skills, resources; of our democratic capacity for change and growth; of the effectiveness of both private enterprise and government and their ability to cooperate; of the intelligence of consumer and voter as well as producer and administrator. If we in America with all our resources cannot even solve our own housing problem, what hope is there?

—National Public Housing Conference
February 1948.

THIS IS A STUDY of how some important decisions were reached in a large American city. The city is Chicago and the decisions had to do mainly with the location of public housing projects. Through the analysis of this particular case we endeavor to bring empirical and theoretical materials together in a way which will further the development of the theory of decision-making and impart wider significance to the concrete data.

Chicago is the second largest city in the United States and the sixth largest in the world (there are 35 independent nations with smaller populations). From a practical standpoint, therefore, the workings of its government would be worth study even if there were no other municipal governments at all comparable. In fact, of course, many other governments resemble that of Chicago in some important respects.*

The question of how much and what kind of public housing

* Indeed, Chicago combines many of what are usually considered the worst features of American municipal administration: it is only one of several autonomous taxing units having the same geographic base, its legal boundaries do not coincide even approximately with the metropolitan area, it is dominated by the state legislature, it has a weak mayor government, a long ballot, a great many small wards, a large number of virtually independent city departments and agencies, a planning commission with little power, and a political machine with much power.

a city should have and where it should be located is also of practical importance. Public housing is "big business" in the United States (roughly, there are 900 local authorities administering 400,000 units of housing in which 1,500,000 persons live) and slums are on the increase in all large cities. There is a strong possibility—particularly in the event of a major depression—that much more public housing will be built; many cities are facing, have faced or will face decisions very much like those that were made in Chicago.

The reader should be cautioned, however, against inferring that the political history of public housing in other cities has been identical with that of Chicago. Generally speaking, the interests which came in conflict in other cities were very much like those which came in conflict in Chicago. The rhetoric of the conflict was also generally very much the same. But there were nevertheless differences of great importance from city to city: for example, the question of whether Negroes were to be segregated in public housing projects was of great importance in San Francisco as it was in Chicago, but whereas in Chicago it was the Housing Authority which opposed segregation and the City Council which favored it (although not openly), in San Francisco it was the other way around. How far, then, can the facts of the Chicago case be taken as descriptive of the situation in other cities? The best answer to such a question is probably that the Chicago experiences should sensitize the reader to certain influences and relationships which are likely to be found, although not in exactly the same form, in most other cities. In short, acquaintance with what happened in Chicago may give the student of the public housing issue some indication of what to look for in other cities.

Furthermore, even though it does not parallel them exactly, the case of public housing in Chicago should be suggestive for certain classes of issues which do not involve housing. Decisions about site selection are likely to have a certain amount in common whether the facility is a public housing project, a sewage disposal plant, a tuberculosis sanitorium, a superhighway, or even a church or school. And since decisions regarding locations, along with decisions regarding budget amounts, are the form in which city planning usually comes into political focus (a comprehensive plan as such is almost never the subject of serious political discussion or action), issues and problems like those described in this volume are the familiar concern of planners and politicians.

In addition, as the reader of the supplemental note will see, the logic of the planning process is essentially the same whether the planning be done by an agency like a housing authority which is concerned primarily with a single function and secondarily with other functions or by an agency like a city planning commission which is no more concerned with one function than with others.

Viewed in a still more restricted focus, i.e., as a measure for relieving the congestion of the inner city, the public housing site selection issue has further general significance. All measures for reducing congestion or for rebuilding central areas must move people to unbuilt areas which are most often on the outskirts of the city. This is everywhere likely to be fraught with political difficulties since a population equilibrium—and thus a political one—is altered; this is especially true if the people who are to move are of different class or ethnicity than those who already live in the outlying areas. Thus, any city which undertakes to "decant" its population is almost sure to encounter problems similar to (although of course not identical with) those encountered by public housing in Chicago.* In the northern industrial cities of the United States where the inner congested slum areas are largely inhabited by Negroes, the parallel will probably be especially close.

Obviously we can not describe or "explain" all of the decisions pertinent to public housing in Chicago. Even if one omits decisions made by individual members of the electorate, thousands of people participated in this decision-making process and some of them have made thousands of decisions. Some of these decisions were of little or no consequence (e.g., a carpenter's decision to drive a particular nail into a particular board).

We have used various criteria to decide which decisions to

---

* The English "New Towns," for example, have met some difficulties very similar to those which were met in Chicago. See the account of Stevenage by Harold Orlans in *Utopia Ltd.*, Yale University Press, New Haven, 1953.

examine and which to ignore. We focus on certain decisions made by the Chicago Housing Authority and on certain related decisions made in the local political structure (particularly the City Council, the Mayor, the Plan Commission and influential opinion-interest groups) and made by the Public Housing Administration and others in Washington. These selected decisions deal mainly with the kind of housing program aimed at under the terms of the general Housing Act of 1949, especially as related to location of projects and racial composition of occupancy, and to a small degree, architectural type.

Another set of criteria for the selection of relevant decisions derives from theory: we take account of decisions only if, and only insofar as, they have to do with "politics," "planning" or "the public interest," conceptions which are explained in a supplement which is the work of Banfield. The index to concepts which appears at the end of the book should help readers see the relations between the theoretical and empirical materials.

Some practical-minded readers may be disappointed that we have not ended the study with a list of specific "major recommendations for action." The reason is that our purpose has been both to describe how administrative and political decisions are made and to provide a framework of analysis which will enable the reader to see how better decisions might be made. In other words, we are not interested—except incidentally and mainly for illustrative purposes—in making specific recommendations having application to the Chicago scene (to do this would require much more time and far more facilities than we have possessed) but in developing a perspective for the analysis of decision-making processes in general.

We chose site selection in Chicago as the case to be studied partly because Meyerson was in charge of planning for the Chicago Housing Authority during the period with which we are most concerned. We expected that this circumstance would afford us a more intimate view of that decision-making process than we could obtain of any other; in some respects it did, but the very closeness of Meyerson's connection with the Authority was in some ways a handicap: we have been prevented by certain obligations from saying some things which an outsider would have little difficulty in discovering and perhaps no hesitation in saying. The present study contains nothing, so far as we know, that an energetic investigator outside of the organization could not have learned from published materials, from public records and from interviews with the decision-makers themselves. All of them, we found, were quite willing to talk about the way decisions were reached.

What we have written illustrates the impossibility of achieving full relevance to immediate and practical issues while avoiding judgments which are not rigorously substantiated and which perforce often cannot be so substantiated. We have made extensive use of participant-observation and of interviews with leading actors. We have also relied heavily on documents—minutes, memoranda, speeches, newspaper files and so on—to supplement first-hand accounts. We have not been able to avoid the necessity of making judgments, however, and where it seemed necessary in order to achieve relevance, we have not hesitated to make conjectures or to record the conjectures of informants. While we have indicated conjectures by signal-words such as "perhaps," "seems to be" and so forth, we have not always documented the source of the conjecture because to do so might violate someone's privacy.

It should be kept in mind, that the events described here occurred several years ago and that the agencies mentioned may have changed considerably since.* The reader perhaps also should be warned that our standard of good planning—rational decision-making—is an ideal one; the standard is, we think, useful for analysis, but real organizations (like real people), if the truth is told, do not make decisions in a substantially rational manner.

* Indeed, since this study went to press, Elizabeth Wood, the staff head of the Chicago Housing Authority and a main actor in our account, was replaced by Lieutenant General William B. Kean.

Left High and Dry

CHAPTER ONE □ □ □ □ □ □

BACKGROUND TO THE CASE STUDY

OUR PURPOSE in the following several chapters is to describe in detail how decisions were reached regarding sites for low-rent public housing in Chicago after passage of the general Housing Act of 1949. To put the Chicago events in the perspective of national trends in public housing policy, a brief note on the development of public housing in the United States may be helpful.

The Federal government first provided public housing in 1918, when two agencies (the United States Shipping Board and the United States Housing Corporation in the Department of Labor) built 16,000 dwelling units for war-workers. After the war, this housing was disposed of to private owners, but with the next emergency—the Depression—more Federal public housing came into existence. The Emergency Relief and Construction Act of 1932, a work of the Hoover Administration, authorized Federal loans to limited dividend corporations for the building of housing, and the following year the National Industrial Recovery Act provided for slum clearance and low-cost housing. The Public Works Administration of the Department of the Interior, after a brief effort to gain its ends by subsidizing private builders, built about 50 projects amounting to well over 20,000 units in 30 cities. PWA policies were sharply criticized by people who believed that, although it ought to be subsidized by the Federal government, public housing should be controlled locally. Eventually most of the PWA housing projects were deeded to local housing agencies.[1]

In 1937 the National Housing Act was passed. This encouraged the creation by communities of independent, special purpose authorities chartered by the states and empowered to receive Federal grants and to build and manage housing. The Federal government was prepared to pay the difference between what it cost the local authorities to build and operate projects and what they would receive in rent from low-income tenants. The major purpose of the Act was slum clearance.[2] During the Depression, when many families were doubled up to share expenses, there did not seem to be a shortage of housing, and so the Act did not propose to increase the housing supply; for each new unit constructed, a slum structure was to be torn down. The supporters of housing reform had the long-awaited satisfaction of seeing some of the worst slums replaced; that the total amount of housing was not thereby increased did not seem important.

Until three or four years after the passage of the Act, it was unclear whether the courts would sanction the use of state powers for building and managing housing projects. The question was whether slum clearance and housing projects could be considered "public purposes" such as would justify exercise of the police power, the power of eminent domain, or the power to exempt from taxes. The courts upheld the public character of the projects, relying on what Myres S. McDougal and Addison A. Mueller called "the well documented facts that slum clearance and the provision of sanitary, low-rent housing decrease danger of epidemics, raise general public health, reduce crime, cut juvenile delinquency, reduce immorality, lower economic waste by reducing health, police and fire protection costs, make better citizens, eliminate fire hazards, increase general land values in the vicinity, cut the accident rate, and prevent the cancerous spread of the slums to uninfected areas."[3]

There was little evidence that slum clearance or low-rent projects would accomplish these things. Nevertheless, the legal basis of public housing was firmly established on the assumption or, as some said, the myth, that slum clearance and low-rent projects were clearly instrumental to the health, safety, and moral welfare of the public.*

About 170,000 dwelling units were built under this program

* In his account of "the myths of housing reform," John P. Dean remarks that "social reformers hoped that the USHA [United States Housing Authority]

in more than 260 communities between 1939 and 1942. During World War II, the Federal government financed the building for civilians of 805,000 units of housing, of which about 195,000 were of permanent construction. Much of this was built and managed for the Federal government by local authorities; in some cases projects which had been intended for low-income people were turned over to war workers. Of the housing that was built under the Housing Act of 1937, 89 per cent was on slum sites and only 11 per cent on vacant land sites, so that little was added to the total housing supply.[4]

Many people feared an immediate depression after the war. Urban redevelopment plans, under which private enterprise would rebuild the blighted centers of cities with Federal subsidies to defray part of the cost of land, were discussed as a way of preventing or mitigating the expected depression. Public housing appeared in these plans as a way of providing quarters for people who would be displaced either by private redevelopment or by public works improvements (such as superhighways) and who could not find adequate housing at rates they could afford to pay. Thus, public housing came to be regarded as desirable not only for the sake of the slum dwellers themselves, but also, and in some quarters primarily, as a prerequisite to private redevelopment, i.e., as "relocation housing."[5]

As the war veterans returned it became clear that the wartime shortage of housing was rapidly growing more acute. New families were being formed at an unprecedented rate, and people were no longer under the financial necessity of "doubling-up." Supporters of public housing, accordingly, pointed to the need for low-cost housing for veterans and expected that politicians would respond with large new appropriations.

Meanwhile, the slums of the northern cities had become in-

---

would introduce a new way of life for the slum family. They believed that many personal and social maladjustments would wither away in the new life of the community." The reformers, he says, uncritically assumed that because substandard housing is generally linked with high death rates, high proportion of juvenile delinquency, high rate of sex offenses, high rate of gambling arrests, high rates of divorce, high rates of alcoholism, and so on, removal of the slums would remove these social ills. "Without question," he concludes, "public housing has provided rehoused families with structures more comfortable and decent and more healthful and safe to live in; but the anticipated improvements in social welfare have failed to materialize." John P. Dean, "The Myths of Housing Reform," *American Sociological Review,* Volume 14, No. 2 (April 1949), p. 286.

creasingly Negro, and so public housing necessarily became involved in decisions the effect of which would be either to extend or curtail segregation. "By the end of the Second World War," Charles Abrams has written, "the shift in the character of slum occupancy had become more marked. Millions of white slum dwellers had moved to the burgeoning new suburbs. The Negroes remained. More than two-thirds of the slum families in many of our larger cities were nonwhite. But by that time the movement for slum clearance had already developed so irrepressible a momentum that no politician local or Federal could ask for its curtailment. Demolition of slums was accelerated by public works programs and by private and public developments. In 1949 an urban redevelopment program tore down more slums, replacing them with expensive dwellings for which few of the new slum dwellers were eligible.

"Meanwhile the constant immigration of minority families, coupled with the continued demolition of slums, intensified the housing shortage for the minorities, increased overcrowding, and forced many of the families to pay rents among the highest in the cities. The proportion of overcrowding for nonwhites in 1952 was already more than four times as great as for the whites, and the proportion of the substandard housing they occupied was six times as great.

"Some relief might have come from the new building boom in the suburbs. But building and real estate men ever since the 1920's had advocated racial segregation. Up to 1950, the code of ethics of the National Association of Real Estate Boards imposed an obligation on realtors to keep minorities out of the new neighborhoods. Dozens of texts and more than a hundred real estate courses in colleges from coast to coast emphasized that when nonwhite families go where they are not wanted, they threaten real estate values and become undesirable neighbors.

"The Federal Housing Administration and the Home Loan Bank Board adopted these policies, and from 1935 to 1949 openly advocated racial segregation of minorities, the barring of 'inharmonious groups' from new neighborhoods, restrictive covenants, and other exclusion devices. The official manual of the

FHA during this period read like a chapter from Hitler's Nuremberg laws.

"In a desperate quest for shelter, the minorities tried to expand the boundaries of their slum neighborhoods. They succeeded in some cities where their numbers were not too challenging. But their efforts were met by resistance or violence in many other cities. Often land they acquired was condemned by local authorities for parks, public works, or on other pretexts; they were harried by private restrictions, zoning ordinances, and a host of other oppressions which have now become common in real estate practice. The decisions of the Supreme Court against racial zoning ordinances and racial covenants, while helpful, have not stemmed the adoption of new exclusion practices.

"In the twenty-five years preceding the end of the Second World War, no less than seventy-five per cent of the new home developments were built in peripheral sections. But these neighborhoods are almost exclusively for whites. Often the political fate of public officials depends on their ability to keep out minorities."[6]

As the migration to the northern cities continued, many Negro and white organizations came to attach more importance to the elimination of segregation than hitherto. During the Depression and the war, fair employment practices had been their key objective. The leaders of the race relations organizations wanted Negroes to have their fair share of public housing, but their demands did not go much beyond that; they did not, for example, make an issue of the fact that most public housing projects in northern cities were segregated. Until the end of the war, a policy of "neighborhood conformity," i.e., of maintaining the pre-project racial composition of a neighborhood in the selection of tenants for a project, was generally accepted by them without protest.

Then, in the middle forties, there was a change in opinion about race relations.[7] Job discrimination was no longer quite so important when there were jobs for all. Human relations commissions had been created in many cities, and, although some of them may have been intended to be "window-dressing," the people who ran these agencies were often effective in creating and directing pressure for bettering race relations. Housing was a field where reform was obviously needed, and public housing was obviously a convenient place to begin. Accordingly, the professionals and others concerned with race relations pressed for more public housing and also for an end to segregation and discrimination in such public housing as already existed. When in 1948 the Supreme Court acted against racially restrictive covenants,[8] public housing was indirectly affected: if the law could not be invoked to enforce discriminatory covenants against Negroes, what justification was there for discrimination by public agencies?

There were at this time other important changes in public opinion which had their effect on public housing. During and after the war, people were prosperous as never before and their prosperity tended to change their view on many matters, among them housing. The 1950 Census showed that for the first time since the United States began industrializing more people owned houses than rented them (this increase in home ownership was also related to changes in opinion). In Chicago, for example, while the number of owner-occupied dwellings increased by 44 per cent from 1940 to 1950, the number of tenant-occupied dwellings increased by a very much smaller proportion.[9] Government was meanwhile becoming less involved in welfare programs. The Truman Administration was preoccupied first with foreign aid and then with military programs. The passage of the Taft-Hartley Labor Act helped cause the trade unions to think more about organizational maintenance and less about welfare goals such as housing. The liberal-left was distracted by charges that some of its leaders, spokesmen, and adherents were dupes of the Soviet Union. Public ownership meanwhile had been losing its appeal.

As the liberal-left retreated, members of the conservative-reaction advanced into some of the positions it had recently held.* Some conservatives supported a large-scale housing program in which low-rent public housing played an important part. The Housing Act of 1949, the original sponsors of which included Senator Taft, the Republican leader, and Senator Ellender, a conservative from the South, along with a survivor of the New

---

* We use the terms "liberal-left" and "conservative-reaction" to indicate relative placement on a continuum of political outlook and to avoid saying or implying how far to the "left" or "right" it may be.

Deal, Senator Wagner, could not have been passed without the support of conservatives. As some conservatives backed public housing, some liberals who had fought for it for many years lost interest and went into other activities; their places in the housing agencies were taken by bureaucrats whose concern was not to win acceptance for controversial goals, but merely to attain goals that had been agreed upon.

The end-products of several lines of policy development were brought together in the Housing Act of 1949. Title I of the Act provided for Federally-subsidized private redevelopment of blighted land and the use of Federal credit for the development of vacant and other land; Title III amended the Housing Act of 1937 by authorizing loans and subsidies for approximately 810,000 units of low-rent housing to be built in six years and managed by local authorities. (As under the 1937 Act also, the public housing could be built on either slum or vacant land sites.) Other titles provided for housing research and for farm housing.

As of November 30, 1953, four and one-half years after the passage of the Act, preliminary loan contracts had been approved for about 350,000 dwelling units of public housing in 1,100 communities in all but a few of the states and territories. By that date, about 110,000 units had been completed. Many more were under construction. Sites had been approved for 263,875 units in 1,761 projects.[10]

This was a smaller achievement than had been anticipated when the Act was passed. After the start of fighting in Korea, President Truman issued an executive order (July 18, 1950) limiting "starts" to 30,000 for that year. Congress, influenced by anti-public housing forces, in the subsequent year limited "starts" to 50,000 and to 35,000 for each of several following years. If it had not been for these restrictions, the achievement under the Act might have been somewhat greater, although it is by no means certain that it would have been much greater.

Some cities—notably New York—built all the public housing for which they could get funds and did so without hesitation. But in many others, among them Chicago, there was energetic and persistent opposition to public housing proposals; in these cities the reservations that had been made for housing were sometimes cancelled or the planned housing programs were drastically cut or otherwise altered.

Between the passage of the Act and February 1954, in at least 70 communities (most of them small ones) opponents of public housing brought the issue before the electorate in referenda or similar measures. In other communities (Chicago was one) the opponents of public housing did not collect enough signatures on petitions to get the issue on the ballot. Where referenda took place, public housing lost in five cities for every three in which it won.[11] It should be kept in mind, however, that these votes usually occurred in off-elections when the voting was light and conservative. Moreover, the opposition groups which sponsored such referenda often managed to frame the question in such a way that the voters passed on what seemed to be socialism or property tax exemption but not in any very meaningful sense on public housing itself.

In Los Angeles and Detroit as well as in Chicago, the controversy over public housing was particularly heated. In Los Angeles the Mayor and City Council entered into an agreement with the Federal government by which the city agreed to build 10,000 units. The next year the California electorate voted to amend the state constitution in such a way as to require voter approval of all public housing projects for which contracts had not yet been signed. (It is of passing interest that some of the middle and upper income precincts of Los Angeles voted heavily against this amendment while some of the poorer precincts voted heavily in favor of it.) Then the City Council, after having spent $12,000,000 on sites for the public housing, dropped the undertaking altogether even though this meant losing the investment already made in it. This decision the voters of Los Angeles sustained, 378,343 to 258,718.[12]

In Detroit, where racial segregation was an important aspect of the issue, a 14,350-unit public housing program planned in 1949 was very much reduced, especially in vacant land sites, by an opponent of public housing who was elected mayor.[13]

It is difficult to make generalizations about the cities which accepted or rejected public housing. Some communities readily accepted all of the housing they could get while others that were similarly situated in many important respects (e.g., racial and ethnic composition, political structure, housing need, and so on) rejected the housing, accepted only a small amount and that after a bitter fight, or located it where public housing supporters thought it ought not to be. Where there was controversy, the precise form of the issue varied widely: in some places the housing was put on vacant sites because slum owners wanted to keep their profitable properties and in other places it was put in the slums because people in outlying neighborhoods did not want it near them.

The controversy frequently centered on whether public housing should be built on vacant sites. This was an issue because middle and upper income and status groups were generally unwilling to permit the movement of lower class or minority groups into new neighborhoods. In the northern industrial cities especially, the question of where public housing was to be located was closely connected with the question of whether the residential segregation of Negroes was to be maintained. Race appeared again and again in the deliberations of those who supported public housing and of those who opposed it.[14]

One other generalization may safely be made. In almost no city was a public housing program developed as part of a long-range plan for all types of housing or as part of a reasonably detailed comprehensive plan for the growth and development of the community.[15]

Nationally there was a well-financed and well-organized campaign in opposition to public housing; the supporters of public housing were also active but their resources were considerably less than those of the opposition. Locally, however, neither the supporters nor the opponents of public housing seem to have been very well organized in most communities. The opponents had plentiful supplies of "canned" promotional material—cartoon mats, editorials, speeches, and so on—which were provided from national headquarters, but there is some question whether this gave them very much of an advantage locally.

Although they were less well organized and financed nationally, the professionals of the housing movement and the supporters of public housing were nevertheless in close communication through associations and through an organ of professional opinion, *The Journal of Housing*. Long before the passage of the Housing Act of 1949 both the supporters and the opponents had formed comparable systems of national communication and there had come into existence a national public opinion respecting public housing. Both sides knew the main arguments that would be used for and against public housing under various circumstances.

For this reason and others, the points made in the controversies over public housing in the various cities were often similar.* One would only have to change proper names to make some of the testimony given in hearings in other cities indistinguishable from some of that given in hearings in Chicago. In the northern cities at least, the public housing issue seems often to have had similar essentials.

The events that constitute the case history are a complicated tangle. The reader may therefore find it easier to follow the narrative if he has a brief chronological summary of it in advance.

The essential facts are these:

In July 1949 the Chicago Housing Authority put before the Mayor and City Council a preliminary proposal which called for building 40,000 units of low-rent housing over the next six years. In the autumn of that year the Authority selected sites for the first 10,000 units, and in November it submitted them to the City Council for approval. A committee of the Council held public hearings on the sites in February; it withheld approval from five of the seven sites. In March a sub-committee of the Council went looking for other sites; its recommendations, however, proved unacceptable to almost all concerned. Then, at the beginning of April, the Authority submitted a revised proposal to the Council. Council never voted on this proposal. Instead, the leaders of the Council framed a compromise. When the Authority demurred at the compromise, the Mayor in May appointed as consultant to the Council an engineer who proposed building projects in "stages" in order to avoid the necessity of relocating slum-dwellers. Late in May this consultant persuaded the heads of the Public Housing Administration in Washington not to hinder the compromise he

* The same can be said of some of the controversies over private redevelopment. See, for example, the account of the Milwaukee and San Francisco projects in Coleman Woodbury (ed.), *The Future of Cities and Urban Redevelopment*, University of Chicago Press, Chicago, 1953, pp. 377-383.

and the Council leaders were urging upon the Authority. Although the staff of the Authority considered the compromise program undesirable, there seemed by the middle of June no alternative to it other than to give up the housing altogether. The heads of the Authority accepted the compromise accordingly, but it turned out that before the Council itself would ratify it (as it did in August 1950) more public hearings would be held and changes would be made in the terms of the compromise. After the Council had finally approved the sites, some further efforts were made to have the Public Housing Administration reject the program, but these were unavailing. By early 1952 the questions which had been raised in the middle of 1949 were largely decided.

In following the narrative the reader may find it helpful to consult the general index frequently, especially such key entries as "Negro," "Kennelly," "Site Selection," "Taylor," and "Wood."

'Where Do You Want It?'
PUBLIC
HOUSING
BURCK
©1949 CHICAGO SUN-TIMES

CHAPTER TWO □ □ □ □ □ □

THE ORGANIZATION AND ITS TASKS

ON THE DAY that Congress passed the general Housing Act—July 8, 1949—the Chicago Housing Authority (CHA) put before Mayor Martin H. Kennelly a proposal to build 40,000 units of low-rent public housing over a six-year period under the terms of the Act. The new housing might cost as much as $500,000,000 (the difference between the operating costs of this amount of housing and what tenants would pay in rent was to come from the Federal government); there was to be enough of it to shelter a population about the size of New Haven, and if decisions were made promptly, the first of the new dwellings might be occupied within a year.

Housing had been considered a problem in Chicago for more than half a century. For most of this period, many influential people favored the reduction of slums; slums they argued, were a cause of crime, poverty, and disease. Later the housing problem was seen to involve more than slum clearance—among other things, the replanning and rebuilding of the central residential areas of the city was needed, and some way had to be found to enable low-income people, especially the Negroes who were coming to Chicago in steadily increasing numbers, to get decent dwellings. By the end of the second World War the housing problem—the usual word for it now was "crisis"—came to have a new dimension, shortage; in 1949, CHA estimated that there were 1,178,000 families* requiring housing in Chicago but only 906,000

* The population of Chicago in 1950 consisted of 3,620,962 persons, an increase of 6.6 per cent over 1940 (the white population decreased slightly in this

"standard units."[1]

Chicago, like practically all American cities, had spread from the center outward, and so the oldest and most dilapidated housing and facilities were in the inner city. The Chicago Plan Commission classified 9.3 square miles of Chicago as "blighted" and another 13.3 "near-blighted."* [2]

These slum areas lay in a half circle around the Loop (the downtown district of about a square mile in which most of the central offices, hotels, theatres, restaurants, and department stores were concentrated), and around the wholesale and light manufacturing areas adjacent to the Loop. The half circle of slum areas was irregular, but for the most part it extended about five miles from the Loop. About one-fourth of Chicago's population lived in these areas, although they comprised only about 15 per cent of the land in Chicago devoted to residential use.

---

period and the nonwhite population increased by over 80 per cent). These figures and those in the text refer to Chicago proper, not to the Metropolitan Area, which by census definition includes six counties in Illinois and Indiana, and had a population in 1950 of 5,495,364 persons. Although they were inextricably one, the Authority could not consider the housing problems of Chicago as part of the housing problems of the Metropolitan Area, for its jurisdiction was only city-wide.

* The Plan Commission classified an area "blighted" if it met *all* of these conditions: 1. was at least 50 per cent residential; 2. at least 50 per cent of the structures (not dwelling units) were built before 1895; 3. at least 50 per cent of the dwelling units (not structures) were "substandard," and 4. of the substandard units, at least 20 per cent were substandard by reason of being "unfit for use." A unit was substandard if it was either: a) "unfit for use" (lacking heat, light, or private toilet or needing major repairs), or b) overcrowded. A unit was overcrowded if either: i) it was occupied by as many as 1.5 persons per room plus an "extra" family of two or more persons, or ii) it rented for less than $40 per month and was occupied by as many as 1.5 persons per room or by an "extra" family of two or more persons. The definition of "near blighted" was similar but less restrictive. In this study we use the term "blighted areas" or "slum areas" to include both those areas which the Plan Commission defined as "blighted" and those defined as "near blighted."

Despite its seeming clarity, the definition of blight left a good deal to interpretation: e.g. which of the more isolated blighted blocks to include within the boundaries of blighted areas (if they were all included, the bulk of the city might fall within the boundaries). In a court case it was once charged—but not proved—that when in doubt the Plan Commission classified blocks blighted if they were occupied by Negroes.

Moreover, the validity of the criteria was doubtful: old structures, for example, even ones with low rents, might be desirable residences. And there might be many good units of housing within a blighted area and many very poor units outside of the blighted areas.

Extending from the blighted and near-blighted areas almost to the city limits were areas which the Plan Commission classified as "conservation," "stable" and "new growth." These terms referred to the life expectancy of the structures in the areas—from one to two or more generations. Roughly two-thirds of the population of Chicago lived in these areas, most of them (over half the total population) in the conservation districts.[3] For this reason we will henceforth refer to all of these districts together as "conservation areas." (See Appendix, Map No. 1.)

The worst part of the slum areas was the so-called Black Belt, a district of about six square miles (according to our estimate) on the South Side back of the Lake Front where most of Chicago's Negroes lived. (See Appendix, Map No. 3.) The Black Belt was only slightly larger in 1950 than at the end of the first World War, although the number of nonwhites in the city had increased dramatically—from 109,595 in 1920 to 277,731 in 1940 and to 519,437 in 1950. It always had been very difficult for Negroes to get housing in areas that had been occupied by whites, and when rent control prevented them from out-bidding whites for rental units, it became virtually impossible. After rent control was undermined and restrictive covenants were declared unenforceable, Negroes could sometimes buy or rent in white neighborhoods, although it was still difficult to do so. If they would sell to Negroes at all, whites—usually real estate operators who served Negroes—found it more convenient to deal only in housing at the periphery of the Negro districts, and a Negro who moved into a white neighborhood had reason to fear violence from which the police would not be likely to protect him. These restrictions accounted in part for the fact that the Negro districts showed little sign of dissolving as the older colonies of Jews, Poles, Italians and other ethnic minorities had done or were doing. To some extent, however, the segregation of the Negroes was self-imposed. For reasons that were certainly not unrelated to the treatment they had received and were still receiving at the hands of the whites, they did not want to live among whites or to be cut off from the kind of community life which only a concentration of Negro population would make possible for them.

Furthermore, segregation was on the increase. In 1950, most Negroes lived in blocks that were predominantly Negro. The proportion segregated was higher than ever before.[4]

Under the conditions that existed in Chicago—an expanding Negro population and a fixed area of occupancy—overcrowding was inevitable. The population density of the Black Belt was 75,000 to the square mile—several times that of the city as a whole, and in some neighborhoods it went as high as 90,000.[5] "In this black man-heap there is no such thing as a vacancy," a Negro writer complained bitterly in 1949, "though outside there are twenty square miles of vacant land labelled 'white.' "[6]

This vacant land was mostly in the outlying areas of the South Side, away from both the Loop and the Lake Front. (See Appendix, Map No. 4.) In the slum areas themselves there were no sizeable tracts of vacant land suitable for residential use, although there were many scattered vacant lots. On the North Side, where property values were very high, there was a small amount of vacant land, but practically none of it was in tracts large enough to accommodate large projects.

Mostly because they could not, but also, as we have said, to some extent because they would not move away from the Negro community, Negroes paid high rents and high prices for land. Their housing, however, was very poor. There was some scattered good housing in the Negro slum areas, as there was in other slum areas, but in general the condition of Negro housing was much worse than that of other slum-dwellers or of other people at the same income level.*

In order to house the people who lived in substandard dwellings and another 95,000 families who were doubled up, and to provide a reasonable vacancy reserve, CHA estimated that 272,000 units of new housing were needed.[7] Of these, about 50,000 units should be for sale and the rest for rent. And of the rental units 51,000 should rent for less than $33 a month, according to CHA estimates. Private enterprise could not meet this need for low-

* In 1947 a Census study showed two per cent of white and 12 per cent of Negro occupied dwellings in Chicago in need of major repair; nine per cent of the white and 22 per cent of the Negro dwellings lacked one or more designated facilities (lighting, heat, flush toilets, etc.), and two per cent of the white and 13 per cent of the Negro units contained 1.51 or more persons per room.

rent housing; if it were not met by public action it would almost certainly not be met at all.

The 40,000 units requested by CHA under the six-year program of the Act were not sufficient to meet this minimum need. This discrepancy between what was needed and what was proposed arose from the fact that the Housing Act provided for the construction of about 810,000 units in the United States as a whole with no more than 10 per cent of this total to be built in any one state. Illinois, then, could not possibly have more than 81,000 units. And Chicago, although it had much more than half of the state's slum-dwellers, could not expect to get more than half of the Illinois quota. Hence the figure 40,000, which, by coincidence, had been CHA's 1945 estimate of the city's immediate need for low-rent housing. The Federal government reserved 21,000 units for the first two years of the program in Chicago; this was more than it reserved for any other city.

The Authority's proposal to the Mayor, the City Council, and the Federal government's Public Housing Administration (PHA) was the product of a long history of thought and action. Ten years earlier such a proposal might have given more emphasis to slum clearance; the new Housing Act recognized in both its public housing and its redevelopment slum clearance titles that the problem was not only poor quality housing, but also lack of housing. Accordingly, the Authority's proposal called for building two-fifths of the new housing on vacant land:

Units to be Ready for Occupancy

YEAR	ON VACANT SITES	ON SLUM SITES
1	3,000	—
2	4,000	—
3	4,000	2,000
4	4,000	3,000
5	—	10,000
6	—	10,000
All	15,000	25,000

If it had not been partly for sentiment—sentiment, it will appear, which had to be taken account of as a political reality, the Authority might well have put the traditional goal of slum clearance aside altogether and have planned to build all of the new housing on vacant land: it did not make sense to tear down houses, even substandard ones, as long as the housing shortage remained acute. But there were many prominent people, including aldermen and commissioners of the Authority itself, who took pride in wiping out slum neighborhoods and replacing them with clean and spacious projects. "It had always been an aspiration of the Board to clear slums," one of the commissioners later explained. "Here was the golden opportunity."[8]

But even though slum clearance was the main objective of many supporters of public housing, it was essential that much of the new housing, especially the first of it, be built on vacant land. For one thing, it was necessary to build housing into which the slum-dwellers could be removed *before* demolishing the slums; to tear down old housing before new housing was ready would create intolerable hardships for the evicted families. For another thing, housing could be built on vacant land much faster than on land from which people had to be relocated and on which old buildings had to be demolished; any housing which was to come into service in the first two years of the program would have to be built on vacant sites. And finally, of course, there was the obvious and urgent need to increase the total supply of housing. A slum clearance program would almost certainly decrease it, for one of the principal objectives of a clearance program would probably be to give slum-dwellers more living space, i.e., to reduce the density of residential population.

There was another factor which, depending on how one looked at it, constituted a strong argument for or against building on vacant land. By far the largest group of the officially defined slum-dwellers were Negroes. Most of the large vacant land tracts available were in lower-middle class (both income-wise and status-wise) white neighborhoods in the outlying districts of the South Side. Building on vacant land would introduce Negroes into white neighborhoods. Whether one liked it or not, public housing built on vacant land sites would break down some of the residential racial segregation which existed in Chicago. And the contrary course—to build projects in the slums—would, whether one liked it or not, stabilize, extend, and perhaps even give a quasi-official standing to the existing patterns of segregation.

There was no way of avoiding the problem; the race issue and the housing issue had to be dealt with together. This was a circumstance which some parties to the impending struggle viewed with satisfaction and which others deplored. Some, like the Chicago Plan Commission, which in its lengthy report, *Housing Goals for Chicago,*[9] never discussed the Negro, might try to ignore the problem or at least to evade responsibility for taking a stand on segregation. But, whether one liked it or not and whether one ignored it or not, the housing problem and the race problem were inseparably one.

In the Housing Act of 1949 Congress defined in very general terms the goals of the Federally-aided housing program. "The Congress hereby declares," the Act said, "that the general welfare and security of the Nation and the health and living standards of its people require housing production and related community development sufficient to remedy the serious housing shortage, the elimination of substandard or other inadequate housing through the clearance of slums and blighted areas, and the realization as soon as feasible of the goal of a decent home and suitable living environment for every American family, thus contributing to the development and redevelopment of communities and to the advancement of the growth, wealth, and security of the Nation."[10]

In attaining these goals, Congress further declared, private enterprise would be encouraged to serve as large a part of the total need as it could, governmental assistance would be extended to help private enterprise serve an even larger part, and the government would encourage local public bodies to develop well-planned neighborhoods. That part of the statement of national policy which referred particularly to low-rent public housing said that it was Congress' policy "to provide adequate housing units for urban and rural non-farm families with incomes so low that they are not being decently housed." Federal agencies, the Act said, should use their powers to encourage: the production of housing of sound designs, materials and techniques; the development of well-planned, integrated residential neighborhoods and the development and redevelopment of communities; and the stabilization of the housing industry at a high level of residential construction. The Act made no mention of any objectives in respect to race relations. The Fourteenth Amendment of the Constitution provided that no state might deny to any person within its jurisdiction the equal protection of the laws, but this, of course, was not a sufficient statement from which to derive a race relations policy.

While it set forth objectives of national housing policy and the general conditions under which the Federal funds could be used, the Act did not create local authorities in Chicago or elsewhere. These had been created earlier under state legislation. The Illinois "Housing Authorities Act" under which CHA was organized as a municipal corporation in 1937 and subsequent legislation specified the powers which local authorities might exercise: (1) investigate housing conditions, determine standards of decent housing, and make plans in cooperation with any public planning agencies for the redevelopment of substandard areas; (2) plan, build and operate housing projects; (3) borrow money through the issuance of notes and bonds, sue and be sued, make and enter into contracts; (4) conduct hearings and subpoena witnesses; and (5) enter into agreements with the city with reference to tax exemptions and payments in lieu of taxes.[11]

If the state or city financed the construction of housing by the Authority (as they did in 1948 to relocate slum-dwellers who were living on sites designated for various public improvements), they could approve sites and exercise a general supervision over expenditures. Similarly, the City Council could assign responsibilities to CHA and set up such controls over the city-financed undertakings as it desired. (Immediately after the war, for example, the city financed in part the construction by CHA of emergency housing for veterans.) But when, as would be the case under the Housing Act of 1949, the projects were financed by the Federal government, the powers of both the state and the city were sharply limited.

Regardless of the source of funds, state law forbade housing authority officials from discriminating on grounds of race. ". . . No officer or employee of the State," the law said, "or of any political subdivision thereof, . . . or of any municipal corporation in the

State, shall deny or refuse to any person, on account of race, color or religion, the full and equal enjoyment of the accommodations . . . facilities . . . or of any property under his care."[12] This was a good deal clearer in its intention than the Fourteenth Amendment, but it was still far from being a specific statement of objectives—one could not tell from it, for example, whether public housing projects should be developed which would encourage the movement of Negroes into white residential areas.

The Mayor could appoint, subject to approval by the State Housing Board, five unpaid commissioners to direct the work of the Authority, but only the State Housing Board had power to remove them and then only for incompetence or malfeasance.

The city had no direct control over the Authority except that it might give or withhold its consent to certain undertakings. In the case of CHA (but not of any other Illinois housing authority) the City Council under terms of a state law passed in 1948 had to approve the location planned for each project.[13] Such other formal authority as it had over CHA the city got by virtue of Federal law and regulations which provided: (1) that the Authority's application for a loan from the Federal government must be approved by the city, and (2) that, as a condition to receiving a Federal loan or grant, the Authority and the city must enter into a cooperation agreement by which the city would typically agree: a) to exempt projects from taxes, b) to furnish city services such as fire and police protection to the projects without cost, c) to grant needed waivers to the building code, to vacate streets, and to accept dedication of new streets, and d) unless a critical housing shortage existed, to eliminate as many slum units as there were units added by the program. For its part, the Authority agreed to make payments to the city in lieu of taxes up to 10 per cent of the "shelter rentals" (gross rent minus utility charges) paid by tenants.[14]

Although projects might be (and in some instances actually were) financed by both the state and the city, the Federal government was the principal source of financial aid for most of the projects. The Housing Authority sold bonds having a maturity of not more than forty years which were its own direct obligations. The primary security behind these bonds, however, was an obligation which the Federal government's Public Housing Administration assumed: namely, to pay to the Authority annual contributions (subsidies) sufficient to amortize the Authority's debt.* The Authority used project rental receipts to pay operating and maintenance expenses.

The independent local authority was the form of organization through which public housing was administered in most cities. There were a number of reasons why this form of organization had become popular. When new governmental activities were being tried, there had always been a tendency to make use of citizen boards to protect the new activity from opponents who wished to destroy it and to mediate between the public at large and the professional staff of the new agency; public libraries and schools, for example, had been set up in this way in most places. When public housing got underway, there was the usual need for this protection but it was made all the more urgent by the circumstance that many city governments were run by corrupt and unimaginative party hacks. An innovation such as public housing, the supporters of public housing thought, should be administered apart from these existing agencies and by people who were sensitive to its special requirements and, of course, entirely non-political.† The alternative, from the standpoint of the public

* After a local housing authority has demonstrated that there is a need for low-rent housing that is not being met, the Public Housing Administration makes small preliminary loans for the planning of specific projects. As projects get into construction, temporary loans are obtained, usually by selling notes of the authority to private investors. The Federal government guarantees these notes. When the project is under construction and costs can be accurately determined, the temporary notes are retired and the authority sells long-term bonds to investors. These are secured by the Federal government's pledge to pay to the authority annual contributions not exceeding the amounts which are needed to make up the difference between annual rents and annual costs (including interest and amortization of all capital loans but not local taxes, from which the projects are exempt). Under the 1949 Act the maximum repayment period is 40 years. When amortization is completed, the authority may operate the project without Federal regulation. The maximum annual contribution by the Federal government is limited to a percentage of the development cost of a project; this percentage is the rate currently charged to the government for long-term credit plus two per cent.[15]

† Luther Gulick has pointed out that the use of unpaid boards with overlapping terms and independent taxing powers has been a favorite device for "taking administration out of politics." He has observed that the professional people in each field of public endeavor tend to form "guild" identifications which are an additional reason why new agencies are given independent status. "It is a central dogma of each of these guilds," he writes, "first, that what is good for them is

housing movement, was to let the Federal government administer housing and this, after a brief experience, was widely opposed. But aside from these considerations, there was an additional and often compelling argument for the independent authority: most cities — Chicago among them — had exhausted their borrowing power; a municipal corporation, the obligations of which would not be obligations of the city, was often the only feasible way to get around this difficulty.

Since the Authority was independent and since the laws that created it were very general in their terms, it was impossible to say precisely whose purposes or what purposes it was to serve. State law required it to make an annual report to the Mayor concerning housing conditions within its jurisdictional area and to include in the report suggestions for remedying any shortage of adequate housing. But this, of course, did not in any way mean that the Authority was to look to the Mayor for direction. There was nothing in the state law itself which specified a hierarchy of ends which it was to seek to realize; the law did enumerate certain powers and, of course, some inferences could be drawn from these as to the general purposes which the legislature intended the Authority to serve. There was no way of telling from this list of powers, however, whether it should build much public housing or little, whether it should build on slum or vacant sites, whether it should build high-rise or row houses, or, indeed, whether it should build new units at all—perhaps it should rehabilitate old ones or in some other way achieve the general purpose of the Act. So far as the law was concerned, the commissioners had very wide freedom within which to decide what means to employ. They could cooperate with neighborhood bodies on matters relating to neighborhood development, act as a land acquisition agency for a private organization such as Michael Reese Hospital, undertake such additional tasks as running a housing rental center, and they could carry on research and planning projects that fell outside the realm of immediate housing needs altogether.

---

good for society, and second, that they know their own business and that no nonmember of the guild is qualified to make any comments or suggestions. . . . With such a foundation, then, of group consciousness, it is almost inevitable that each guild should desire to pull the government apart so that the guild may take to itself the management and the control of its special part of the governmental system." "Politics, Administration, and the 'New Deal,' " *Annals of the American Academy of Political and Social Science,* v. 169, September 1933, p. 56.

If it took money from the city, state, or Federal governments, the Authority would have to agree to certain conditions—conditions which would in effect fix the range of possible ends in respect to some, but by no means all, important choices. Thus, as a condition to receiving Federal aid the Authority would have to accept certain Public Housing Administration standards governing construction costs, quality of construction, income and other tenant eligibility requirements, tenant selection policies, and management policies generally. In addition, PHA would supervise the procedures under which contracts were awarded by the Authority and it would reserve the right to decide whether the schemes were consistent with some of the requirements of sound city planning and with the special needs of all groups within the city's population. These limitations, important as they might be in many matters, did not at all mean that the Federal government would provide a hierarchy of clearcut ends which the Authority would seek to maximize.*

PHA did decide, *after* the first Chicago sites had been selected, that, while it would be left to the option of the local community to decide whether to segregate by race, the total supply of public housing, even if in only one project, would have to be apportioned equitably between whites and nonwhites. "We are not attempting, by our regulations to do what Congress did not see fit to do," a PHA spokesman said[16] in explanation of the agency's failure to prohibit segregation in Chicago.† Of course the Authority was in principle (though not in actuality) perfectly free not to ask for Federal funds—or for that matter for city or state funds; in principle, it might have its own end-system quite separate from those

* In the early years of public housing, especially, Federal regulations were so detailed and all-inclusive as in effect to fix the ends of a local authority. Bryn Hovde wrote that the United States Housing Authority (the predecessor of PHA) "completely dominated all but a very few of the local authorities, prescribing not only the outside limitations of their expenditures and the general conditions to be observed in the development and management of their projects . . . but dictating minute details as to materials, design, and procedures." "The Local Housing Authority," *Public Administration Review,* Volume 1, No. 2, Winter 1941, p. 170.

† This policy was based on what PHA took to be legislative intent. When the bill was under consideration, Congressional opponents tried to kill it by attaching a non-segregation feature which Southerners were sure to oppose. Accordingly, supporters of public housing, who themselves mostly favored the non-segregation feature, opposed the non-segregation feature for reasons of strategy.

of all other governmental bodies. Only as it needed money would it come under the direct control of legislative bodies.

From a formal standpoint, then, the end-system of the Authority was to be defined by the five unpaid commissioners. The law did not specify, however, where or in what manner the commissioners were to discover the ends that the agency was to serve. No legislation directed the commissioners to regard the Mayor and the City Council as the legitimate authorities. The Mayor appointed the commissioners, to be sure, but he had no power to remove them, and so there was no more reason from a formal standpoint for them to serve the Mayor's or the Council's ends than anyone else's. Similarly, the State Housing Board had little formal control over the Authority—it could only remove a commissioner for incompetence or malfeasance.

However, for an agency to spend hundreds of millions of dollars—perhaps eventually billions—to achieve purposes which were not specified by a legislature would be contrary to the fundamentals of the American political system. Such a thing would be an unconstitutional delegation of the legislative power. The Authority was not in this position, however, for the courts had ruled that the act under which CHA was created included adequate standards for the guidance of the commissioners and that, since standards were provided by the legislature—even though they were in such general terms as "the public interest," what was delegated was not legislative but "quasi-legislative" power. Legally sufficient though they were, the vague guides provided in the act left the commissioners to decide as best they could what specific ends should be served. In the CHA, as in most organizations, these questions of how and where ends were to be discovered and given operational meaning were not formally raised.

Legally the commissioners were in charge of all CHA activities; in principle none of its affairs was beyond their reach. The direct management of the Authority, though, was in the hands of an Executive Secretary employed by the commissioners. According to the formal arrangements (which were not always the basis of their actual practice), the commissioners established all major policies by resolutions which were recorded in Authority minutes.

In addition to establishing policies, the commissioners exercised control by authorizing the execution of official documents, by approving certain controlling documents including the budget, and by reviewing or auditing operations.*

The organization of CHA under the Executive Secretary included the usual staff aids (legal counsel, public relations, personnel, and accounting) and three operating departments—Land Acquisition, Management, and Development. Neither Land Acquisition nor Management (the latter of which had two-thirds of the Authority's personnel and was responsible for tenant selection and project management) played an important part in the decision-making process by which new sites were selected and new projects were planned. These matters were handled by Development. With the passage of the Housing Act of 1949 it was clear that Development would have to be expanded very rapidly.

As in any organization, there was, of course, only a rough correspondence between the formal arrangements and the principles by which behavior within the organization was actually governed. Relationships and understandings which did not appear on the organization chart or in the procedure manual were always of the utmost importance. These relationships and understandings arose to a considerable extent out of the characteristics of members of the organization (i.e., characteristics which had no formal connection with the requirements of the organization) and the roles they saw for themselves.

The chairman of the Authority (he had been elected chairman in 1943) was Robert R. Taylor. In his late forties in 1949, Taylor was prosperous, upper-class and a Negro. He had studied architecture at Howard University, had an undergraduate degree from the University of Illinois and had taken courses in business and economics at Northwestern. He had participated in the designing and building of small groups of houses, had helped develop

* Citizen boards are intended as checks on professional administrators, but not uncommonly the administrator is given enough power to make him a check on the board as well. Illinois law, for example, makes the Chicago Board of Education responsible for "general supervision and management" but it gives the Superintendent of Schools power to appoint teachers, select sites, and choose textbooks unless overruled by a two-thirds vote of the full board. The CHA Executive Secretary had no such powers; the position was entirely dependent upon the board.

and was the manager of a large housing project established privately by Julius Rosenwald for Negroes, and was the secretary-treasurer of a savings and loan association. Although still firmly committed to public housing, he had in recent years come to attach increasing importance to other ways of improving the housing of Negroes and of breaking down residential segregation. One of these ways was to increase the Negro's "consciousness of economy."[17] Taylor believed that if Negroes saved and invested enough money, they could solve their housing problems for themselves. As the executive of a savings and loan association, he helped moderate income Negroes find and finance homes outside of the segregated areas.

Taylor was influential because he was a successful man in whom Negroes could take pride and because he had the power to give or withhold favors. He was not, however, particularly dependent upon the opinion of the Negro community and, although it was well-known that he was a Democrat, he was not politically active. While he was well aware of his responsibilities as a prominent Negro, he was not what was called a "race man."* Taylor was probably by temperament one of those very many people who want to be liked and admired by everyone, whites as well as Negroes.

Wayne McMillen, who had been appointed to the Board by Mayor Kelly in 1943, was a professor of social service administration at the University of Chicago. A native of Iowa and a graduate of Iowa State College, McMillen had once run unsuccessfully and without machine support for the Democratic nomination for state senator. This was his only venture in politics. In general his views were those of a "liberal" or "New Dealer," but on some issues his position could not be so easily classed.

Claude A. Benjamin, who had been appointed to the Board in 1946, was a prosperous small businessman. His point of view was not unusual among businessmen—he favored free enterprise, econ-

* Samuel M. Strong makes a distinction between a "race leader" and a "race man." The race leader is devoted to the welfare of the race; the race man exploits the race issue for his own special purposes. The race man is a good deal more aggressive—or at least a good deal noisier—than the race leader. Taylor would probably be regarded more as a race leader than as a race man. "Social Types in the Negro Community of Chicago," Unpublished Ph.D. dissertation, Department of Sociology, University of Chicago, Chicago, 1940, pp. 68-82.

omy, and scrupulous honesty in government. As a member of a minority group, he was sensitive to intolerance; he was vice-president of the Chicago Council Against Racial and Religious Discrimination and a contributor to and an active member of a number of Jewish and other philanthropic organizations. Benjamin was occupied with problems other than the welfare of the Negro, but it was well understood that he would never approve a housing program which involved segregation or which was otherwise discriminatory.

Henry A. Kruse, secretary-treasurer of the Chicago Flat Janitors' Union (AFL) was a conservative labor-politician. At the beginning of 1950 at a meeting of the commissioners, he recorded a statement of his views on the role of publicly aided housing:

"Public housing [he wrote] should not compete with private housing or the realty interests. Public housing should be built in inlying areas where public housing is needed; in close proximity to industry so a worker need not spend extra hours each day traveling to and from work.

"Public housing is needed in areas that are now slum and blighted. In these areas public housing will enhance the character of the neighborhoods and the neighboring dwellings, and it will add materially to the economic welfare of the city.

"Private investors and realty interests do not invest in and develop slum areas, therefore public housing in these areas will not compete with the private or realty interests."[18]

Kruse probably understood that if public housing were built in the slums it would tend to keep Negroes where they were and that those projects which were located in the Negro districts would be all-Negro. Kruse, there seemed reason to believe, was opposed to bi-racial housing.

Another commissioner, Charles Kellstadt, a vice-president of the Sears Roebuck Company, rarely attended commissioners' meetings. He resigned in 1949 when he was transferred from Chicago.

Wilfred Sykes, an Australian-born engineer who was chairman of the board and former president of the Inland Steel Corporation, succeeded Kellstadt in March 1950. Sykes, who had been the chairman of the postwar planning committee and an officer of the National Association of Manufacturers, soon familiarized himself with the affairs of the Authority and came to be regarded by its staff as an able executive. To many of the staff Sykes seemed unenthusiastic about public housing (in 1953 when he resigned he said that he was not particularly in favor of public housing because there were 20 miles of slums upon which public housing could make little impression) and not especially in favor of a policy of non-segregation.

A majority of the commissioners (Taylor, McMillen, and Benjamin) favored a large and unsegregated housing program which would be built on both vacant and slum sites. However, only one —Benjamin—was known to be unwilling to accept any compromise which would entail an important sacrifice of any of these ends.

From the inception of the Authority, its Executive Secretary was Miss Elizabeth Wood. Born in 1899, she took B.A. and M.A. degrees in English literature at the University of Michigan. After teaching at Vassar College, doing editorial work for the Home Modernizing Bureau and then case-work for a charity agency, she became head of the staff of the Metropolitan Housing Council, a citizen-sponsored Chicago association concerned with housing problems, and, in addition, the Executive Secretary of the then newly-organized State Housing Board. In 1937, when CHA was organized, the commissioners, acting on the advice of Walter H. Blucher, Executive Director of the American Society of Planning Officials, Louis Brownlow, head of the influential Public Administration Clearing House, and other leaders of the good government movement, employed her to direct their small staff.

By 1949 Miss Wood had been on the job longer than any of the commissioners. With a staff of 600, she administered 10,000 units of housing. It was she, more than any other individual, who had given the Authority its special character and standing, a character and standing which made it a widely acknowledged leader among the several hundred local housing authorities of the United States.

Miss Wood was a fighter. A newspaper columnist once described "her candid stare, her determined chin, her crackling speech and taut vitality."[19] When one of her subordinates died, she wrote of him (italics added):

He was a good *fighter.* He *headed* into every problem with a *cocky* kind of cheerfulness; he was *jubilantly* proud of every gain he made, not because he expected from it personal congratulation or reward, but because it *strengthened* the *ramparts* of the Authority. Few people had any recognition of the quality of the job he did. He was a good *fellow-warrior;* we loved him.[20]

Edward Fruchtman was CHA's attorney. Then in his middle thirties, Fruchtman had worked for the National Labor Relations Board, had been a captain in the army and in that capacity had helped to rehabilitate trade unions in post-war Europe, had returned to Washington as assistant counsel to the NLRB and had later moved to a position in the Housing and Home Finance Agency. Although he very rapidly mastered housing law, much of Fruchtman's work did not involve purely legal questions. He was relied upon to raise appropriate questions and to supply good judgment in all kinds of matters.

John G. Vaughan, Jr., was Director of Development during the initial phases of site selection. An engineer by training, Vaughan had held a series of major Federal housing posts in Washington and New York and, as a volunteer, had participated actively in a citizen-sponsored city planning association in New York. He became ill early in the site selection program and did not continue work on a full time basis.

Martin Meyerson, who was hired by Vaughan to head the Planning Division, became head of the Development Department when Vaughan resigned. He was the technical specialist in charge of, among other things, site selection and site planning. He had been one of the planners of a community redevelopment and rehabilitation program for the Michael Reese Hospital in Chicago and had been on the staff of the Philadelphia City Planning Commission and the American Society of Planning Officials. He was on the faculty of social science and planning at the University of Chicago, a post from which he took a leave of absence to work for CHA. His role, he thought, was to give the policymakers (Miss Wood, the commissioners, and the City Council) complete and reliable technical information. Meyerson had decided personal views: for example, he was convinced that public housing which violated the standards of good city planning might be worse than no public housing at all. Along with Vaughan and Fruchtman, Meyerson was Miss Wood's chief staff aide in matters relating to site selection.*

Communication between the commissioners and the staff took place through meetings of the heads of each body (Taylor and Miss Wood) and through joint sessions of the whole Board with the principal staff members. In 1949 and early 1950, it was the practice of the commissioners (Taylor, McMillen and Benjamin, with Kruse rarely present and Sykes not yet appointed) to meet regularly once a month and at such other times as the Authority's business required. While the process of site selection was under way most intensively, these special meetings were very frequent; sometimes there were periods of a week or more when the CHA Board met almost every day and when the members were in contact with each other and with the staff by telephone between times.

Taylor, as chairman, was informally empowered to act for the Board in minor matters. In 1949, when the site selection process began, he promised not to make any important commitment which was not first unanimously approved by the Board. Until this rule of unanimity was lifted, no faction could control the Board.

Ordinarily, the Executive Secretary and those of the principal staff members who were especially concerned with site selection met with the Board. The agenda of these meetings was arranged in advance by the Executive Secretary in consultation with the

---

* Leonard Reissman in "A Study of Role Conception in Bureaucracy," *Social Forces,* Volume 27, No. 3, March 1944, pp. 308-9, has described four types of bureaucrats: 1. the *functional* bureaucrat looks for recognition to a reference group outside of the bureaucracy; Fruchtman, a lawyer, and Meyerson, a city planner, were probably both of this type; neither expected to make a career of working for housing agencies or even for public agencies; 2. the *specialist* bureaucrat identifies with the bureaucracy as well as with a professional group; the CHA comptroller, a man who expected to work in public agencies but not necessarily in housing authorities, may have belonged to this type; 3. the *service* bureaucrat is oriented both to the bureaucracy and to an outside group but the group is one which renders some special service to the society (Reissman's example is aid to handicapped children), not a profession; Miss Wood probably belonged to this type: she was an administrator of public housing, not an administrator "in general"; 4. the *job* bureaucrat looks for recognition within the bureaucracy itself and, like Max Weber's ideal-type, tends to regard functional efficiency as an end in itself. These types, incidentally, correspond fairly well to what seem to be the self-conceptions of the CHA employees; none of the top staff was a job bureaucrat, however, and none would have wanted to be thought one.

Chairman. It included presentation of reports on CHA activities and, very often, formal memoranda recommending policy positions. Here, the staff's function was hardly distinguishable from the policy-making function itself. As in all such organizations, the staff was in the very nature of things of great and often of paramount importance in the making of basic decisions. The advantages of the staff in its dealings with the commissioners were that it consisted of full-time employees, that it was intimately acquainted with the situation, that its members were in close and continuing contact with each other, and therefore able to act in concert, and that it had detailed and often technical knowledge that was indispensable. It was inevitable therefore that the staff would decisively influence the making of some of the most important policies, and it was inevitable, too, that this would be resented by some of the commissioners.

If the staff often entered the realm of "policy," the commissioners often entered that of "administration." In fact there was never any way of knowing what would be of interest to a commissioner and therefore "policy." One commissioner liked buildings with pitched roofs, another had views on heating systems, a third gave advice on a statistical study, and a fourth helped design an accounting form. Sykes, the commissioner with the most administrative experience, suggested to a staff member soon after his appointment that the Board confine itself to the determination of general policy, leaving all other matters to the staff with the understanding that if it did not administer the Board's policies satisfactorily it would be dismissed. This suggestion was warmly approved by the staff. The commissioners, however, apparently preferred to act as they had been acting.

CHA Board minutes (like the board minutes of most organizations) reported only actions taken. The minutes of most formal Board meetings were clear, but sometimes, even with regard to these formal meetings, the commissioners could not agree among themselves as to the specific intent of the conclusions they had reached at some previous meeting. Very often such misunderstandings were of a subtle sort: policies were remembered inexactly, and so, frequently, they were unconsciously modified by restatement to fit the immediate issue at hand.

There was a reason why minutes were not kept of the informal meetings. Some of what was discussed—racial policy, for example—was highly controversial, and, since the Board minutes had to be matters of public record, the commissioners could not have spoken their minds to each other with entire freedom if minutes had been taken. Without a written record of all that was said the commissioners could talk more freely, and they may have felt that they could talk without danger that what they said would be accurately remembered later when they might feel differently.

Since the law did not say precisely what ends it was to serve and since it was formally independent of the Mayor and the City Council, the commissioners had to decide as best they could what should be the Authority's end-system. They were what may be called a quasi-legislative body, and as such they were an anomaly in a political system which presumes that legislators have constituents with power to turn them out of office and whose wishes they must accordingly respect.* The commissioners of the Authority were "legislators" who had no constituents or, at least, no constituents who could turn them out of office. How then were they to decide whose ends, among the many conflicting ends at issue, should be taken into account or given most weight?

The commissioners did not deliberately discuss the procedures by which the relevant ends might be determined. They seem to have taken it for granted that they needed only to do what conscience said was "best for the people of Chicago as a whole." Certainly none of them thought that purely private or self-regarding ends were the proper basis for Board decisions, and so far as we know there was only one commissioner who ever attempted to use his position for purely personal ends.

The commissioners included a Jew, a Catholic, a Negro, a small businessman, a big businessman, a labor leader, and a social worker-intellectual. No one supposed that this diversity was acci-

* Although anomalous, such bodies are of course numerous and have had a long history in the United States. Thirty or forty years ago, there were independent boards in charge of school, health, police and fire departments in many cities, and even today education is generally administered by citizen boards, some of them elected but many appointed, with taxing powers. Moreover, the popularity of the special authority as a mode of organization is probably increasing.

dental, and so the commissioners were in varying degrees self-conscious representatives of interest groups concerned with public housing. How specific the claims of these special interests were, depended to a large extent upon the nature of the interest involved. It was hard to say how "small business" or "big business" could as such make any special demand upon the housing program through their "representatives" on the Board. In the case of the Catholic Church, however, the interest and the means of communicating it to the "representative" (if there was one) were somewhat more concrete and direct: for example, some Catholic spokesmen had discouraged high-rise projects because these might tend to interfere with family life. As a Negro, Taylor represented an even more apparent interest; his fellow commissioners took it for granted that he would have the special needs of the Negro constantly in mind. Kruse was nominally the representative of labor; however, he was chiefly interested in the Flat Janitors' Union and he saw to it that they were not adversely affected by the public housing that was built.

The standards by which the commissioners and others decided what kind of representation was proper and what was improper were highly particularized. Thus Kruse was once criticized editorially for participating in decisions in which his union was concerned. But Taylor, who represented an interest group which was far more important in the affairs of the Authority, was expected to participate in decisions involving the Negro. The difference was in part legal (the law said that no commissioner might have an interest in any contract for services to any project and Kruse's union had such contracts), but the real point seemed to be that a commissioner might represent a special interest appropriately only if it comprised a sizeable sector of the population (e.g., Negroes, Catholics, small businessmen, union labor, etc., but not the members of the Flat Janitors' Union), only if he sought to protect the interest group from unfair or discriminatory treatment and not to secure some special advantage for it at the expense of others, and only if he would receive no direct, and especially no material, remuneration for his services as a representative.

That they saw themselves to some extent as representatives of different and sometimes opposed interests tended to prevent the commissioners from attempting to define a clear and consistent end-system for the Authority. They could say what the Authority ought *not* to do (for each commissioner could see how any concrete proposal might affect the interests he wished to protect), but to elaborate a single positive conception of the public interest was something that they could not do. This was partly because they were oriented toward the protection of special interests and partly because they could not have agreed upon the concrete details of any conception of the public interest. The Board was, therefore, a mechanism for criticizing and amending a conception of the public interest and for giving or withholding approval of one rather than for creating one.

If the Board had been able to act in secret, its members might have been somewhat more able to free themselves from the claims of special interests and to try to agree upon a clear and explicit statement of ends. But since its minutes were open to the public, the commissioners knew that any agreement that they might reach on controversial matters would provoke a reaction that would destroy the agreement and weaken their own standing with the groups they represented. As long as there was any chance that the record would be made public, Taylor, for example, could not, even if he had wanted to, have agreed to any statement of ends that did not declare that the Authority would seek to improve the position of the Negro.* But such a statement, of course, would have only provoked a public argument. "If anyone had proposed that we declare it our policy to use public housing as a way of breaking down segregation in Chicago (and no one ever did propose this), I don't think any member of the Board would have agreed," McMillen once said.[21] "A statement like that would have had to go into our minutes, which are open to public inspection. There never was any formulation as a public statement required, except the one on non-discrimination. The issue never came up."

The Development Department, as it was reorganized to meet

* Commenting on this sentence in a manuscript version of this work, Taylor remarked that he saw his role as chairman as that of representing "broad city-wide interests" and that only in this way could he obtain the respect and support he needed to help the Negro people.

the new demands of the Act of 1949, consisted of five divisions: Construction, which would play its main part after the site selection process was over; Statistics and Research, which would collect and interpret data for all departments of the Authority; Design, which would supervise the design of projects after the sites were selected but would also be somewhat involved in the selection of sites; Standards, which was organized in mid-1950 and would assemble and formulate technical standards for the guidance of the other Development divisions; and Planning. The wide scope of the Planning Division was something of an innovation. There were hardly any housing authorities that had tried to make their projects part of a comprehensive program for the proper development of a city as a whole. It was evidence of a forward-looking and thoughtful approach (particularly on the part of Vaughan and Miss Wood) that the Chicago Housing Authority should try such a thing.

As described in a memorandum to the less planning-minded commissioners, the Planning Division was to have (in addition to the major task of project planning) three main programming functions: 1. either directly or through the Chicago Plan Commission to develop a complete inventory of sites appropriate for public housing; 2. to correlate CHA's plan with the plans of other agencies, public and private, which were building housing; and 3. to correlate CHA's plans with those of other city agencies, such as the Board of Education and the Park District. The budget provided for a planning staff of about 30 persons. The Development Department as a whole had about 100 staff members.

Meyerson, the head of the Planning Division, was more inclined than Miss Wood to emphasize the importance of a comprehensive city plan as a basis for the location of public housing. According to the doctrine of the city planning movement, to which he fully subscribed, every city should have a "comprehensive" or "master plan" which would show how the city should develop in the future. If every important decision regarding public investment were made with due regard to the master plan, then all decisions would be reciprocally related or "integrated," since the master plan, by definition, was a set of key decisions each of which was made with reference to all of the others and to all of the principal aspects of city life. The fact was that, although a number of cities had documents which were called master plans or comprehensive plans, very few of these so-called plans even roughly approximated the planning movement's definition of a master plan.* This, however, did not prevent the staff of the Development Department from believing that a master plan was not only possible and desirable but, if public housing was to be properly located, essential. The first housing sites would have to be selected without the benefit of a full-scale plan, Meyerson admitted, for Chicago had none. But there was a large background of information about Chicago and at the end of a year it should, the staff thought, be possible to bring a comprehensive residential development plan to an advanced state of preparation. The first 10,000 units could not be located according to a plan, but the remaining 30,000 hopefully would be.

"The Planning Division," Meyerson said at this time, "should serve as a gad-fly to bring this over-all planning about. If the Plan Commission and other agencies cannot be stimulated into making such a comprehensive residential plan, then the Housing Authority, perhaps in conjunction with the Land Clearance Commission will have to do it itself."†

---

* In describing the master plan, Ladislas Segoe wrote, "This plan showing in outline form the city's desirable future development—the appropriate uses of private land and the general location and extent of all necessary or desirable public facilities, all in appropriate relation one to another and in scale with the expected growth of the community and its financial resources—constitutes what is called the comprehensive city plan or master plan." *Local Planning Administration,* The International City Managers' Association, Chicago, 1st ed., 1941, p. 43.

Despite the doctrine of the city planning movement, "most planning commissions never got beyond the stage of drawing up a zoning ordinance" according to Robert A. Walker. (*The Planning Function in Urban Government,* University of Chicago Press, Chicago, 2nd ed., 1950, p. 46.) The New York charter, for example, required that all capital improvements conform to a master plan unless approved by a two-third vote of the Board of Estimate, but no such plan has ever been prepared. The New York City Planning Commission approved a plan for transportation and one for redevelopment and regarded these as parts of the master plan that would eventually be prepared. But of course a piece of a master plan which is prepared apart from the whole is a contradiction in terms: transportation must be planned *with reference to* redevelopment, etc.

† The National Association of Housing Officials in its guide for local housing authorities, *Planning for Low-Rent Housing* (Public Administration Service, Chicago, 1938) took very much the same view as the planners. It advised that if

As Miss Wood and Meyerson understood it, one function of planning, and especially of comprehensive planning, was to assert the supremacy of the public interest over private, partial or special interests. "The idea that corrupt politicians or 'special interest' groups should not direct the growth of the community but that the 'general interest' of the community as a whole should be enhanced is inherent in current community planning thought," Meyerson wrote at about this time. "It has become a constant task of community planning to sift the proposals for community development, to separate out those that will be of value just to a few persons from those that will be of value to all, and to recommend honest procedures for achieving desired proposals."[22]

The Planning Division's task, whether it was to encourage the making of a comprehensive plan for residential development or simply to "correlate" CHA's plans with those of other agencies, was bound to be a very difficult one. Chicago had not one but six governments. There was the city government proper, a very loosely joined collection of departments and boards owing allegiance more to the City Council than to the Mayor, and there were five other quite separate bodies (the Board of Education, the Board of Trustees of the Sanitary District, the Chicago Park District, the Board of Commissioners of Cook County and the Forest Preserve District of Cook County) each with independent taxing powers and with officers who were either elected or, if appointed by the Mayor, virtually independent of him. Most of these governments were concerned somehow, even if only tangentially, with the housing program, and of course all of them had interests of their own to serve and to safeguard and ample legal authority and political power with which to do so.

Furthermore, half a dozen public or quasi-public bodies were very directly and substantially concerned with housing. The City Council was one. It had several standing committees which would have to be taken into account: Housing; Building and Zoning; Local Industries, Streets and Alleys; and Planning. Housing was

---

a city planning department could not supply the needed data "a housing authority should first assist the city planning department in obtaining the funds necessary for such work. If the city planning department is unable to make the necessary data available to the housing authority, the latter should proceed independently and promptly to obtain them. This relationship recognizes the fact that housing is an integral part of city planning." pp. 8-9.

the largest of these committees with at one time 32 of the 50 aldermen as members.

The Land Clearance Commission was another such body. Like CHA itself, the Land Clearance Commission was to a large extent independent of the Mayor and City Council. It could assemble blighted land in tracts of two acres or more and sell it at "re-use value" (for example at 50 cents a square foot, which might be a third or less of what the land cost the Commission) to a redeveloper who presented an acceptable plan. The cost of this "write-down" was to be shared by the local and the Federal government on a one-to-two ratio. In 1949 one such project, Lake Meadows, was being developed by the New York Life Insurance Company, and the Land Clearance Commission hoped to find investors for more. Since CHA and the Land Clearance Commission would both be looking for sites it would be advantageous for them to work closely together; this was all the more true because by good timing each agency might relieve the relocation problems created by the other. The director of the Land Clearance Commission's staff had once been director of planning for CHA, and so it seemed reasonable to suppose that the two agencies would coordinate their programs carefully.

However, in 1949 the Land Clearance Commission was not quite ready to select a program of additional sites and its small technical staff did not begin to function fully until the middle of 1950; by that time it was too late to do much coordinating with CHA on the initial public housing sites under the 1949 Act. But even if this had not been the case, there were other difficulties that would have stood in the way: the CHA planning staff was still in the process of recruiting personnel; the Land Clearance Commission had committed a large proportion of its planning budget to work being done by the Plan Commission; and very likely the Land Clearance Commissioners were in fear that close association with the then controversial public housing program might be a political liability.*

---

* Coordination between the corresponding Federal agencies—although they were responsible to the overall administrator of the parent agency, the Housing and Home Finance Agency—was also very imperfect, partly for political reasons. The Public Housing Administration had been set up apart from the Federal Housing Administration to avoid the influence of the home-builder, mortgage banker in-

The Chicago Dwellings Association was another agency concerned with housing. It had been created in 1947 to produce a limited amount of "middle-income" housing on a non-profit basis for veterans. CDA had only little relationship, formal or informal, with the city government. The Chicago Housing Authority kept accounts for CDA and provided it some technical assistance.

The office of the Mayor's Housing and Redevelopment Coordinator had been created in 1947 to bring some order out of the chaos that resulted from having so many agencies working on similar problems. The office required power to succeed, but no one knew what powers, if any, the Mayor had given the Coordinator. During most of 1949 and 1950, the duties of the post were being performed by an Acting Coordinator.

The Chicago Plan Commission was an advisory body which had no operating powers. It consisted of 34 unpaid commissioners appointed by the Mayor, of whom 20, an ample majority, were *ex officio* representing city departments and committees of the City Council. The Commission included three very well known architects who often had a professional interest in city development schemes, as well as several businessmen and bankers who had special neighborhood and other property interests to protect. One of these architects, Nathaniel Owings, a partner in the firm which was designing the Lake Meadows redevelopment project, was chairman of the Commission in 1949 and 1950. Eight powerful aldermen were *ex-officio* members of the commission; some of them were known to be opponents of public housing and especially of bi-racial public housing.

Although one of the earliest city plans had been made in Chicago in 1909, little effective planning had been done subsequently. The Commission had, however, made a rather complete land use inventory and had published in 1943, *The Master Plan of Residential Land Use of Chicago*. The title was misleading, for, while it contained a great deal of information about residential land use, this document was not detailed enough to serve as a

---

terests which dominated the latter agency. Then the Division of Slum Clearance and Urban Redevelopment was set up apart from other operating units so that subsidized private rebuilding would not be unduly influenced by them. The lack of coordination nationally made it all the less likely that the local agencies supervised by these national ones would work closely together.

basis for decisions and it was more descriptive than prescriptive. Insofar as it contained proposals, these were delineated mainly in three maps: one showing where housing areas of various conditions (e.g. conservation, stable, etc.) would be located in the future, another where housing of various types (e.g. tall apartments, single family dwellings, etc.) would be located, and one showing future population densities in areas of residential land use. The most fundamental point it made was that the density of population in the congested inner core of the city would be reduced; although the plan did not say so, this could only take place by a migration to outlying undeveloped and partially developed residential areas. But whether this reduction of density was a prediction of something that was likely to happen or a recommendation of something that ought to happen was not clear. The plan did suggest that public powers be used to acquire and clear land and reduce its costs, but it specified few concrete steps, and a great many circumstances that would have to be taken into account in any action program were altogether ignored: there was no attention paid to the special problems of the Negroes, for example, or to the costs of developing transportation, utilities, schools, and other facilities for new residential areas. Some of the assumptions on which the plan was based were questionable; this was true, for example, of its population estimates (by 1950 the city's population had already exceeded the figure projected for 1965). But the most serious failing of the plan was that it implied relocating the slum population and it did so without pointing out—and presumably without considering—the consequences of this relocation. No one wanted congestion or slums, but these could not be eliminated without to a considerable extent breaking down racial segregation. The Plan Commission proposed higher densities for Negro than for other areas, but, either from timidity or for other reasons, it failed to point out that a choice would have to be made between congestion and the breakdown of segregation. Its report, therefore, did more to obscure than to clarify the choice the city faced. The City Council voted to "accept" the report, as it did other Plan Commission documents, but it did so without discussion and apparently without any thought of measures to effectuate it.

A *Preliminary Comprehensive Plan* had also been published by the Plan Commission. It described a highway network, a gross designation of future residential, commercial, and industrial land use and an indication of areas for parks and some other facilities. It was very generalized and was often pointed to more as a description of what already existed than of something the city government intended to bring into existence. Although the Plan Commission sought to have new undertakings, including housing projects, conform roughly to this comprehensive plan, it was never made the basis of detailed decisions. It was too general and, in the view of the Plan Commission, too preliminary for that.

For several years prior to the passage of the Housing Act of 1949 the Plan Commission and the Authority had rarely worked together. In 1944 the Plan Commission declared in a formal resolution that in passing upon any CHA proposal it would "commit itself only to the extent" of finding that the proposal did or did not conform to the master plan of Chicago.[23] Since Elizabeth Wood, Vaughan and Meyerson believed that the support of the Plan Commission was important for the public housing program, they determined to establish close working relations with the Plan Commission's staff. They knew that the Executive Director of that staff could not ignore the conservative and generally anti-public housing character of his Commission to which he was responsible, but since its budget was small (it was only $150,000 a year), there was reason to believe that the Plan Commission staff might provide technical aid to CHA if that agency could offer operating funds.

As matters stood on July 8, 1949, the day CHA submitted its general proposal to the Mayor, the legislative steps that would have to be taken before the architects and engineers could go to work were few and—one might think—simple. The City Council, consisting of the Mayor and 50 aldermen, would have to approve CHA's application to the Public Housing Administration for a "program reservation" of up to 21,000 units (the amount of housing that was to be started, but not completed, during the first two years) and for an advance of loan funds to cover the costs of site selection and planning. At the same time, the Council would have to enter into a cooperation agreement with CHA by which it would undertake to provide city services for the number of units reserved.

These first steps were taken by the Council exactly one week after the Authority put its proposal in the Mayor's hands. This was, as it happened, the same day that President Truman signed the Housing Act, making it the law of the land.

The Housing Authority—that is, the commissioners and the appropriate staff members—had now to select sites for the first year's program, 12,000 units. In the course of this process, the sites would have to be reviewed by the Plan Commission and to some extent by other agencies such as the Board of Education—all agencies whose powers in this regard were only advisory, but which nevertheless, because of their political positions, would have to be taken fully into account. Then the specific sites would have to be approved by the City Council. Finally, the Public Housing Administration would have to accept the program as a whole.

If no serious disagreements turned up and with good luck in matters of routine, it might be possible to move some of the slum families into the new housing within a year. "Let's make it fast," the *Sun-Times,* Marshall Field's newspaper, urged in an editorial on July 11, 1949. "The public looks to the mayor to see to it that the CHA program is approved before the City Council quits for the summer on July 22." The *Daily News* took a less hopeful view. Some public housing is necessary, it said, but the amount proposed seems excessive. "Past and current experience with site selection and other red tape makes it extremely doubtful if 30,000 units could actually be produced in six years."[24]

"He Certainly Can Take It!"
LA SALLE
RANDOLPH
CITY HALL
MAYOR KENNELLY
CHICAGO'S PRESSING PROBLEMS
1951 • CHICAGO SUN-TIMES

CHAPTER THREE □ □ □ □ □ □

THE POLITICIANS

THERE WAS much reason to expect Mayor Kennelly to press for early acceptance of the Authority's proposal. It would be hard for any politician not to accept so large a gift to his city, especially to a city so much in need of housing as Chicago. Moreover, experience indicated that support of public housing might be good politics. Back in 1915 Mayor William Hale Thompson had demonstrated a formula for winning elections which had proved itself time and again; it called for (among other things) assiduous cultivation of the Negro vote and an energetic appeal to the booster spirit which gloried in vast public works.[1] Politicians of both parties had not forgotten this time-tested formula, and public housing seemingly fitted the formula perfectly since it was presumed to appeal both to Negroes and to boosters. Boss Kelly, Kennelly's predecessor, had made himself the great friend and protector of public housing and it was expected that Kennelly would do the same. In his campaign he had in fact stressed the housing shortage and the voters had given him the biggest total vote and the biggest margin of victory in the city's history. The vote in the Negro wards gave the new Mayor less endorsement however: Kelly, who had established himself as the Negro's friend, had received 61.1 per cent of the vote in these wards in 1943; Kennelly, who had yet to prove himself, received only 56.3 per cent.

Kennelly's stand on issues other than housing, especially that of political interference with the schools, was no doubt chiefly responsible for his success at the polls. But apparently he felt that emphasis on the housing problem had brought him votes. At his first press conference after the election, he called housing Chicago's "number one problem and emergency" and soon after taking office he appointed a 16-man Committee for Housing Action, the chairman of which was the president of the Chicago Title and Trust Company. "Controversies of any nature," the Mayor told the committee, "such as those over the principles of public and private housing, have no place in an action program."[2] The committee quickly brought in a report which urged, among other things, more low-rent housing. Acting on one of its recommendations, the Mayor appointed a Housing and Redevelopment Coordinator who, reporting directly to him, helped secure passage of a $30 million slum clearance and rehousing bond issue which the Mayor's forces placed on the ballot. The bond issue was supported by all four of the city's large newspapers, by the State Street Council (a merchants' organization), the Civic Federation (a taxpayers' association), and the labor, church, Negro, and women's organizations which were regular supporters of housing legislation. The Real Estate Board (an association of realtors) remained neutral, although some of its members did not. The voters approved the bond issue by a nearly two to one majority.

This general enthusiasm for a housing program seemed to be shared by the aldermen. They voted 28 to 16 to memorialize Congress in favor of the Housing Act, and their vote on CHA's application for a preliminary loan was even more encouraging: 35 to 9. As delegates or alternates to the 1948 national convention, four of them had helped to frame the Democratic Party platform, which unequivocally promised public housing. Two of the aldermen were Negroes and many others had slum area constituencies.

With elections to be held the following November, the Democratic Party seemed to want a housing program which could be pointed to as an accomplishment. The Party as a whole seemed to want a housing program, and so did certain individuals in key places. There was Alderman John J. Duffy, for example, chairman of the Council's finance committee and as such its chief leader, who hoped to be elected president of the Cook County Board, a job which had been described as "the juiciest plum in all Chicago." It was thought that Duffy needed the support of the *Sun-Times* to win. But unless he gave some support to public housing, he could not expect the paper's backing, for the *Sun-Times* was campaigning hard for public housing.

And yet, in another view, the case was not so clear; there was, in fact, much reason to doubt that the Housing Authority's proposal would win ready acceptance, and there was even some reason to believe that it would not be accepted at all.

Candidate Kennelly had said much about housing, but remarkably little about *public* housing. So too had some of his chief supporters; they also were for housing, but not necessarily for public housing and not necessarily for as much housing as was requested in the CHA proposal. Thus, for example, the Plan Commission, which often reflected the sentiments of the business community, had in its 1946 report, *Housing Goals for Chicago,* concluded that the quickest and most effective way to provide relief for people who could not afford to buy or rent new houses "is through the building of new dwelling units for those thousands of families who are able to pay for them." "As these new houses and apartment units are constructed," the report said, "the acute tension in the housing market will be relieved; there will be greater freedom of movement; and there will be thousands of good dwellings units vacated and made available for the occupancy of families with somewhat smaller incomes."[3] This was what was widely known in the literature of housing as the "filtering down" process.

This "filtering down" view did not take account of the most numerous class of slum-dwellers, the Negroes, who for a variety of reasons (but chiefly because of patterns of segregation) were not at liberty to move into the houses that might be vacated, and it did not take account of the fact that there were many more slum-dwellers than there could possibly be vacancies—that the base of the income-pyramid was larger than its top.[4] The Plan Commission had not ignored these people entirely however. For the 10,000 families it estimated were living in structures unfit for habitation, "a reasonable amount of new construction through public aids must be provided to enable them to enjoy decent living conditions and to permit the rapid elimination of unsightly, unsanitary, and dangerous residential structures."[5]

If, as seemed not unlikely, the Mayor shared this opinion, the Housing Authority might have trouble persuading him to sponsor a program of 40,000 public housing units. There was in fact reason to believe that the Mayor and his Housing Action Committee did share this view, and that both the Committee and the Housing and Redevelopment Coordinator (the first Coordinator was a vice-president of the Marshall Field and Company department store) were more interested in curbing the Housing Authority than in helping it. It was due in part to the Housing Action Committee that the new private redevelopment slum clearance program was established outside the Authority in a specially created Land Clearance Commission.

The City Council, the body which would have to pass upon any sites proposed by the Authority, consisted of 50 aldermen, with the mayor as presiding officer. The aldermen were elected for four-year terms from wards of roughly 25,000 to 65,000 registered voters, only about a third of whom usually voted in aldermanic elections. (The number who voted in mayoralty elections was about twice as great.) Nominally the office of alderman was non-partisan. Actually, however, no one could win an election without the support of a powerful organization and (with some rare exceptions) the only powerful political organizations in the wards were the Democratic and Republican parties. An alderman who did not have the support of his party "machine"* ordinarily had no hope of reelection.

---

* Although written almost two generations ago, Lord Bryce's description of machines applies both in general and in detail to the Chicago machines of the present day. See *The American Commonwealth,* 1917 ed., Macmillan, New York and London, Vol. II, Ch. LXIII for Bryce's account of the circumstances which give rise to machines.

"The elective offices are so numerous that ordinary citizens cannot watch them, and cease to care who gets them. The conventions come so often that busy men cannot serve in them. The minor offices are so unattractive that able men do not stand for them. The primary lists are so contrived that only a fraction of the party get on them; and of this fraction many are too lazy or too busy or too careless to attend. The mass of the voters are ignorant; knowing nothing about the personal merits of the candidates, they are ready to follow their leaders like sheep. Even the better class, however they may grumble, are swayed by the inveterate habit of party loyalty, and prefer a bad candidate of their own party to a (probably no better) candidate of the other party. It is less trouble to put up with impure officials, costly city government, a jobbing State legislature, an inferior sort of congressman, than to sacrifice one's own business in the effort to set things right. Thus the Machine works on, and grinds out places, power, and opportunities for illicit gain to those who manage it." *Ibid.,* p. 110.

The Democratic "machine" had ruled Chicago since 1923. Catholics were in control of it; since 1930, with a few exceptions, they had held the major city offices: the mayor, city treasurer, county clerk, more than half of the county commissioners, and two-thirds of the aldermen were Catholics.[6] And among the Catholics it was those of Irish extraction who were dominant in politics: one-third of the Council, including most of its leaders, were Irish-Catholics. The other aldermen were mostly of Polish, Italian, Bohemian, Lithuanian, Slovak, or Greek extraction (in descending order of importance, these were the principal nationality groups in the Democratic party) or of German extraction (these were Republicans).[7] A few aldermen were Jews (unlike the Poles, Italians, and other ethnic minorities, the Jews did not usually endeavor to be recognized as a group on the party slate or in the award of patronage).[8] Two were Negroes. The numerical importance of the Irish in the Council was to be accounted for not so much by their numbers in the electorate as by the fact that in wards where no one ethnic group had a clear majority they made the most acceptable compromise candidates. As one politician explained to an interviewer, "A Lithuanian won't vote for a Pole, and a Pole won't vote for a Lithuanian. A German won't vote for either of them—but all three will vote for a 'Turkey' (Irishman)."* [9]

A few of the aldermen aspired to higher political office, especially (among those who were lawyers) to judgeships, but most of them were in the business of being aldermen as other men are in the business of selling shoes. Being an alderman was supposed to be a full-time occupation, but the salary was only $5,000, so most aldermen supplemented their salaries by selling something

* A candidate's ethnicity was often a decisive asset or liability; in mixed wards he was most fortunate if his name was such that he could be represented as belonging to more than one ethnic or nationality group. Thus, Alderman Benjamin M. Becker's ward committeeman introduced him to voters of German extraction as of German extraction, stressed to voters of Swedish origin that Becker's wife had lived in Sweden and must have Swedish blood herself, pointed out to Catholics that Becker was a graduate of the DePaul University College of Law and a teacher there (thus implying that he was a Catholic), and presented him to Jews as a Jew. If the Catholics were fooled, no great injustice was done, for Becker's predecessor as alderman for many years was Dr. Joseph Ross, a Catholic whom the Jews assumed was a Jew.[10]

—most often insurance or legal service (more than half of them were lawyers). Being an alderman was, of course, very good for business.

Ordinarily, even if he were so inclined, an alderman could not concern himself deeply with the larger issues of city government or take a city-wide view of important problems. If he wanted to stay in office, he had to devote all of his available time and attention to the affairs of the groups that made up his ward. He was in the Council to look after the special interests of his ward and to do favors for his constituents: to get streets repaired, to have a playground installed, to change the zoning law, to represent irate parents before the school authorities, and so on. In addition to activities of this kind, he had to take an interest in the social life of his ward—to appear at weddings, funerals, and neighborhood occasions, and to say a few well chosen words and make a small donation when called upon. If he had any time left, he might think about the problems of the city as a whole. But whatever he thought, he was expected to work for his ward first.

From a formal standpoint, the 50 aldermen governed Chicago.* The Council made appropriations for all municipal purposes, it awarded franchises to and regulated the rates of public utility companies, it passed on appointments presented by the mayor, and (within the authority given it by the state) it could create new city departments at will. The mayor could send or read messages to the Council, he could vote when there was a tie (or when more than one-half of the aldermen had already voted for a measure), and he had a veto (including an item veto over appropriations acts) which could be overridden by a two-thirds vote. In principle, each alderman was the independent agent of his ward. From a formal standpoint, then, the Council was a good deal like a league of independent nations presided over by a secretary-general.

In fact, however, there existed two sets of informal controls by which the aldermen's independence was very much limited and qualified. One set of controls was the leadership of the Council

* The city could exercise only those powers doled out to it by the state legislature, however, and so it might be more accurate to say that the city was governed by the state. See Barnet Hodes, "The Illinois Constitution and Home Rule for Chicago," 15 *Chicago Law Review* 78, (1947).

itself. Half a dozen of the most powerful Democratic aldermen—the "Big Boys," they were sometimes called—working usually with the mayor, effectively controlled the whole Council when matters of interest to them or to the mayor were at stake. They did this in part by controlling committee assignments. Unless an alderman could get on an important committee, his power in the Council was small. And unless he cooperated with the chairmen of the important committees and especially with the chairman of the Finance Committee (whose salary was $8,500, who was provided a limousine with a police chauffeur, and who had an office second only to the mayor's in splendor), he could not hope to get anything done for his ward. Any measure that required an appropriation had to go to the Finance Committee, and so, as one alderman explained, the chairman of that committee "sits at the gate of accomplishment for any alderman. . . ."[11] Indeed, if an alderman fell foul of the Finance Committee chairman or of any of the "Big Boys" he might be punished by having some city service to his ward reduced or suspended. On the other hand, even if he were a Republican, he could expect generous treatment from the leadership if he "played ball."

The other set of informal controls operated through the party or machine. An alderman had to stay in favor with his ward committeeman—i.e., the party leader in his ward—or else be the committeeman himself. The ward committeeman made all of the important decisions for the party within the ward. The committeeman was elected in the primary every four years (usually he could keep an opponent off the ballot by raising technical objections to his petitions) and so his power rested in part upon a legal foundation. From a legal standpoint, he was entitled to receive and disburse party funds, to manage campaigns, and to represent the leaders of the party within the ward. In fact he was commonly the "boss" of the ward; the party organization in the ward "belonged" to him. He decided who would run on the party's ticket within the ward, he appointed and dismissed precinct captains at will, and he dispensed patronage. As a member of the City and County Central Committees of his party, he participated in selecting its candidates for all city, county, and state offices and for Congress. (Half of Illinois' 26 Congressional districts were in greater Chicago.) In each of the party governing bodies his vote was in proportion to the total primary vote for his party in the last election; this of course gave him an incentive to "turn in" the biggest vote possible.

No salary went with the office of committeeman, but most of the committeemen held one or more public jobs and some of them ran businesses which were profitable because of their political connections.

William J. Connors, Democratic boss of the 42nd ward (the district described by Zorbaugh in *The Gold Coast and the Slum*),[12] may be taken as reasonably representative of at least some other ward committeemen. In 1950 Connors, who was in the insurance business, was on the public payroll in two capacities: as a state senator and as a bailiff of Municipal Court. His way of running his ward was described as follows:

> That Connors provides well for his workers is undeniable. Not only does he have a great many jobs to distribute, but he is a source of funds if any of his men need to borrow. He supports them when they are in difficulty with the law, as sometimes happens, and takes an interest in their family affairs. His relationship with them is that of a benevolent despot. He holds the power to withdraw their source of livelihood and to banish them from active work in the party and from their power positions in the community. He is the sole dispenser of the campaign funds from the party superstructure and the candidates. He may establish the assessments of the jobholders at any rate he desires without consulting them. He makes the party commitments to the county and city organs without a canvass of the captains' opinions and then demands complete obedience to these decisions. He may move a captain from one precinct to another at his discretion and is, of course, the sole source of patronage distribution.
>
> The committeeman generals his workers much like a military leader might. He plots the strategy of the campaign, estimates the difficulties that may be encountered, and decides the amount and allocation of money to be spent. He shifts captains from one point to another when called for. He attempts to "build" good precincts over a long period of time. Such building requires several years and may involve extensive trials and changes. Jobs are distributed not only on the basis of the effectiveness of the captain but in regard to the total effects such distribution may have. It happens occasionally that a strong Democratic captain has a smaller number of jobs allotted to him than one who is attempting to build up a Democratic precinct in the face of strong Republican competition. Thus in one precinct which casts a

heavy Democratic vote, there are only two jobs besides the captain's, while another precinct that turns in only a slight Democratic majority is staffed by nine jobholders in addition to the captain.

The committeeman respects the unity of the precinct organization and the authority of the captain and his workers. As long as the captain's activities are successful and his conduct does not threaten the party's vote-getting power, Connors does not interfere with the internal structure. The captain selects his own assistants and nominates his choices to receive public jobs. He assumes the responsibility for building an effective precinct organization. He decides how party funds allocated to him will be distributed and to a certain extent how they will be obtained. He and his men must share the responsibility of contributing whatever additional money is necessary beyond that sent from the party's headquarters. Connors respects the autonomy of the captain in this area of personal influence. Captains may or may not distribute campaign literature, pay cash for votes, engage in fraudulent activities, or arrange precinct meetings of the voters. The only important check on the captain's conduct is the final tabulation of votes at each election.[13]

Any ward committeeman who cared to could have himself nominated alderman. If he chose not to run for the office himself (like Connors, he might prefer to be on the public payroll in another capacity), he made sure that the candidate was someone who would work closely with him in ward affairs and offer no challenge to his control of the organization. "Naturally," an alderman once explained, "he (the ward committeeman) doesn't want to get a man who will build himself into a power so he can take the organization away from the committeeman. If the alderman doesn't do what the ward committeeman wants him to do, then the committeeman will dump him at the next election."[14] Some committeemen treated their aldermen as errand boys, other paid little attention to them, and still others treated them as friends, partners, and collaborators.[15]

If an alderman became powerful enough, he might unseat his committeeman and become the ward boss himself. But even in this case he could not be independent of the machine. The leaders of the Central Committee could bring him into line by withholding patronage or discharging public employees from his ward, by denying him financial support from the party's general coffers at election time, or by allowing an investigatian of graft and corruption to take place in his ward. If it saw fit, the Central Committee could destroy a ward organization—and thus a ward committeeman—by these means, but it could do so, of course, only at the cost of impairing, at least temporarily, the effectiveness of the machine. Since its purpose was to win elections, a major concern of the machine was "harmony." Only if a committeeman failed to support the party's slate was he likely to be disciplined severely. If they wanted a favor from him, party leaders would offer him a favor—usually patronage—in return.

To increase their power *vis-a-vis* the Central Committee leadership, ward committeemen formed factional alliances or "blocs." Usually these alignments were on a geographical basis—thus, for example, there were South Side and West Side blocs of ward committeemen.

In order to maintain itself and to accomplish its purposes, any organization must offer incentives of the kinds and amounts that are necessary to elicit the contributions of activity it requires. It must then use these contributions of activity so as to secure a renewed supply of resources from which further incentives may be provided—it must, in other words, maintain what Chester Barnard has called an "economy of incentives" or else cease to exist.[16]

In Chicago a political machine distributed "gravy" to its officials, its financial backers, and to the voters. In this way it induced them to contribute the activity it required—to ring doorbells on election day, to give cash, and to go to the polls and vote for its candidates—and in this way it gained possession, through its control of the city or county government, of a renewed supply of "gravy."

As the word "gravy" suggests, the incentives upon which the machines relied were mainly material. Some prestige attached to being a ward politician; there was "fun" in playing the political "game"; there was satisfaction in being "on the inside"; and sometimes there was even an ideological commitment to an issue, the party, or a candidate. But these non-material incentives were not ordinarily strong enough to elicit the amount and kind of activity that a machine required from its workers. "What I look for in a prospective captain," a ward committeeman told an interviewer, "is a young person—man or woman—who is interested in getting some material return out of his political activity. I much prefer this type to the type that is enthused about the 'party cause' or all 'hot' on a particular issue. Enthusiasm for causes is short-lived, but the necessity of making a living is permanent."[17]

The "material return" that the party offered a worker was generally a job on the public payroll. Committeeman Connors, for example, had at his disposal in 1952 an estimated 350 to 500 jobs and the total public payroll to Democratic workers in his ward was conservatively estimated at $1,320,000.[18]

Although jobs were the most visible of the material returns the party gave its workers, other opportunities to make money may have been more valuable. An alderman or committeeman who was a lawyer, an insurance man, or a tavern owner could expect to profit greatly from his association with the party. Whether he was profiting lawfully or unlawfully it was often impossible to tell. Alderman Sain and his ward committeeman, County Commissioner John J. Touhy, for example, were partners in an insurance business. "We handle a lot of business, no question about it," Touhy once blandly told a reporter. "I assume its just good business in the ward to carry insurance with us."* [19]

Even with the voters the machine did not make its appeal on the basis of issues or ideology. It offered them certain non-material incentives—chiefly the friendship and protection of its precinct captains—but in the main with them, as with the party workers, it relied upon "gravy." Just as it gave its workers jobs and opportunities to make money in exchange for their services, so it gave its loyal voters "favors"—special services and preferential treatment at the hands of its members and dependents who held city or county jobs—in exchange for their votes.

The party's agent in exchanging friendship and favors for votes was the precinct captain.† In 1950 a representative captain described his work as follows:

---

* Some years earlier the *Chicago Daily News* compiled a list of the ordinances introduced by Sain over a five-month period and then inquired of the people who were specially benefited by these ordinances whether they had recently bought insurance of the firm of Touhy and Sain. It turned out that many of them had. (September 24, 1940.)

† In a vivid account by David Gutmann, the Chicago precinct captain is described as a "salesman." "Mr. Dolin [the precinct captain] is a go-between between his party, which has services and favors to sell the public in exchange for the

I am a lawyer and prosecuting attorney for the City. I have spent 19 years in precinct work and have lived and worked in my present precinct for three and a half years.

I try to establish a relationship of personal obligation with my people, mostly small shopkeepers and eighty per cent Jewish. I spend two or three evenings a week all year round visiting people, playing cards, talking, and helping them with their problems. My wife doesn't like this, but it is in my blood now. I know ninety per cent of my people by their first names.

Actually I consider myself a social worker for my precinct. I help my people get relief and driveway permits. I help them on unfair parking fines and property assessments. The last is most effective in my neighborhood.

The only return I ask is that they register and vote. If they have their own opinions on certain top offices, I just ask them to vote my way on lower offices where they usually have no preferences anyway.

I never take leaflets or mention issues or conduct rallies in my precinct. After all, this is a question of personal friendship between me and my neighbors. I had 260 promises for Korshak in this primary.

On election day I had forty or fifty people to help me because this was a "hot" campaign. All they had to do was to get out their own family and friends. I used to lease an apartment near the poll where I gave out drinks and cigars, but I don't do this any more.

I stayed inside the poll most of election day, especially during the vote counting. If something went wrong, you could have heard me yell all over the precinct. Actually there isn't as much fraud now as there used to be.

Abner (the PAC candidate) was not really a threat in my precinct. He had seven workers but they contacted only their friends. No one feels obligated to them and they worked only during the campaign. Abner's campaigners were naive. They expected to influence people by issues, and they relied on leaflets and newspaper publicity which is not effective. Besides, Abner (Negro) is not hard to beat in a white precinct. I just carried a picture of both candidates around with me.

I can control my primary vote for sure because I can make the party regulars come out. I don't encourage a high vote here, just a sure vote. In the general election there is much more independent voting, and I can't be sure of control.[20]

---

public's votes, and the public, or at least the segments of it which are willing to exchange their votes for services—often enough to swing a close election. In this relationship the vote stands for currency, the party is the manufacturer or the supplier, the public is the consumer, and Mr. Dolin the door-to-door salesman. . . . To the party the vote has 'commodity' or exchange value, in that it represents a fraction of the total sum of votes needed by the party to gain exclusive control over the 'tons' of patronage whereby it holds power, and to gain access to the financial resources of the community." David Gutmann, "Big-Town Politics: Grass-Roots Level," *Commentary*, 17:1, February 1954, p. 155.

In the conservation areas, especially, the precinct captain was often active in the neighborhood improvement association and a leader in efforts to keep "undesirable people" out of the neighborhood. An interviewer who spoke to 30 precinct captains in 1951 found that 16 of them had been approached by voters who wanted help in preventing Negroes and Jews from moving into the neighborhood. Some of these captains invented slogans and ran campaigns on an issue such as: "The ——— neighborhood is a good clean neighborhood. Let's keep it that way!" A captain was likely to learn about it almost immediately if a landlord rented to an "undesirable"; very often the captain would go to the landlord to urge in the name of civic pride that he discriminate and to point out that property values would decline if he did not.

In heavily Democratic precincts the owners of rooming houses sometimes consulted with their precinct captains about new roomers and assisted the party workers with their canvass at election time. In some cases these owners refused to permit Republican workers to enter their buildings. The loyalty of the rooming house owner to the Democratic party was not a matter of ideology: the owner who did not cooperate with the precinct captain could expect a visit from the city building inspector the next day.[21]

In addition to the services of party workers and voters, the machine needed cash. (It usually cost about $40,000 to elect an alderman.) This it raised by assessing the salaries of people who owed their jobs to the party, from the proceeds of ward-sponsored affairs such as picnics, boxing matches, and golf days, and in contributions from individuals and organizations who wanted to be on good terms with the party or, perhaps, even to help its candidates win.[22] These were all considered legitimate sources of revenue. In some wards, however, money was raised by promising favors or threatening injury to business interests, especially to those interests—e.g., taverns, hotels, and nightclubs—which were subject to inspection and licensing laws. Business people who wanted favors—a change in the zoning law, a permit to operate a tavern, a tax adjustment, and so on—were expected to pay for them in cash. In some wards there was even said to be a fixed schedule of prices for such favors. Whether the money so received went to support the party or to support personally the ward committeeman, the alderman, and their cronies was seldom clear; indeed, in many wards no real distinction could be made between the coffers of the party and the pockets of the boss: the ward organization "belonged" to the boss.*

The most profitable favors were of course those done for illegal enterprises. In giving protection to gambling joints, unlawful taverns, and houses of prostitution some politicians joined with racketeers to form a criminal syndicate.† A by-product of their activity was the systematic corruption of the police force; in one way or another officers were either bribed or discouraged from doing their duty. "After you find out how many places are protected by the ward politicians," a patrolman of long service told an investigator, "you just stay out of the way so you won't be around when something happens."[23]

The machines were most effective in delivering votes in the precincts where they were most corrupt. In general, these were in the "skid-row" districts and the slums, where votes were cheapest and illegal activities most numerous. The "river wards" in the decaying center and on the West Side of the city were the most solidly organized and the most corrupt. Here "social absenteeism"—the departure of socially articulate leaders of the community—had reached such a point that the machine politicians had the field to themselves.‡ It was almost unthinkable that an

* If he thought the transaction was likely to be profitable, the ward boss might sell the services of his organization to the opposition. He might be criticized for doing this, but he was not likely to be unseated; after all, the organization "belonged" to him.

† ". . . the criminal syndicate," according to Aaron Kohn, chief investigator for the Emergency Crime Committee of the City Council, "can be described as consisting of political officials, having the power and responsibility to enforce the laws, who maliciously withhold that power in exchange for money and support from hoodlums, vice operators, professional gamblers, and other community enemies, to aid them in their political ambitions." Independent Voters of Illinois, *The Kohn Report; Crime and Politics in Chicago,* Chicago, 1953, p. iii. However, after two months inquiry a grand jury in the Spring of 1954 gave up its efforts to uncover specific links between crime and politics in Chicago. "If an alliance exists," the jurors said, "it might be disclosed with funds to conduct undercover work. . . ." *Chicago Sun-Times,* May 1, 1954.

‡ See the discussion of social absenteeism in Morris Janowitz, *The Community Press in an Urban Setting,* The Free Press, Glencoe, Illinois, 1952, p. 214. Janowitz notes that social absenteeism contributes to the decay of the ideological element in politics, thus creating "a new kind of hoodlumism in politics" and making possible sudden shifts from one party to another which have no significance in terms of the traditional political allegiances.

alderman in one of these wards might lose at the polls because he took an unpopular stand on an issue. If he lost, it was because his committeeman "dumped" him, because the committeeman sold out to the opposition, or because the opposition managed to build a more powerful machine, but it was not because the voters disliked his stand on any issues. These "river wards" were in sharp contrast to the so-called "newspaper wards" particularly on the North Side where voters usually split the ticket in the way a newspaper advised. The aldermen in the "river wards" could afford to be contemptuous of the newspapers; in their wards editorials were words wasted.

Although corruption in varying degrees was widespread in both parties, it was by no means universal in either. Some Democratic and some Republican wards were probably almost entirely "clean" and even in wards which were not "clean" there were aldermen and other officials who were not parties to the "deals" that were made in the back rooms. The honest aldermen, however, got little credit or encouragement from the voters. Many people seemed to think that all politicians were corrupt and that if an alderman did not use his office for personal profit it was because he was a fool. When a North Side alderman bought his boy a football suit and helmet the other children in the neighborhood said, "Look at the alderman's son," suggesting ill-gotten funds. The alderman himself drove a two-year-old Dodge instead of the Cadillac that he could well afford, but even this did not convince his constituents that he was honest.[24] * This widespread cynicism tended, perhaps, to give the aldermen a low conception of their calling and to encourage irresponsibility on their part.

Some of the honest men, the Mayor among them, did less than they might have done to put a stop to corruption. The fact was that they needed for themselves or for their party the support of the powerful bosses in the corrupt wards. So, for that matter, did many other interests, both liberal and conservative, in city, state, and nation.

---

* As this study went to press a committee of the Chicago Bar Association filed charges against this very alderman after the *Sun-Times* had accused him of fee-splitting in zoning cases.

Negroes had less power in the Council than their numbers in the city warranted. In 1950 there were 10 wards where their vote was more than 20 per cent of the total and 10 other wards where it was from 10 to 20 per cent. In four wards (the 2nd, 3rd, 4th and 20th) the vote was overwhelmingly Negro; two of these wards had Negro aldermen. If they had not been so much concentrated in these few wards—if, instead, they had been spread evenly over the whole city, the Negroes, although they might not have had any of their number in the Council, might have had more representation there: instead of having virtual control over two aldermen and a good deal of influence over several others, they might have had some influence over all 50 of the aldermen. When the voting was not on a ward basis, i.e., in city-wide, state, and national elections, this mal-distribution was no handicap; Negro leaders often claimed that they held a balance of power between the parties in the city, state and national scenes.*

The two Negro aldermen were Archibald J. Carey, Jr., a Republican, who was both a minister and a lawyer, and who was generally regarded as among the best educated, the most eloquent, and the most intelligent men in the Council, and William Harvey, a Democrat, who had been secretary to Congressman William L. Dawson, the political boss of the Black Belt.

Dawson knew how to build an organization that would deliver votes. He was the committeeman of Harvey's ward (the "mother ward" it was called by the Negro politicians because from it the Negro political organization had spread) and Harvey and other Democratic Negro politicians reputedly took orders from him as a matter of course. His Federal patronage and his close ties with top leaders of the Democratic machine (he was vice-chairman of the Cook County Central Committee and of the Democratic National Committee) gave him a position of great power within the party. In return for what it gave him, Dawson was expected to

* After Truman's victory in 1948, Walter White of the National Association for the Advancement of Colored People wrote: "There can be no doubt . . . that Illinois' 312,000 Negro voters gave the President his 51,000 majority (seventy-six per cent of the vote in the 11 wards where Negroes live went for Truman). . . ." *Chicago Daily News,* November 13, 1948.

deliver the Negro vote for the party, and thus, for those of the party's candidates who ran against Negroes and even for those who were covertly anti-Negro.

Dawson's organization was built in part on patronage and in part on financial contributions from "policy kings" and, perhaps, from other illegitimate enterprises as well. "Policy" or "numbers" was a form of gambling in which small sums—often as little as 10 or 20 cents a day—were bet against large odds, and it was very popular and widespread within the Negro community.

Policy had created the capital that was the foundation of many legitimate businesses and it was the support of many churches and welfare organizations.* Dawson took the position that as long as it was legal to place bets at race tracks in Cook County or to play bingo for money in churches, there would be no interference with policy in his district. He protected the policy kings not only from the law but from rival racketeers as well. Once when the Capone mob bribed police captains to enforce the law against the Negro policy operators (the white gangsters were then trying to "muscle in" on the Negroes), Dawson went to the Mayor and got the policemen transferred to other districts. At the time he remarked that, while he would not take money from numbers racketeers for personal gain, he would accept political contributions from them.[25]

Having this financial backing, Dawson could afford to be generous in his contributions to churches and other organizations that might bring him support at the polls. "If I asked Carey for some money for the church," a minister told an interviewer, "Carey would hem and haw and would finally say he would try and get it. But Dawson would write out a check without any

---

* "The 'policy king' knows his position and tries to be accepted among the upper respectable groups. Look at H. Y. who has established two drug stores, J. K., a shoe store, the J. brothers, a department store, which all indicates that the attempt is entrenchment. It also means, though, jobs for people. . . . The 'policy king' makes the highest contribution to the NAACP. The churches don't dare talk against him because he contributes heavily. The whole thing is so intertwined and interconnected that it would be quite difficult to make a distinction between the various sources where the money for the support of various institutions and organizations comes from. The 'policy king' or 'policy baron' is a symbol of success and power." Quoted from a member of the editorial staff of the *Defender,* in Samuel M. Strong, *op. cit.,* p. 122.

question." Under the circumstances, the minister explained, "even if you hoped Dawson would lose, you'd still make speeches for him."[26]

Having an efficient organization in the precincts, Dawson did not need to be much concerned with what the Negro voters thought about issues. He took pains to introduce bills dealing with civil rights, FEPC, and other matters of special concern to Negroes, but he rarely took the floor and he was frank to admit that he was more interested and involved in the affairs of his district than in purely national matters. Washington simply happened to be the most satisfactory place from which to run his organization and to assist his Chicago constituents.

Housing was one matter that interested his constituents. Dawson spoke out against the Lake Meadows redevelopment project which would displace many more Negroes than it would house, but he did not try to kill it. He was, he said, very much in favor of public housing, although he believed that the Chicago Housing Authority was to blame for the existence of segregation in its projects in the past.

Dawson and other Negro politicians paid little or no attention to the Negro press. They ignored it because their constituents did. Even thoughtful Negroes—ones who were likely to read editorials and serious news—usually disregarded the Negro newspapers.

Some Negro leaders thought it was too bad that Chicago Negroes, and therefore to some extent all Negroes, were represented in Congress by a man who was organization-minded, whose alliances were dubious, and whose concern with large national issues was small. But while they might regret these shortcomings, some Negroes among Dawson's critics were apt to feel that it was a good thing for the race that it had a man with the courage and skill to play the political game effectively.*

* "Negroes, [in Chicago]" two Negro social analysts have written, ". . . have seldom supported the reformers. They have preferred to deal with hardheaded realists who are willing to trade political positions and favorable legislation for votes. A cynical realism has pervaded Black Metropolis which sees democracy as something granted to Negroes on the basis of political expediency rather than as a right. In the past this has meant dealing with the 'corrupt' machines, and even the clergy have not hesitated to play the game." St. Claire Drake and Horace R. Cayton, *Black Metropolis*, Harcourt, Brace and Company, New York, 1945, p. 377.

Nevertheless, there were few rewards for the underlying population in Dawson's game.

Dawson's own view of the matter was candid and intelligent. "Political organizations are not matters of chance," he told an interviewer. "They set up candidates and issues. I don't know what you can substitute for political organizations unless you are going to substitute the view of those who control radio and television. You know we no longer have a free press. If we don't have political organizations, then we will have control by the radio and television. Politics is what you make it. It is an honorable activity. In politics you make commitments and you have to stick by commitments. People who can't make commitments can't get along in politics. If the intelligentsia—the widely trained—if they see incompetent people run politics, it's their own fault."

During his 14 years as Mayor, Edward J. Kelly had been the undisputed boss of the Democratic Party in Chicago and in Cook County. Through an alliance with Patrick A. Nash, chairman of the County Central Committee, Kelly controlled all patronage and thus the whole machine. As an admiring alderman once remarked, "Kelly walked around with 9,000 jobs stuck in his back pocket."[28]

As Mayor and as boss of the machine, Kelly was in full control of the Council. He saw to it that his men had all of the important committee posts and if a Democratic alderman dared to oppose one of his measures he would call the man's committeeman to demand that he be made to conform.

In 1947, faced with a hard campaign—public opinion was aroused by corruption in the school system—Kelly retired. Jacob Arvey, a West Side lawyer who had been his chief lieutenant and who succeeded him as chairman of the County Central Committee, maneuvered successfully to have the party nominate as Kelly's successor a candidate who would stand for reform and who would not disturb the balance of power among the factions then struggling to inherit Kelly's power.

Martin H. Kennelly had the qualifications that were wanted. He was of Irish extraction and a Catholic, he was a successful businessman (he had been in the trucking and warehouse business all his life), he had never been prominent in politics although he had been active in one wing of the Democratic Party and a generous contributor to it, and he was favorably known as the head of the city Red Cross drive. All of this, of course, made him a good reform candidate. But from the standpoint of the factional leaders who were fighting for control of the party, it was perhaps an even greater advantage that he was not allied to any of them and that he clearly had no inclination to participate in the struggle for control of the machine. Indeed, Kennelly is supposed to have accepted the nomination on the explicit understanding that he would not be expected to act as a machine leader or to take directions in policy matters from the machine.

Kennelly made a campaign pledge that he would respect the independence of the City Council and after his election, when the leaders of the Council met to choose the committee heads, he made a point of being on vacation in North Carolina. Kelly had always attended meetings of the important committees of the Council; Kennelly did not even attend meetings of the Finance Committee. Moreover, Kennelly in effect declined to take a place on the County Central Committee and he seldom attended party conferences.[29] He even extended the merit system to cover a large number of minor jobs in the city government. Whether from expediency, prejudice, or principle, the new Mayor apparently believed that the aldermen should run the city with as little direction from him as possible.

Without the Mayor's help, Arvey, the chairman of the County Central Committe, could not hold the remnants of the Kelly organization together. Thomas D. Nash, committeeman for the 19th ward, formed a coalition of several South Side Democratic and Republican ward bosses to take control of the Council away from the Kelly-Arvey forces, and shortly after Kennelly's election, the alderman of Nash's ward, John J. Duffy, was elected chairman of the powerful Finance Committee over the Kelly-Arvey candidate.

For many years Duffy had had to defer to Kelly. "Kelly was a good mayor," he once told an interviewer, "but he became too powerful—the same thing happened to him that ruined Hitler and Mussolini. Kelly said, 'If you don't run the organization and its members, they'll run you.' He argued that you have to be the boss to be successful. Kennelly is a different type. He says it's the responsibility of the Council to make decisions. We get together and we throw out our views—exchange them—and we learn a lot from listening to each other."[30]

Some of the aldermen who did not, like Duffy, gain power thereby were not so sure that it was an advantage to have a weak mayor. "What he (Kennelly) is trying to do," one of them said, "is introduce a new philosophy into Chicago government of letting the legislative branch take care of itself. The trouble with that is we have been so used to being led around that we haven't gotten used to working out our own problems. Take when Mayor Kelly was in; when I needed something I could say, 'We have to have this,' and in twenty-four hours we would have it. Today, it takes a lot longer to get something. Maybe his position is right, but it will take a lot longer to catch on."[31]

Critics of the Kennelly administration, including the liberals, most of whom had voted for him, were often exasperated by the Mayor's way of doing things. They criticized him for acting like a discussion leader instead of a politician. "Kennelly's idea of a beautiful world," one of the public housing leaders once said, "is to sit around a table and have the opposing parties come to an agreement for which he would take the credit without ever having opened his mouth."[32]

The way the Council worked under Kennelly at the time of the public housing site selection struggle was described by Thomas Drennan, a seasoned observer of City Hall who was the *Sun-Times'* political columnist:

"As finance committee boss in control of over $200,000,000 a year for city expenditures" Drennan wrote, "Duffy has been able to set up some order among the rambunctious lads in the council.

"But this is limited mainly to deciding who gets to the jam pot first—and how much he gets. This also stops the overly-playful ones from setting fire to the aldermanic house.

"A select number of the 'big boys' are entrusted with enforcing Duffy's policies. They include Alds. Francis Hogan; Clarence Wagner; Harry Sain; William J. Lancaster and P. J. Cullerton. Important, too, because of their seniority are Alds. George D. Kells and Dorsey Crowe.

"When Edward J. Kelly was mayor and aldermanic brats were punished by the baseball-bat-in-the-woodshed system, those in this group used to dine daily in the Bismarck Inn, across from the LaSalle street entrance to the City Hall. The place featured a 75-cent lunch.

"But things have changed. Since Kennelly got in, the group may be found in the same hotel's Walnut Room where the a-la-carte lunch items run into three figures.

"These aldermen, good Democrats all, are the 'works' in operating the city's business. Through their control of key subcommittees created by Duffy, they pass on every vital measure—especially those involving spending of public money on contracts.

"So far Duffy has been able to use these lieutenants to 'deliver' the City Council for legislation wanted by Kennelly. Some liberal measures had to be crammed down their throats on the grounds of expediency. But despite long delay—the building code revision, for instance—they eventually went along.

"The rest of the aldermen, with about six exceptions, usually fall in line because of Duffy's influence with key department heads, one of whom, Lloyd M. Johnson, is superintendent of streets and electricity. He decides which streets should be repaired and maintained and how often the garbage will be collected in the wards—important decisions to an alderman."[33]

Most of these aldermanic leaders represented, it should be noted, lower middle-class wards on the South Side—wards which were mainly in conservation areas. Duffy himself came from a South Side ward where there was much vacant land and a small colony of upper-class Negroes. Wagner, his close friend and chief lieutenant, probably could expect to win only one or two more elections, so rapidly was the Negro population increasing in his ward. Horan's situation was similar. Lancaster did not come from the South Side, but his ward was a conservation area and his allegiance had been shifting from Arvey's West Side Bloc. The aldermen from these South Side wards and allied areas were a minority but possessed most of the power that was exercised in the Council, for they were its leaders.

By 1949 the Authority had awarded many millions of dollars worth of contracts, rented thousands of units of housing, and given thousands of jobs. This was the raw material from which a mighty political machine could have been built in a city so favor-minded as Chicago. But the Authority had never been political. It had done favors, but it had done them seldom and only in trivial matters. (Curiously, no very important favors seem ever to have been asked of it.)

One reason why the Authority remained non-political was the close supervision provided by the Federal government. But there were few of these controls that could not have been evaded in one way or another, and a more important reason was that the commissioners and Miss Wood took pride in the fact that their agency was "clean." There was only one commissioner who would not have been indignant at a suggestion that the Authority be a source of patronage and favors; Miss Wood, of course, was determined to administer the agency according to the best professional standards.

In its first few years of existence the Authority, fearing party spoilsmen and jealous of its independence, had as little as possible to do with the City Hall. Many people supposed that CHA was a Federal agency run principally from Washington. Some aldermen, including ones who favored slum clearance, were antagonized by its aloofness. Mayor Kelly usually ignored it, although now and then he intimated to Taylor that his intentions were friendly.*

By 1941, however, Kelly not only took an active interest in the Authority but made himself its sponsor and protector. CHA and the Plan Commission, he made clear, were to be "clean" agencies in his otherwise motley establishment. When Kelly talked to liberal groups—Negroes, labor, church people, and so on—he would point with pride to the Authority. When he talked to the real estate men and the downtown business community he would point with pride to the Plan Commission.

---

* Writing of the situation as it existed in 1940, Annette Baker Fox concluded, "In the past the Chicago Housing Authority has tried to pursue its own ends without let or hindrance from any municipal agency. It has even been reluctant to seek financial aid from the city. But although the role assumed by the Authority was relatively narrow—'Manager and Builder of Low-Rent Communities'—it could not be played without contacts with other groups. Chief among them was the city council. Yet friends of housing on the council have been antagonized by the reticent attitude of the Housing Authority. The Authority's obvious fear that its 'impeccable administration' would be contaminated by too close contact with municipal agencies may actually have been detrimental to the housing program as well as to the coordination of local governmental activities. Certainly the achievements of the Chicago Housing Authority were insignificant compared to other large cities. Not only did it have little to show for three and one-half years' work, but it was still widely regarded locally as an instrument of U.S.H.A." "Coordination of the Local Housing Authority with the Municipal Government," Unpublished Ph.D. dissertation, Department of Political Science, University of Chicago, Chicago, August 1941, p. 116.

Milton Shufro, the Authority's public relations man, was one of the people responsible for encouraging the Mayor to take the Authority under his protection. If the Mayor wanted an agency to point to before the liberals, it was not surprising that he should choose the Authority, and so the attention the Mayor paid to Shufro was probably an effect rather than a cause of his decision. At any rate, by 1941 Shufro had established a liaison with the Mayor and had come to be Miss Wood's principal staff adviser.

Shufro was a graduate of the University of Missouri school of journalism. Early in the Depression, unable to find a newspaper job, he had been attracted into social work because, as he later explained, he liked to work with people. He took courses in social service administration at the University of Chicago, became a case-worker, and then a director of the Transient Bureau. Later, after a period as a public relations man for the American Association of Social Workers, he worked as a labor and social legislation reporter for a Chicago newspaper.

As a newspaperman, Shufro, he once explained, "saw the terrific lack and inability of people who were trying to tackle social problems—they didn't know how to express their point of view, how to get it before the public." His newspaper training and what he described as his "social sense" led him to believe that he could perform a much-needed service by mobilizing public support for the social service agencies. In 1938 he got a temporary job with the Authority. Soon he was put in charge of arranging dedications of new projects. Instead of having 300 people at a dedication as before, the Authority now commonly had 5,000.[34] Shufro later was made director of public relations. During the war, he became assistant executive secretary.

When a commissioner of the Authority resigned, Shufro went to the Mayor to suggest the appointment of his friend and former teacher, McMillen. Shufro later reported the discussion as follows:

SHUFRO: Look, Mr. Mayor, here's a guy, a University of Chicago social worker. He almost knocked your guy out of the primary, but I think he'd be a good man on the commission.
THE MAYOR: Is he a poor man's man?
SHUFRO: Yes, he's a damn good poor man's man.[35]

McMillen was appointed. Meanwhile, Taylor, who had been

vice-chairman, was elected chairman by his fellow commissioners, who may have been encouraged to do so by Mayor Kelly.

The appointment of McMillen and the election of Taylor to the chairmanship reinforced a public relations approach which Shufro brought to the Authority. Miss Wood had given little attention to public relations.* "My conception," Shufro explained later, "was to get the people who actually lived in the slums, the Negroes, the church, labor, civic and women's groups, the college professors, teachers, social workers and medical men to become interested in and identified with our program."[36] In discussing Taylor with the Mayor, Shufro later explained, "my primary interest was in the racial field. The Housing Authority could and did lead the way in this area. It actually stood out, and civic groups followed with commendation. With a Negro chairman, it would have to do a good job in that particular field."[37]

Shufro's public relations work had results. "After a while, Negro organizations, labor organizations, civic and church organizations became the core of our support," he said later. "We became symbols. This became true not through any particular magic, but due to the fact that our program and administration was good in the sense of being decent and honest, forthright, just and fair."[38]

As assistant executive secretary, a position to which he was promoted in 1944, Shufro had five principal duties: to supervise the management division, to supervise the statistics department, to control and coordinate the personnel functions, to supervise and establish policy for the public information program, and to act as executive secretary when Miss Wood was away. In practice, his main jobs were management and public relations.

However, beginning in 1947, after Kelly left office, Shufro no longer had access to the mayor's office. Indeed, the very fact that he and the Authority had been Kelly's proteges, or had at least been protected by Kelly, weighed heavily against him with some of the City Hall figures whose power was now greatly increased.

---

* The National Association of Housing Officials' *Housing Yearbook* of 1940 stated (p. 42): "In the field of public relations the Authority has confined itself to a report of activities from its inception to 1940 and to the preparation of a simple brochure for distribution to prospective tenants and agencies."

Alderman Duffy, for example, the leader of the South Side Bloc who soon defeated the Kelly-Arvey candidate for the chairmanship of the powerful Finance Committee, did not like Shufro and had always bitterly resented the dictatorial way in which Kelly had forced CHA proposals through the Council.[39] Duffy's friend and principal lieutenant, Clarence P. Wagner, another South Side alderman, had in fact once successfully opposed a Kelly-sponsored slum clearance ordinance and in doing so had distinguished himself as one of the few Democrats ever to clash with Kelly on the floor of the Council.[40]

The new leaders of the Council made it plain that Shufro was not welcome in City Hall. "If you send Shufro here," they told Taylor, according to Taylor's later account, "you will get nothing."[41]

In part because Shufro now had no influence at City Hall and was in fact a liability there, Taylor and McMillen thought that the Authority should have, instead, a business man as its assistant executive secretary. Shufro was one of the many who had lost power in the break-up of the Kelly organization, and, like most of the others who lost power, he soon lost his place too. He was not fired, but seeing that the commission was hostile to him, he regretfully resigned in 1948 to take a better paying job with a large architectural firm which did work for housing authorities.

Shufro's influence on the Authority and on Miss Wood had been great. It was, as he himself said, largely due to him that they became symbols—symbols, it may be added, to which ideologists of both the left and the right would energetically react.

After his departure, Miss Wood continued to rely upon him for advice. During the site selection struggle he was to be, among those outside of the staff, one of her two or three most intimate advisers.

As they prepared the ambitious new six-year program in 1949, the heads of the Authority anticipated a difficult time with the politicians. Under Kelly it had never been necessary to get the Council's approval of specific sites; the change in the state law which gave the aldermen a veto power over sites was made after

Kelly's retirement and it was an unmistakable sign that the Council meant to put an end to the Authority's independence.

By 1949 it was clear, too, that Mayor Kennelly would not give the Authority effective support. Whatever his views on public housing might be, Kennelly was pledged to let the Council run things in its own way.

Many of the aldermen were frankly hostile. One reason for their hostility, Miss Wood thought, was that the Authority was honestly and efficiently administered. "They really hate us," a newspaper quoted her as saying in 1950. "They'd love to have that gravy."[42] "If CHA were willing to play politics on jobs and contracts and to permit the 'boys' to have an in—things would be simple," the newsletter of the Public Housing Association (a voluntary association in Chicago of public housing supporters) said at about that time. "The 'boys' would be demanding a public housing project a day. But in Chicago we have a Housing Authority whose integrity is infuriating to the 'boys.' "[43]

The aldermen who came from the outlying white neighborhoods—the conservation areas in the South Side—had an additional reason for hostility. If the Authority was to build on vacant land, it would have to build in their wards since there was no suitable vacant land elsewhere. And if it built, it would inevitably bring Negroes and other "undesirable people" into neighborhoods where people had been endeavoring for years to keep them out and thus presumably to protect property values. (Of course, even if it built within the congested Negro slum areas, the Authority would inevitably displace some Negroes who would probably find their way into the outlying white neighborhoods. This possibility, however, was not widely recognized and therefore not so much feared.)

Many of the aldermen came from conservation areas. Moreover, as we have mentioned, a South Side bloc of ward bosses had challenged the remains of the Kelly-Arvey organization and had gained control of the Council. Aldermen Duffy and Wagner, the two most powerful men in the Council, were both South Side leaders. In 1949, it can be seen in retrospect, they were gaining and consolidating power at the expense of the Kelly-Arvey faction.

In 1949 the principal leader of the Kelly-Arvey faction was

William J. Lancaster, chairman of the Rules Committee and of the Housing Committee of the City Council, but he was shifting to the South Side bloc. Two years before, when the Kelly-Arvey faction was still dominant, Lancaster had been an effective supporter of the Authority.[44] Now he had cooled. "I am not essentially a public houser," he remarked in the summer of 1949 when the Authority put its proposal before the Council. "I believe that any family which through no fault of its own cannot live in decent housing has the right to live there. It is our duty to give them decent housing, but public housing should stop there."[45]

Lancaster's coolness was a sign of the new distribution of power within the party and the Council, and it was a portent of what was to come.

BURCK 1951, CHICAGO SUN-TIMES

OUTGROWN IT ALREADY

CHAPTER FOUR □ □ □ □ □ □

THE CLIMATE OF NEIGHBORHOOD OPINION

IF ONE LOOKED at figures on housing supply and demand, there was good reason to suppose that a big public housing program would be popular. According to one official definition, 144,000 Chicago families—about a half million people—lived in "slums."[1] There were besides, everyone knew, many thousands more who were uncomfortably crowded in housing that was not classified as slum. One might think that here was a fundamental political fact—that, however reluctant they might be, the politicians would have to do something about housing or else face the voters' wrath.

As an indicator of the demand for public housing, however, this estimate was somewhat misleading. It was based upon a housing market analysis (the pre-war decennial Census was, of course, useless and it would be four years before all of the tabulations on housing in the 1950 Census became available) which had been made in collaboration with some of the best-known real estate research consultants and had cost about $30,000; nevertheless it was of necessity a hurried job. (It had been made largely in two months prior to the passage of the Act and was rushed to completion so that the Authority would have figures to back up its proposals to the Council and the Public Housing Administration.)

Moreover, the market analysis was easily subject to misinterpretation. "Housing need in Chicago," it began, "arises from the fact that there are 1,178,000 families requiring housing and only 906,000 standard units available to satisfy this demand."[2] The equating here of "need" with "demand" was confusing, for it might be that people who by the Authority's standard (and perhaps by their own as well) *needed* housing might nevertheless *demand,* i.e., be willing to spend their money for, new cars or television sets rather than better housing. It might be that the Authority's standard of need ("every family in the city should have a standard dwelling unit to itself") was useless as an indicator of the choices that people would actually make between slum housing and public housing.

That many of the slum dwellers did in fact prefer other things to improved housing was strongly suggested by the family income figures contained in the market analysis itself: 55 per cent of the slum families had incomes of $3,000 or more and 35 per cent had incomes of $4,000 or more. Among these, of course, were many Negroes who could have obtained non-slum housing only by paying much more for it than whites would have had to pay, as well as many families, both Negro and white, whose expenses for essentials such as food and clothing were so great that a family income of $3,000 did not leave enough to rent or buy a decent place to live. Nevertheless, we think that a sizeable number of slum-dwellers were prevented from moving out of the slum only by the fact that they preferred to spend their money for other things than improved housing.

The heads of the Authority were of course aware that many of those who "needed" public housing would not "demand" it. But, even so, they probably did not regard their figures with enough caution. The Authority, like most such organizations, had what may be called a "producers' bias": having a product to sell, it tended to persuade itself, as well as others, that this product was very much in demand. A bias of this kind is perhaps an aspect of high morale in such an organization.

If, as we suspect, the Authority somewhat overestimated the potential demand for public housing, this "producers' bias" was perhaps one reason why. But another and related reason was that the Authority, like almost all housing agencies, was not in the habit of doing rigorous research: it was, after all, an action agency, not a research organization. Moreover, rigorous research could be embarrassing, for it might lead to conclusions which ran counter to the assumptions on which the agency's very existence was predicated. Thus, for example, a housing market analysis which concentrated on demand for public housing, rather than upon need for it, might not at all have served the principal reasons for which the analysis was made, i.e., to support the Authority's proposals for a large program.[3]

The commissioners were apt to be impatient with the very idea of research, and when the staff proposed that the National Opinion Research Center be engaged to gather data on consumer preferences in housing, Miss Wood, although she seemed to favor the idea herself, decided that it would be better not to suggest it to them.

But even if the Authority had been quite unbiased, rigorous in its research, and willing and able to spend the very large sums that would have been necessary to collect accurate and detailed data on both supply and demand, the data might still have had little or no value for the making of some of the most important decisions that had to be made. In late 1949 and early 1950, for example, there was good reason to believe that an economic recession had begun; if this had occurred (and it probably would have except for the war in Korea), the demand for public housing would probably have risen very sharply. People who were quite unwilling to live in public projects in 1949 might have been very glad to live in them by 1951 if unemployment had spread then. Uncertainty was a fundamental feature of the situation and one which no amount of research could have eliminated.

Some people would oppose public housing because they considered it ugly—so ugly as to ruin the appearance of a neighborhood and depreciate surrounding property values. People who lived in small free-standing brick pillboxes which stretched line upon line over the plain were especially severe in their criticism of public housing projects. Pillbox dwellers found row houses intolerable. Similarly, people who lived under conventionally pitched roofs found flat roofs offensive. Thus a project which was praised in the *Journal of Housing* was compared to a row of saloons in a small mining town by an irate citizen whose letter Mayor Kennelly, who had made similar criticism himself, took the trouble to forward to the commissioners.

It was sometimes said that the projects were "cheap-looking." In fact, although there was nothing shoddy about their construction, they were built to be inexpensive and to look so as well. Rooms in the projects were small. There was often no storage space for suitcases, tools, and large toys; ceilings were not plastered; floors were of troweled concrete; woodwork was waxed rather than painted; bathtubs were not provided with showers; most closet doors were eliminated; heating and other pipes were exposed; and in some projects there were no dividing walls between living room, kitchen, and dining space.

In order to avoid criticism from realtors and builders who thought that public housing should not compete in cost or amenity with private housing, the government's Public Housing Administration insisted, as a condition to the granting of Federal funds, that projects include no features not found in the lowest-priced new private housing in the city. "Anything is extravagance," the PHA manual said, "which is not necessary to decency, safety, sanitation, or adequate standards of family life. . . ."[4]

In general the PHA regulations served the realtors' purposes admirably: public housing could often be pointed to by private builders as an example of bureaucratic bungling and inefficiency. Thus, when a leader of the anti-housing forces went to the state capitol at Springfield to testify for an anti-housing measure he took with him some slides of a Chicago project and some of the houses he had built himself. "The legislators are mostly from the farm areas, you know," he explained later, "and they don't know or care anything about what happens here in Chicago. So I asked them to tell me when they thought the project was built and I had guesses from a year to 60 years. (You can take photos in certain ways to make it look real old.) They are pretty nice houses inside of course, but in trying to be too economical on the outside the Housing Authority really led with their chins."[5]

The PHA regulations also helped give the projects an institutional appearance and so to contribute to their "project" character, a character often objectionable to pillbox dwellers and prospective tenants alike. During the Depression, when even many of the middle-class were on relief, living in a public housing project entailed no loss of social status. At that time projects were, especially from the slum dweller's point of view, relatively high-status neighborhoods. But during and after the war, when very few of the middle-class were on relief and most slum dwellers had incomes so high that they were ineligible to live in public projects, the situation became very different; to live in a public housing project then came to mean, even among Negroes (although less among them than among whites), that one was marked as "low income" and hence "low class." To some extent it was not the projects themselves but the neighborhoods in which they were situated that stigmatized people. But even where this was the case, the projects were likely to be blamed.

The Housing Authority was aware of these objections to projects. "It is of prime importance that our projects do not consist of the sterile and stereotyped buildings that many people have come to think of as public housing projects," the CHA manual for architects said. The architecture that was wanted was "domestic in appearance, non-institutional, different, economical."[6]

One might have expected, no matter how various the objections that others might make, that the people who lived in public housing or had once lived in it—a number that reached many thousands of families—would be the Authority's ardent and active supporters. There were indeed many among these who were supporters, but there were also many who were not. Some of the people who lived in projects resented the investigation—snooping, they called it—which the Authority had to do to establish the continued income eligibility of tenant families. "The people living in public housing can't afford to take a pay raise," a "CHA Tenant" complained in a letter to the *Sun-Times*. "The minute they get a raise in pay they get a rent increase that either matches or betters the raise. Many men who could advance themselves in their work have to stay where they are because they cannot take a chance of putting their children out on the street if they earn more than the maximum. . . ."[7] And, of course, when a family was compelled to move because its income was too high, public housing was damned. It was not surprising that many people should feel this way: after all, nobody likes the landlord.*

---

* George Orwell observed in 1937 that sometimes a tenant from a filthy hovel no sooner got into a Corporation house than he wanted to be back in the slum. The trouble was, he said, that necessary restrictions (you could not keep pigeons and every garden had to have the same kind of hedge) made the new houses seem cold, uncomfortable and "unhomelike" to the tenants. "On balance," he

Those who were most active in the politics of public housing can be roughly divided into five principal opinion-interest groups—groups which in part corresponded to various geographic areas of the city. One such group consisted of people who had business interests in the Loop—especially the department store executives who ran the State Street Council. Some of these executives, alarmed by the steady exodus to the suburbs, wanted the slum areas near the center of the city—areas which were largely Negro—redeveloped into "high-class"—and therefore white—residential neighborhoods for people who would spend more money in the great downtown stores and pay more taxes for the support of city services.* These executives had a considerable measure of influence by virtue of their own wealth and by virtue of their allies, principally real estate and management interests connected with Loop property. However, they were not unanimous in their opinion; some of them depended largely on Negro customers.

Because they lived in the fashionable suburbs rather than in Chicago proper† and for other reasons as well (perhaps because they were accustomed to buying what they wanted), the department store executives and merchants did not in most cases appear

---

concluded, "the Corporation Estates are better than the slums; but only by a small margin." *The Road to Wigan Pier,* Gollancz, London, 1937, p. 73.

An anthropologist who studied the new town of Stevenage found that some people "disliked a completely modern, antiseptic, and—let the truth be said—moral town, without its quota of ill-lit narrow streets, easy old pubs, pool rooms, and other dens of moderate iniquity." Harold Orlans, *op. cit.,* p. 163.

* Joel Goldblatt, a former president of the State Street Council, wrote in the *Daily News* of Feb. 25, 1954: "To businessmen like me, slum elimination is important economically as well as morally. Rebuilding of huge sections of a city is expensive, but not to rebuild it would be far costlier. As things are now, we actually pay taxes to support slums rather than to destroy them. The city's businessmen and property owners must pay for the increased police, fire, and health services necessary for slum areas."

† In Chicago as in most American cities, the executives and the professionals had been steadily moving to the suburbs. Wayne Andrews suggests that these suburban residents possessed community-regarding views but lacked vigor in implementing them partially because of the lack of an upper class tradition of public-spiritedness furthered through church ideology and organization. "As for the leading professional men, most of whom are suburbanites, while not indifferent, and often acutely conscious of the pressure of the *Tribune,* they find it next to impossible to rouse the city from its lethargy. The fact that neither the Presbyterian nor the Episcopal Church possesses anything like the prestige of the Episcopal Church in New York is one indication of the remarkable absence of social responsibility." *Battle for Chicago,* Harcourt, Brace, New York, 1946, p. 320.

openly on the political scene. A few of them, perhaps, made "fixing" politicians a part of their normal business practice; others, including some who would not think of bribery, were accustomed to "exercising influence." "The big names on State Street," a politician told an interviewer, "are usually generous with their contributions."[8]

North Side residents were another opinion-interest group. The city's high-income neighborhoods were mainly on the North Side, especially in rental areas near the Lake Front and the suburbs. The people of these neighborhoods, unlike people in some other neighborhoods, did not speak of the aldermen as "dirty politicians"; indeed aldermen from these wards—Becker, Freeman, Geisler, Hoellen, Weber—had been to Harvard, Northwestern, and other universities of high prestige and were middle-class and "civic-minded" like most of their constituents. These neighborhoods were in large measure Republican.

These North Side wards (as well as a few others on the South Side, e.g., the ward in which the University of Chicago was located) were sometimes called "newspaper wards" by the politicians. The voters in these wards were likely to take seriously what was said in editorial and news columns. They often voted a split ticket following the newspapers' recommendations.

North Side opinion about public housing was not unanimous, but—especially in the early stages of the site selection struggle—it generally supported public housing. There were relatively few Negroes on the North Side and little prospect that any would come there in the foreseeable future. Nor was there any significant amount of public housing there. North Side people had nothing to lose by a public housing program and no doubt many of them were anxious to see the lot of the slum-dwellers improved. The spokesmen for numerous church and civic organizations lived on the North Side; they had a representative as well as a personal interest in the public housing issue and they tended to take a community-regarding rather than a self- or neighborhood-regarding view of it.

The slum dwellers themselves were by no means united in their opinion or interest regarding public housing. In most slum districts only about one-third of the families were eligible to live in it. Some were not citizens. Many had incomes that were too high; the 1949 admission limit (which had not kept pace with rising prices) in terms of a tenant's annual income was a maximum of $2,900 for a family of five or more. Most leaders of the slum community were excluded for this reason. Some other slum dwellers, though eligible, were rejected for various reasons: because they had no children or, in special cases, because they were criminals, mentally unstable, or otherwise clearly unsuitable as tenants. Still other people, although acceptable to the Authority, were prevented by their special circumstances from living in projects.

The Authority could not provide places of business for known prostitutes, gamblers, dope peddlers, and the like. Such people were supposed to be beyond the ken of all except the police and some social agencies. Yet many of these people lived in the slums, and some of them performed services which others valued. As the slums were torn down, they would be forced into a more concentrated and specialized "skid-row" district, an inconvenience about which some of them—as well as some of their employers and customers—could be expected to complain.*

Respectable people, also, would have their way of life disturbed by the destruction of the slum, whether for public housing or for other purposes. The widow who subsisted by renting rooms would not be able to survive in a housing project. The peddler

---

* "Any objective study of slum phenomena would show that slums perform a set of functions for the city, and that these functions are carried out in response to values that are common throughout the population. Some of these functions are morally 'residual'; nevertheless they are prized—not banned—as a part of the urban structure. They are banded together and located in particular areas in order that the whole city can have access to them. The 'red light' district and concentrations of gambling activities, for example, are an aspect of the city's functional organization. They develop in response to values existing among non-slum as well as slum residents. The slum also functions as a place of residence for the population with the lowest income status, but the process by which low incomes are assigned to particular families, and the size of that income, involves values of people outside as well as the values of people inside the slum community. Only in a romantic sense can anyone say that these activities and conditions are dissociated from the physical fact of the slum. Since the larger society calls slums into existence, and by its systems of values causes them to grow, slum areas cannot be eliminated without changing these values." Joseph D. Lohman, in *Needed Urban and Metropolitan Research,* Donald J. Bogue, editor, Scripps Foundation, Oxford, Ohio, 1953, pp. 28-29.

who required an inexpensive and conveniently located barn for his horse and wagon would have no place in a housing project. Neither would the old Italian who made his living by selling sausages from a sidewalk cart. The priest would be left without a parish, for of course the new project would be occupied by eligible families from all over the city, not from the old section itself. The old neighborhood would, in fact, be scattered. People who could not live in public projects somewhere else would have a hard time finding places to live even though the Authority would try to help them by maintaining a relocation program. To the politician, the storekeeper, the minister and others who had some stake in the slum neighborhood, its destruction was especially to be feared. For such people, the passing of the old neighborhood meant the loss of power and place that had been hard won. In some cases it meant also the loss of a valued cultural heritage: the dispersal of a Greek slum, for example, meant an end to the shadow plays which, to the deep satisfaction of the older men, portrayed Greek history, scenes of peasant life, and the glories of strife with the Turks.

As for the labor unions, their national offices had been staunch supporters of public housing. However, in Chicago, though the CIO's office provided considerable help in fighting for the CHA sites, the locals and members of the separate unions played a minor role. (The CIO Packinghouse Workers' Union was an exception: its leaders happened to be close associates of some of the main public housing supporters.)

That the unions, which were in most cases favorably disposed to CHA, were not more active is easy to understand. We have suggested before that in the period under discussion unions were so pressed by adverse governmental action (as well as by political schism in their own ranks) that they had little interest in other directions. Moreover, in the post-war prosperity union members in the major industries had incomes above the eligibility ceilings for public housing. Unless these income limits were changed and unless vastly more public housing units were built than ever contemplated by anyone, the union rank-and-file could have little expectation of ever obtaining public housing units for themselves.

In addition, some union members had ties with neighborhood associations which on this issue may have taken precedence over union affiliation.

Among the Negroes (who constituted the largest group among the slum dwellers), especially, there was a further division of interest between the underlying population, a large proportion of which was eligible to live in public housing, and the middle and upper classes—the property owners, businessmen, professionals and politicians. The underlying Negro population had much to gain by the destruction of the slum. It was indicative that in 1949 the vote on the redevelopment bond issue in two solidly Negro precincts showed 11 to one and seven to one majorities for slum clearance and redevelopment, whereas in the city as a whole it was only two to one.[9]

Except when the issue was to be decided by ballots, the opinion and interest of the underlying population did not count for much, however. The people who spoke for the Negro were middle and upper class, and it was these classes that they mainly represented. Many prosperous and influential Negroes were actively opposed to slum clearance and to projects which would move Negroes to outlying vacant areas. In 1948 some Negroes voiced fears that "the whole slum clearance program is a veiled effort to transfer Negroes from the center of the city to the outskirts."[10] The "Champions" and the "Vigilantes," secret organizations of Negro property owners, and the Park Lake Council of Neighborhood Clubs insisted that relocation housing be built within the Black Belt; they favored "maintenance of community lines." Only one predominantly Negro organization, the Urban League, and only one Negro politician, Alderman Archibald Carey, vigorously attacked relocation plans on the grounds that they would preserve segregation.[11]

"Are there groups that . . . resist the breakdown of the ghetto?", a writer in *Crisis* (the magazine of the National Association for the Advancement of Colored People) asked in 1949. "They are principally certain of the property owners, businessmen and professionals, preachers, and politicians who serve the South Side. Property owners, especially those resident in areas likely to be cleared, are open supporters of the policy of keeping the ghetto intact. Professed property owners lead the Champions and the Vigilantes and as such constitute the several allied groups of these two foremost pro-ghetto organizations. The businessmen and professionals, who support the protectors of the ghetto, do not usually themselves appear on platforms or get their names in print. But the ministers and the politicians match the property owners in blistering, open attack on those who would destroy the ghetto.

"The property owners obviously represent a vested economic interest. Their properties, moreover, are rarely single family homes and often produce income as rooming houses, multi-family structures, or makeshift kitchenettes, so notoriously present in Chicago. The businessmen and professionals likewise fare well in the busy and monopolistic markets stemming from restraints on Negro living space. The ministers of the larger congregations, housed in big, costly edifices can make easy appeal to the communities of ownership involved. The politicians, of course, thrive in districts where the precincts are heavy and grow larger week by week."[12]

That some Negro leaders had a private stake in the maintenance of congestion (and therefore of segregation) did not necessarily mean that they did not also have disinterested reasons for opposing slum clearance. Many believed that what the white man wants always turns out to be harmful to the Negro—that after the slum was cleared, the whites would take the centrally located, Lake Front district for their own use, as certain whites had publicly advocated, leaving the Negro nowhere to go. ("How simple for them to believe that whites from whom space was taken will take it back at the first opportunity," the writer in *Crisis* from whom we have quoted remarked.)[13] Housing projects would offer fewer places to live than had the slum: this reduction in density was one of the objectives that public housing was intended to achieve. "Slum clearance is Negro clearance," a slogan that appeared on posters in many shop windows in the Negro district—sank into the consciousness of the colored slum-dwellers. Lake Meadows, the New York Life Insurance Company's redevelopment project, was a case in point; because it was planned to reduce congestion, it was displacing many more Negroes than it could possibly house. Public housing would do the same. One day in 1948 more than 1,800 people gathered at the Pilgrim Baptist Church, the biggest and one of the more fashionable Negro churches, to hear Reverend J. C. Austin criticize the city's slum clearance plans. "It is less the duty of Chicago to clear its slums than to house all its people," Reverend Austin declared. "We are more interested in people than in land, in homes for all now than in building a beautiful city for the future."[14] Austin had tried without success to persuade a group of wealthy Negroes to buy a strip of land on the South Side and to build low-rent cooperative housing. Public housing would be run by whites; Negroes, Austin maintained, would not be fairly treated except by landlords of their own race.[15]

Some Negro leaders who supported slum clearance and other measures that would help to break down segregation did so for ideological reasons. As long as they would not be treated as equals by whites, Negroes would want to live in districts which were close to the center of Negro social and cultural life. But they wanted to know that they were free to live in any area. "I want to be able to walk where I please," Alderman Carey, the leading Negro supporter of public housing, once said.

Another active opinion-interest group—and by far the most influential one—consisted of owners and residents in the conservation areas. These neighborhoods were mainly white and the percentage of single family dwellings and of owner-occupants was relatively high in them. (See Appendix, Maps Nos. 1 & 2.) Catholics were the largest single religious denomination in these areas and generally Irish-Catholics were predominant.* The leaders of the wards in the conservation areas, as we have indicated, were the most powerful figures in the City Council.

Against these conservation areas, the Negro slum areas which had been overcrowded in 1940 but had since doubled in numbers without increasing significantly in size, exerted a steady and irresistible pressure to expand. The white residents of the conservation areas had for the most part themselves escaped from the slum and from ethnically segregated or semi-segregated districts only a generation or two earlier and were, accordingly, dismayed at the prospect that the "nice" neighborhoods into which they had

* Chicago was in 1949 the largest Catholic diocese in the western hemisphere. Catholics were spread out fairly evenly over the whole city; parishes were often the forms of community—including political—identification. Of the approximately 300,000 Jews, one-third lived on the West Side, one-fourth on the North Side, one-fifth on the Northwest and one-fifth on the South Side. Protestants were concentrated on the western and northern fringes of the city, although many lived in other parts as well.

arduously climbed would be engulfed by the advancing slum.* All along the boundaries of the Negro districts wherever there was the prospect that Negroes would penetrate into the white conservation areas, there were "racial incidents." Frequently the houses of Negroes in these areas were bombed.†

The supporters of public housing supposed that the resistance of these neighborhoods to the entry of Negroes was a manifestation of "race prejudice." To a large extent it undoubtedly was: the people of the conservation areas no doubt generally took it for granted that dark skinned people were their inferiors. But to a significant extent what was called "race" prejudice was really dislike of certain characteristics which were associated with lower class people—not only lower class Negroes but lower class whites as well. The prejudice of the people of the conservation areas probably included the following components: a) fear of criminals, b) dislike of people who were dirty and disorderly in public places, c) dislike of people with whom they could not readily communicate and resentment that these people should replace as neighbors other people with whom they could readily communicate, d) dislike of people of lower social status, e) dislike of people of different customs, manners, and ways of dress and speech, f) dislike of people of different physical type, and g) dislike of people of different skin color.‡ Probably most people will

* See Samuel Lubell's account of the place of housing in the political psychology of the "'new' immigrants," i.e. those who came or whose people came to the United States after 1885 from Poland, Russia, Greece, Italy and the Hapsburg Empire. *The Future of American Politics,* Harper, New York, 1952, esp. Ch. 5.

† Of the 485 "racial incidents" reported by the Mayor's Commission on Human Relations between January 1, 1945 and January 1, 1950, 73.6 per cent had to do with housing.

‡ In 1950 Shirley A. Star studied interracial tension in two communities of Chicago, one (Greater Grand Crossing) which was adjacent to the main Negro community and which was being occupied by Negroes and one (Auburn-Gresham) which was of stable racial composition and in which there were no Negro residents. From 619 interviews she concluded that most people were disturbed at the idea of sharing their neighborhood with Negroes, that this feeling was as widespread in the so-called uninvaded community as in the so-called invaded one, that the people in closest proximity to the invasion felt less fear of possible physical and economic deterioration of the community and more fear of close social relationships between whites and Negroes, than did people who were more remote from the invasion, and that flight, apathy, and hopelessness were the predominant individual reactions to the question of how to cope with the disturbing aspects of the racial movement even though the majority wanted to see that movement combatted (pp. 153-54). In explanation of why they were or thought they would

agree that these components are arranged here in ascending order of moral significance and that the first four items on the scale, at least, ought not to be called "race" prejudice. It may be that the attitude of the people of the conservation areas toward the Negro was mainly "race" prejudice, i.e., that its most important components lay toward the "g" end of the scale, attributing all these characteristics to all Negroes. However, we suggest that there were important attitudinal components based on class rather than on race; there was also some reason to believe that the relative importance of the components toward the "g" end of the scale were declining from year to year. If this was so, a fundamental improvement in race relations might be in the offing, for the national income was so high and was increasing at such a rate that lower class people, Negro as well as white, could very rapidly be assimilated to the standards of the middle class. If indeed color was no longer the principal basis of objection to the Negro, he might prove to be only the latest of a succession of slum dwellers to be assimilated into Chicago's life. The transition of a neighborhood from one group to another had always been marked by conflict; there were some grounds for hope that the long-term experience of the Negro would not be essentially different from that of other minorities who had by now made their way out of the slums.*

be disturbed by the invasion, people most often reported "the presumed harmful effect that Negro residence would have on community standards and property values. About equally important as a reason for feeling distress over the presence of Negroes in the community was the notion that white people are antipathetic to Negroes and would just feel uncomfortable or agitated to have them around. Fears about crimes committed by Negroes and the threat to personal safety if Negroes lived in the community and concern over white children associating with Negroes and other possible social mixing were the remaining more frequent sources of distress at the idea of invasion." "Interracial Tension in Two Areas of Chicago: An Exploratory Approach to the Measurement of Interracial Tension," Unpublished Ph.D. dissertation, Department of Sociology, University of Chicago, Chicago, December 1950, p. 49.

* Father Luigi, the priest of a Sicilian parish which was broken apart by the building of Cabrini Homes, a project which came to be occupied partly by Negroes, complained bitterly to a newspaper columnist that the project had "encouraged immigration of a group alien to this community in blood, faith, and color. . . ." A generation earlier the Lutheran minister of a church in the same area had objected when the Lincoln Park Commission proposed to put a playground there. "This is our neighborhood, a Swedish neighborhood," the minister had said. "The dark people have come in farther south in the ward. If a playground is put in our neighbrohood we fear these people will come with their

It was true, however, that lower-middle class whites in conservation areas objected to the coming of Negroes even when the Negroes were professional people who built expensive homes and even when these homes were far removed from those of the whites. But even in these cases the objection was perhaps more to the status disadvantage that the coming of Negroes was thought to give the area in the eyes of some abstract public than to the Negroes themselves.

Many people in the conservation areas identified strongly with their neighborhoods or "communities"—they thought of themselves as residents of Roseland, Morgan Park, Lawndale or one of the approximately 80 other districts of Chicago which, although not legal political subdivisions, nevertheless were well-recognized (by public agencies as well as citizens) and had long-established identities.* Some of these people had been born and brought up in their community: others had lived there for a long term of years and expected to remain indefinitely. In some communities one could even find people who had seldom or perhaps never ventured beyond the community boundaries.

There was some reason to believe that among the community-minded people the level of political competence was high: their opinions, at least about local affairs, tended to be better informed than those of people whose local community identifications were weaker.

In every community there was a local elite of merchants, bankers, real estate men, lawyers with neighborhood practices, clergymen, and ward politicians. These local leaders were mostly

---

children to live in our neighborhood. . . ." The "dark people" were the Sicilians who were to be Father Luigi's parish and who would have to make way in their turn for a still darker people. Harvey W. Zorbaugh, *The Gold Coast and the Slum,* University of Chicago Press, Chicago, 1929, p. 160.

* Those who had strong identifications with the community were probably a minority; in one part of the Southwest Side an interviewer found that only 30 per cent of the people knew the name of their alderman and only a minority knew of any voluntary associations in the locality. But, of course, it required only a minority to make a community. In another study, Janowitz concluded that the community "leaves relatively untouched only a minority of residents, heavily involves another perhaps smaller group in the community, and creates varying degrees of involvement for the bulk of the residents." Morris Janowitz, *op. cit.,* p. 225. Of course, many people may identify with the "ethos" of a locality, but not with its institutions. Furthermore, identification need not result in participation.

people who had lived in the community for 20 years or more; of course they knew each other and most of the community-minded residents of the district. In addition to this informal system of communication, there was in every community a formal one: in 1950 there were 82 community newspapers with a total weekly circulation of more than 983,000. These were devoted to the affairs of the local communities.

In most areas there were one or more neighborhood improvement associations. (There were 200 such associations in Chicago in 1949, most of them in the conservation areas.) These were led and principally financed by the merchants, real estate men, and bankers who had a "booster" spirit and, of course, a direct financial stake in the prosperity of the neighborhood; only when an issue of particular interest arose was the ordinary home-owner urged to contribute to support his neighborhood improvement association or take an active part in it. Naturally, the associations sought issues that would attract widespread interest and support: they carried on campaigns for better street lighting, they developed community playgrounds, and in some cases they even sponsored social affairs. The activity which was surest to attract support, however, was one called "maintaining property values."

Actually "maintaining property values" was somewhat of a misnomer. It would be more accurate to describe the activity as "maintaining status values" or, more accurately still, "maintaining *status quo*." For the fact was that the associations often opposed changes which would probably increase property values but which in doing so would change the character of the neighborhood. (The movement of Negroes into an area, for example, would often increase property values, for it was taken for granted that a Negro should pay more than a white.) Not uncommonly improvement associations opposed the building of new schools and hospitals. When they did, it was always in the name of maintaining property values.*

---

* Thus, for example, Alderman John C. Burmeister, Jr., of the 44th ward, in order to prevent the building of a hospital in his ward ("It will depreciate badly the value of surrounding property") introduced a resolution to prohibit school, church, and hospital construction in apartment areas throughout the city without prior public hearings before the zoning board of appeals. *Chicago Sun-Times,* March 8, 1954.

Of all the ways of "maintaining property values," the one which was most likely to build membership in and support for the improvement association was that of discouraging the entrance of "undesirable people"—especially Negroes—into the neighborhood.* From 1928 until 20 years later, when the Supreme Court ruled them unenforceable, most of the neighborhood associations actively promoted the spread of residential racial covenants. By 1949, opposition to the entry of Negroes had become the principal business of most of the associations.[16]

Most of the neighborhood associations belonged to one or more of a dozen federations. These, together with the community newspapers and other interests with which they were actively allied, were centers of political power in the districts where home-owners were most numerous. Five of these federations (see Appendix, Map No. 5) were particularly powerful in 1949 and it was from some of them—the Southtown Planning Association, the Southwest Neighborhood Council, and the Taxpayers Action Committee—that the most strenuous and effective opposition to public housing would come during the site selection struggle.

The leading spirit of the Southtown Planning Association was Frank C. Rathje, president of two community banks, past president of the American Bankers Association, and vice-chairman of the Chicago Plan Commission. Rathje was very much interested in a large community shopping center at 63rd and Halsted Streets, directly in the path of Negro expansion. For many years he and his business associates had labored to keep Negroes out of this district. Along with William McDonnell, editor of the *Southtown Economist,* a community weekly devoted to housewifely rather than to scholarly economics, Harry S. Himmel, a furrier, and Bernard Sack, a realtor, Rathje was an officer and leader of the Southtown Planning Association. In 1947, the Association's budget was $60,000 of which half was earmarked for use in contracting racially restrictive agreements. (The Association was conducting a "Choose Your Neighbor" campaign that year.) Several neigh-

---

* A member of the Morgan Park Improvement Association told an interviewer that the only block captain to obtain a 100 per cent membership in 1950 was a man who based his solicitation on the danger that Negroes would move into the neighborhood.

borhood improvement associations and a number of businessmen's clubs were affiliated with the Association and it was supported financially by (among others) the Sears Roebuck Company, Wiebolt's Department Store, the Chicago City Bank and Trust Company (one of Rathje's banks), the *Southtown Economist,* and several aldermen.

In 1946 the Southtown Planning Association began a campaign to "build the Negroes out of Englewood." Its leaders formed the Southtown Realty and Development Corporation and made plans to build a 1,100-unit apartment building in a Negro area in the heart of Englewood. The new housing was intended for middle-income whites. The Negroes who had lived there would be encouraged to move to Robbins, an all-Negro community just south of the city limits. The Southtown Planning Association had gone to a great deal of trouble to attract Negroes to Robbins: it had helped set up a building and zoning commission there, it had promoted a $650,000 bond issue for water and sewage improvements, and it had persuaded the State Housing Board to buy and clear 22 acres of slum and blighted land for private redevelopment.*

---

* A somewhat different plan for the welfare of the Negro was advanced by the Chicago Lawn Businessmen's Association (another neighborhood improvement association) in 1947:

> Now therefore let it be resolved: That the Chicago Lawn Businessmen's Association does hereby subscribe to and offer the following plan . . . to be submitted to Municipal, State and Federal officials, neighborhood improvement associations . . . and individuals whose activities are aimed at a solution of racial problems and the preservation of the principles of our National Constitution and Bill of Rights. Said plan is as follows:
>
> 1. The practice of placing colored families in the midst of white families should be discontinued because (a) this practice is a fuse that sets off race riots; (b) this practice is sponsored by persons who are attempting to foment race riots to break down our form of government . . . (c) this practice depreciates the value of property in the neighborhood where it is carried out.
> 2. Additional good housing should be furnished the colored people by the following processes:
>   (a) All vacant lots in neighborhoods presently occupied by colored people should be built up. . . . All lending agencies should pledge (funds) for construction loans on new housing in colored neighborhoods.
>   (b) Old, unsanitary and dilapidated structures in colored neighborhoods should be condemned and wrecked, a block at a time, and new housing erected in their stead immediately.
>   (c) When the neighborhood has reached its saturation point of population it should be expanded immediately adjacent to it in an orderly manner.

The Southwest Neighborhood Council was another important federation of improvement associations, and one which came into being principally to fight public housing. One of its leaders and organizers was George Stech, a truck owner and driver who was also president of the United Home Owners of the Twenty-Third Ward. In the summer of 1950, when the Council was nearly a year old, Stech was interviewed in the two-story bungalow where he lived and he told about the United Home Owners activities. It had worked for a long while to get the city to pave certain outlying streets and to install city services. When they made him its president, he obtained better garbage pick-up service and he persuaded the city to wash streets that had not been washed for years. Stech showed his visitor a stack of his correspondence with city and county departments in which he asked for services and made complaints on behalf of the neighborhood. The county, it seemed, had dug up the street in order to lay water pipe on Archer Avenue and it had never put the street back in suitable condition. Stech had threatened to sue the county if the street was not fixed. It was fixed. The trees along the road presented another problem; they were so large that they were dangerous to both drivers and pedestrians. When a man broke his glasses on a protruding branch, Stech again threatened suit and the trees were promptly trimmed. Then the Santa Fe Railroad built a pig pen in the area; Stech and his organization made such a commotion that it was soon removed.

It was probably the energy he showed in these causes that brought Stech the chairmanship of the Southwest Neighborhood Council. The Council consisted of a delegate from each of 20 property owners' associations in the southwest section of the city. Public housing was the issue which brought the associations to-

---

3. Colored neighborhoods should be furnished with recreational and educational facilities comparable with white neighborhoods.
4. Colored neighborhoods should be furnished with street lighting, garbage collection, street cleaning, and other public services comparable to white neighborhoods.
5. Sites for new subdivisions for colored people should be acquired in a manner similar to the plan outlined under No. 2(c) . . . at the appraised evaluation, with the understanding that none of the acreage will be purchased by colored, at any price, until the appraisal figures have been publicly advertised. (Quoted in *Chicago Defender,* January 4, 1947.)

gether. By early 1950 the Council had a budget of about $3,000; later in the year it seemingly had a good deal more.

Stech said that there were many reasons why he opposed public housing—"reasons" typically employed by the opponents of public housing. The first reason, he said, was its unsightliness. "The houses are close together and ugly to begin with," he said, "and they are not taken care of properly. Garbage is thrown all over, mops are hanging out of windows, curtains are torn, windows are broken. This ugly picture is not pleasant to live with and it decreases the value of the property." His second argument was about the kind of people who lived in projects. "They have no sense of responsibility, they don't take care of their houses or their children, and they have no initiative. A social worker came up to me one day and said that I should feel sorry for these people and that I should take some responsibility for them. Now, I'm not a rich man, but I worked hard to raise a family. I went to work when I was 16 and I supported three younger sisters. When they grew up and got married, then I got married and now I'm raising a second family. I told her this, and she didn't have any answer for me. How can she tell me that I owe these people something?

"If these people would work and save they could have a house of their own. Before the war you could buy a little house like this one for about $6,000. They say they couldn't pay the rent on a house like this, and probably they couldn't now. But if they'd got a place before the war it wouldn't cost them any more than they're paying now and they could have a place of their own. You know, a lot of these people came up from the farms and from the South during the war. They made a lot of money working at war plants. But they took their checks into the bar to be cashed. The bar-keeper probably cashed it for them because they owed him $10 or so. He took his money out, and they probably drank up another four or five dollars and by the time they got home they didn't have much left.

"You know, a lot of people say it's the colored we don't want, but the kind of whites who live in public housing are just as bad. It's not the colored alone. It's the whole class of people who live like that. I talked to a colored woman who spoke against the site at Lake Park and 43rd. She called me to ask if we could give her any help. I asked her what her reasons were for being against public housing, and she said, 'We're high-class niggers, Mr. Stech, and we don't want any low-class niggers living next to us.' "[17]

Stech, some of his associates in the Southwest Neighborhood Council later agreed, was a promoter who hoped that his record of community activity, and especially his fight against public housing, would serve to launch him into politics. (After the site selection struggle was over Stech did, in fact, try to run for alderman, but his name was stricken from the ballot because of irregularities in his petitions.) He was able to head the Council because, whatever his motives, he was willing to work. "Stech worked awfully hard at it, every single day in the week," one of the other anti-public housing leaders later recalled.[18]

Ralph J. Finitzo, a prosperous realtor and builder (he estimated that he sold about 100 houses a year), was, some people said, the behind-the-scenes head of the Southwest Neighborhood Council. Shortly after its organization, he became executive secretary of the Council. He was also a member of the Chicago Metropolitan Home Builders' Association and chairman of its public relations committee, a post that was given him because he was the only one in the Association who was excited enough about public housing to want to take action. There were 30 members on the public relations committee, Finitzo once explained, but they were all wealthy, "big" builders who had "lost touch with the neighborhoods" and cared little about public housing and related issues. Since the "big" builders were apathetic, Finitzo organized the "small" ones as the Small Builders' Council on which were represented builders who sold from several houses to 100 a year. This was often called "Finitzo's organization."

Finitzo was, he once told an interviewer, making a financial sacrifice for the sake of opposing public housing: he could make much more money, he said, if he were to encourage the location of a large public housing project in the area where he operated. Then, by building houses for sale to the Negroes who would come into the area once it was opened for Negro settlement, he could get higher prices, for he believed it was well-established in the real estate business that "if Negroes want housing, they will have to pay for it."

In his various capacities, Finitzo worked closely with the neighborhood improvement associations. "If it weren't for these," he once said, "we could not get any support for our stand against public housing at all. . . . It's all a question of property values. Nobody wants to live near a housing project, and we just drum that into them. I wish we had more support, though; we are badly organized and the aldermen tend to vote the party line. We have to get the property owners stirred up to put the pressure on the aldermen."[19]

Finitzo had engaged an attorney, Arthur Sachs, to represent the Southwest Neighborhood Council. Sachs had not previously had any special concern with housing issues and he had hardly any political experience. Like Stech and Finitzo, he claimed to take a disinterested view of the issue. "For all the time I spent," he said later, ". . . and I spent a good part of a year working on it, I got not more than $1,200."

At first Sachs (so at least he claimed later) was not opposed to public housing in general; he was opposed only to a proposal to locate a project at a particular site. In principle the idea of slum clearance appealed to him, although he thought projects should not be built where there was private development or a reasonable prospect of it and he was fearful that public housing would mean higher taxes. By the time the site selection struggle was over, however, he had become persuaded that all public housing was undesirable.

Sachs was aware that much opposition to public housing was based on racial prejudice, but this was not, he said, his reason for opposing it or the reason of the Southwest Neighborhood Council. "I can honestly tell you," he told an interviewer afterward, "that there was no discussion at which I was ever present at which the racial issue was mentioned. It wasn't really the problem. Even if there had been a guarantee on the part of CHA that the projects would have been all white, there would have been no difference. Had there been a race issue, I would have taken no part."

Sachs, like Finitzo, was exasperated to find that business organizations with money and power were faint-hearted in their opposition to public housing at least on the local scene. He went to a dozen mortgage houses and savings and loan associations to solicit support for the Council. "The only one that had any guts," he said later, "was Talman Federal. The others were mostly afraid to get up and say that public housing would reduce land values. They were afraid of the Federal Housing Administration. They were afraid that they would meet disfavor with Federal agencies." Other opponents of public housing thought that Sachs and the Council were fighting a lost cause. "I admire your guts," Sachs remembered a member of the Chicago Real Estate Board as saying to him, "but I think you're crazy—you can't get one unit cut off the program." This, Sachs found, was the prevailing view among the realtors. "The Real Estate Board," he said later, "gave zero assistance." All in all, he concluded, the anti-public housing forces were fortunate in having their power greatly overestimated. "We had no public relations at all," he said. "It was a midget fighting a couple of giants."[20]

The fourth principal leader of the anti-housing forces was Cornelius Teninga, a prosperous realtor and mortgage banker whose firm was founded in 1895 by his father, a then recent immigrant from Holland. Teninga, a graduate of the University of Chicago in both economics and law, was chairman of the Taxpayers Action Committee, which was a federation of several neighborhood associations, the South End Chamber of Commerce, the Kiwanis Club of Roseland, and two lodges of the Knights of Pythias.

Teninga opposed public housing because he feared it would displace Negroes and bring them to his area. "Here in our community (Roseland)," he told an interviewer, "we have always had a reasonable number of colored who have come and used the facilities of our community—our parks and our shops. The Negroes we have had in our community have owned their own homes. We get along with them all right. But CHA has shoved Negroes into neighborhoods where there weren't any Negroes. Our people do not support rent control or public housing. When we see a lot of Negroes coming out here with money in their hands trying to buy property that Negroes have never bought, we inquire where the money is coming from." The implication of this remark was that by buying the property of Negroes preparatory to slum clearance, the Land Clearance Commission (and CHA) facilitated the movement of Negroes into Roseland. If public housing could be built in the slum districts without displacing Negroes, Teninga would not, he said, be opposed to it, although in his opinion it made little sense to give the newest housing to the lowest income group.

The Taxpayers' Action Committee had about $15,000 to spend in 1950. About half of this money came from home owners and the rest from builders, merchants and others who, as Teninga put it, "don't want to see the whole thing go black (Negro)." The Committee attempted to assess its contributors one per cent of their tax bills. Landlords, Teninga found, were reluctant to contribute; they were interested in the abolition of rent control, but not of public housing. The Real Estate Board was also indifferent. "It is not a lobby," he once explained. "A lot of people who are members of it say, 'Why should we beat our brains out on public housing or rent control? The owners ought to. We don't manage even 10 per cent of the properties. We are only intermediaries.' "

The trouble with the real estate business, Teninga had long since concluded, was that real estate men were too individualistic. Instead of helping each other and working together, most of them were anxious only to prevent the other fellow from getting ahead or getting more publicity. "There are," he once said, "a few real estate men who are altruistic. They are public spirited. The same is true of myself. We just provide some leadership for the owners of this community. We have a mailing list of 20,000 names."[21]

During the struggle over sites, Stech, Finitzo, and Sachs worked together closely. Their association, the Southwest Neighborhood Council, had little to do with Teninga and the Taxpayers' Action Committee however. "I have great respect for Teninga," Sachs once said, "but I didn't want him on our side. His approach didn't make sense."[22] Although Sachs did not see fit to say so, he was probably referring here to Teninga's emphasis on preventing the spread of Negro residence. Teninga, at any rate, was a liability from Sachs' standpoint.

The heads of the Authority and the supporters of public housing were well aware of the opposition that existed in the conservation areas. There was not much that they could do to avoid it, however. They could not build housing without moving Negroes into these areas: the only available vacant land was there. They might build in the slums, of course, but if they did so—this was a crucial point which the opposition never seemed fully to grasp—they would not only cause hardship to the people who were displaced but they would also inevitably cause Negro families to increase their pressure on the conservation areas.

But although they took it for granted that there would be strenuous opposition from property-owners in the outlying areas, the public housing strategists believed that their most influential opponents were the big city-wide and nation-wide building, banking, and real estate interests. These, they believed, had joined forces with other interests who, for ideological reasons, wanted to discredit and destroy all welfare programs. Taken altogether, these interests, in the view of the public housing leaders, comprised a well-organized and well-financed conspiracy, a conspiracy which was national in scope.*

There was some truth in this view. The State Street Council

* The public housing leaders seem to have supposed that the power structure of Chicago was something like that described by Hunter in "Regional City": there the persons who "set the line of policy" for the community are industrial, commercial, financial owners and top executives of large enterprises ("first rate" power holders) and operations officials, bank vice-presidents, public relations men, small businessmen, top-ranking public officials, corporation attorneys, and contractors ("second rate" power holders). The understructure professional people (civic organization personnel, newspaper columnists, petty public officials, professionals such as ministers, teachers, and social workers) "hold the line" on policies set by the top structure (pp. 109-110). "The understructure may be likened to a key-board over which the top structure personnel play, and the particular keys struck may vary from project to project." (p. 94.) Floyd Hunter, *Community Power Structure,* University of North Carolina Press, Chapel Hill, 1953.

As the reader will see, we found no evidence that a "top structure" made policy respecting public housing. This may be because the top structure was so subtle and devious that we failed to discern its workings, because it was occupied with matters it considered more important than public housing, or, as we think most likely, because in Chicago, a city which is larger in population than any of 35 independent nations, there are so many "top" power-holders—and these have so little in common and are so little in communication—that consciously concerted action by them is all but impossible. But even though concerted activity may not be feasible, some power-holders, as we show, exercise great influence in some spheres of activity.

was indeed a group of powerful merchants who were able to act in concert. The Chicago Metropolitan Home Builders' Association, the Chicago Real Estate Board, the Chicago Mortgage Bankers' Association, and the Civic Federation of Chicago all had great influence which it seemed could readily be turned against public housing. These organizations were linked together through interlocking directorships and they had ties to the many property owners' associations throughout the city (the Real Estate Board and the Title and Trust Company had in fact collaborated actively with the associations in promoting restrictive covenants).[23] Moreover, the community weeklies went far toward connecting the anti-public housing forces into a single system of communication of which hundreds of thousands of neighborhood-minded readers were a part. No doubt some of the people who were active in some of the property owners' associations were members of Chicago's secret native fascist organization, the White Circle League.

The Chicago anti-public housing interests, moreover, had ties with national organizations such as the National Association of Real Estate Boards, the United States Savings and Loan League, and the National Association of Home Builders, organizations which in the last eight months of 1949 spent more than $200,000 on their Washington lobby. Indeed, Chicago was headquarters for the national anti-public housing lobby and one of the leaders of the lobby, Morton Bodfish, head of the United States Savings and Loan League, was a vice-chairman of the Chicago Plan Commission. (Getting its leaders appointed to local planning commissions was part of the lobby's publicly announced strategy.)[24] Herbert U. Nelson, the $25,000-a-year vice-president of the National Association of Real Estate Boards, was also prominent in Chicago affairs.

The national real estate lobby was, of course, part of a larger "big business" lobby with which Chicago business leaders had many connections. The working connections between the real estate and other big business interests were not especially close, however. "Big business is not a particular asset to us in fighting socialism," Nelson once explained. "If we had the support of big business it would hurt us and not help. I have talked this over with one of the representatives of the steel industry and he agrees. Some of the smartest leaders in NAM also think this is true."[25]

On the fringes of the anti-public housing movement were the native fascist organizations, especially the Committee for Constitutional Government, and Gerald L. K. Smith. These, probably, were also regarded as public relations liabilities by the real estate men.

Elaborate and ramified as it undoubtedly was, the national real estate lobby and its Chicago affiliates would have little direct influence in the struggle over sites in Chicago. In part the reason was that the real estate men were not all in agreement or all very much interested: whether for business or personal reasons, a few of the leading members of the Chicago Real Estate Board and of the Chicago Mortgage Bankers' Association would fight for, not against, public housing, and the organizations themselves would stay somewhat aloof from the struggle. Other leading members of these organizations fought against public housing not through their national but through their neighborhood groups—a "grass roots" approach advocated by the lobby. Later events showed that there was less effective communication among the opponents of public housing than the public housing supporters had supposed, and this of course affected the ability of the opponents to make themselves felt. (There also proved to be less effective communication among the supporters than the opponents supposed.)

The national real estate lobby would do little on the Chicago scene: its representatives would make small donations to local groups and distribute "kits" of anti-public housing pamphlets and other literature.[26] There were, Bodfish explained after the struggle was over, carefully considered reasons why the national lobby did not participate more actively in the Chicago fight, where the largest single program reservation for public housing was at stake.

"I thought the problem was in Washington," Bodfish said. "There is no popular demand in this area or any other that I know of for state-owned housing. My thinking was that the centralist—the socialist—planners gave public housing its impetus. The people who favor public housing are not particularly concerned with slums; they are concerned with the extension of public enterprise into the area of real estate, and for some period they could get Federal funds for this purpose." If the supply of funds from Washington could be shut off, Bodfish believed, public housing would soon become a lost cause. "At the local level public housing would not amount to anything. They had paid staffs and some starts, but no local support. Cities by themselves [i.e., without Federal aid] would not have public housing programs."

But although public housing programs would soon end without Federal funds, it would be useless, Bodfish thought, to try to stop them locally as long as the subsidies were flowing from Washington. "I thought any city council would take anything from the central government that it could get for nothing," he remarked afterward.

There was one possible advantage in using the lobby's resources on the local scene, Bodfish said. Local anti-public housing campaigns would be "a way to get an increased understanding of this thing [public intervention in housing] and of its implications." But even in this regard there were certain disadvantages in operating in the context of a local controversy. Local people tended to see the issue in concrete rather than in ideological-symbolic terms: they wanted to discuss what to do about slums in Chicago whereas the main issue for Bodfish was not slums in Chicago but the extension of public enterprise into the real estate field and the even larger question of whether everyone was entitled to a good living at the hands of the Welfare State whether he worked for it or not. Bodfish was unwilling to spend much of his time discussing the pro's and con's of public housing in Chicago because the setting of the discussion would enable the public housers to take advantage of the undeniable—but to him irrelevant—fact of slums. "I wouldn't get out and debate with Elizabeth Wood and my good friend Robert Taylor," he said afterward. "Hell, I knew there were slums in Chicago." Though Bodfish's own position was largely ideological he nevertheless pointed to the supporters of public housing as "left-wingers" whose prime concern was the ideology of extending governmental ownership of property.[27]

"LOOK – IT'S CATCHING UP ON US!"

CHAPTER FIVE □ □ □ □ □ □

THE DEVELOPMENT OF POLICY

In almost all of the opinion concerning public housing—the opinion of the State Street merchant, the industrialist, the neighborhood banker, the real estate man, the politician, the labor official, and others—there seemed to be one question in common: Where would the CHA program move Negroes?

This question had a history. In 1937 CHA had inherited three projects from the Federal government's Public Works Administration. The transfer was hardly complete when nine Negro families applied for apartments in one of them and the alderman, whose ward had hitherto been all-white, expressed alarm. The manager of the project received the applications from Negroes on the same basis as those from whites; however, he limited the Negro families to one building or section.[1] Soon afterward the commissioners issued a policy declaration: "Resolved, that colored families be accepted for occupancy in the Jane Addams Houses in the same proportion as they are at present represented in the neighborhood."[2]

The Board had acquired this policy, along with the projects, from the Department of the Interior. The "neighborhood composition rule," as it was called throughout the country, had been formulated by Interior Secretary Harold Ickes and his advisers and was apparently accepted by Negro leaders and active advocates of public housing. It meant that a housing project would not be permitted to alter the racial character of an area. How precise the correspondence should be between a project's racial composition and that of the slum area it replaced, and whether the "neighborhood" should be defined as the general area of a project or as the project's exact boundaries, were subject to interpretation.

CHA, like other authorities, gave a narrow interpretation to the policy. Two of the PWA projects were in what had been white neighborhoods and were accordingly filled with white tenants. The third project presented a difficult problem. Twenty-six Negro families had lived along one edge of that site. CHA, applying the neighborhood composition rule, admitted 26 Negro families to the project. These families were housed in segregated stairwells. Later, when some eligible Negroes threatened to sue, the number accepted was increased to about 60 families. The additional families were largely segregated in one part of the project.

Subsequently, CHA built a sequence of five new projects. By application of the neighborhood composition rule two of these were all-white (except for less than one per cent Orientals), a third was all-Negro, a fourth was all-white, and the fifth was bi-racial. These projects were completed by 1943. Of the next group of projects to be built (between 1944 and 1949), one was all-white (with a few Japanese) and two were all-Negro (except that one of these had a token white occupancy of five per cent).

CHA was aware that in choosing the sites for these projects it was fixing their racial composition. At first the Authority took it for granted that the projects should be all-white or all-Negro; there were, actually, few parts of the city where it was possible to build a project which under the neighborhood composition rule would be bi-racial. Nevertheless, despite this assumption, there had always been vigorous opposition to public housing sites. Thus, in 1938, when CHA built its first project under the 1937 Act, white property owners from nearby areas bitterly objected to the rehousing of Negroes on the site, although it was one which had been almost all Negro.[3]

The growing pressure from Negroes who came to Chicago to do war work and the trend of policy in national government toward equal treatment for Negroes inclined the Authority to seek sites which would form bi-racial projects. That most of the later projects became Negro was a circumstance not intended by the Authority when it chose the sites.

The Cabrini and Brooks projects, for example, were both intended to be bi-racial: following the neighborhood composition rule Cabrini would be occupied by 80 per cent white tenants and 20 per cent Negroes, as in the surrounding areas; Brooks, following the same rule, would have 20 per cent whites and 80 per cent Negroes. But when Cabrini, a project for defense workers, was completed, it proved to be very difficult to persuade a full complement of white families to live there. There were, however, more than enough applications from Negroes. The 20 per cent ratio was relaxed and the number of Negroes was allowed to rise without hinderance. It rose to 30 per cent (a few years later it had risen to 40 per cent) and Cabrini became the one permanent project which (in 1949) was bi-racial.

In the case of Brooks, where 80 per cent of the occupants were to be Negro, it proved impossible to obtain and retain a sufficient number of white tenants. Most whites refused to live in a project which was predominantly colored; those who tried it generally left as soon as they could, often with the encouragement of the Negro families, who felt that the whites were occupying places that should rightfully have been given to Negroes. Finally, despite the intention of the Authority, Brooks became entirely Negro. From this and similar experiences, the Authority concluded that unless a project had many compensating advantages from the point of view of whites and unless the percentage of Negro occupancy was small—not more than 20 per cent—whites would not apply or would move out and Negroes would move in until the project became all Negro.*

In 1946 CHA changed its racial policy. Through day-to-day decisions based on what circumstances seemed to require, the Authority shaped a new racial policy, one which was to prove of great importance in its affairs.

The Authority was authorized by the City Council in 1946 to

---

* Subsequently, the situation changed in two important respects: the Authority appealed to new sources of white tenants and there was a change in the attitude toward Negroes of many whites, especially veterans. In 1954 the Authority had some projects which, although predominantly Negro, nevertheless had a stable bi-racial occupancy. Racine Courts, for example, had 76 per cent Negroes and 24 per cent whites. It was on the edge of a Negro district in a neighborhood that was not badly deteriorated and it was designed especially for large families: whites with large families were, of course, harder pressed for housing than others.

construct and manage, under contract from the Federal government and subject to its regulations, temporary housing for veterans. The temporary housing had to be built on vacant land since it was needed in a hurry. Mayor Kelly, concerned about the city budget, told the Authority that it was to use only land which was already in the possession of the Park District, the Sanitary District, and the Board of Education. These sites were mostly in outlying residential districts—districts occupied by whites. There were only two small sites available in the Negro areas. Since over 20 per cent of the veterans needing housing were Negroes and since the Federal Housing Expediter insisted that Negroes receive a fair proportion of the total (although he left the city free to decide whether housing should be segregated or not), it was necessary to set the neighborhood composition rule aside and to bring Negroes into white areas under CHA auspices. The veterans' housing was to be temporary, and so, presumably, the Negroes would move away in a few years. Nevertheless, there was certain to be opposition.

Projects were built on 21 sites in 11 wards. Although Kelly assured the Authority that it could depend on his full support in cases of racial trouble, the commissioners and staff were somewhat apprehensive. They decided to house Negroes in the larger projects only—those of 150 units or more. The idea was to reduce the potential trouble spots to a manageable number. The Authority would not refuse to admit a Negro to one of the smaller projects in the unlikely event that he insisted upon living in one, but it would not direct Negroes to the small projects.

In many white neighborhoods, therefore, the projects would be all white and in a few white neighborhoods where there were large projects there would be some Negroes. Even in these large projects, however, the number of Negroes would be fairly small. Kelly himself suggested that Negroes be limited to 10 per cent of the total amount of the housing, this being the percentage of Negroes in the total population.

The policy was adopted without being formally passed upon by the commissioners. "We felt that the veterans' projects represented a new era," Miss Wood said later, "and there could not be the same adherence to the neighborhood composition rule that there had been in the old program."[4]

The staff, with Taylor's close collaboration, began elaborately to prepare for the opening of the first bi-racial project. They carefully selected the families who were to be the first Negro arrivals: generally former officers with combat records whose wives were known to be competent housekeepers were chosen for admission. The white veterans, too, were screened, although much more casually. This first veterans' project was opened with what appeared to be great good will and harmony.

The second bi-racial project was Airport Homes, consisting of 185 units on the South Side. CHA tenanted the first 125 units with white veterans. Then, because the carefully selected Negroes were not yet ready to move in, it interrupted the tenanting, giving as its reason that the builders had some finishing touches to add to the remaining units. During the delay, 59 white veterans from the adjacent neighborhood, presumably with the connivance of some policemen and ward politicians, seized the keys to the vacant units from the CHA caretaker and moved in as squatters. The press (which took its position from the Mayor's Commission on Human Relations) treated the affair as a spontaneous reaction to bureaucratic delay. Actually it was a maneuver to forestall occupancy of the project by Negroes. Anti-Negro feeling in the neighborhood was being excited by local politicians who hoped apparently to create an incident which would embarrass Mayor Kelly in the coming elections.[5]

CHA gave places in the project to those squatters who were eligible and for about a month it tried unsuccessfully to persuade the others to leave. Finally, when it was clear that a court order would be issued, the squatters left. But when CHA moved two Negro families into the project there was an immediate hostile reaction. A crowd of about 200 persons, most of them local housewives, threw stones and shouted profanity and threats. Soon 1,000 spectators gathered, and a force of 400 policemen was assigned to the project to keep order. For two weeks the Negro families courageously lived in the project under guard. Then they succumbed to the pressure and moved away. CHA could find no more Negroes who would run the risk of being mobbed, and accordingly Airport Homes remained a white project.[6]

After Airport Homes, however, there were always at least a few Negro applicants for almost all of the projects. Hitherto, the Authority had been able to keep some projects all white merely by taking no positive steps to encourage Negro applications. The trouble at Airport Homes changed this. Airport Homes was a challenge to "race men" among the Negroes and to their supporters among the whites; these people made it clear that the question of segregation or no segregation would have to be openly faced henceforth at every project. When there was no avoiding the question, the Authority would, of course, have to support the principle of non-discrimination.

This was the situation in May 1947, when Miss Wood was called upon to answer questions at a public meeting sponsored by the Fernwood-Bellevue Civic Association. She told 350 indignant property owners that in all projects, regardless of their location, both Negroes and whites were welcome. She said that no assignments had yet been made to the Fernwood project (which was then under construction) and that she did not know whether any Negroes would choose to live in that particular project. "We must," she concluded, "invite them all in the exact order of their priority and on the basis of their need."[7]

With her talk of "inviting" the Negroes, Miss Wood angered the property owners. She seemed to be telling them that CHA would encourage Negroes to move into their neighborhood. "I would have been satisfied with this answer," Alderman Reginald DuBois told the meeting after Miss Wood had been heard, "if it were on the basis of equal rights for all—but it isn't. Negroes would not seek housing in white neighborhoods if they were not being prompted to do so by some group. I believe that Negroes would not ask to be assigned to this project if they were not pushed to do so. We all want to protect our homes, and the people of this community will put up a stout fight: The burning question is whether or not Negro veterans are to be located in this project. . . . I believe, Miss Wood, that, considering the fact that there are other projects that are now 100 per cent colored, you could go down the list of 25,000 veteran applicants and, without bothering your conscience a bit, find 87 white tenants for the local project."[8]

It was true, of course, that CHA had selected special families from among its Negro applicants for those projects which, for strategic reasons, it had chosen previously to make bi-racial. And so it was true, too, that CHA could at one time have decided in advance that there were to be no Negroes, or a certain quota of Negroes, assigned to the Fernwood Project. (Indeed, of the 20 projects which were completed by August 1947, only 11 were bi-racial although all completed after that date would be bi-racial.) As we have explained, afterward it was no longer possible for CHA to have altogether excluded Negroes from any project. It could have found ways of limiting their numbers, to be sure—perhaps of limiting them drastically, but it could not admit this in public. To bring the Authority officials before a public meeting was to oblige them, in keeping with the American creed, to declare themselves unalterably opposed to discrimination.[9] The more disturbance the Fernwood neighborhood made about Negroes, the more CHA would feel compelled to offer Negroes places there. That it would make a major disturbance was clear; this section of Chicago had always opposed the coming of Negroes through restrictive covenants, and even physical violence.

On August 13th CHA began moving the first 52 families, eight of whom were Negro, into the Fernwood project. Warned by the rumblings of anger and the open threats that had been emanating from the neighborhood for months, the CHA staff and the Mayor's Commission on Human Relations had applied an approach that had worked well elsewhere. They brought teachers, librarians, church leaders and others together for "orientation" in advance. They distributed explanatory pamphlets in the schools, alerted the police, and organized a Community Goodwill Council (despite the great difficulty of finding sponsors for it in the Fernwood neighborhood) which would set up a canteen and distribute coffee and doughnuts to the families as they arrived.

Despite these preparations, there was serious trouble at once. When the first Negroes appeared a crowd began to gather. By late evening the project was surrounded by a mob of 5,000. The next day the mob disappeared, but it gathered again the next night and the next, erupting in sporadic acts of violence. A thousand policemen held it precariously in check the first three nights. It was two weeks before the police could be reduced to 700 and six months before the Negro families could be considered safely established in the project.

Events had made the Housing Authority the hero—or the villain—of these dramatic scenes. Hitherto, the Authority's racial stand, while it was probably no more discriminatory than that of most other government agencies, had been conservative; certainly no one had ever seriously claimed that the Authority was trying to change race relations in any fundamental way. But now, after the events at Airport Homes and Fernwood, CHA was hailed by pro-Negro and damned by anti-Negro organizations for its "aggressive leadership" in the struggle to end racial discrimination. Alderman DuBois introduced a resolution in City Council in which he charged that CHA "persists in theories of housing which are shared by no other representative local government agencies in Chicago, and are not in accord with those of a great majority of citizens."[10]

It was largely the pressure of events that was responsible for bringing the Authority to a new racial policy. Indeed, so far as any formal declaration by the commissioners was concerned, the racial policy was still the one that had been obtained from Washington in 1937: the neighborhood composition rule.

In the period between the Airport and the Fernwood riots Mayor Kennelly succeeded Mayor Kelly. This was an important change. Kelly had encouraged the Authority not to be concerned about opposition; he was the Boss, and he would see that the CHA program and projects were protected. When the Airport Homes riot occurred, he had at first wavered, saying that it was a Federal and not a municipal matter, but then he had issued a strong statement prepared by the Commission on Human Relations which endorsed CHA's policy of selecting tenants "according to need" and he had declared that "all law-abiding citizens may be assured of their right to live peaceably anywhere in Chicago."[11]

Kennelly took a different view. When the much more serious Fernwood riot occurred, he had no public statement to make. He was exasperated with the Authority for what he seemed to think was its intransigent and unreasonable stand. He told Miss Wood he could see no sense in calling a thousand policemen to duty at a fantastic cost per day just to protect eight Negro families. Couldn't they, he asked, be taken care of in some other way?[12] When the CHA commissioners recommended that he issue a public statement supporting their position, he did not respond.*

This was the setting in November 1947, when at the Mayor's urging the citizens of Chicago voted nearly two to one in favor of a bond issue to finance relocation housing and subsidized private urban redevelopment. A redevelopment program would probably necessitate relocation—the rehousing of those persons residing on redevelopment sites—for unless there were low-rent projects into which the slum-dwellers could be moved it would be futile to talk of rebuilding the old areas. Even without redevelopment, relocation projects would be needed to accommodate the families who would be displaced to make way for certain major public works, e.g., the Congress Street super-highway and the Medical Center development.

Relocation housing would have to be built on vacant land if it was to serve its purpose; it would be almost absurd to choose relocation sites from which still additional families would have to be relocated. Vacant land for residential use was to be found chiefly in the outlying, white districts. In relocation, therefore, there was the making of another set of conflicts.

A month after the bond issue was approved by the voters, CHA made tentative relocation housing site proposals to the Housing and Redevelopment Coordinator. The sites it recommended were large parcels of vacant land in outlying areas. The Coordinator was expected to appoint an inter-agency committee to consider these and other sites. No such committee ever met. Instead, Mayor Kennelly and the "Big Boys" of the Council made it clear to CHA that the proposed sites were not acceptable.

Six months after submitting the first list of sites, CHA sub-

* However, after another incident occurred he did issue a statement supporting CHA on March 9, 1948.

mitted a new list, this time directly to the Housing Committee of the City Council. Mayor Kennelly wrote that these new sites —three small ones in slum areas and a large one in a public park —were a "good selection." But after the Mayor and the members of the Housing Committee took a bus trip to inspect the sites, he decided that the selection was not as good as he had at first thought. Three of the aldermen in whose wards projects were planned were strongly opposed to them. A crowd of 5,000 gathered to protest the selection of the one large, vacant-land site. Observing these portents, the Mayor changed his mind, cancelled the public hearings which had been announced, and withdrew the sites from consideration by the Council.

This second set of sites was a compromise which had brought protests from some of the pro-housing forces. (The South Side Planning Board, for example, declared that "no sound technical evidence was submitted to support the recommendations.")[13] Furthermore, CHA came under pressure from the opponents of public housing to compromise still further.

After five weeks of negotiation, Taylor, McMillen and a few key aldermen agreed to nine other sites—sites which the CHA staff disapproved. The new sites met the one criterion which the Coordinator had put forward—that they "should be in areas least likely to interfere with potential private development or neighborhood construction"[14]—but they met none of the usual planning criteria. They were relatively small (eight averaged 7.7 acres; one was 34 acres) and two-thirds were in slum areas adjacent to railroads, factories, and traffic arteries. Only four were completely vacant; on all of the others there was some housing which would have to be razed before construction could be completed.

The supporters of public housing were uncertain as to what stand to take on the compromise relocation program. One organization's spokesman called it "laudable" while another remarked that "progress comes slowly." The CIO, the American Veterans Committee, and the Independent Voters of Illinois urged that the worst sites be discarded and more suitable ones substituted. The Chairman of the Commission on Human Relations said six of the sites were satisfactory from the standpoint of racial policy, but he urged adoption of all nine on the grounds that the others represented some gain. Homer Jack, a Unitarian minister who represented the Chicago Council Against Racial and Religious Discrimination, objected, believing that the relocation housing program should be used to develop new areas where people could live without segregation. "This is not a new principle unique to Chicago," Jack said of the policy he recommended. "It reflects the accepted inter-group relations goals across the country."[15]

After a quick and vociferous public hearing the City Council approved the entire "package" of sites by a 40 to five vote.

Five of the relocation sites were in white areas. These had been approved by aldermen who had often publicly sworn that they would never agree to bringing Negroes into white areas. To an outsider, it must have seemed that the aldermen had suddenly and unaccountably cast aside their prejudices—and, incidentally, their political futures. This was not the case however. Taylor had privately reached a compromise with the Mayor, Duffy, and a few other aldermen. At first Taylor agreed to limit Negro occupants of the projects in the white areas to not more than 20 per cent of the total. After agreeing on this figure, the Mayor told Taylor that he found he could not persuade the aldermen to accept so high a quota of Negroes. They would agree to a range of from 10 to 20 per cent, the Mayor said, but no more. Taylor accepted this. But then the Mayor and Duffy found that they still could not obtain Council approval for two of the projects. In that case, Taylor said, the deal was off: there would be no projects at all. Hearing this, Kennelly and Duffy thought they might be able to persuade the two most difficult aldermen to agree on a quota of 10 per cent, and on that basis the deal was concluded. (Taylor pointed out afterwards that in the situation then existing—the almost complete segregation of Negroes in Chicago—he had good grounds to regard the 10 per cent quota as a significant gain for Negroes.) Once Taylor and the Mayor had come to these terms, the voting in the Council was a formality.[16]

CHA's director of planning at this time was a former real estate man named John M. Ducey. Ducey believed strongly in planning, and so, even before selection of the relocation sites, he wrote a memorandum proposing that the Authority and the Plan Commission take steps toward preparing a long-term plan for Negro residence location. Ducey's idea was that the planning agencies should prepare and make public three maps showing, each on a different assumption, the probable distribution of Negroes at the end of a 10-year period. One map would be based on the assumption that the Negro ghetto would continue to grow at its perimeter by jumping boundary lines. A second would show the distribution that would result if new segregated communities were to be developed in certain vacant or sparsely populated districts. The third would show the distribution of Negroes on the assumption of "complete integration."

Ducey regarded these maps as a device to make it clear to the people of Chicago that there had to be some settlement of the question of where Negroes were to live and that it would be wiser to have a deliberate settlement—not necessarily one planned by the Plan Commission, but rather one planned by all community interests—than to leave the question to be settled "accidentally" by the working of various pressures. He was proposing that the city agencies help the people of Chicago to see the implications of the rate of expansion of the Negro population and to make a conscious choice to which the Authority and other agencies, both public and private, might then relate their policies.

Ducey's proposal was never acted upon by the Authority, and so it was never sent to the Plan Commission. Informally Ducey received comments from members of the Plan Commission staff. "It's a nice idea," he later remembered their saying, "but we couldn't touch it with a 10-foot pole. The farther the Plan Commission stays away from the racial issue, the better off it will be."[17]

After his experience with the relocation program, Ducey resigned.

A city agency which did try deliberately to formulate a comprehensive racial policy was the Commission on Human Relations, an agency which, while it could advise the city government, had no administrative authority. The Commission made the removal of segregation the active purpose of its policy—at least it did so before 1949, when its outlook began to conform more closely to the Mayor's wishes. Redevelopment, it argued, would inevitably necessitate the movement of Negroes into white residential areas. Rather than have them spread by jumping boundaries and "taking over" block after block, a process which caused friction with the whites, it was desirable, the Commission felt, for the Negroes to scatter in various locations among the whites. This kind of movement was not likely to occur except as the result of an explicit policy on the part of the city. If the city declared its purpose to stop the advance of the Negro slums by encouraging the spread of Negroes into white areas, it could implement that purpose by a wise administration of the relocation program. If, on the other hand, the city chose sites which would freeze the existing patterns of segregation, private redevelopers could be expected to act similarly. The spread of housing segregation would mean the spread of school segregation. Children who went through school without ever having any contact with children of another race, the Commission pointed out, would not fit in easily in factories, stores, and offices where there was no discrimination. Thus, the long-run effect of segregation would, in circular fashion, be even more segregation.

On the basis of these considerations the Commission recommended a site selection policy that would, "(1) open up new areas of vacant land throughout the city where low-income families displaced from slum clearance areas may live regardless of race, creed, or ethnic origin, and without segregation—thus avoiding extension of the presently constituted ghettos on the South and West sides, and (2) create no new segregated patterns such as would result from clusters of Negro families located adjacent to Negro communities."[18]

These recommendations were based on reflection rather than on research. The two recommendations were very difficult to achieve, for past experience indicated that it was hard to establish permanent bi-racial communities of low-income people: the whites would move away and the Negroes would move in until the new areas became small ghettos. Even if the whites would permit it, most Negroes might not, under existing conditions, want to be dispersed in predominantly white neighborhoods. There were many Negroes who felt that, while it would be well to have many small scattered Negro communities rather than one or two large ones, there were advantages for Negroes in living together. At any rate, no one knew whether, in the unlikely event that it should try, the city could persuade Negroes to end segregation, a practice which, although it had been forced upon them by whites, had —as we have noted—taken root in their psychology and in their economic and social organization.[19] The ghetto was a place where, among other things, one did not have to compete with whites, and this had its advantages, at least for many among the Negro leadership.

Miss Wood maintained that the compromise by which CHA agreed to limit Negro occupancy of relocation projects in white areas to 10 per cent was improper and she was surprised that the Negroes did not resist it. But she also held that the quota might have a reassuring effect—that it might help the cause of public housing and thus, of course, the Negro. "It may very well be that fidelity to that low percentage will make a difference by reducing the fear that aldermen have of the coming of a project," she said in an interview at a later time. "The aldermen are not particularly worried by a 10 per cent Negro occupancy. Practically all of them have some Negroes in their wards. It may be that a firm stand on a low percentage will in time mitigate the terror that a lot of people have. I don't know whether that is true or not, and in any case there is a very real reason why the Negro people should repudiate a policy that establishes any percentage at all. It is a kind of gamble that we have made, a gamble that may or may not pay off. There is no question in my mind but that a few of the aldermen have completely recovered from the feeling that what we intended was to take these housing projects and fill them up 100 per cent with Negroes or mostly with Negroes. We won't know until we get a little further along whether this policy—which is a bad policy essentially—will ease the pressure in the next site fight."[20]

Quite apart from these tactical considerations, there was good reason for CHA to accept a quota on Negro occupancy in the white area projects. The experience of the Authority suggested, as we have indicated, that if there were more than about one-third Negroes in an otherwise white project, the whites would leave until the project eventually became almost all Negro. This was an outcome which the Authority was as anxious as the aldermen to prevent and it was one reason why Taylor had allowed the Mayor and Duffy to persuade him to accept the quota. "I put up a big fuss about the idea of any quota at all," Taylor said afterward. "I talked a lot about freedom and so forth. But I was not too worried. I knew what had happened in those projects that were supposed to be 50-50; the whites had never moved in, and so they had become all-Negro projects. I saw that Cabrini was successful with 30 per cent Negroes. I figured that more than 30 per cent wouldn't work, but between 10 and 30 would work all right. More than 30 would tip it over."[21]

Both sides, then, were agreed that the occupancy of Negroes in white area projects should be limited by a quota: the difference of opinion—whether there should be 10 per cent or 30 per cent Negroes—was, it would seem, one upon which agreement might be reached.

It was unfortunate, perhaps, that this coincidence of interest between the pro-Negro and the anti-Negro forces could not be made a matter of general public knowledge. If the Housing Authority had been able to explain publicly that it would not permit Negro occupancy to rise above 30 per cent in predominantly white projects, a good deal of suspicion and fear might have been dissipated. Some people, of course, would be outraged at the prospect of even one Negro family entering their neighborhood, but many people, probably, would have been satisfied to know that the Negroes would be prevented from "taking over" the neighborhood in its entirety.*

---

* In its public statements the Authority maintained that its policy was nondiscriminatory. But not until the summer of 1953 did the commissioners decide to let Negroes into all projects. Then, after a riot at a project into which a Negro family had been inadvertently admitted, the commissioners on August 26 voted to open all projects to nonwhites as soon as "consistent with the maintenance of law and order." Violence continued at this project, and nearly a year later (April 7, 1954) the City Council passed a resolution declaring that there should be no discrimination at any public housing project.

Chicago had not had an integrated program comparable to that in certain other cities. By "integration," housing professionals mean the mixture of racial

Whatever might have been the advantages of a public statement of this kind, CHA felt that it could not make one. Such a statement would have been viewed in many quarters—both pro- and anti-Negro quarters—as a qualification of the principle of equal treatment of races. It was necessary above all to maintain in public the fiction that any law-abiding citizen could live wherever he pleased and that in public housing projects no account would be taken of race, color, or creed. Here the importance of the symbolic function far outweighed that of the real function. The special value of secrecy—of what the politicians called a "deal"—was that it permitted the making of "practical" gains without the loss of advantage in the war of symbols.

The City Council could force the Authority to accept inferior sites for the relocation projects because that program was financed by the city and the state. Under a national housing act, the passage of which could be foreseen in 1948, the Council, if it agreed to any public housing program at all, presumably would have to permit the Authority to choose sites without interference. The Authority would, the politicians seemed to think, use this opportunity to build large bi-racial projects in outlying white neighborhoods.

On March 15, 1948 the Council took action to prevent this.

---

groups without spatial segregation either through agency action in placing residents according to quotas or through free choice by tenants and prospective tenants as to the projects in which they will live.

Furthermore, some local authorities whose programs have been no more discriminatory than the Chicago one have been bitterly attacked by Negro groups and their supporters. In Detroit, for example, where the facts of discrimination are not much different from what they are in Chicago but where the local authority has not claimed an ideological commitment to the principle of non-discrimination, the authority has been bitterly attacked in the press, and, more important, in the courts.

Probably, if the staff of the Chicago Authority had not been so vigorous in proclaiming its commitment to the principle of non-discrimination, it would have been attacked for its practices. But it must be emphasized that the CHA staff tried hard to develop an integrated program. The principal obstacle was unsuitable sites: most of the sites were in Negro areas, areas of low status, or areas lacking community facilities, and it was virtually impossible to get whites to live in such places. If it had had large outlying sites with good community facilities where a majority of tenants would have been white in the normal course of events, CHA might have had an integrated program.

Nevertheless, despite the Authority's good intentions, faster progress toward integration might have been made if the Negro groups had attacked the Authority.

Alderman Lancaster, the chairman of the housing committee, informed the state legislature, which was then considering a bill to prepare the way for the anticipated Federal program, that the City Council wanted authority to approve or disapprove each site. The legislature obligingly included a provision in the legislation giving this power to the governing bodies of all cities having a population of 500,000 or more; Chicago, of course, was the only city in Illinois of that size. At the same time, the Mayor and the principal aldermen arranged to place the new urban redevelopment program in a new agency, the Chicago Land Clearance Commission, rather than in CHA. If CHA had been more popular in the Council, it might well have been considered the logical place for that function.

Meanwhile Alderman Carey, one of the two Negroes in the Council, provoked a brief but bitter battle by a resolution to require non-discrimination in all housing built with city funds or on land obtained (as redevelopment project land would be) by the exercise of the city's power of eminent domain. Some of the leaders of housing organizations thought the Carey resolution unwise and unnecessary. The ends it sought could be obtained under existing laws and it might discourage private investment in redevelopment. Nevertheless, his resolution received considerable support, for this was seemingly a case where failure to fight would mean to suffer an irreparable loss in the war of symbols even though to win the fight might have small "practical" value.*

The Housing Committee of the Council voted favorably on the Carey resolution, but after the *Sun-Times* questioned its wisdom and legality and Mayor Kennelly spoke out against it, the Council voted the resolution down 31 to 13. Carey and his supporters had hoped that its passage would help define the situation in such a way as to discourage those who favored segregation.

* We believe that those housing organization leaders who took this view were mistaken. Existing laws did not prevent redevelopers from discriminating after land came into their possession and private investment in redevelopment would probably not have been discouraged once the issue was settled. Carey's intention was to strike a blow at racial and religious discrimination, and the resolution he introduced did have practical importance even though it was defeated: apparently because of it, the New York Life Insurance Company voluntarily accepted a non-discrimination clause in its agreement covering the Lake Meadows project.

Its defeat probably did just the opposite; it probably encouraged people to believe that the question was still an open one and that resistance to the spread of Negroes was not hopeless.

Very likely this controversy strengthened the politicians' conviction—a conviction that had been spreading among them for several years—that some of the supporters of public housing and related measures were intent on altering the pattern of racial segregation.

As the passage of the national housing bill approached, the supporters of public housing began to muster their resources in preparation for the impending struggle over sites for the new public housing program.

The most vociferous of the public housing groups was the Public Housing Association, most of the members of which were leaders of organizations concerned with social problems. The Association had been founded several years before.* For a while

---

* The Chicago association had its counterpart in many other cities. In *Building A Citizens Housing Association* by Alexander L. Crosby, National Housing Conference, Washington, 1954, likely candidates for the nucleus of a local association are listed:

"The Reverend John Earnest, the young minister whose sermons are being talked about.

"Arthur Bookman, head of a private school that emphasizes citizenship in its curriculum.

"Sidney Blackstone, the lawyer who helped draft the new city charter.

"Wurster Wilson, an architect who discussed slums at a meeting of the Lions Club.

"Mrs. Henrietta Parent, the PTA president who browbeat the school board into replacing a firetrap 10 years sooner than planned.

"Ira S. Profitt, a progressive businessman who ran as a nonpartisan candidate for city council.

"Miss Lucretia Houghton, active in the League of Women Voters and surefooted in local politics.

"Miss Frances W. Jones, a social worker with firsthand knowledge of slum conditions.

"Robert Workman, a labor union official who lives in a sub-standard neighborhood.

"Dr. Philip Bagley, who has worked for improved health facilities in the public schools.

"James Peck, a newspaperman who writes about welfare issues.

"Mrs. Lucinda Banker, who knows every influential family and doesn't mind influencing them."

The pamphlet suggests that four other classes of candidates should be considered: 1. Plain citizens without any claims to titles or celebrity; 2. Residents of the slums ("Oddly, few housing associations ever enroll anybody who knows the slums from the inside."); 3. Representatives of minority groups; and 4. Real

it had had a full-time executive director, but gradually its resources had dwindled.

Shufro, the CHA public relations man, and others had persuaded some friends and acquaintances to take leading parts in the Association. These included Elmer Gertz, a lawyer who was president of the Association at the beginning of 1949, Saul D. Alinsky, executive head of the Back-of-the-Yards Council, who succeeded Gertz as president later that year* and Alexander A. Liveright, director of a University of Chicago adult education program for labor union members, who in 1950 was chairman of the Strategy Committee. This committee was a body to which various organizations supporting public housing—the Packinghouse Workers Union, the Congregational Union, B'nai B'rith, the Catholic Youth Organization, the Chicago Council Against Racial and Religious Discrimination, and others—were invited to send representatives, and which was established by the Public Housing Association to coordinate the action of these groups in the site selection fight.

The Association was financed mainly by a few believers in the cause of public housing, among them Gertz and the elder Marshall Field, the publisher of the *Sun-Times*. From time to time contributions came from a few employees of housing agencies and from architectural and engineering firms. The Association's budget was a very small one however—too small to support an office or a regularly employed staff worker. Alderman Duffy once called it, "a paper organization," but since it included representatives of well-established organizations, it was to some extent an organization of organizations.

For the leaders of the Association (as well as for other parties to the issue) the site selection issue had intrinsic, instrumental, and ideological significance. To house people adequately was an

---

estate men ("Find out where he stands before inviting him because uninviting later would be awkward.") pp. 6-7.

* The Back-of-the-Yards Council was a stockyards-area neighborhood improvement association which Alinsky, backed by the Packinghouse Workers Union (CIO) then in its initial organizing drive, and Bishop B. J. Sheil, head of the Catholic Youth Organization, had organized in 1939. In theory the Council was a social worker's or community organizer's version of "grassroots democracy" (the theory was set forth by Alinsky in *Reveille for Radicals,* University of Chicago Press, Chicago, 1945); in practice it was, like other neighborhood organizations, run mainly by a few professional and semi-professional leaders.

end in itself, and one which most of the leaders of the Association valued highly. But the particular issue also had significance for larger issues such as the long-run standing of public housing and the breadown of racial segregation. All of the leaders of the Association were aware of the instrumental significance of the site selection issue for these larger issues, and some of them were primarily interested in the larger issues and, accordingly, willing to use the particular issue to further the larger ones.

But the public housing and site selection issue had a further and even more general significance: it was a symbol which stood for a wide range of diffusely formulated ends, for a point of view, or an ideology. Most of the leaders of the Association seemed to attach some symbolic importance to the issue, seeing in public housing something more than a way of distributing a commodity —housing—which the market had somehow failed to distribute satisfactorily. In their eyes it was also a way of showing concretely and dramatically what government could do for the common man; people who saw the slums swept away and new neighborhoods created would be likely to realize that, if it were not for ignorance and apathy and the selfishness of special interests, the power of government could be used to realize much more fully the democratic ideal. "Public housing," Gertz wrote in a letter to the Authority in 1949, "is more than a means of providing shelter for those unable to pay a fair, or economic, rent. It is a visible proof that this is a country which believes in the dignity of all human beings, a living testimonial to the America for which Jefferson, Jackson, Lincoln and Roosevelt dreamed and fought." That the least powerful of persons, he went on to say, is entitled to live serenely and decently—that is the ideal of public housing.[22]

Although most of them probably felt that the issue had some of this symbolic significance, only a few of the principal leaders of the Association were primarily interested in ideological ends. Gertz himself, for example, was probably mainly interested in the intrinsic significance of the issue. Shufro, although he attached intrinsic importance to the issue, seems to have been principally concerned with the larger issue of the long-run future of public housing in Chicago and elsewhere.

As is usually the case in American political discussion, it was good strategy for the Association leaders to justify public housing on all three grounds—intrinsic, instrumental, and ideological—at once. Since they are still to some extent Puritans, Americans want to be assured that a position on an issue has wide and acceptable moral implications. But since they are pragmatists as well, they also want to be assured that it is a purely practical matter. Thus after the passage of the Housing Act of 1949, Gertz, writing in the Association's newsletter, stressed that the housing issue should now be considered a practical one (i.e. one having intrinsic rather than instrumental or ideological significance):

Sensible people know that the time is now past for ideological discussions about public housing. Provision for public housing is the public policy of the United States, the State of Illinois and the City of Chicago, as expressed in laws. Sensible people recognize that public housing meets not only the needs of human beings for shelter, but is good business as well. It is a means to restore this community to financial solvency. The other day Prentice Hall, Inc., a clearing house of information for business people of the nation, sent the following communication to a large number of people. We quote the statement because of the common sense in it.

> "Here's your cue for action on the NEW HOUSING ACT—
>
> "If You Can't Lick 'Em, JOIN 'EM!
>
> "This realistic approach is your key to profitable operation under the HOUSING ACT OF 1949, just passed by Congress. Smart real estate men already admit they're going to *get on the public housing bandwagon* NOW. . . ."[23]

Alderman Duffy did not take very seriously the claim that the significance of the housing issue for its supporters was mainly intrinsic rather than instrumental or ideological. "Some of the housing people are on the square," he told an interviewer, "but there are as many more who are interested in stirring up trouble. By putting a project in every section of Chicago they could infiltrate Negroes—stir up trouble and keep the pot boiling—never let it stop."[24] Presumably he meant that the public housing supporters wanted to do this because they were primarily interested in the larger issue of race relations reform or because they wanted to promote an ideology. If this was his opinion, Duffy was almost certainly mistaken with regard to many and probably most of the public housing supporters.

However, even if their interest in the issue had been wholly practical, the political success of the public housing supporters would have had ideological significance merely because it would be interpreted (rightly or wrongly) as evidence of the power of the liberal-left. In short, as long as public housing was supported actively from the liberal-left, it could not be altogether divested of ideological significance. As long as many people associated with the liberal-left supported it, many people associated with the conservative-reaction would attack it.

Those public housing supporters whose interest in the issue was largely or mainly ideological were particularly opposed to premature compromise. Compromise, while it might provide some kind of housing, would not strengthen the symbols of the democratic ideal around which support could be rallied. Indeed, if a choice had to be made, it would be better, in the opinion of the few who were most ideologically-minded, to have the issues put before the public in a clear-cut fashion at the risk of getting little or perhaps even no housing than to get a less-than-satisfactory program—albeit a program—without any public airing of the issue. But the main leaders of the Association were confident that this choice did not have to be made; in their opinion, the strategy which would bring the issue before the public most effectively was also the one that would result in the most satisfactory housing program. Thus the more practical-minded (i.e. those who were interested in the issue for its intrinsic significance) agreed with the more ideologically-minded that there should be no compromise which would prevent putting the issue before the public. "I would like to wave the banner of practicality," Shufro said at a large banquet in his honor when he resigned from the Authority. "To be practical you must follow principle and not compromise. On the day that CHA compromises, you'll be slapped on the back. And that night, the Housing Authority will be alone on the back porch."[25]

Alinsky was also opposed to compromise. "There are certain points on which a human being cannot compromise—moral issues without which we have nothing," he told the Association in his inaugural address as its president. "Housing is one of these."[26]

Perhaps Alinsky was here using the term "housing" to include "non-discrimination." At any rate, when the issues were purely practical ones, Alinsky, people who had followed his career said, had never shown himself unwilling to compromise when there was advantage in doing so.[27]

As the leaders of the Public Housing Association saw the situation, it would be good strategy for the public housing forces to fight publicly in order to clarify the issues and force the opposition to yield. "It is the duty and obligation of the commissioners," Gertz wrote them on April 26, 1949, "to publicly press for action to get housing even in the face of hostile attitudes. No battle was ever won without fighting and it is becoming increasingly apparent that additional public housing is not going to be built in this city unless the Housing Authority Commissioners lead in the initiation of steps to open a battle where necessary."

Another organization which was to play an important part in the struggle for public housing was B'nai B'rith, a national Jewish fraternal and service organization, the Chicago chapters of which had about 35,000 members. B'nai B'rith was the parent organization of the Anti-Defamation League (ADL), the purpose of which was to combat anti-semitism and racism in general. Within the framework of a national policy, ADL's local program was decided upon by a committee of 50 community leaders. Housing problems, insofar as they seemed to be connected with racial or religious discrimination, had long been a matter of active interest to the organization. Its leaders had vigorously supported the Carey resolution and they were in favor of a large—and of course unsegregated—public housing program.

The ADL official (he was one of 16 professional staff members in the Chicago office) who was assigned to look after housing matters was Samuel D. Freifeld. He had studied history and sociology, held a high position in OPA and then in the criminal investigation division of the Army in western Europe, and at his father's death had inherited a business in insurance, real estate, and the management of syndicated property. "I have had a very lively interest in liberal politics since campus days," he once remarked. "I can tell which splinter groups a person belongs to by his vocabulary and by asking polar questions."

Prompted by protests from a small number of public housing opponents among the membership of B'nai B'rith, the policy committee of ADL reviewed the grounds of its support of public housing and issued a set of instructions to its staff. Taking account of the argument that bad housing increases insecurity and that insecurity in turn increases anti-semitism, the policy committee decided that, while this justified B'nai B'rith's support of public housing, it did not justify support by ADL, the purposes of which were a good deal more specialized; as some of the committee remarked, on the basis of this argument ADL might work for an extension of the social security law. The second reason—and the one which the policy committee decided was sufficient justification for ADL's interest in the issue—was that people who oppose public housing tend to do so (as an ADL official later said) "not on grounds that it is something like socialism, but rather on a racial basis."[28] The policy committee cautioned the staff, however, to confine its efforts to those aspects of the issue which were most affected by racial discrimination. For Freifeld the public housing issue was not only a strategic approach to the larger issue of anti-semitism but a symbol as well. "Interracial housing," he wrote early in 1950, "is brotherhood spelled out in terms of bricks, mortar and people living together as neighbors in a community. . . . Not until all the forced slum dwellers have been transplanted to decent, ratless houses, surrounded by white cabinets and sanitation facilities, will our responsibility taper. Only upon the realization of a community that provides minimum decent conditions can we expect a world of disappearing disease, reducing tensions and incipient brotherhood. . . . How do we dare have the effrontery to treat one of the basic commodities of life so lightly, so indifferently, so callously, so immorally, so politically, so 'economically'?"[29]

Like all such voluntary organizations, B'nai B'rith was continually in need of program material. Its leaders were probably looking for popular issues.* It is no reflection on their sincerity

* An ADL official has written the following comment on this passage: "I do not want to give the impression that as a mass membership organization we do not have a problem in providing useful program for our members. This, however, was not the motivating factor in this instance, though it may have contributed to the same end. There are certain interests which our organization has

to suggest that they may have wanted to use the public housing issue to which, as we have said, they had long been firmly committed, to build a stronger and more active leadership in the local chapters of the organization—a leadership which, because of its renewed commitment to the ends symbolized by public housing, could later be utilized in connection with other, related issues or simply to maintain the organization. To be sure, some members of the organization would probably be alienated by a campaign in favor of public housing, but these would be relatively few and their loss would be more than offset by other gains. One of the leaders of B'nai B'rith said later that a small amount of financial support for the organization might have been lost, "but it was good ideological education for the thought leaders."[30]

Freifeld represented B'nai B'rith on the Strategy Committee which the Public Housing Association set up. But Freifeld's own style and that of his organization were somewhat different from the style of some other Public Housing Association leaders. He did not want to make himself or B'nai B'rith conspicuous by aggressive statements or demonstrations, and he was sometimes embarrassed by the (as he thought) too unrestrained and high-pitched note of the Association. "Many members of the Public Housing Association are congenital activists," he once observed, referring to their verbal behavior. "They say something violent and think this is the solution to all problems. They pass resolutions."[31]

The Chicago Metropolitan Housing and Planning Council, another pro-housing organization, had its own distinctive style, a style which it took mainly from its president and leading sponsor, Ferd Kramer.

Kramer, who had studied at West Point, was president of one of Chicago's largest realty firms and a resident of Highland Park, a fashionable North Shore suburb. He had been Deputy Defense Housing Coordinator during the war and was a past

in fair employment practices, etc., which impel us to get into public issues even if our membership is so swamped with projects that we can expect very little material assistance from it at a particular moment. You should know, too, that the B'nai B'rith also had departments concerned with hospitals, religious foundations on college campuses, vocational and youth services, etc. The complaint of the B'nai B'rith, more often than not, is that it is asked to do too much, not too little."

president of the Chicago Real Estate Board and one of its board of directors. He had been instrumental in establishing an institutional and community planning program at Michael Reese Hospital in Chicago's South Side.

The Metropolitan Housing and Planning Council was nominally governed by 40 directors, most of whom were prosperous lawyers, architects, bankers, and industrialists. Some members of the Council believed that Kramer and others, anxious to keep the Council acceptable to people of wealth, power, and social standing, went to some pains to see that there would not be an undue proportion of supporters of public housing on its board of directors; at any rate, the "balance" on the board was such that it was not likely to take an extreme stand on any issue. Support for the Council—it had an annual budget of $16,000—came from about 500 contributors, of whom about 100 (including numerous corporations) contributed half. The Council had a downtown office with three full-time employees (headed by Mrs. Dorothy Rubel) and it published a newsletter—a printed one, not a mimeographed one like the Public Housing Association's. The newsletter was sent to about 4,000 persons believed to be interested in housing and city planning.

Kramer and the Council regarded public housing not as a symbol of a better world, but simply as places for low-income families to live. They had even suggested at one time—much to the dismay of some of their supporters—that some temporary housing for veterans be built in the Negro slums.[32] "We are interested in action, not pious lip service," the director of the Council once remarked, comparing the Council with the Public Housing Association. "There is a less emotional type in this organization. Recently one of our board members resigned because she felt that our approach, particularly on race relations, was too intellectual. She wanted to be with people who were more emotional about it, so she went over to the Public Housing Association."[33]

The more genteel character of the Council and its more limited objectives reflected a different style of operation from that of the Association. The Council was not interested in forming "mass" opinion. Kramer testified at public hearings and the Council issued occasional statements to the press and published the newsletter, but the main effort of the Council was to exert influence through people who had power, particularly financial power. When the Strategy Committee invited it to send a representative, the Council declined. "We don't think that rallies and mass meetings and that kind of publicity get anywhere," an official of the Council later explained. "We send important people out to harass the Mayor and to talk to the leaders of both parties."[34]

The Council was not adverse to compromise. Kramer supported the relocation housing program with the remark that "progress comes slowly" and, presumably, he would favor another compromise if one were necessary to get housing. To some of the leading members of the Association, the readiness of the Council to compromise appeared unprincipled.

Kramer held that a citizen's organization should not be on very close terms with the public agencies with which it dealt; only in this way, he believed, could such an organization retain full freedom of action. Consequently, he did not invite Miss Wood or any of the CHA commissioners to meet with the Council's board and he rarely communicated with them.

Kramer was of the opinion that CHA should be headed by a $25,000 or $50,000 a year business executive. CHA was big business—bigger than any real estate enterprise in Chicago—and should accordingly, in his view, be managed as other big businesses were managed.[35]

There were other organizations, especially organizations dealing with religious or labor union affairs, which would support public housing. The three that have been described, however, played the most important roles in the battle for public housing.

Among the supporters of public housing it was the leaders of the Public Housing Association—especially Shufro, Liveright, Gertz, and Alinsky—who were closest to Miss Wood and the staff. In her opinion, they were a citizen group in whose judgment she could place great confidence.[36] "Her ear is bent one way," one of the public housing supporters to whom she paid little attention remarked in an interview after the site selection struggle was over.[37]

Miss Wood wanted to make practical rather than ideological

gains. She was convinced that the way to do so was to put the public housing issue squarely before the public. This had been her opinion even before the relocation housing struggle; after that fiasco she was all the more sure that there was nothing to lose and much to gain from fighting the issue out in public. In this she was in full accord with the opinion of the leaders of the Public Housing Association and that of her principal staff advisers.

The Public Housing Association leaders distrusted Taylor and McMillen. They had compromised too easily on the relocation housing program and there was every reason to believe that they would compromise too easily again. "The commissioners," Gertz wrote them early in 1949, "have failed to take aggressive leadership and have been content to accept the dictates of those who are not particularly concerned with housing the poorer people of this community."[38]

In the fight over relocation housing, the commissioners had revealed themselves (the Association leaders maintained) so anxious to demonstrate political sagacity that they had been easy marks for the tough political professionals in City Hall. As some of the leaders appraised the situation, it was essential to prevent the commissioners from concluding another deal in private. The issue would have to be fought in public, for if the commissioners were permitted to negotiate with the politicians in private they would surely capitulate. But if the site selection process were carried on in the open and if the issue, especially as it concerned the Negro, was fairly and clearly explained to the public, the politicians would not be able to force upon the commissioners the kind of a "deal" that they (the politicians) undoubtedly had in mind.* The leaders of the Association did not make the mistake

* The top staff of CHA generally held this position also. In this relationship to the commissioners, the top staff was not exercising that self-denial which, according to Weber, was crucial to the whole apparatus of bureaucracy. ("The honor of the civil servant is vested in his ability to execute conscientiously the order of the superior authorities, exactly as if the order agreed with his own convictions." Max Weber, Gerth and Mills trans., *Essays in Sociology,* Oxford, New York, 1946, p. 95.) In the opinion of the top staff, housing professionals had a right and a duty to fight for a certain kind of public housing even if in doing so they ran counter to the wishes of the commissioners. This unbureaucratic conduct is to be explained partly by the fact that the staff owed its ultimate allegiance to the standards of the public housing profession rather than to the board and by the fact that the board, which consisted of part-time amateurs, seemed more an appendage to the organization than a part of it.

In 1952 Miss Wood observed that housing authorities were being criticized for

of supposing that their cause was widely popular—that all they needed to do was to sound the alarm to bring the slum-dwellers and the Negroes to the defense of public housing. They did hold, however, that by mobilizing their organizational allies—the church, labor and other civic organizations—they might be able to prevent the politicians and the commissioners from settling the issue in a wholly unsatisfactory way.

Accordingly, the Association decided to fight on three fronts. 1. There would be a campaign of city-wide publicity in the newspapers and on the radio, and by rallies, mass meetings, and picketing. 2. In every neighborhood where sites were proposed the people would be organized to support public housing with messages to their aldermen, testimony at hearings, and letters to the press. 3. The Association would put pressure on the Democratic Party by arranging for civic organization leaders to meet the Mayor and other party officials in face-to-face conferences.

In this strategy Marshall Field and the *Sun-Times* were to play a key part. Representatives of the Association called on Field and got his promise to make public housing a major campaign in his newspaper if the issue arose. The collaboration between the paper and the Association was to be extremely close. David Anderson, the reporter assigned to cover housing, would often attend meetings of the Strategy Committee. When special needs arose, one of the leaders of the Association—this leader later claimed—would sometimes call his New York cousin, who was Field's lawyer and who was able to intercede with the *Sun-Times*.[39]

That their strategy might not secure a very satisfactory housing program the public housing leaders were well aware. It might, however, get a better one than the relocation program had been, and it was certainly not likely to get a worse one.

Taylor was told that the *Sun-Times* would support him if he fought the issue in public and criticize him if he did not. Although he believed that he could obtain a better housing program by negotiating with the politicians than by fighting them, Taylor, who was sensitive to the attacks that had already been made upon

---

performing a leadership or political function. "The public agency may no longer fight," she remarked in a public address. "It must take what is given; to fight is undemocratic, to plead its function is propagandistic, illegal, improper."

him and to the promise of more to come and whose position of leadership probably depended at least as much upon whites like Marshall Field as it did upon Negroes, reluctantly agreed to follow the Public Housing Association-*Sun-Times* strategy.

"I didn't feel I could alienate the *Sun-Times* and so forth," Taylor later said in explanation of his decision to make the site selection fight in public. "They were already suspicious of me. They said they could help me get a better deal than I got before, and I couldn't prove they were wrong."

While he was considering what his approach should be, Taylor consulted the Mayor.

"Are you really going to help us in this fight?", Taylor asked.

"Yes, I am," the Mayor replied, as Taylor later recalled. "You can count on me."

"Then we'll give you a list of the sites we want and you negotiate for them. When you come to an agreement with the aldermen, we'll propose publicly the sites you have agreed upon."

"No," the Mayor said, as Taylor recalled. "Do your own negotiating. But I'll stand behind you."

After his visit with the Mayor, Taylor told the Public Housing Association leaders, "All right, we are going to fight it out in public. Let's make our recommendation on an ideal situation—an ideal program—to start with."[40]

On the one hand, the *Sun-Times* encouraged Taylor to refuse to negotiate privately with the leading aldermen and, instead, to agitate the issue in public; on the other hand, it piously called for collaboration between the Authority and the City Council. "The first step toward a better relationship is mutual understanding and respect," it editorialized. "It is time for the Authority to take the Council into its confidence, and for the Council to quit sabotaging public housing by undermining the Authority. . . . The Authority should be prepared to work with the aldermen in choosing sites. The aldermen, for their part, have a duty to approach the site problem from the point of view of Chicago's general welfare. Too many aldermen, including some who profess to support public housing, are too adamant in the attitude that their main job is to prevent projects from being located in their wards."[41]

'Wottsamatter With THAT Building Site?'

CHAPTER SIX ☐ ☐ ☐ ☐ ☐ ☐

THE STRUGGLE BEGINS

THE PRELIMINARY PROPOSAL which CHA presented to the Mayor on July 8, 1949—a proposal which called for building 15,000 of the 40,000 units on vacant land—reflected the decision to present the kind of a program which most of the supporters of public housing believed represented the needs of the people of Chicago. Taylor held that it might be wiser to negotiate in private, but he was committed to fight in public, if necessary, and so it was important to choose the initial sites with care.

As we have indicated, if there had existed a detailed comprehensive plan of development for Chicago, this might have provided a defensible basis for the choice of sites. The aldermen might not have agreed about particular sites, but it would have been possible to demonstrate to them that the Authority's decisions were not capricious—that they rested on general principles which had been chosen with care. But unfortunately there was no such plan.

Although Miss Wood and her chief staff members were also aware of the importance of a specialized plan for housing in relation to other aspects of the city's development, they had not been in a position, prior to the passage of the 1949 Act, to make such a plan themselves. They previously had had no funds from the Federal government with which to hire a planning staff of the size and quality that would be required for such an undertaking. City Council and the State did make some planning funds available after World War II, but these were largely devoted to project planning.

The heads of the Authority had considered various courses of action that were open to them for improving the housing of low-income people. Building and managing new housing projects was not the only way to achieve CHA's purposes. Instead of building projects, the Authority might have repaired old structures and rented or sold them to needy families; or it might have built new housing in a highly decentralized fashion, developing small vacant sites with a few units on each. These were two possibilities; there were, of course, many others.

The Authority had in 1945 (and also before the War) investigated in detail one such possibility, that of rehabilitating a slum block rather than replacing it with new houses.* It had not systematically investigated many other possibilities in such detail, partly because it had no special funds or staff with which to do so and partly because it was unclear as to how far its legal authority permitted it to employ means other than building and operating projects.† The city might have provided funds for such investigations if it had been asked (the study of rehabilitation was made with a special grant from the city) and the state legislature might have enlarged the Authority's powers if it had been asked to do so. It was, however, taken for granted on all sides, by the heads of the Authority no less than by the officials of the city and state, that the Authority's principal reason for being was to build and operate projects of the kind that had been familiar in Chicago and elsewhere since the thirties. In its acceptance of the widely held ideal of public housing, the Chicago authority was no different from other authorities elsewhere. Even the Federal government's Public Housing Administration did not seriously study alternatives.

Although they did not engage in detailed systematic inquiry into the consequences that might be expected to follow from

---

* This study was summarized in *The Slum . . . Is Rehabilitation Possible*, Chicago Housing Authority, 1946. It showed that rehabilitation would be cheaper than new construction, but that under existing laws the annual Federal subsidy required would be greater than for new construction. Thus it concluded that "public housing can provide homes for low-income families in new buildings at lower rents than in rehabilitated structures."

† Miss Wood, herself, held that the terms of the Authority's charter permitted it to consider other courses of action than projects. "The Authority," she told a Housing Institute meeting, "is given very broad powers to plan, originate and administer public housing projects, even broader powers to undertake such other activities as may be necessary or desirable to remedy and provide housing for the lowest income group." Address of February 8, 1940.

various alternative approaches, the top staff of the Authority and especially Miss Wood did give such possibilities a great deal of attention. In fact, CHA had participated in certain alternative approaches, e.g., in transferring units to private ownership, in clearing an area for a redevelopment program by Michael Reese Hospital, and in fostering a non-profit middle-income housing program.

The commissioners, however, in contrast to the staff, had very limited knowledge about housing and had few principles on the basis of which to select among alternative policies—and what principles they did have were not necessarily ones held by the staff. Both the commissioners and the staff realized, for example, that there were certain important advantages to be had from using small sites. Small projects seemed to be favored by politicians and property-owners because they did not dominate the area as big projects did and because the project dwellers were more easily integrated into existing neighborhoods or at least more easily endured. (Local "in-groups" would, of course, tend to be opposed to any changes in the neighborhood: to large private projects as well as to large public ones.) Moreover, it was much easier to find small vacant sites in slum areas than large ones. The disadvantages of small projects were that they would almost certainly be segregated, that they often could not be provided with adequate community facilities, that they would soon be engulfed by the surrounding blight, and that the costs of building (and managing) them would probably be higher with the result that fewer units could be built. The problem was that if all these advantages and disadvantages were systematically examined by both the commissioners and the staff, the commissioners might make a different choice from that of the staff—the commissioners might choose small sites in order to avoid controversy, whereas, in the view of the staff it was essential to build medium or large projects in order to create new and better neighborhoods, and racially integrated neighborhoods if possible.

Miss Wood had probably thought as intelligently and as imaginatively about the uses and limitations of projects of various types as had anyone in the United States. Her reflection had brought her to the conclusion that under the conditions then existing the best course of action for agencies dealing with public and private redevelopment was entirely to rebuild blighted areas into protected residential neighborhoods.

In 1945 Miss Wood made a speech explaining why she favored this course of action.[1] She began by pointing out that principal ends (to house people in wholesome and attractive neighborhoods)—not incidental ones—should be decisive in the making of a plan. "You do not make plans that show the blighted areas rebuilt for the purpose of restoring purchasing power to the central business districts," she said. "You do not make plans for the purpose of restoring municipal income. You do not draw plans for the purpose of giving private enterprise new areas in which to operate its business. The plans cannot be directed or prejudiced by any single wish or objective, however respectable and right that wish may be. They must be related to the realities I have described.

"But how do you make these plans? The result to be obtained by the rebuilding, if its extraordinary costs are to be justified, is a series of residential neighborhoods so attractive (I mean in terms of grass, flowers, shrubs, land patterns, etc.) as to compare favorably with the suburbs. If the results are not that good, the expenditures are wasted.

"If this is the result to be obtained, one cannot ignore the sour and rubbled ground and smoky air, which, together make nearly impossible the kind of growth of trees and grass and flowering shrubs that transform a neighborhood. One cannot ignore the impact of the crisscrossing by trucks and buses and street cars and passenger traffic with all its accompanying fumes, noise, and danger. One cannot ignore the poverty of the poor people—their inability to pay $65 or $55 rents. You cannot ignore their undisciplined garbage habits.

"Therefore, your planning must cover all these items. It must be bold and comprehensive—or it is useless and wasted. If it is not bold, the result will be a series of small projects, islands in a wilderness of slums beaten down by smoke, noise, and fumes.

"What is this bold planning? It consists of the following:

"1. An unalterable determination to relocate all transit and traffic in such a way that the blighted areas are subdivided into superblocks averaging, let us say, about 80 acres, through which no street car or other public transit passes, through which no traffic goes; in fact, so designed that entrance to interior streets discourages traffic. You have only to examine the present and proposed street and transit plan for the city of Chicago to recognize what a bold requirement that is. Planners say: 'We can't take the street cars off Indiana or State Streets or Taylor Street.' They say: 'If we put in new quiet street cars or buses, it will be all right.' The answer is: 'It won't.' On the basis of experience with large urban redevelopment, we know that if blighted areas are not rebuilt in these protected superblocks, all expenditures will be wasted; the project will decay. Little plans will require a redoing of the total job within three generations.

"The public taste is clear and is evident by the trend that every competent subdivider and realtor knows; the public desire is for the amenities of grass, trees, protection from noise and danger of traffic. The public has had little chance to express that desire but the expenditure of vast public subsidies must be directed by it.

"2. An unalterable determination to clean up the nuisance impact of industrial slums—their smoke, physical decay.

"3. A head-on facing of the problem of poor people: and that means public housing. You cannot let them shift for themselves or stick your head in the sand and say: 'Well, they ought not to be poor. If they were like our Pilgrim Fathers, they wouldn't be poor. If they were true Americans, they wouldn't be poor.' The fact is there are poor people. Poor people can be housed in physically bad houses which have a malevolent effect on the community or in good houses which have a benevolent effect.

"4. A head-on facing of the problem of the cultural (to use a fancy term) level of the slum dweller. This means that there shall be instituted an educational program for slum dwellers through every available medium in relation to their living habits. A recognition of the urgency of this educational program has been forced upon public housers, who have, in many cases, had to fight hard to keep their projects from becoming slums because of the living habits of so many ex-slum dwellers.

"I can best illustrate this in terms of garbage. Garbage disposal in slum areas is a simple and primitive thing. A child is sent with an overflowing container to the alley and he may dump it on a pile or throw it in the general direction of an overflowing container. If orange peel, ashes and tin cans are dropped along the way, nobody cares. When this same family moves into a public housing project, it brings along the same indifference about dropped orange peel and tin cans, and the ultimate disposition of the garbage in incinerator or can. If the wet bottom of the paper bag falls out and spills coffee grounds in the hallway, the family cares little until a few visits from the management have impressed upon it a new standard. If this same family were to move to another house, not under management, there would be no one to comment upon or much less discipline the sloppy habit. It is in just such homely ways that neighborhoods deteriorate.

"The educational program that public housing takes on includes many other things. The encouragement of the feeling for making the neighborhood one with flowers, trees, etc.; the encouragement of good habits of paying rent; the development of a sense of responsibility in regard to the behavior of all children in the neighborhood, not just one's own.

"Of course, it is fantastic to think that public housing must care for the total educational load. It can only care for its own share, but it must continue to point out the urgency of this program and stimulate public schools and other institutions to carry it on.

"5. A head-on facing of the fact that the process of tearing down the slums is the process of pulling the roofs from over the heads of thousands of families. There must be some place for these families to go. Many public works, not housing alone, tear down slum dwellings. It is estimated, for instance, that the minimum proposed public works for Chicago will tear down some ten thousand dwelling units. The cost of re-housing these families is an integral part of the cost of public works. It must be planned for. In this city, therefore, and I am sure in most others, there must be short-term and long-term provisions in the total housing program. Suggestions have been made for using various types of temporary housing for relocation centers.

"A major necessity, in my opinion, is the construction of

planned, permanent communities on vacant land that can be used for this purpose. This means that there must be encouraged as a part of the slum clearance program, a program of building both public and private low and moderate rental housing on vacant land—in the outskirts of a town if this is necessary."

This was Miss Wood's idea of what a public housing and redevelopment program should be. To a large extent it was also the idea of her top staff. But whether and to what extent the commissioners shared her views was not clear, for they had not discussed fundamental matters in a systematic and continuing way. Whether the Mayor and the "Big Boys" of the City Council would agree with any of her premises was doubtful, but even in their case no one was clear or certain as to what agreement or disagreement existed; the staff and commissioners had not sat down with the leaders of the Council for serious and sustained discussions. Neither did the heads of other city agencies discuss policy fully with the Council heads; such a thing would hardly have been possible, for there were too many agencies and too many policy problems.

In view of the fact that the 21,000 units reserved for Chicago by the Federal government represented a vast and sudden expansion of public housing, there was good reason for the CHA staff to consider afresh and more systematically than before the courses of action that were open to them. There was good reason, too, for them to reach as much understanding and agreement on essentials with the commissioners and the "Big Boys" as was possible, for no housing program could possibly be carried into effect without their approval.

It was known that when the Council reconvened after its summer adjournment, it would be necessary to submit sites for the first year's program. Even if a prompt beginning were made, this would be difficult, for Vaughan was new to the job and new to Chicago, and Meyerson would not assume his duties as head of the Planning Division until the end of September. Besides, the full board of commissioners would not meet during the summer.

Vaughan joined the staff in April 1949. It seemed very likely that the Housing Act would soon be passed; however, it had seemed likely in previous years as well, and so its passage could not be taken for granted. Vaughan found that there was much that needed to be done in anticipation of the passage of the Act. A great deal of information on particular sites, especially on slum sites, was in the Authority's files; much of it, however, was out of date—some sites described in the files as vacant, for example, had since been built upon. The most serious handicap, however—and one which perturbed Vaughan, was that the Plan Commission had made no firm decision as to what vacant land —and in some cases, even what slum districts—would be available for residential building. There was no way of knowing for sure which sites the Plan Commission would approve.

The planning staff then consisted principally of three technical persons. They had been working on the details of the relocation program and on other project work. They had been too busy to make any systematic preparations for the new program.

Vaughan believed that the most important single thing he could do prior to the passage of the Act was to get a housing market analysis made. The analysis would be needed to justify a large program to the City Council if the act passed (Vaughan once considered proposing that 50,000 to 60,000 units be built over a 10-year period) and to support an application to the Public Housing Administration.[2] Accordingly he spent much of his time working with other public agencies and private organizations in the making of the market analysis.

After the passage of the Act assured that funds for the program would be available, Vaughan engaged the Plan Commission to make a detailed inventory of all vacant land sites of 10 acres or more. It would be several months before the results of this would be available. Also, as funds became available, he began the difficult and time-consuming task of recruiting staff for the expanding Development Division. As his staff increased, he set it to collecting systematic data on many sites: as rapidly as possible the Planning Division would accumulate a file of up-to-date information on each vacant land site studied by the Plan Commission.

After the passage of the Act, Vaughan suggested to Miss Wood that it might be well for him to discuss the Authority's intentions with some of the leading aldermen before detailed planning got underway. Miss Wood discouraged him from this, however, partly on grounds that he was too new on the job to talk to the aldermen, but mainly on grounds that the aldermen would harm the housing program if they were brought into the planning of it too early.[3]

On the second day of September, Miss Wood placed the site selection problem before the commissioners. By the 12th, she wrote them, the staff would have data prepared on four sites. The Council was to meet on the 19th. That would give the commissioners very little time to study the site proposals, she observed, "yet, it would be advantageous to keep up our record of prompt action and the very favorable press that has resulted therefrom." The commissioners, she suggested, might spend as much time as they liked with staff before the 12th and, in the following week, have additional meetings with other public officials.[4]

At the same time she sent them a memorandum on criteria for site selection.

"It would be fortunate," she wrote, "if site selection could be put on a purely scientific basis. However, the fact is, that too little is known of the reasons why people live where they live, or choose one neighborhood rather than another. It is generally presumed that people live where they live because they are in reasonable proximity to their job, or to jobs; or to other ties of church, family or friends. But it is also generally known however much we may presume that families would *like* to live in proximity to their jobs, they do not either because they can't or because they give up this desire for a greater. We simply do not know the extent to which people actually do live where they live because of proximity to church, family or friends. The logical conclusion is that it is most humane to develop a housing program which allows wide choice particularly when it is a program designed to serve people who are being forced to move out of their present quarters.

"The first rule of site selection used to be 'housing projects should be located in convenient relationship to schools, transportation, utilities, churches, shopping,' but when one is building or rebuilding a city with a hope that one is building communities of lasting good quality, the first rule is different. Housing should not be built to fit inflexibly into the existing pattern of transportation, utilities, or existing school and park plants. Frequently such patterns must be redesigned, relocated, and created anew in order to build communities that will not deteriorate. New school buildings in outlying areas, new or rebuilt schools in slum areas, new street patterns, and transportation routes may be the first things needed to make a new community good for a long time. Determination as to what is kept, or what is cleared must also be made with an eye on the taxpayers' pocketbook. One cannot underestimate the impact of 40,000 new houses (not to mention the Land Clearance Commission's program) on the planning, physical and financial, of the Board of Education and Park District, street and utility departments, CTA, and utility companies.

"On the basis therefore of this general point of view, the following would seem to be a list of workable principles:

"1. The total program of the Authority should include both in-lying and out-lying projects in order that there may be a wide choice by applicants.

"2. In the total program there probably should be more in-lying than out-lying sites (actually this means more slum clearance sites than vacant land sites).

"The reasons are as follows:

(a) the largest pool of low wage paying jobs is in the center of the city;

(b) the institutions and other ties of slum dwellers tend to make them wish to remain where they are, or nearby, i.e., close to the center of the city. Census data on nationality movements over the years seems to substantiate this feeling; and

(c) private enterprise has not yet indicated sufficient interest to insure rebuilding of the slum areas.

"3. In spite of the number of reasons in support of a slum clearance program, the fact is, however, that it cannot even begin until there is building on vacant land.

"4. In general, it is desirable that public housing projects shall not result in large scale economic segregation. Therefore, in large developments of new construction, public housing projects should, so far as possible, be developed co-incidentally with other private or semi-public developments, such as those undertaken by the Land Clearance Commission and the Chicago Dwellings Association.

"5. The principle of providing choice to the applicants requires a distribution of projects throughout the city to the extent allowed by sound principles of land economics and within the limitations of availability of land. The chief limitation on distribution is the fact that it is poor business to build public housing projects on expensive land, either vacant or slum. On the other hand, it is certainly not desirable to have all the public housing projects in one section of the city.

"6. Just as it is desirable to develop public housing projects where possible in connection with other housing enterprises, so it is desirable to give preference to location of such developments where it is possible for the Board of Education and the Park District to develop their facilities co-incidentally with the housing construction. In any case no housing project should be initiated until adequate school facilities are firmly planned for by the Board of Education. The production of 40,000 units in a six-year period will have a terrific impact upon the capital budget of both of these agencies, particularly the Board of Education. It is, therefore, necessary that there be close contact with these agencies in coming to conclusions about site selection.

"7. It should be noted that public housing projects properly situated, could well serve as buffers between areas designed for various uses, i.e., industrial and residential. This indirect but vitally important contribution to the overall city rebuilding program should not be overlooked."[5]

By the middle of September the commissioners chose to forego the advantages of a reputation for great promptness in order to be able to present to the Council in a single "package" all or most of the sites that would be needed for the 12,000 units which were to comprise the first year's program. The commissioners decided that the gain from a "package" proposal would offset the disadvantages of delay. They maintained, however, that because the public at large—and especially the politicians—felt there was a housing crisis, the agency should work fast. Acting in haste, its plans could not be detailed.

Meanwhile, Meyerson started on the job a few days ahead of

schedule, before any sites had yet been definitely selected. The commissioners and the staff at this point decided in a general way what kind of program they wanted. They were sure they wanted some sites on vacant land; these were essential to provide for the relocation of people who would be displaced by slum clearance. There had been some suggestions that the entire first year program be on vacant land. This was assumed to be a political impossibility, and, anyway, it was the intent of the six-year program to emphasize slum clearance: if projects were to be developed on slum sites during the coming two or three years, it was necessary to begin acquiring sites fairly soon. To acquire title to the land, relocate the families, and demolish the structures would take at least two or three years.

Having decided that the first year's program should be partly on slum and partly on vacant land, it was next decided that the proportion of slum-site units to vacant-site units should be about half and half. Vacant land projects, the commissioners and the staff knew, would be opposed by those residents of white areas who disliked housing projects, Negroes, and people of the lower class. Slum projects, on the other hand, would be relatively popular both because slums were offensive to people who had to pass by them as well as to some of the people who lived in them and because slum projects kept the slum dwellers where, in the opinion of many property owners, they belonged. A program which was half slum and half vacant land could be called "balanced."

After discussion of the memorandum on criteria for site selection, the staff and the commissioners revised it into a statement of general principles to guide further planning:

"1. Sites should be located throughout the city; this is desirable to prevent concentration of building types and concentration of economic groups as well as to provide tenants with some choice of neighborhoods. However, too close a proximity of widely divergent economic groups should also be prevented.

"2. Sites should be selected during the first few years predominantly on vacant land; this is essential to carry out the main purpose of the program; clearance and rebuilding of occupied slum areas (should occur) after homes have been built into which to move families occupying slum sites.

"3. Projects should be designed as integral parts of well-planned and complete neighborhoods; the Chicago Housing Authority proposes to accomplish this by joint development and close cooperation with the Chicago Plan Commission, Park District, Board of Education, Sewer and Water Department, and, to the greatest extent feasible, with housing programs of the Chicago Land Clearance Commission, Chicago Dwellings Association, and independent private builders.

"4. Size of projects should be determined by the following factors: (a) economy of development; (b) economy of operations; (c) such planning factors as the availability of land, condition of the surrounding neighborhood. Our experience shows that most economically developed and operated projects are generally those containing from 750 to 1800 dwelling units.

"5. Sites should be selected and projects designed only in terms of such important principles of design as will permit the project to be an asset and not a stumbling block to the future development of Chicago.

"6. Building types should provide for variety, within limits. There should be variety for the different needs of tenants between elevator apartments, three-story walk-up apartments, row houses, and, possibly free-standing houses. Generally, the denser inlying neighborhoods should contain more high-rise buildings than the outlying neighborhoods, but all projects should be designed with variety of outline and form so as to contribute to the beauty of neighborhood and city."[6]

It was surprising, one might think, that after so many years of experience in major cities throughout the United States there did not exist a body of tested principles for the selection of public housing sites under various circumstances and on various assumptions. Certainly, the general criteria set forth by the staff and the commissioners did not in any precise sense represent an application of what had been learned in Chicago, to say nothing of New York, Philadelphia, Detroit, Los Angeles, and the many other cities with similar problems. Perhaps nothing of significance had been learned in these places; no one, however, had ever tried systematically to find out.

At any rate, the criteria produced in Chicago (in most cities no explicit criteria at all were formulated) were not concrete and rested on certain assumptions which were perhaps not defensible. Why, for example, should so much importance be attached to "economy" as a criterion governing the size of projects? (The Federal agency, probably on the defensive against the attacks of the real estate groups, required that projects be built at the lowest possible costs, and this was a practical reason for the criterion; however, there is no doubt that most of the commissioners approved of it in principle also.) If perchance, most people, not only project residents but neighboring property-owners and residents as well, preferred small projects, would there indeed be any "economy" in building large ones, even if the large ones cost less? Did not "economy" have to be measured as a ratio between costs and satisfactions rather than in terms of costs alone? Similarly, perhaps CHA (admittedly under the mandate of the Washington agency) was wrong in concluding that it was "poor business to build public housing projects on expensive land"; it might be that, measured in relation to the satisfaction (or absence of dissatisfaction) accruing to the community from the use of one site rather than another, expensive land (i.e., high-priced land) would, in some instances, be much "cheaper" than other land. Costs were meaningless and therefore deceptive except in relation to benefits, but what benefits ought to be taken into account and how could they be measured? Some classes of ends may be regarded as immoral or otherwise unworthy of satisfaction, thus the end of not having Negroes in one's neighborhood should not, if satisfied, be counted as a benefit. But if, for reasons which were not immoral (and it was part of the problem to decide which were and which were not immoral), a neighborhood would be better satisfied to have a certain project located on a relatively high-priced site (one which would necessitate the building of a school, perhaps), how many extra dollars ought to be spent to satisfy the people of the neighborhood? The usual practice, which the staff and the commissioners, in accord with Public Housing Administration policy on economy, were accustomed to regard as "good business," did not ordinarily take account of either social benefits or social costs (i.e., benefits or costs the incidence of which was indiscriminate, so that those who benefited or lost could not be charged or compensated accordingly). But it might be that the usual business practice was not appropriate for a public agency, which presumably was under an obligation to attach some weight to everyone's wishes, or even that the usual business practice was wrong and ought to be changed so that it would take account of social costs and benefits.

The commissioners were now ready to consider particular sites. There were some seemingly obvious possibilities—sites, both vacant and slum, which had been inherited from previous operations of the Authority. The Development Department had assembled some data on three such sites.

One of these was a strip of vacant land which lay between the existing Trumbull Park housing project and a railroad. This seemed to be a site which private enterprise would not want and it was near a school and a park. But a circumstance which the staff pointed to as a "sound and practical reason" for expanding the Trumbull Park project was that the Public Works Administration, which built the project, had installed a high pressure heating plant which required as much labor for its operation as would be required if the project were very much larger. Expanding this project would make possible pro-rating this operating cost against more units, thus reducing the per-unit operating costs greatly. Another advantage from the point of view of the staff and some of the commissioners was that the site was in a white area. It was essential that the housing program accommodate a certain number of whites (otherwise, for one thing, it would not be approved by the Federal government); if all projects were built in Negro slums, it would be impossible to get any white tenants, for not only were there more low-income slum dwellers among Negroes than among whites, but, according to regulations, families displaced by projects had the first claim upon new ones. It was good to build projects that would be bi-racial, the staff asserted, but it was imperative to build projects in which a reasonable number of whites could and would live.

Another vacant land site which was "on hand" as a result of past operations was at 44th Street and Cicero Avenue. The reasons given in favor of this site were that the Land Clearance Commission and the Chicago Dwellings Association had made tentative commitments to develop it jointly with the Authority, that the Park District owned an undeveloped park site there, and that the Board of Education had preliminary plans for a new school. Other arguments for the site could also be made.

The Authority was then constructing a 350-unit relocation project adjacent to this area; this project was believed to be too small for economical maintenance and for the support of adequate community facilities; expanding it would remedy this situation. Much of the proposed site was a "dead subdivision" the taxes on which were delinquent and some of the titles of which were "lost." Because of the difficulty of assembling land under these conditions, the site was unattractive to private enterprise and was likely to remain so indefinitely. Here, too, some housing could be provided for whites—a strong argument for the site in CHA's view.

A third site was at 43rd and Halsted Streets. This was partly a slum site, but it included some vacant land. The advantage of this site in the eyes of the staff and of the commissioners was that the City Council had approved it on a previous occasion. Presumably the Council would let its endorsement stand.

These three sites were accepted by the commissioners, who, meanwhile, were screening other possibilities. Most of these possibilities were put forward by the planning staff but some were suggested by Miss Wood and other officials of the Authority. In a few instances a site was suggested by a commissioner who had heard about it in a casual fashion. Ordinarily, some of the commissioners, with Miss Wood, Vaughan, and Meyerson, visited the suggested sites in a hired car; later, at the CHA offices, they discussed what they had seen and examined the data supplied by the Planning Division. Particular sites were sometimes eliminated because one of the commissioners objected to them. Later, if another commissioner became enthusiastic about a site, it was returned to the agenda for further consideration.

By the beginning of October the commissioners, in addition, had decided on three slum sites which the Authority already owned either in whole or part (including the partly vacant 43rd and Halsted site mentioned), and on a fourth slum site (an extension of the Cabrini Homes project), which it did not own but had long had under consideration. These four sites would accommodate about 5,000 units. That meant (since it was decided that the first year's program should be a "balanced" one with about half the units on vacant and half on slum sites) that, adding the proposed 3,000 units on the two vacant sites which were also on hand, enough more vacant land would be needed to accommodate about 2,000 units. Most of the ensuing discussion about sites, discussion which went on continuously during the first two weeks of October, centered on the selection of this additional vacant land.

The commissioners decided that the additional land should be in a single ward if possible; they believed it would be foolish to antagonize more aldermen than necessary, and putting a project on an outlying vacant site would, it was assumed, surely antagonize any alderman whose ward was chosen. Desirably the land should be in the ward of an alderman who was firmly committed to vote for public housing or firmly committed to vote against it—if an alderman was in the doubtful category, it would be foolish to goad him into active opposition by locating a project in his ward. Only three aldermen—Carey, Becker, and Merriam—were known to be so friendly to public housing that they would support it under virtually any circumstances, and in none of their wards was there a suitable site; in Carey's and Merriam's wards there were no large tracts, and the commissioners believed residential property values in Becker's ward were so high that they would be seriously impaired by public housing—the area, in their opinion, was too good for public housing.

A good possibility seemed to lie in the ward of the Council's "powerhouse," Alderman John J. Duffy. No one supposed that Duffy was a friend of public housing. Nevertheless, it seemed reasonable to suppose that, since he was a principal leader of the Democratic Party, the Mayor's floor leader in the Council, and a candidate for the office of president of the County Board (a circumstance which it was assumed would make him unwilling to antagonize pro-housing voters and, especially the *Sun-Times*), he would have to support the program even though he might not like it.

Meyerson, the head of the Planning Division, had recommended a site at 115th Street and Ashland Avenue in Duffy's ward. At first examination the site seemed to have very few qualifications other than this political one. It lay in a triangle between two major railway lines on the very extremity of the city. Next to it was a big drop forge plant which made so much noise and vibration that pebbles two blocks away bounced in sympathy with the hammer. But the site had some seeming advantages. It was very large. There were already many Negroes living in the area, a circumstance that made this almost unique among vacant sites and seemed to obviate the strongest objection that was likely to be made to a vacant site. The Plan Commission, had classified the area for residential use; industry, therefore, could not very well claim that it had been deprived of a place to build. Another positive advantage in the opinion of the CHA staff was a tentative promise which Meyerson had obtained from a Negro builder to develop part of the site for private housing if the rest of it were developed for public. By this collaboration, community facilities could be planned for an integrated public-private, bi-racial project—an arrangement which seemed very desirable to Meyerson, the other staff, and the commissioners.

The seven sites thus chosen provided for a total of about 10,000 units, 2,000 less than the number endorsed by Council and granted by the Federal government for the first year. The total was in part fortuitous: the slum sites which the Authority had on hand happened to provide for about 5,000 units and enough vacant land had been selected roughly to balance this number. The Authority could have found other slum sites and more vacant land to balance them, but to avoid further delay in submitting a program of sites it did not do so.

The seven sites would be stoutly defended in the coming weeks by people who would argue that the Authority made its decisions on "technical" grounds while the aldermen made theirs on "political" ones. In fact, of course, some of the considerations that were decisive for the Authority were also—and necessarily—political. But the political factors the Authority took into account sometimes proved to be politically unrealistic. Thus, for example, in the case of the Trumbull Park site, the staff soon found that the aldermen cared little about economy; in the case of the 43rd and Halsted Street site, the existence of a previous agreement did not at all exempt it from opposition in the Council; and in the case of the large vacant site at 115th and Halsted, industry did claim it, there was opposition to the movement of Negroes there, and Duffy did not hesitate to oppose it.

Nevertheless, once the sites had been made public, Meyerson and the others could not admit that they were selected in part on the basis of political judgments. Indeed, as time passed the criteria used in site selection receded in the consciousness of some of the CHA planners; they seemed to believe that the package really was what the *Sun-Times* described, "an orderly, long-studied plan,"[7] and they found themselves angered at the aldermen's presumption in substituting political judgments for technical ones. Of course, CHA required that each site meet technical as well as political criteria; for the aldermen only political considerations counted.

At the end of October, Taylor, with the Authority's proposals, called on the Mayor. He asked him to present the sites to the Council with a strong endorsement.

"Go talk it over with Duffy," the Mayor told him as Taylor later recalled. "Work it out with Duffy—it's the aldermen's affair."

"No," said Taylor, "the commissioners think the matter ought to be discussed and decided upon in public. We have decided to present the program to the Council publicly."

"I differ," the Mayor said, "but if that's the way you want it, go ahead."

"We want you to look over our selections and give us your personal opinion," Taylor remembered saying to the Mayor: "Then we would like to have you present the sites to the Council with your endorsement."

"Give me a week to think it over," the Mayor replied, putting the documents Taylor had brought in a drawer of his desk.

Three weeks passed following this interview before the Mayor found time to see Taylor again. Then he opened the drawer of his desk and pointed. Taylor saw the CHA documents in the very spot where the Mayor had put them before.

Thinking the matter over, the Mayor explained, it occurred to him that the aldermen would be resentful if he took a stand on the sites before they learned of them. He had, accordingly, taken pains to learn nothing about them because he did not want to get in a position where he might have to commit himself. He had even avoided reading any of the newspaper stories about the sites for this reason.

"Those newspaper fellows will pry and pry," he told Taylor. "They will ask me point blank if I know anything about the sites. I want to be able to answer 'No.' "[8]

It was clear enough now that the Mayor could not be persuaded to present the sites to the Council as a program which he endorsed. If there was going to be a fight, it would be between the Authority and the Council. The Mayor indicated that he was not going to be a party to it if he could help it.

It was now too late for Taylor to turn to Duffy or to Duffy's lieutenant, Alderman Lancaster, the chairman of the housing committee. For, contrary to Taylor's wish, the site program had "leaked" to the press.

Taylor had failed to give the staff a full account of his first meeting with the Mayor. He told them that the Mayor advised against any publicity on the sites before they were put before the Council and he said that he fully agreed with this judgment. But whether the Mayor would support the sites or not—or even whether he had presented the sites to the Mayor—the staff could not learn.

The staff members were afraid that Taylor might be preparing to agree with City Hall. Publicity, the staff decided, was needed for the very reasons that the Mayor and Taylor were opposed to it—to forestall such a capitulation. Accordingly, some stories reached the press. Releases of the Public Housing Association were one avenue of publicity; David Anderson, the *Sun-Times* housing reporter, who was on familiar terms with Public Housing Association leaders, was another.

This publicity made it impossible for Taylor to agree privately to any significant changes in the program. There was, therefore, no reason now for him to see Duffy and Lancaster, if (and it is not clear whether or not this was the case) he had intended to do so.

The Authority's conduct exasperated Duffy and Lancaster. Duffy felt that, especially as they were proposing a large project for his ward, the commissioners were high-handed in not coming to consult him before they made their final decision. Lancaster probably believed that the housing committee should also have been consulted. That, one of the committee members said later, would have been the polite thing to do.

"We would have been glad to talk it over with the Authority in advance," Duffy said afterward, "but we never got the chance. They assumed the attitude that they could do what they wanted. They could hand us a package, or could bring pressure to force their program on us. This attitude was the result of the way things were done in the Kelly Administration. Under Kelly, whenever the Authority submitted a proposal, that was it. That's what he thought, anyway. He found out in the last four years of his career that there were some fellows in the Council who would get up and tell him that this was a Council-governed city, not a Hitlerite or Mussolini one. Under Kennelly, everyone is given an opportunity to determine for himself where he stands."[9]

Taylor now formally submitted the "package" (as the seven sites came to be called) to the Council. He did this by addressing a letter to its presiding officer, the Mayor. "It is the hope of the commissioners as they know it is yours," he wrote on November 23, 1949, "that the Chicago Housing Authority will be enabled to proceed quickly to begin building the housing that so many of its citizens need so urgently."

The Mayor forwarded the proposal to the Council. "In view of the serious lack of housing," his letter of transmittal said, "I urge you to give prompt consideration to this important matter."

A few days later the housing committee of the Council held a hearing. Taylor, Miss Wood, Fruchtman, Vaughan and Meyerson appeared for the Authority. Taylor began by reading a formal statement which had been drafted for him by members of the staff. The statement was addressed to the newspapers as well as to the aldermen, and it was aggressive in tone.

"The people of Chicago are watching today to see whether this program of low-rent housing is really going to get started," Taylor began. Then he went on to describe in general terms the kind of a housing program the Authority favored: it should be predominantly on vacant sites (he did not explain why); it should make for "well integrated and complete neighborhoods" (he did not say what this meant); and it should conform to sound and established housing policies regarding recreation and other facilities. He added that the projects should be of a size which could be economically developed and operated (he gave no estimate of the added costs that might be incurred by building small, decentralized projects). In conclusion, Taylor urged haste: the Federal government's promise of funds would expire in August and there was danger that by delay the city would lose a large sum of Federal aid. (This was a point which had been stressed to Taylor by the staffs of the Authority and of the Public Housing Administration in Washington.) This argument was perhaps specious; while it might alarm newspaper readers, the Mayor and the aldermen, who suspected that such a deadline could be extended, were probably impressed not with the deadline but with the political maneuvering of the Authority in stressing such an argument.

The aldermen at once made it evident that they did not like or trust the Authority. For example, when Taylor mistakenly referred to a building shown in a sketch as high-rise, Lancaster, the chairman, took him to task at once, implying that the fuzziness of the sketches and Taylor's misstatement were evidence of a disposition on the part of the Authority to deceive the aldermen.

Alderman Pacini, from whom CHA had expected moderate criticism but not direct opposition, was one of three aldermen who spoke strongly against particular sites at this time. Another was the South Side Republican, Reginald DuBois, long a bitter critic of the Authority, who spoke in opposition to the site in Duffy's ward; Duffy himself said nothing for the record, but it was understood, the *Sun-Times* said, that he was strongly opposed to the site and that DuBois was performing a friendly service by "fronting" for him.[10] The third opposing alderman was something of a surprise to the CHA representatives. He was the Democratic Negro alderman, Harvey, who had told Vaughan and Meyerson that he would support the program with certain modifications, but in an angry outburst now said that the people of his ward had no confidence in CHA and that he would not rubber-stamp CHA's plans.

Lancaster adjourned the hearing after two hours. The committee, he said, wanted more information from the Authority: it wanted to see all of the data which the Plan Commission had prepared for the Authority on potential vacant sites and it wanted to know how many and what kinds of buildings the Authority proposed to build on each of the sites.

Five weeks later the housing committee held a second hearing and Taylor appeared again with another statement which also seemed to annoy the aldermen. "Whether the homeless and ill-housed families in Chicago will get a low-rent housing program or not rests now with the City Council," he said. "Continued delay in approving these and additional sites may jeopardize seriously the securing of Federal money. In fact the Federal Public Housing Administration has already expressed concern about the rate of progress on project development."[11]

Lancaster and his committee seemed not to care about the Public Housing Administration and its concern. The committee would require still more information, the chairman said. Moreover, there had been requests for public hearings on the sites; hearings would be held some time after the chairman's return from a winter vacation in Florida.

The public housing supporters believed that the aldermen were delaying in order to test public opinion. They were trying to find out how poor a public housing program they could get away with. The time had come, therefore, the public housing supporters decided, to show the politicians the full strength and determination of pro-housing sentiment among the people.

The Public Housing Association had already intimated what the politicians could expect if they failed to do what the people required of them. "If our politicians do not produce soon," Alinsky had warned at his inauguration as the Association's president, "this organization will go out into the wards. We will see if the political machine preventing housing can stand up against an unhoused public."[12]

In January the Strategy Committee sent 25 representatives of its associated pro-housing organizations to see the Mayor. A Unitarian minister led the delegation. The Mayor told his callers that in a democracy a mayor doesn't put pressure on the aldermen—he lets the people's representatives decide for themselves.

After this meeting, the public housing strategists had no remaining doubt about the Mayor. He was, as Liveright later phrased it, "only cutting ribbons" (i.e., performing ceremonial functions). There was nothing to be gained by talking sensibly to him. He would have to be pressured by newspaper publicity and in other ways.[13]

The Strategy Committee went next to Jacob Arvey who had until recently been chairman of the Cook County Democratic Committee and who was generally believed to be still the *de facto* boss of the machine. Arvey, the public housing supporters thought, was a "smart politician" who would surely see that the Democratic Party would gain or lose mass support by its handling of the public housing issue. Moreover, since Arvey was a Democratic National Committeeman from Illinois, he would tend to look at the matter from a national as well as from a local standpoint. Accordingly Liveright and others pointed out to Arvey that Chicago's failure to produce a large and satisfactory public housing program would embarrass the national Administration. Arvey seemed receptive, but Liveright was disappointed by the note on which the conference ended.

"All very nice," Arvey finally said, as Liveright later recalled, "but you guys that want me to crack the whip now are the same guys who were after me a couple of years ago for pressuring the Council." He went on to say that Kennelly had agreed to run for Mayor on the understanding that he would be offered no advice from the Democratic Party unless he asked for it. So far, Arvey said, he had not asked for any.[14]

Next the Strategy Committee went to see Duffy. This interview was altogether unsuccessful. Duffy later recalled it as follows:

"There was a clique of Reds—well, tinted at least—who came

in one night and told me I was going to vote for public housing or else.

" 'I thought you are interesting in housing,' I said.

" 'We are,' they said.

" 'But,' I said, 'you are telling me to vote for the seven sites or for nothing.'

" 'Yes,' they said.

" 'Then,' I said, 'you're for nothing.'

"They proceeded to tell me they would do everything they could to see me voted out of office. I congratulated them.

" 'That's the American way of life,' I said."

Duffy saw no reason to regard the Public Housing Association or the Strategy Committee as serious threats. He felt that these organizations were the creatures of the Authority, or at least partners of it, and they had no real membership support. "Some of the pressure was coming from groups spurred on by employees of the Authority," he said afterwards. "I forget the set-ups. They had names, but they were just paper organizations."* [15]

Whether paper organizations or not, they could issue press releases and this, Duffy would probably have admitted, gave them a certain amount of influence at a time when the newspapers, especially the *Sun-Times* and the Negro press, were devoting much attention to the housing issue. In publicity the public housing supporters had a major advantage over their opponents, for, because of their close ties with the Authority staff, they were usually primed in advance about coming decisions and supplied with the arguments that could be made for or against these decisions. Moreover, David Anderson, the *Sun-Times* housing reporter, and housing reporters of other papers, who rarely went to the anti-housers for stories, were on close terms with members of the staff and other public housing officials and sometimes attended meetings of the Strategy Committee.

The City Hall was extremely sensitive to criticism in the press. On several occasions the Mayor called Taylor and Miss Wood on

* At about the same time a small delegation of opponents to public housing visited Duffy. "He was friendly," Sachs, who was one of the delegates, later recalled. "He complimented us on our clean fight (i.e., for not exploiting racial antagonism). I would say that I left with the impression that *as a man* he was against the program."[16]

the telephone to remonstrate with them for the unkind things that were being said about him in print and to ask if the Authority woudn't please see to it that the newspapers did not get any more stories that would embarrass him. Taylor always assured the Mayor that as chairman of the Authority he was most eager to avoid undue publicity, but others believed that the Mayor's anguish showed that the pressure was accomplishing results.

Anderson (as well as other housing reporters) wrote stories every day on some aspect of the developing struggle. He interviewed all of the aldermen in whose wards sites had been selected. Two declared that they were in favor of them; four said they were opposed, and one, Duffy, had "no comment." The *Sun-Times* then addressed editorials in the form of "memos" to the aldermen who were opposed, illustrating each memo with the appropriate alderman's photograph.

Alderman Tourek said he was against the project planned for his ward because a number of veterans then living in trailer camps would be ineligible for it. "Isn't that a dog-in-the-manger attitude?" the *Sun-Times* asked. "What's your *real* reason for objecting to construction of a housing project in a sparsely populated area that private enterprise isn't the least bit interested in developing?"[17] With Alderman Pacini, who said the project should be built on slum land rather than vacant land because otherwise it would attract people from outside his ward, the *Sun-Times* took an understanding and sympathetic tone, but it warned, "You ought to be out 'selling' your constituents and other aldermen on the idea of solidly backing up the housing authority's efforts to make Chicago a better place in which to live."[18]

Harvey, the Negro alderman, was opposed to the site in his ward because "to build a project there you would have to tear down too many good houses." "It's not a slum," Harvey argued. "It means that too many Negroes would have to be displaced and that would cause more racial tension. The CHA says it is non-discriminatory but it really forces people on other people. That causes bloodshed. Forcing people out of their homes as is intended in this neighborhood is unconstitutional. I stand for my people. They're against this project and I'm against it. I'll fight it until I drop." In its memo to Harvey, the editors said they couldn't believe that his constituents would not be willing to trade their slum hovels for modern, clean, safe apartments. "Why the sudden change of heart about public housing, Ald. Harvey?" it asked.[19]

With Duffy, who had no comment, the *Sun-Times* was severe. It reminded him that he was a candidate for president of the Cook County Board, a circumstance which made his views on public housing of special concern to the whole community. "If the aldermen continue to hem and haw over the first sites proposed, as they are now doing, they may fluff the entire program for our city," the memo to Duffy said. "If that happens, the tens of thousands of Chicagoans who are suffering from the housing shortage will have some questions for you to answer as a Democratic Party leader, and they'll expect more than 'no comment.' "[20]

Editorials criticizing the Council also appeared in the *Chicago Daily News* and even the Hearst *Herald-American,* but the ones in the *Sun-Times* were those that probably most hurt the aldermen, for the *Sun-Times* named names. Once Taylor found Duffy ruefully reading one of the "memos" that the newspaper had addressed to him. "This makes me want to forget all about public service," Duffy said. "It makes me want to get out of it and stay out of it."[21]

The *Sun-Times* did not criticize the Mayor, however. He was what the city room called a "sacred cow." Marshall Field had been one of those who persuaded him to run as a reform candidate, and Field's managing editor was one of the Mayor's admirers. When stories were written that suggested the Mayor was stalling, they were edited in such a way as to relieve the Mayor of responsibility. The *Sun-Times* was, however, willing to report statements by officers of the Public Housing Association and others who criticized the Mayor. Not for two years would the *Sun-Times* attack the Mayor himself. "Whose side is Kennelly on?", it asked then. "Job was a man of monumental patience. But would he have made a good mayor?"[22]

Delegations and press releases were not the Strategy Committee's only weapons however. It intended to fulfill Alinsky's threat: to go out into the wards—especially into the seven wards for which sites were proposed—to organize neighborhood groups to support the housing program at the "grassroots level."

For this purpose B'nai B'rith, which had chapters and lodges in many wards seemed well suited. The announcement that there would be public hearings for four days beginning February 23 set the B'nai B'rith machinery into motion. At the end of January its Joint Council on Housing sent all chapter and lodge presidents a model letter which was to be mailed by them at once to every member. In addition, the central office supplied the chapters with a B'nai B'rith Area Housing Directory containing the names, addresses, and telephone numbers of the people designated to organize support for the seven sites in each part of the city. A "ward assignment sheet" was enclosed; this listed the lodges and chapters which had been selected to lead the fight for each of the seven sites. The chapter and lodge presidents were asked to appoint "ward action committees" at once. "You will be called upon for progress reports within the next 15 days," the central office memorandum concluded.[23]

While these requests were being distributed, B'nai B'rith published a mimeographed "action and information kit" which summarized briefly the status of the housing program, located the seven sites on an outline map of the city, suggested types of action by priority (set up a housing action committee within each lodge, direct visits to aldermen and ward committeemen, send letters and postcards to aldermen and ward committeemen, hold meetings—city-wide, area-wide or local ward, send letters to the Mayor, to newspapers and to members), and indicated which aldermen were favorable, doubtful, or unalterably opposed to public housing.

When B'nai B'rith planned to sponsor a rally at which Miss Wood, Louis Wirth, a well-known University of Chicago sociologist interested in race relations, and Waitstill Sharp, a Unitarian minister and civic organization leader, would speak, Arthur Sachs, the lawyer for the Southwest Neighborhood Council, let it be known that if the rally were held he would pack it with opponents of public housing. This caused Freifeld and the head of the Anti-Defamation League, A. Abbot Rosen, to ask Sachs to discuss the matter with them privately. In what Sachs later described as a "star chamber" session, the ADL heads pointed out that it would be "irresponsible" for him, acting as a B'nai B'rith leader, to air the organization's internal disagreements in public. The ADL leaders, according to Sachs, asked whether he was being paid to oppose public housing. Acknowledging that he was employed as an attorney to represent the Southwest Neighborhood Council, Sachs said he would be opposed to public housing on the sites in question anyway, although he probably would not take the time and trouble to assert his views if he did not have a client to represent. He was told that as a citizen and a lawyer, he could of course do as he pleased about public housing and the meeting.[24] He did not pack the meeting, perhaps because he could not.

So active were Freifeld and some of his associates on the Strategy Committee—especially Adrian Robson of the Congregational Union, Bernice Fisher of the CIO, and Father Cantwell of the Catholic Labor Alliance—that the other leaders of the Public Housing Association began to fear that it would be swallowed up. Freifeld and his associates, for their part, were also made uneasy by the collaboration. It bothered them that such usual allies as the A.F. of L., the American Jewish Committee, the American Veterans' Committee and the Catholic Labor Alliance, among others, were not strongly represented on the Board of the Association. It would be better, they thought, if the Association were more representative of these "mass" organizations and less of individuals who were not acting in any organizational capacity. What made them most uncomfortable, however, was the presence on the Strategy Committee of representatives of the Progressive Party, who were planning to picket City Hall, a move which would embarrass them and their organizations acutely. Unless the Progressive Party people agreed to follow only those lines of action approved by the Strategy Committee, Freifeld said, B'nai B'rith would disassociate itself from the Committee and he himself would resign his directorship in the Association. The ADL was supported by its allies. Others leaders of the Association and the Committee, however, thought this was an unreasonable demand. The Congregational Union, some of them pointed out, had invited Mayor Kennelly to be the guest of honor at one of its meetings without having asked the Strategy Committee for its approval. Why, then, should another group ask permission to picket? But Freifeld and his associates insisted, and, since B'nai B'rith and the organizations informally allied with it could not be spared, this demand was accepted.[25]

At the hearings, the gallery was filled with several hundred angry spectators, most of them housewives, many of whom came in organized fashion by chartered buses and sat through the four days of testimony, clapping, shouting, hissing, pounding and booing. The gallery's indignation was directed, however, not against the opponents of public housing or the politicians, but against the Authority. Whenever a public housing supporter spoke his words were likely to be drowned by cat-calls from the gallery.

Many individuals and organizational representatives testified in favor of the package of seven sites as a whole: the Church Federation of Greater Chicago, the Cook County League of Women Voters, a representative of the State Street Council, a vice-president of the First National Bank, a vice-president of Armour & Company, and many more. But many of these people lived on the "Gold Coast" or in the fashionable North Shore suburbs and, while they had views on public housing in general, they knew little about particular sites and they could claim no direct and personal interest in any of the projects. Although the officers of these organizations read prepared statements, their membership was not there to cheer and applaud them and to boo and hiss the opposition. Even B'nai B'rith, which had invested much time and effort in preparations, had only a scattering of supporters in the gallery.

The anti-housing forces were represented by some city-wide organizations—the Chicago Real Estate Board, for example. But most of those who testified for the opposition represented district or neighborhood associations (the Taxpayers' Action Committee, the Southwest Neighborhood Council, the West Lawn Women's Club, and so on) and so they could talk, not only about public housing in general or the package of sites as a whole, but about particular sites as well. It was these neighborhood associations that had crowded the gallery with irate women who hooted and screamed whenever a public housing supporter took the floor. The Southwest Neighborhood Council had sent out 12,000 notices urging people to attend the hearings and it had a petition said to be signed by 4,600 persons who opposed the Cicero Avenue site.[26]

Chairman Lancaster ruled that the first three days of the hearings would be devoted to testimony on particular sites while the last day would be reserved for those who wanted to be heard on the package as a whole. This, of course, gave a great advantage to the opposition: there would be 67 speakers opposing particular sites and only 20 (some of them hastily recruited from among the Public Housing Association leadership) favoring them. On the last day the tables would be turned, although briefly; then 63 speakers would favor the whole program and 12 would oppose it.

Arthur Sachs, the lawyer engaged by Finitzo and Stech on behalf of the Southwest Neighborhood Council, was on hand to coordinate the testimony of the opposition to the first site considered, the one at 44th Street and Cicero Avenue. Sachs introduced a number of "experts"—real estate appraisers, brokers, representatives of local Federal savings and loan associations and so on —who made about a dozen principal points, points which were repeated over and again (and which often were all but lost in a welter of verbiage about socialism, rent control, and other irrelevancies) by others of the opposition in the following days. These were the following: 1. Rezoning the neighborhood for row houses would lower re-sale value of existing houses; 2. The effect of public housing would be to create, rather than to clear, a slum in the neighborhood; 3. Property owners would have to bear higher taxes to support facilities for a project—and would have to suffer from resulting crowded schools and other facilities; 4. The city would lose the additional revenue that might be obtained from private development of the area; 5. A project would depreciate property values; 6. A project would soon deteriorate because of the irresponsibility and negligence of the tenants; 7. CHA was inefficient; 8. Public housing would penalize thrift and the desire for home ownership; 9. Public housing was not the only way to end tax delinquency on land; 10. Small public projects would be better than large ones because they would have less adverse influence on the neighborhood; 11. Private builders would refuse to enter an area where there was a project; and 12. Ninety-five per cent of the people of the ward opposed the site.

The people who spoke in favor of this site included John Ducey, CHA's former planning chief, who represented the Public Housing Association; representatives of the National Negro Congress, the South Side Planning Board, the Chicago Board of Amalgamated Clothing Workers, the American Veterans' Committee, the Progressive Party, and two "individuals," one of them a Negro. When they managed to make themselves heard against the jeers that came from the gallery, these speakers, whose statements contained references to social justice and to racial equality, made a dozen main points in reply: 1. The housing shortage was acute; 2. Vacant sites were essential to permit relocation and subsequent slum clearance; 3. Chicago's zoning was outmoded; 4. Public housing would not lower property values; 5. A project would enhance the neighborhood; 6. Housing could and should be planned as to prevent development of slums; 7. Private enterprise was not building fast enough; 8. Low-rent housing necessitated subsidy and would provide substantial revenue to the city through in-lieu-of-taxes payments; 9. The cost of providing municipal services to slum dwellers was greater than for other groups; 10. It was desirable to distribute minority groups throughout the city without segregation; 11. Interracial projects were successful elsewhere; and 12. Housing was a city rather than a ward issue.[27]

The Mayor and most of the aldermen made it clear that their sympathies lay with the opposition. Lancaster was cordial to the opponents, but abrupt, even rude, to the proponents. During the first three days of the hearings the Mayor appeared only when the anti-housing people were being heard; on the fourth day, when most of the testimony favored the entire program, he did not come at all. Meyerson believed that the Mayor, Duffy, Lancaster, and most of the other aldermen identified themselves with the real estate men and neighborhood lawyers; they wore the same kind of clothes, smoked the same kind of cigars, and told the same kind of jokes. With the ministers and other "do-gooders," the aldermen were not comfortable; the very look of a man like the Unitarian minister who headed the Chicago Council Against Racial and Religious Discrimination, was enough to make them uncomfortable.

But regardless of their likes and dislikes, the aldermen and the

Mayor were in the business of getting votes, and this might be enough to account for most of their behavior. On one occasion it was called to the Mayor's attention that 89 ministers had appeared in behalf of the housing program. "Those are just ministers," the Mayor was said to have retorted. "They are not property owners."[28] In the opinion of some of the public housing leaders this remark showed that the Mayor was not a good politician. A good politician, they thought, would count noses rather than property and on this basis 89 ministers would be more important than a smaller number of property-owners.

The professional politicians, however, seemed to agree with the Mayor. They may have been unduly influenced by their prejudices, but it is possible, too, that they had discovered by experience that a property owner is more likely to be moved to action—and therefore more likely to be politically dangerous—than a person who is moved by love of his fellow men or by the desire to represent an organization. Moreover, the aldermen may have had reason to believe that the property owners were more likely to generate and organize political opinion in the wards than were the ministers.

There was, however, another possible explanation for the aldermen's very apparent bias. This was that the aldermen were well aware that they would eventually pass a housing program of some sort—a program which surely would offend the property owners—and that they therefore viewed the hearings not so much as an opportunity for the property owners to exert influence as a means of giving them the only satisfaction they were likely to get, that of "shooting their mouths off." The opponents to public housing were, perhaps, being indulged by Lancaster, very much as a condemned man is indulged by the authorities on the night before his execution. Quite possibly, too, the politicians attached less importance to words than did the liberals and intellectuals, most of whom were aghast at the proceedings.

Nevertheless in the course of the hearings there was a fuller canvass of the arguments for and against—especially against—the sites than had so far been made at any stage of the planning process. The aldermen, despite CHA staff technical reports to them, seemingly had absorbed little besides the general statements put forward by Taylor in his presentation to the housing committee and in his subsequent answers to their questions. The hearings were very far from being a reasonable discussion however. This was so because the setting (especially the presence of the mob in the gallery) and the rhetoric made them an exciting contest rather than a serious effort to find a basis for compromise and agreement. Since they were engaged in a contest, both the public housing supporters and opponents had to state their cases in the strongest possible terms and the Authority, of course, could not concede any merit to an argument which tended to discredit public housing. If there was to be reasonable discussion, it could not take place in such an atmosphere. And this meant that it could not take place in public.

If the hearings had any effect at all, other than that of relieving the feelings of the opponents to public housing, it was probably on the minds of the commissioners, especially that of Taylor, the only one who attended regularly. Apparently Taylor was more convinced than before that it would have been wise to reach an agreement with the politicians. The other commissioners, when they heard what happened at the hearings, appeared to agree with him in large measure.

When the hearings were over, the housing committee recommended two slum sites (both extensions of existing projects), but by a vote of 13 to seven it refused to approve the package as a whole. One of the seven who favored the package explained that he did so to insure the ultimate defeat of all of the sites.

The two slum sites that were approved were useless, of course, without vacant land areas to accompany them; there were about 3,500 families living on these two sites, and until there was housing into which these people could move, the Authority could do nothing with the sites.

The committee's action did not mean that the other sites were finally rejected. Reporting to the full Council on March 2, Lancaster explained that the five sites which had not been approved were still under consideration; in fact, a special subcommittee had been appointed to examine these and other sites more closely. Lancaster said he was disappointed in the attitude of many people toward public housing. It was wrong to be against it, he said. "We have to have public housing, although it cannot be dictatorial. We must approve it, but it is not necessary to approve the full package."[29]

The Mayor also made a brief speech to the Council. Whenever a conflict arose between CHA or other city agencies and the City Council, he would be on the side of the Council because it consisted of the elected representatives of the people, he said. It was not within his province to approve or disapprove of any particular sites, but it *was* within his province to urge the Council to approve a plan for the number of units under consideration. "Public housing is definite," the Mayor concluded. "We have to have it. And I'm sure that a large majority of the Council will want to take advantage of the Federal funds which the government is in effect sending back to us."[30]

When the Public Housing Association's leaders learned that the Mayor was urging the Council leaders and the Authority heads to get together, they wrote him a letter which they made public. In it they asked him to allow them to have an observer at any negotiations over which he might preside.[31] This, of course, was a way of saying that they did not think he would act fairly unless he was being watched by a representative of the "public." Obviously there was no longer any possibility of reasonable discussion between the Mayor and the Association spokesmen.

'What Can Be Sweeter, Boys—It's In NOBODY'S Ward'

CHAPTER SEVEN □ □ □ □ □ □

CLIMAX

AFTER APPROVING the two slum sites and, in effect, though not formally, rejecting the rest of the package, the housing committee of the Council delegated the site selection problem to a subcommittee of nine, all but one of whom were opposed to public housing. Alderman Emil V. Pacini, who had vigorously opposed a site in his ward, was chairman of the subcommittee, the task of which was to suggest sites to the housing committee and, through it, to the Authority. In the second week of March, the subcommittee chartered a bus and, with Meyerson and a staff member from the Plan Commission as technical consultants and with some interested aldermen and newspapermen as observers, made several trips to inspect some 40 sites which through various avenues had come to the attention of the Mayor and other Council leaders or were known to the subcommittee members.

The aldermen were in a carefree mood on these excursions. They pointed out a notorious brothel, told of famous pranks that had been played by certain salty characters, and remarked facetiously on the opportunities they saw for enterprising aldermen to increase their bank accounts in particular wards. The "boys," as they called themselves, were frank to say that they were out to "get" the Authority and the seven aldermen who had voted for the package. The way to get a fellow alderman was to locate a site in his ward, and the way to get the Authority was to find sites CHA would regard as so unsuitable that the public housers would be forced into the awkward position of having to oppose public housing. Under the circumstances the aldermen were not much concerned with the usual criteria of site selection—e.g., presence or absence of schools, parks, and transportation facilities; the main requirement was that a site should embarrass the appropriate people.

To a certain extent, the search for impossible sites was simply prankishness. But Pacini and a few of the aldermen probably intended the pranks to hurt—even to cause the defeat of the pro-public housing aldermen if possible. When Aldermen Becker and Merriam, two of the principal public housing supporters, were in the bus, the other aldermen teased them constantly. Merriam, whose father was a distinguished professor at the University of Chicago, was not altogether at ease with his fellow aldermen, who were mostly of another social class. When members of the subcommittee suggested putting projects adjacent to the University of Chicago in his ward, Merriam did jokingly counter by proposing a site in the ward of Alderman Keane, one of the "Big Boys" of the Council. Becker got angry when he was teased; he thought perhaps that through him the Jews were being made a butt.

On March 23, after several days of bus travel, the subcommittee and other members of the housing committee met in a closed session which began early in the evening and lasted until after midnight. As soon as Pacini suggested a site, it was moved and seconded by Harvey or Bieszczat. Pacini, Harvey, Bieszczat and the others were about to confront the public housers with the choice between nothing and worse than nothing when Alderman Cullerton, one of the "Big Boys," intervened. "Parky" Cullerton was no friend of public housing, but he was not willing to see the Council make itself ridiculous. By raising objections and making counter-proposals, he almost single-handedly prevented the committee from endorsing the most outlandish of the proposals that were being made, e.g., from locating a project on the University of Chicago tennis courts.

Even with some of its worst absurdities eliminated, the *pot-pourri* of sites was indefensible. It included several on the Lake Front near the fashionable Edgewater Beach Hotel; a site which lay in the path of a projected superhighway; others that were densely covered with valuable non-residential property; and still others that were badly cut by transportation lines or totally lacking in community facilities. One of the sites was among those that had been proposed by the Authority: this was a Negro slum area adjacent to the Ida B. Wells project for which the subcommittee recommended 480 dwelling units rather than the 1,665 units the Authority had proposed.

After this midnight session the housing committee delivered a list of 13 sites to the Authority, taking care to make no formal recommendation because Federal regulations required that sites be proposed by the Authority.

The subcommittee's list was sharply attacked in the press. The *Sun-Times* scolded the aldermen vigorously and even the conservative *Chicago Daily News* observed editorially that the subcommittee consisted of determined opponents of public housing. "Such public housing as we require—and we require some," the *Chicago Daily News* said, "ought to be undertaken as part of a systematic plan for the rehabilitation of the city. It must not be treated as a nuisance to be swept into odd corners here and there or hidden behind industrial ruins. The result should not be something to be concealed. It should stand out in civic pride, as the great housing developments in New York do today, and as those in Pittsburgh soon will."[1]

Due to the foolishness of the Pacini subcommittee, the position of the Authority was now considerably improved. The aldermen had shown that they were incapable of selecting satisfactory sites themselves; if there was to be public housing, evidently, it would have to be on sites selected by technically qualified agencies.

Even before the "bus-window" committee was appointed, Meyerson had become convinced that the Authority had blundered in proposing a 10,000-unit first year's program without giving the aldermen any definite idea of what was to come in the following years. Some of the aldermen had complained bitterly at not "knowing where they stood," and the complaint, Meyerson felt, was justified. If they were shown that the Authority intended to build extensively on slum sites later and that the long-term plan for public housing had some significant relation to plans for private redevelopment, for traditional private housing, and for schools, parks, transportation and other facilities, the Mayor and the "Big Boys," if not the other aldermen, might pay more attention to CHA's recommendations.

Miss Wood agreed with Meyerson, now that the planning staff

was reaching its full complement of 30 staff members, that a long-range plan was at least worth trying, and so, after informing the commissioners of the intention, the planning staff during the winter embarked upon an intensive effort to outline a comprehensive plan for the rest of the six-year 40,000 unit program, with special emphasis on the 21,000 units projected for the first two years.

Meyerson had also arranged for the CHA planning staff and the Land Clearance Commission to aid the Plan Commission in preparing a plan for residential densities. Such a plan was an essential basis for future site selection. Over a period of several months, two and, at times, three CHA planners worked with the Plan Commission on this study. However, when the density plan was completed, the Plan Commission, which was wary of the implications of some of the proposals contained in it, did not publish it.

Meanwhile, when he found that the subcommittee had only worsened the site selection problem, the Mayor was disappointed. He publicly called Duffy and Lancaster to his office to discuss matters with Taylor. These gentlemen, he told the press, pounding his fist on his desk, would work together continuously, beginning in the next week, until they came up with an acceptable housing program for Chicago. He had intended to take a vacation in April, the Mayor said, but he would postpone it until the housing problem was solved.[2]

The supporters of public housing were appalled to think of Taylor being closeted with Duffy and Lancaster. So, evidently, was Taylor himself, for he and the other commissioners readily agreed with the staff that the Authority should take the offensive by publicly rejecting the so-called "bus-window" sites and putting forward in their place a revised CHA package. The planning staff had by now made some progress in selecting sites for the second year's program and Meyerson urged the Commissioners to submit to the Council the entire 21,000-unit program for the first two of the six years. The commissioners, however, decided that some of the sites the planners had in mind were too good for public housing (i.e., that they should be reserved for private enterprise) and they were too hopeful, at this point, of getting the Council's approval of a first year's program to be willing to run any unnecessary risks. Accordingly, they wrote Lancaster accepting the one site which had been in their original proposal and rejecting the others. Having disposed of the "bus-window" sites, CHA proceeded to submit its new package. It included some of the vacant sites from the first package. "We were present at the public hearings on these sites," the commissioners wrote Lancaster, "and took note of the various objections and points of view expressed. We found no sound reason which causes us to revise our judgment."[3]

In addition to these sites from the first package, the new proposal contained others which brought the total number of units to 12,000, the whole of the first year's allocation. The new sites were taken from the 21,000-unit two-year plan that the planning staff had been preparing. Two-thirds of the units in the new package were on vacant land. One large site accounted for most of the new vacant land units; this was part of a vacant square mile on the edge of the city on the South Side. The new package also included an extension of the large existing Altgeld project in Alderman DuBois' ward. Because of the larger amount of vacant land that it contained, the commissioners and the staff felt that this second package was very much better than the first one.

The new package was made public shortly before Taylor (together with McMillen and Benjamin) was to meet with Duffy and the other City Hall leaders. Once again the Public Housing Association and the other pro-public housing groups were relying on publicity to prevent the commissioners from making what the group regarded as an unfavorable compromise.

The Mayor and Duffy were annoyed when, just before their meeting with Taylor was to take place, they read about the new package in the newspapers. The Mayor told reporters that he would not take a position regarding the new proposal,[4] and when Taylor, McMillen, and Benjamin arrived at his office they found not only Duffy and Lancaster there but two other "Big Boys" as well—Wagner and Keane, both of whom were among the bitterest opponents of public housing.

"After the CHA members presented their program," the *Sun-*

Times City Hall reporter wrote in an account of the meeting which both Taylor and McMillen later said was substantially accurate, "Wagner lit into them. He blamed them for the council's failure to adopt a housing program and pulled no punches in expressing his opinions of the CHA as a whole and of some of its members and employees.

"Kennelly, miffed at the package proposal of the CHA representatives, made no effort to restrain Wagner. When the alderman finished there was a moment of silence as the mayoral appointees to CHA waited for Kennelly to back them up.

"When the mayor didn't, CHA member Claude Benjamin tied into Wagner. Kennelly interrupted immediately with:

" 'Remember, you're in the office of the mayor of Chicago.'

"Then the mayor swung his chair around so that his back was to the other conferees. After the meeting broke up, Kennelly administered a private scolding to the CHA members. The resultant freeze has showed no sign of thaw to date—but Kennelly has indicated he won't ask for any CHA resignations."[5]

Several days after this meeting the new package was considered by the housing committee of the Council. The Mayor, perhaps relying on advice from his floor leader, Duffy, indicated he felt it would be rejected in a way that would end all consideration of future public housing. Presumably to prevent this, he asked the committee not to vote on the proposal at that time, but, instead, to appoint a new subcommittee to negotiate further with the Authority. (Some thought that the Mayor was really opposed to public housing and that his actual fear was not that the package would be rejected, but that it would be accepted.) "For three or four months I've been trying to get the various agencies together with the aldermen," the Mayor said. "I don't think much progress has been made. I'm not criticizing any of the agencies. We have to get closer together. This is only going to be solved around a table. I suggested this some months ago. We are where we started out, but now everybody knows more about the problem than before. I ask you to appoint a committee of the smallest possible number and devote full time to getting an agreement on the sites so that we can take the people out of the slums of Chicago."[6]

Alderman Carey, an able supporter of public housing, agreed

with the Mayor. But he said that more than the appointment of a new committee was needed. "There has to be a new influence to reconcile this problem. I don't think just using your office will do it. I think there has to be a new face, Mr. Mayor, your own winsome face, to lend leadership in this situation."[7]

The Mayor, however, declined. He would be in his office at 8:30 in the morning, he said, and he would remain there until 10:30 at night in order to encourage the committee to resolve the difficulties. But he would not chair the committee.

Until the Mayor intervened, some of the leading opponents to public housing expected that the new package would be accepted by the Council although there seem to have been no very good grounds for thinking so. "We had practically come to the point when everyone was ready for a vote and we all of us wanted a vote even if we knew we were going to lose," Ralph J. Finitzo said afterward. "At least we would know how we stood and everyone in the Council would stand up and be counted. And they had us licked. Then along comes Kennelly and says that we should not vote in the atmosphere that prevailed right then, and he stopped them from voting on it. That saved us. . . ."[8]

This incident may have persuaded some of the real estate and other anti-public housing interests that there was real hope of defeating the housing program altogether. At any rate, Finitzo said that in the week following the Mayor's intervention he was able to collect twice as much money as he had in the entire previous period.[9]

This was the situation when Alderman Egan, in whose ward the 44th and Cicero site was partly located, caused a flurry of excitement with a resolution which the Council passed inadvertently and which would have ended the site selection struggle if the city's corporation counsel had not ruled it invalid. The resolution declared it the Council's policy to approve only sites in or adjacent to areas that had been designated slum. His idea, Egan said, was to eliminate uncertainty about the Authority's intentions: the residents and investors in any non-slum neighborhood ought, he believed, to be assured that no public housing project would be located near them.

Duffy now took full command. He and Lancaster and a few

of the other "Big Boys" put the Authority's second package aside and began choosing sites in their own way.

"I called the leaders together," Duffy later recalled, "—actually it was Lancaster who called them, but I was there—and I told them what would happen if we scuttled the ship. They gave us some good arguments for being against housing. Then we talked it over and weighed it for awhile. Then we had a recess for a couple of days. Then we came together again. Over a period of time we convinced them—convinced them legitimately."

The people who had to be convinced were the other "Big Boys." As Duffy later explained, "Out of the 50 aldermen you get 12 or 15 who you have confidence in—who you can trust and who are able; some of them are able, but you can't trust them—you wouldn't be out of a room 15 minutes when the newspapermen would know all about it." The able and trustworthy aldermen were (Duffy said) "the fellows who do the thinking in the Council" and most of them were also chairmen of important committees. It was with this inner circle of leaders and powerholders that he collaborated in shaping a compromise housing program.

Duffy's criteria of site selection, which the other "Big Boys" apparently accepted, were very different from those of the Authority. In Duffy's opinion, public housing was necessary, but only to a limited extent. "We need some public housing," he explained after the site struggle was over, "but we shouldn't have so much of it that Chicago becomes a public housing town with no one left to pay the taxes." Projects should be provided for the poorest people in the worst slums, but it should not be carried much further than that. At present the middle-income groups, he felt, were being ignored. "All the public housing people can talk about is public housing," he once complained. "They never talk about the fellow who is just above and is not eligible. There are two classes of people that are neglected. First, there is the fellow who, although he is not eligible for public housing, can't purchase a house. And then there is the fellow who can pay $1,500 down on a bungalow and pay his way. He is the substantial citizen. He will pay taxes, and without taxes our system of government will collapse."[10]

On the one hand Duffy and other aldermen were concerned that many of their constituents were excluded because of income from public housing; on the other hand they wanted the quantity of public housing to be no greater than necessary to provide for the destitute or near-destitute—any more than was necessary for this purpose would attract more poor people, particularly southern Negroes, to Chicago. Above all, projects should not be located where they would interfere with the private housing of "substantial" taxpayers.

"Public housing should not be placed where it will stymie the growth of a community," Duffy once said. "It shouldn't be put on virgin territory—it's to outlying districts that Chicago must look for the kind of development that will support the city government. To put a public housing project in a vast tract (sometimes they use only 25 acres of a 100-acre tract, and kill the rest of it) and then expect private contractors to go in there is just asinine. Wherever there is a project there is deterioration of the surrounding neighborhood. No one will invest in a $15,000 or a $18,000 house near one of those projects."

It would not be quite so bad to take virgin territory away from potential private development if the poor people of the surrounding neighborhood were to be housed there, Duffy thought, for he shared with other "substantial" citizens a feeling of attachment to a local community. But the Authority would, of course, take its tenants from among whatever slum dwellers might be eligible. "At 115th and Ashland they wanted to put up four, five and six story buildings in a strictly single-family residential neighborhood," Duffy complained. (Actually other single family house areas were many blocks from the site and most of the buildings CHA was proposing were two story.) "But they didn't tell the people there that not one soul would be eligible to live in those places. They didn't tell them that they were going to bring slum-dwellers in there. They were going to use that fine tract of land for outsiders when we ourselves were in sore need of housing."

The place for public housing projects, Duffy concluded, was in the slums, and preferably in those slum neighborhoods where projects already existed. "If public housing will do any harm to a slum neighborhood—and that's questionable—then it has already been done in places where projects have already been built; it's better to add to it than to create a new problem somewhere else. The only thing I am against is construction in virgin territories."[11]

Duffy was not unaware of the problems that would be caused by displacing people from slums without first providing new housing on vacant sites. He judged that, as compared to the presumed damage (by public housing or more likely by Negroes who would live in public housing) to the "substantial" citizens in the outlying neighborhoods, the hardships inflicted upon slum-dwellers (most of whom were Negro) would be the lesser of two evils. At the same time, he knew that any program which made no provision at all for relocation—which contained no vacant land—stood little chance of being accepted by the Authority or by the Federal government.

Since there was a sizeable colony of Negroes in his own ward and since, although he was running for a County office, it was of the utmost importance that he be able to carry his own ward, Duffy took some pains to discuss the public housing proposals with some of his "substantial" Negro constituents. "I had the colored leaders of my ward in for a meeting," he said afterwards. "I submitted the proposition to them: 'You fellows are the ones that have got to live with it. I am only your representative. You tell me what you want.' And they voted against it 100 per cent."[12] Most of these leaders lived in a high income Negro residential district where houses were often priced at $25,000 or more. These people were as much opposed to housing projects as were whites of the same income group—even more opposed, perhaps, since it would be much harder for them than for whites to move away from a nearby project which might mean a loss of status. The Morgan Park Association, representing middle class Negroes in Duffy's ward, was also opposed to having a project nearby.

It took Duffy and the other "Big Boys," who had some help from the Plan Commission's staff, about two weeks to select new sites.

The Duffy-Lancaster compromise program, as it came to be

known, provided for about 10,500 units on slum and 2,000 units on vacant land. There were eight slum sites (including the two the Council had already approved), all in Negro districts. There were seven vacant sites (including parts of three the Authority had recommended), but the number of units to be built on these vacant sites was very small: the largest would have 588 units and most of the others would have only 300. The two vacant land projects of about 2,000 units each which CHA had proposed were eliminated; for the 115th and Ashland site Duffy substituted another in his own ward, but one for only 300 units. The proposed 600-unit extension of the Altgeld Gardens project in DuBois' ward was cut to 300 units. (DuBois, although a Republican, was, Duffy afterward explained, "a very decent fellow.") Becker, on the other hand, although a Democrat, suffered by having the 588-unit and one other vacant land site put in his ward. Both of the sites in Becker's ward had been among the "bus-window" selections; the Authority had rejected them because they were in the path of a planned superhighway. Becker was very much upset to find these two sites proposed for his ward. He was not being treated fairly, he thought, and the reason was perhaps anti-semitism as well as his stand on public housing. He went to Duffy to protest.

"John, you damn fool," he said, "you're running for president of the County Board. Not one Jew will vote for you."

Duffy was not impressed with this argument. He is said to have replied, "The trouble with you Jews is, when you get backed up against the wall you start crying. When we Irish were backed against the wall by the Ku Klux Klan we used clubs, we used bricks, we used stones. But what do you Jews do? You don't fight. You start crying. Well, you asked for it and you're going to get it."[13]

The compromise program, CHA estimated, would displace 12,465 families, almost all of them Negro. It would provide relocation housing (i.e., housing on vacant land sites) for only 2,112 families. And when, finally, the slum site projects were completed, the net addition to Chicago's housing supply would be only 47 units. The density of population in the slum-site projects would be far in excess of Plan Commission recommendations.

This was a program which Duffy and Lancaster were sure the Council would accept. But now—because Federal regulations required that sites be proposed by the Authority—it was necessary to have CHA propose this program as its own before any action could be taken by the Council.

The Mayor, Duffy, and Lancaster called Taylor and McMillen to a secret meeting in a hotel room and urged them to accept the compromise. The commissioners, however, refused to act before getting a report from their staff.

While the staff studied the program and prepared its recommendations, the pressure on the commissioners to accept the Duffy-Lancaster compromise mounted. Only four days after it was made public, the *Tribune* reported that the Mayor and Council were irked by the Authority's delay in acting upon the compromise. At best the compromise had only a slim chance of getting the needed 26 votes, the story said, and every day's delay made its passage more unlikely. One unnamed alderman was quoted as saying that if CHA tried to increase the number of vacant land units over that provided in the compromise, he would introduce a measure calling for the resignation of several key commissioners and officials. The Authority was fortunate to get what vacant land the compromise provided, the story suggested, because there was strong neighborhood opposition to these sites.[14]

The *Sun-Times* strengthened the commissioners' bargaining power with one hand and weakened it with the other. President Truman was soon to visit Chicago, that paper pointed out, and "the nation is watching to see whether Chicago will remove the suspicion that local Democrats are sabotaging the President's important housing program." But having said this, the editors went on to advise the Authority not to reject the compromise. "We believe," they said, "The Duffy-Lancaster compromise, while it falls short of honesty and fails to meet Chicago's needs, should not be rejected by the Housing Authority. Rather, it should be improved. Mayor Kennelly should insist upon its improvement."[15]

The pressure which the CHA staff found most disturbing came

from the Plan Commission. The chairman, Nathaniel Owings, a partner in the large architectural firm of Skidmore, Owings and Merrill, telegraphed for publication from a vacation spot in New Mexico that the Duffy-Lancaster proposal met the requirements of city planning so well that it should not even be considered a compromise. "All those whose basic interests lie with the good of Chicago should go all out for this plan," Owings wired. "It will not displace Negroes, but will actually increase the number of living units in areas concerned."* [16]

The Plan Commission's responsiveness to City Hall was not surprising. Its budget was precarious and therefore it felt it necessary to do routine tasks and favors for particular aldermen. One such favor had been done for Alderman Pistilli while the Council had the Authority's first package under consideration. Without an analysis by its staff, the Plan Commission reclassified an area from "blighted" to "conservation," a change which meant that the area could no longer be considered for slum clearance. Hitherto, the existence of blight had been a technical matter to be determined objectively by analyzing the number of structurally sound and unsound buildings, the number without running water, and so on. Now the technical criteria were replaced by political ones.

Under the circumstances, the CHA staff was pleasantly surprised that the Plan Commission Director, Carl Gardner, in his testimony before the first housing committee hearing supported the classification of land on which the Authority's site proposals were based—a classification which had been prepared by the Plan Commission staff. Gardner declared that while the Commission was not concerned with whether a given vacant site should be devoted to public or private housing, it had determined which vacant land was suitable for residential development. Thus the Authority was able to justify both its own selections and later its rejection of a number of the "bus-window" sites on the basis of the Plan Commission's study.

---

* A few months earlier the *Chicago Tribune* in a front page story quoted Owings' opinion that the slums bordering on the New York Central tracks should be among the first cleared because of the bad impression they gave visitors to the city.

But the Plan Commission's firmness was short-lived. When it became apparent that its stand precluded the use of some of the sites the "Big Boys" intended to propose, the Mayor, Duffy, and Lancaster met with representatives of the Commission and pointedly demanded that it stop being unreasonable. It was shortly after this meeting that Owings (who had gone to New Mexico and therefore could not have been personally familiar with the Duffy-Lancaster sites) issued his blanket endorsement of the compromise.

This endorsement meant that in order to accommodate the Mayor and the aldermen the Plan Commission had to disregard planning proposals which had previously been accepted. The Commission agreed to reroute a planned superhighway, the path of which had long before been decided by the Commission, thus making sites in Becker's ward available with the result that he could be punished by the other aldermen for supporting public housing. Changing the route of the highway would cost millions of dollars because two otherwise unnecessary bridges would have to be built.

The Plan Commission's action made it more difficult for the Authority effectively to oppose the Duffy-Lancaster compromise. If the Plan Commission regarded the Duffy-Lancaster plan as sound, the public would say, why did not the Authority accept it at once? The answer would be simple for opponents of public housing to supply: the Authority, they would assert, wanted to use public housing to alter the racial pattern of Chicago.

As for other operating city agencies and organizations, the planning staff of the Housing Authority worked closely with their officials concerned with planning. There was frequent collaboration between the CHA staff and the staffs of the Board of Education, the Park District, the Welfare Council and other organizations. Nevertheless, the Board of Education, in the period under consideration here—1949 and 1950—gave support to those people who were opposed to public housing or at least to public housing on vacant land sites. The Superintendent of the Board charged in a statement which was widely quoted in the press and elsewhere that the plans of the Housing Authority for vacant land construction would require large expenditures for new schools at a time when: 1) there was a clamor for new schools from areas where citizens paid full and high taxes; 2) the Board of Education was approaching its statutory limit of indebtedness; 3) in some of the areas of the city there were vacant class rooms.[17]

Some of the opponents of public housing used these arguments to maintain that the Housing Authority was arbitrary. It could build in areas where no new schools would be required, they said, but chose instead to build in vacant areas where large additional public expenditures for schools and other facilities would have to follow.

Of course, the vacant school rooms tended to be in stable, built-up areas. Twenty or more years before, the young families who had moved into these areas had had a plethora of children of school age. The children grew up and moved on to other areas, but the older, childless people remained. In these areas there was virtually no vacant land and there was no large number of structures deteriorated enough to warrant demolition. Nor would building in slum areas significantly ease the problem since the older schools and the most inadequate schools in the city were located in slum areas and particularly in the Negro slum areas. (As early as 1938, thirteen of the fifteen Chicago schools running on two or more shifts were in Negro areas.) These schools were so badly deteriorated that they would soon have to be replaced anyway.

However, the criterion, in this as in most political struggles, for a successful argument was that it be plausible, not necessarily that it be valid. The Superintendent of Schools' argument did seem plausible to many and this probably did the Housing Authority some damage.

The staff had little difficulty convincing Taylor, McMillen and Benjamin that the Duffy-Lancaster compromise was unsatisfactory. When early in May the Mayor asked the commissioners to meet with him and the key aldermen to discuss their objections to it, the commissioners took Meyerson with them, for the Mayor had said that Gardner would be present. Meyerson insisted that, apart from its other inadequacies, the compromise would mean too high a population density in the projects built on slum sites;

an acceptable density, he argued, would be no greater than that previously recommended by the Plan Commission. Gardner agreed that the Plan Commission's standard should apply, but he wanted to interpret it differently. The Mayor and the aldermen were unwilling to try to understand the points the two technicians were making. They should get together and stay together until they could agree, the Mayor said.

Nearly a week later the meeting reconvened. Meyerson and Gardner had deliberated with each other but had reached no conclusion. (Some citizen leaders urged that ex-Mayor Kelly be called in to help solve the housing impasse—a suggestion aimed in part to embarrass Kennelly.) The Council was meeting that very morning and the Mayor hoped that a housing program could be placed before it for action at once. Outside the Mayor's office there were hundreds of people who had come to City Hall expecting action. The opposition, 600 strong and wearing white badges reading, "We are Opposed to Public Housing," came from a rally held at a Catholic parish house where it had been decided to pack the gallery. The proponents, on the streets outside, were represented by 150 pickets, who marched up and down in front of almost as many policemen. The pickets carried signs demanding that the Mayor "End Jim Crow Housing" and "Build on Vacant Land."

Inside the Mayor's office, there was a new face. It was that of Ralph H. Burke, a consulting engineer who did much work for the city on airports, parks and other public works (it was to Burke's firm that Mayor Kelly had retired) and who had now been called in by the Mayor, Duffy, and Lancaster to advise them on the technical matters which Meyerson had been putting in the way of the compromise. Burke was a very able man. He had, moreover, an advantage over Meyerson which would count heavily with public opinion: he had many years of experience in the city and a flourishing consulting practice.

Burke now became the Mayor's technical specialist on housing. Within a few days, as soon as he had familiarized himself with the situation, he began meeting with the Authority staff on behalf of the City Hall.

For some time the public housing forces had been seeking to regain the offensive. In order to discourage Taylor and the other commissioners from compromising, some of the Public Housing Association heads invited about 30 Negro leaders to a meeting. Only a few came, but all of these claimed to have great influence with Taylor and all said they were strongly opposed to compromise. N. M. Willis, president of the local branch of the National Association for the Advancement of Colored People, subsequently wrote the commissioners setting forth two basic principles of site selection on which he said the Authority should not yield: 1. All sites should be on vacant land, and 2. The sites should be "large enough to make an impact on the surrounding neighborhood instead of being swallowed up by it." Willis observed in his letter, that, "It is not enough for us to get underway a housing program, just any housing program. It must be a good housing program. . . ." A firm stand by the Authority, he added, would help the Council members understand their role and function in site selection.

Except for Willis, none of the Negro leaders who was at the meeting seems actually to have tried to influence Taylor—at least Taylor could not later remember that any of them spoke to him. The only pressure he was aware of came from Negroes who were opposed to the housing program. There were plenty of these, he said later; indeed, probably many of Taylor's upper class Negro associates were opposed to it.

The public housing group also sought the intervention of President Truman, who came to Chicago in the middle of May to make a speech. The Independent Voters of Illinois pointed out to the President in an open letter that only two Democratic aldermen, Merriam and Becker, had spoken in favor of the Authority's sites. The United Packinghouse Workers Union held a noon rally of 20,000 workers in the stockyards the day of the President's visit to protest the Democratic administration's failure to provide housing in Chicago. Privately several influential people tried to get the President to prod the local Democrats, but apparently they did not succeed. When he reached that part of his prepared address in which he pledged his support of public housing, the President *ad libbed,* "And you sure need it here in Chicago!" But he made no other public statement.[18]

A nearer source of support was the Public Housing Administration, which, since it would have to approve any program that might be agreed to by the Council, was in a highly strategic position. In December, a Washington newspaper had quoted a PHA spokesman as saying that, while local communities might decide whether or not to segregate projects racially, the Federal agency would insist that all races be treated "equitably" in any proposed public housing program. In the middle of May the Authority obtained from the Commissioner of PHA, John Taylor Egan, a telegram which, although somewhat cryptic, gave the Mayor and his lieutenants concern. "The Public Housing Administration," the wire said, "cannot approve a program which does not accommodate various racial groups of low income on the basis of their respective housing needs." This message, taken together with the fact that in another city the PHA had just disapproved an all-Negro housing program, strengthened the Authority's position. However, a more detailed and specific statement was needed from PHA. Accordingly Miss Wood went to Washington with Meyerson to see the commissioner and his first assistant, Warren Jay Vinton.

Vinton had been a leader of the pro-public housing forces on the national scene for many years. He was an energetic, intelligent, and devoted administrator who was the author (with Benjamin Stolberg) in 1935 of a critique of the New Deal called *The Economic Consequences of the New Deal.* Vinton was also a long-standing friend of Miss Wood.

When Miss Wood told the Mayor that she and Meyerson were going to Washington to see the heads of PHA he suggested that Burke go along to present the City Hall's viewpoint. Miss Wood and Meyerson met with Vinton and the assistant commissioner for field operations, in advance of the appointment with Egan. They found Vinton and his associate wholly receptive to the CHA program (the revised package).

But later, when Burke came for the conference with Egan, the prospect changed. Burke declared that he was no politician—

just an engineer—but he happened to have been told by people who *were* politicians that there was absolutely no chance that the Council would accept any program except the Duffy-Lancaster one. When Egan and Vinton heard this, they were obviously distressed. In many cities, public housing, one of the Fair Deal's most advertised accomplishments, was in difficulties. If it should fail in Chicago, one of the great strongholds of the Democratic Party, the President and the Party would be very much embarrassed, for it was the Democrats, as the President and the campaign orators had often said, who were responsible for public housing. Egan and Vinton were uneasy: they wanted the Council to accept a good, or at least a defensible, housing program, but they could not run any risk of killing the program altogether. Chicago had to have public housing—good public housing, if possible, but public housing anyway.

Much to the surprise of Miss Wood and Meyerson, Egan and Vinton were conciliatory in their conversation with Burke. They made it plain that they would approve the program if four conditions were met: 1. The Chicago Plan Commission's standards of density would have to be respected. 2. The total supply of housing in Chicago could not be decreased. 3. The program could not be racially discriminatory. (A 50-50 division of units between whites and Negroes would be "equitable," Egan and Vinton said, but a program which was 60 per cent Negro and 40 per cent white would probably be "approvable." This implied that some "white" slum sites would have to be added to the Duffy-Lancaster program so that some of the people displaced—and therefore some of the people re-housed—would be white. On this point Burke hesitated, repeating that he was not a politician; finally, however, he agreed that it might be possible to add a white slum site to the program.) 4. The displacement of such large numbers of people as would occur under the Duffy-Lancaster plan was serious and could be disastrous, the PHA officials said, and they strongly urged that more vacant land be added. But they carefully refrained from saying that they would reject the program if more were not added.

At the end of the conference, Egan and Vinton advised Miss

Wood and Meyerson to be practical, to take the long view, and to remember that, after all, the basic intent of the Act was just to provide housing.*

A few days later, after Miss Wood had returned to her office in Chicago, Vinton, who had conferred with the race relations advisers in the housing agency, telephoned her. He said that after further discussion with his staff and with Foley, administrator of the parent agency (the Housing and Home Finance Agency), the great hardship that would be brought about by the program, particularly on families who would be displaced without being eligible for public housing, had come sharply to his attention. Accordingly, he wanted to stress the necessity of construction on vacant land.

These later thoughts were not likely to be of much avail now, however. The Authority did not have to be persuaded of the need for more vacant land, and Burke and the Mayor now knew that little change in the Duffy-Lancaster plan need be made to get it approved by PHA. Since now everyone concerned believed that Washington would accept almost any program approved by the Council, the Authority's position was worsened.

Burke and his staff had meanwhile prepared an elaborate and persuasive report (for which the Authority much to its surprise was subsequently billed) in which he claimed that projects could be built on the Duffy-Lancaster sites without causing a relocation problem, and therefore, without necessitating the use of additional vacant land. Burke's idea was to build the projects before tearing down the slums—to build them in stages in the alleys, vacant lots and other interstices of the slum sites, tearing down slum dwellings only as units of the projects became ready for occupancy. In this way the Negro slum-dwellers (although the Burke report did not mention Negroes) presumably could be re-housed without moving them out of their existing districts.

---

* "Dear Warren," wrote Walter H. Blucher, executive director of the American Society of Planning Officials, from Chicago to his old friend Vinton, "What value is there in stiffening the backs of planners if public officials themselves weasel and compromise. . . . When we finally succeed in getting a housing authority which is willing to stand for a decent minimum program, it is pretty sad when the Federal officials won't back up that kind of a program. Political expediency is a very poor rationalization for abject surrender." (May 31, 1950.)

"Probably," the Burke report said, "the most controversial element in the entire re-housing problem and the one which in the minds of many constitutes a barrier to the ready application of re-housing in slum areas centers around the temporary relocation and placement of persons now residing in the slum areas to be redeveloped.

"Some urge that the rebuilding in the slum areas must be deferred until the new 'low rent' housing is built on vacant land elsewhere. Admittedly under the 'low rent' program only a part of the residents of slum areas (those with 'low incomes' as defined in the Act) could be accepted in such new housing. This is therefore not a solution of the problem.

"A careful study of the slum areas has led to the conclusion that rebuilding of the areas can proceed without delay, without demolishing the existing houses and without a tedious and intricate problem of temporary relocation of persons.

"While the existing tenement buildings are grossly overcrowded the areas in which slum housing is located are not overcrowded. In every instance, there are available vacant lots, open spaces and parts of streets which can be closed; and upon these available spaces, the first units of the redeveloped housing can be built, without destroying a single house and without dispossessing a single person.

"In each of the areas under study a preliminary site plan of the new housing has been made and it has proved that a substantial start on redevelopment can be made before any demolition is necessary. A procedure of stage development has been worked out in each area which will permit the completion of new units far in advance of the demolition of old buildings and in much greater numbers at every stage of the program than the number of old buildings removed.

"The result of such a procedure would be not only to avoid costly delays in the program, but also to make permanent homes immediately available without temporary relocations for those residents of the area who can qualify for admittance to a 'low-rent' housing project. It would also create additional units for the admission of other families of 'low-income' now residing in other areas thus freeing up available houses for those families in the next level of income who cannot qualify for 'low-rent' housing but who also cannot pay an economic rent required by private builders of new homes.

"The group enjoying the highest bracket of income who are finally displaced in the last stage of reconstruction may well be accommodated in such projects as the New York Life Insurance Company or the non-profit group now interested in housing or others who might be induced to enter the field with Federal and local aid offered through the Land Clearance Commission."[19]

The attractiveness of Burke's scheme, from the aldermen's standpoint, was that it seemed to keep the Negroes where they were and so prevented the deterioration of property values and the other undesirable effects which were said to come from the movement of Negroes into outlying white areas. But from the standpoint of the public housing supporters, most of whom not only favored public housing but favored public housing without segregation, this was a serious disadvantage. Yet, because the idea of using public housing to break down segregation was not accepted by public opinion generally, the public housing supporters could not be fully open about one of their strongest objections to the Burke scheme. If they had explained that they opposed the scheme largely because it perpetuated existing patterns of residential segregation, not even a majority of the commissioners, to say nothing of the aldermen, would have supported them.

The idea of stage development was not new to the Authority; it had already built one project in stages. But the Authority's conception of stage development was very different from Burke's. He proposed building on cross streets and alleys as well as on vacant land; this involved building across utility lines, something which, if it was feasible at all, might involve a great deal of additional expense. Burke, moreover, was proposing very tall buildings which in many cases would be so close to adjacent structures as to violate the city's ordinances and regulations on housing, zoning, and fire protection; some of these ordinances and regulations could well be suspended temporarily, but others—those concerning access for fire fighting equipment, for example—could not be.

These objections to Burke's scheme were grave, but even more important from the standpoint of the Planning Division was the high density it would entail. Burke himself calculated that after the final stage the density would be 36 dwelling units per gross acre (a gross acre includes roads and other land uses besides housing); in public housing with its families of large size, this might mean as many as 100,000 persons per square mile, which was twice the density the Plan Commission had previously recommended. Burke's sketches showed an abundance of open and play space between units, but when the CHA technicians scaled the drawings they found that they were far from realistic. Moreover, Burke calculated existing density in numbers of dwelling units, a basis which took no account of the large number of families who were doubled up. Thus, although Burke claimed that his proposal would increase the total amount of housing, the Authority calculated on the basis of existing *families* rather than dwelling units, that fewer units would be provided than there were families who would be displaced. Indeed, the Authority found that almost as many Negro families would be displaced as new units would be built; this meant that practically all of the new housing would have to be allocated to Negroes, an arrangement which CHA was loathe to make both because it favored bi-racial projects and because it was obligated to serve whites as well as Negroes.

It was hard for Meyerson to persuade the commissioners and, later, the aldermen that the high density was a significant objection to Burke's plan. They pointed out to him that in the "Gold Coast" neighborhoods the density was even higher. To this he replied that the upper income families who lived there were able to go elsewhere for recreation, whereas low income families (who, incidentally, usually had more children than the upper income people) would have to take their recreation on the site. Meyerson also contended that an increase in density would necessitate a series of further adaptive changes to bring about a new ecological balance: changes in the transportation system would be required, and also changes in the distribution of stores, schools, parks, churches and other features of city life.

From the point of view of many of the aldermen, of course, high density was the chief advantage of Burke's plan. It seemed to keep the Negroes in the Negro area while making it possible for the politicians to claim that they had increased the total number of dwelling units. Whatever might be the merits of the CHA's arguments, the aldermen could see that they were so technical that the Authority would not be able to put them before the public in a persuasive way. That being the case, they could as well be ignored.

Although it did not press the point with the aldermen, another and very important objection that the Authority staff had to the Burke scheme was that the slum buildings among which the projects were to be constructed might not all be torn down. If the housing shortage continued and if no vacant land were provided for relocation projects, it might prove very difficult and perhaps impossible to demolish the old slums. And if the old buildings remained standing, the areas would, of course, be incredibly overcrowded by the addition of public housing.

In advising the commissioners, the planning staff stressed two principal points: 1. The Authority should not develop part of any site, or any entire site, unless and until it had guarantees that the other agencies concerned—especially the Department of Superhighways, the Land Clearance Commission, and the City Council itself—would do their part to carry out the whole program. The staff said Burke's bland assurance that the agencies would do their part once the Authority began building had to be supplemented by statements from the agencies themselves. 2. The Authority should not approve any particular site apart from a program of sites; the acceptability of a site should be decided in the light of its effect upon the whole public housing program.

The commissioners seemed to agree to these principles, and so the planning staff went on to spell out their implications in some detail. This was first done by fixing a set of standards in conjunction with the Plan Commission staff as a basis for discussions with Burke. The standards were as follows: 1. Planning for rebuilding should be in terms of "residential development units"*

* This term was adopted in preference to "neighborhood unit," because Reginald Isaacs, then the planning director of the Michael Reese Hospital in Chicago had indicated that the "neighborhood unit" concept had been employed in city planning as an avenue to racial and class segregation. His position is summarized in "The Neighborhood Theory," *International Federation for Housing and Town Planning News Sheet,* No. X, September 1948, pp. 6-8.

rather than of small isolated sites; 2. The minimum size of such a unit, especially when surrounded by commercial and industrial land uses, should be that required for about 1,000 families—enough to support facilities such as schools and parks adequately; 3. The maximum average density should be about 30 dwelling units per acre (including streets and neighborhood facilities); 4. Rebuilding within a unit should be on a scale sufficient to permit closing of all, or nearly all, through streets; and 5. An area should not be designated for current rebuilding if it contained a large number of commercial and industrial properties which would tend to break the residential development into small segments.[20]

These standards which were agreed to jointly by the Plan Commission and CHA staffs were supplemented by five more policies which referred to CHA alone: 1. In an area containing commercial-industrial properties, CHA would not develop part of a residential unit unless other agencies, public or private, agreed to develop other nearby parts; 2. CHA would not displace a large number of industries or businesses unless suitable relocation areas existed for them; 3. CHA would not spend more than $2,000 per dwelling unit for land acquisition, including demolition and all site improvements; 4. CHA would pro-rate public housing equally between the needs of whites and nonwhites; and 5. CHA would accept no program which would not provide an immediate and sizeable net addition to Chicago's housing supply.[21] The last three of these standards expressed Federal as well as local policy.

With these declarations the planning staff had considerably clarified some of the Authority's ends. Knowing what it wanted, however, was not enough; the real choice now, it was rapidly becoming clear, lay between a version of Burke's program and no program at all.

Burke's scheme had been only a modification of the Duffy-Lancaster one to begin with. On his return from Washington, Burke added one "white" slum site (actually, as the planning staff soon discovered, this site was in rapid transition and would in the normal course of events be almost entirely Negro before a project could be built) and he revised somewhat the number of units planned for the other sites. The program was still virtually an all-Negro one, however, and it violated all of the standards that the

Plan Commission and CHA staffs had set.

At the end of the first week in June, Meyerson believed that the commissioners should reject the City Hall compromise and put forward a new plan of their own. "The staff has attempted in all ways that it could to make this program workable," he wrote. "Until the last days, the staff almost felt that it could succeed in converting this program into a workable program. However, the more the staff analyzed this program the more it became apparent that unless new sites not previously considered were to be included in the program and others excluded, the program would be a discriminatory one." Meyerson concluded that the program, to be feasible and desirable, should be either: a) smaller, with a better balance of vacant land and blighted areas and of units for Negro and white occupancy; or, b) larger—perhaps being a two or more year program—and providing such a balance.

It was now nearly seven months since Taylor had gone to the Mayor with the initial package of sites. During most of this time the Authority's position seemed to the public housing supporters, and to the opponents as well, to have been growing somewhat stronger. The fiasco of the "bus-window" sites had made the Council look ridiculous and the weakness and ineptness of the Mayor had become more apparent every day. The prestige which the City Hall had lost the Authority seemed to have gained.

But somehow the Authority's position had begun to erode by the first of May. Perhaps the erosion began early in April when the Mayor intervened to prevent the housing committee from voting on the Authority's second package. Or perhaps it was the Duffy-Lancaster compromise, and especially Burke's ingenious defense of it, which got the process underway. Again, it may have been the discovery by the Mayor and Duffy that they had no reason to fear a veto from PHA in Washington. At any rate, by the middle of June it was clear to both supporters and opponents that the Council might not pass any housing program at all.

Certainly one reason why CHA's position had worsened was that the press had lost interest in the struggle.

The press campaign reached its crescendo at the end of March, when the aldermen were considering the "bus-window" sites. Not only the *Sun-Times* but other newspapers as well at that time carried the housing news in banner headlines on the front page. But only a month later, when the Duffy-Lancaster plan was announced, the *Sun-Times* devoted little attention to it.[22] The Negro press showed the same loss of interest. It criticized the City Hall proposal, to be sure, but it did so in a half-hearted way; the fury that some of the pro-public housing groups looked for from it was lacking.

At the beginning of May, David Anderson, who had been writing daily news stories and frequent features, was taken off the housing beat by the *Sun-Times*. Apparently the editors had decided that the housing campaign had been carried far enough. It was the *Sun-Times*' promise of support, of course, which had been decisive in persuading Taylor to fight the housing issue in public rather than to seek a compromise. Various explanations were now given for its sudden defection. Field's New York lawyer, who was a cousin of one of the Public Housing Association leaders, had died suddenly, and some said that it was the removal of his influence which had changed the newspaper's policy. Others believed that the change was due to the ascendancy in the *Sun-Times* of the young Marshall Field (the following October young Field became the paper's active head) who was regarded as more conservative than his father. Some of the public housing supporters believed that Taylor and McMillen had gone to the editors of the *Sun-Times* to ask them to stop their campaign so that they, the commissioners, could make a settlement with City Hall. According to this opinion, it was the commissioners, not the editors, who had "sold out."

Any or all of these explanations may have been correct. But there was another factor which, regardless of the weight that might be attached to any of these, may have accounted partly for the action of the *Sun-Times*, the *Daily News* and the other newspapers which lost interest in public housing at about the same time. This was that the struggle had become so protracted and so complicated as to be tiresome to editors and readers alike. To keep track of its vicissitudes—to know which sites were now under consideration, and why they were or were not acceptable—was a full-time occupation. The technical staff of CHA managed to keep abreast of all developments, but people who had other interests—even the commissioners—found it almost impossible to know what was going on. The newspaper editors, probably having themselves become bored with the interminable twists and turns of the housing story, may have felt sure that their readers were bored with it too, as indeed they very likely must have been. Not only had the housing struggle become tiresome, but the issue, now that Burke had embellished the City Hall proposal, was no longer simple enough to be explained in headlines and a few leading paragraphs. To make sense of it required more time and effort than either the editors or readers were willing to spend. "We're not a crusading paper," the chief editorial writer of one newspaper at this time told a reporter who had been covering housing. "It's all right to get on something for a time, but you don't have to make a career of it."[23]

Then in June 1950, the fighting in Korea began and the site selection struggle faded even farther into the background of public interest. Korea was a good excuse, if any was needed, to think about something else. The opposition, which was steadily becoming better organized, now demanded that public housing be stopped lest needed materiel be diverted from Korea.

Anderson later believed that if the *Sun-Times* had continued its campaign a somewhat better housing program would have resulted. "I think we had them on the run—up to a point," he told Meyerson later. "I think if we had kept up the pressure, we'd have gotten a little more." But any victory would have been a partial and temporary one. "They would have got you some other way," he remarked afterward.[24]

By June, Taylor, who had never been fully convinced that a public fight could be won against the "Big Boys," was sure that the longer the struggle continued the less would be the Authority's bargaining power. He had seen in the beginning, he said later, that the Mayor and Duffy, while they might be prodded by editorials in the *Sun-Times*, were under no compulsion to provide any housing at all—and certainly not housing to meet the specifications of the Authority; if they saw fit, the "Big Boys" could ignore the housing issue altogether. As the struggle progressed, Taylor thought he saw that Duffy and the others were increasingly contemptuous of the influence of the public housing forces; the aldermen had not rated the power of the public housing supporters highly at the start, and now they believed that their judgment was confirmed. Taylor felt so too, and the fact that he felt so no doubt helped to confirm the aldermen in their impression. It was the opponents of public housing who had shown—if the galleries were any indication—that they had popular support. The pro-public housers had talked big, but they had not been able to produce. So at least it seemed to Taylor.

Taylor's experience with one alderman was typical, he said later, of his experience with at least five other aldermen. This alderman told him in the autumn of 1949 that he would "go along." In December, the alderman was not so sure. In May he came to Taylor and said, "Every time I go home I get an earful from people who are opposed to the projects—I get it in church, in the grocery store, in the tavern, and even from the kids at school." Finally, early in June, he said, "I'm sorry, but I can't support you."[25]

Becker, one of the three ardent public housers among the aldermen, found that the prospect of two projects being located there had created a good deal of feeling in his ward. Two-thirds of his mail consisted of letters opposing his stand on public housing. Of the letters which approved his stand, half came from outside of the ward. These were mostly from organizations such as the American Veterans' Committee. He was continually embarrassed to see prominent Jews and representatives of Jewish organizations join forces with the anti-public housers. When the rabbi of his own temple complained to him that public housing would destroy the Jewish community in the ward, Becker reminded him sharply that when he (Becker) came into the community 18 years before there were signs here and there which read, "No Jews Allowed" and "Only Gentiles Need Apply." Should the Jews do to the Negroes what the Gentiles had done to them?

Despite his arguments, Becker found that the anti-housing sentiment of the Jewish community was growing. Finally, all of the Jewish organizations in his ward except two had taken a stand against him. He went to Rosen, Freifeld, and other ADL leaders in distress. "What is my responsibility?" he asked. "Should I do what the people of my ward want, or should I do what I know is good for the whole community? Where does my duty lie?"* [26]

The Anti-Defamation League, and on its invitation three other city-wide Jewish organizations—the American Jewish Committee, the American Jewish Congress, and the Jewish Labor Committee—called a meeting of the rabbis and other Jewish leaders in Becker's ward. An ADL spokesman told them that a grave situation existed in the ward. The action of the City Hall in placing two public housing sites in the ward was nothing less than a Machiavellian scheme to test the integrity of the Jews. " 'These Jews,' " he quoted one of the "Big Boys" as saying, " 'they're for FEPC, for civil rights laws, for everything decent; they're even for public housing—except in their own wards.' "[27] It was up to the Jewish community to frustrate this attempt to make Jews appear hypocritical. Finally everyone present decided to support Alderman Becker in his fight for public housing, and also in his opposition to the poorly located sites in the ward.

The ADL representatives were aware, of course, that dislike of the Negro or of "lower class" people was not the only, or perhaps even the main, reason for opposition to the projects within the ward. The Jews of the 40th Ward did not like the idea of being singled out for punishment because their alderman had supported public housing; anti-semitism, they believed, was the only possible ground on which those sites could have been selected. Therefore, some who were not at all adverse to having low-income Negroes for neighbors vigorously opposed the sites.

Meanwhile, the Negroes remained relatively passive. Most of the Negroes, being lower class, were inarticulate or had few opportunities to express themselves. The articulate Negro community—which, of course, was largely middle and upper class—appeared to be very little interested in the housing problem or at least the site problem. "The powerful colored political leaders in Chicago who maintain influence in Washington and also here in Chicago

* "I regarded Alderman Becker's conduct as having noble and heroic proportions," Freifeld wrote later in a letter to the authors. "He constantly contemplated the nature of his responsibilities, locally and city-wide, but never for a moment was there the slightest indication that every decision was not made with integrity and honesty and civic loyalty."

have remained mute and silent on this housing tragedy," the Negro newspaper, the *Chicago Defender,* observed. Some important middle and upper class Negroes were known to be actively opposed to public housing.[28]

If the position of the public housing supporters had weakened, the leaders of the Public Housing Association saw fit to ignore it. Early in June they sent a delegation to the CHA commissioners to insist that there be no compromise and to suggest that the Authority submit a new package consisting mainly of vacant land sites. Benjamin was the only commissioner at all receptive to this suggestion.

From the Metropolitan Housing and Planning Council the commissioners received quite different advice. Its president, Ferd Kramer, wrote them a letter calling the City Hall plan unworkable and saying it would so worsen the city's relocation problem that all other slum clearance programs would have to mark time. Nevertheless, "in the interest of action," he urged the Board to accept those of the proposed sites on which there was agreement and to continue to look for more. By agreeing to a smaller initial program, he said, the Authority might be able to get a workable ratio of vacant to slum sites.[29]

This was a position that Meyerson had taken two weeks earlier. If the Authority wished to insist upon a ratio of 50 per cent vacant land (and he believed that it should), it might achieve its aim by reducing the number of slum site units to 2,000, which was the amount of housing Duffy and Lancaster were willing to build on vacant land.

Meyerson believed that there was even a possibility that Duffy and Lancaster, if they were approached by the CHA staff privately and in a conciliatory spirit, could be made to see that in terms of *their* ends, not those of the Authority, there were serious defects in the compromise program, defects which could be removed by the addition of more units on vacant land. He was sure that the aldermen did not fully realize that a slum clearance program unaccompanied by relocation housing on vacant land would inevitably push the Negroes into outlying white neighborhoods—the very thing the aldermen most wanted to avoid.* He thought, too, that Duffy and Lancaster did not realize what heavy costs in city services their program of high density slum-site housing would entail.

However, it was now too late to discuss these matters with the aldermen. Taylor had told Miss Wood that the time for negotiating was at an end, and she therefore did not—as Meyerson hoped she might—ask him to go see Duffy and Lancaster.

Taylor did not believe that the views of the staff ought to be decisive in the question of whether or not to accept the compromise. "I felt there were three groups we ought to satisfy," he later explained. "One was the commissioners. Another was the *Sun-Times*. The third was Washington."

The commissioners were already satisfied, not that the program was a good one (although apparently it pleased Kruse), but that it was the best that they could get and a good deal better than nothing. When this was clear, Taylor called Marshall Field and explained the situation. Field asked for a day or two to make some inquiries. The next day, the managing editor of the *Sun-Times,* who probably had never been pleased by the paper's public housing crusade anyway, called Taylor back to say that it seemed wise to accept the City Hall compromise.

Taylor then called Washington. Vinton said, as Taylor later recalled, "We ought to try to approach the White House on this. Give me five days to see if we can get the President to intervene."

After several days had passed, the Mayor called Taylor. "What are you waiting for?" the Mayor asked, as Taylor later recalled. "Don't you realize that I'm having a terrible time trying to hold our support together in the Council? Why can't you make up your mind?"

"I'm not quite ready," Taylor replied.

"Why not?"

"Well, I'm sorry, but I'm just not ready."

Finally Vinton called back to say that everything had been done that could be done and that Taylor should accept the compro-

* By 1953 the spread of displaced Negroes had so alarmed the politicians that the Plan Commission passed a resolution urging that slum area redevelopment be discontinued until additional housing could be built.

mise if it were not racially discriminatory, if densities were not too high, and if certain technical requirements were met.[30]

What happened in Washington, according to one source, was that Egan, the PHA commissioner, asked a vice-chairman of the Democratic National Committee to intervene with Kennelly. "OK," the vice-chairman said, "you just clear it with Dawson first." Dawson, it will be recalled, was the Congressman who was the political boss of the Black Belt and himself a vice-chairman of the National Committee. Dawson, according to our informant, was unwilling to have the Committee intervene. He is supposed to have said that he would do nothing until the people of his district "squawked"—when they got hurt, then he would be for vacant land sites.[31]

Dawson himself later denied this account. He said that he was never approached in regard to the housing controversy by anyone connected with the Democratic National Committee. He added that he and Alderman Harvey had been in perfect agreement on the public housing issue (Dawson was Harvey's ward committeeman, it will be remembered) and that both of them had always staunchly supported CHA proposals, including the proposal to build on vacant land. Harvey had in fact, for a long time, opposed the site in his own ward (*supra,* p. 175) and also played a major part in trying to substitute the "bus-window" sites for those proposed by the Authority (*supra,* p. 190). Dawson's statements about the parts he and Harvey played in the site selection struggle were made several years after it was over and his memory may have been faulty.

On June 16, since there had been no Washington intervention, immediately after hearing the formal report which Burke was to present to the Mayor later that day, Kruse moved acceptance of the City Hall sites. Taylor and McMillen voted for the motion. Sykes was absent but had indicated to Taylor that he was in favor of the compromise program. Benjamin voted against it on the grounds that it was unfair to both whites and Negroes and could not be completed in a reasonable time.

"The critical housing condition," Taylor wrote to Lancaster now that the decision had been made, "necessitates an end to the impasse which has existed. Accordingly, even though the site approvals we are requesting here vary from the program we originally advocated and though we still believe that greater emphasis should be placed upon building on vacant land in the beginning stages of this six-year federal program, nevertheless we believe the program we are submitting will be of benefit to the city when achieved."[32]

"AW, THEY WON'T BUILD—LET'S PLAY HOUSE"

CHAPTER EIGHT ☐ ☐ ☐ ☐ ☐ ☐

SETTLEMENT

THE STRUGGLE was not over, however. The compromise had still to be approved by the housing committee and by the full Council, and there were some who believed that the Mayor and Duffy could not—or would not—muster the necessary 26 votes.

Indeed there seemed to be more opposition to the compromise than there had been to the Authority's first proposal. The property owners, the realtors, and the local merchants—and so of course the aldermen responsive to them—were as much opposed as ever, perhaps even more. The size of the projects on vacant sites had been cut very drastically, but the property owners objected to these smaller scale projects as much as they had to the larger ones. They would, it was plain, try to defeat the housing program altogether or at least to eliminate all of the vacant sites.

To the votes of the irreconcilable anti-public housers were now added those of several middle-of-the-roaders who had been expected to support the program. The long delay in reaching the compromise had made it more difficult for some friendly aldermen to withstand the pressures put upon them. And then at last the most ardent supporters of public housing—Becker, Merriam, and Carey—declared they would vote against the compromise. As Ralph J. Finitzo, the building contractor who was one of the leaders of the opposition, afterwards remarked, nobody liked the compromise. "The Mayor told the Housing Authority they could have a bone and be happy," Finitzo said, "and then they told me that at least they had cut the size of the project in my neighborhood down to 300 units and that was my bone. So no one was happy."[1]

Becker was perhaps the least happy of all. When the compromise was brought before the housing committee he accused the CHA commissioners of "chicanery" and "hypocrisy" and demanded public hearings on the new sites. The committee approved the compromise after a three-hour wrangle, but Lancaster agreed to hold further hearings in the middle of July.

The situation was now badly confused. The Authority was defending a program which it had opposed only a little while before. Becker, who had been one of its most devoted supporters, was now its foe. The pro-public housing forces—the Negro, church, labor, and other liberal groups—were divided and uncertain. Should they agree to a housing program which would maintain and extend and by implication even make official, residential congestion and segregation? Or should they oppose the program, and so lose an opportunity to get more public housing than had yet been built in Chicago?

Now that no one was any longer enthusiastic in support of the program and many were opposed to it, there seemed to be a good chance that it would be voted down. Even if it were not voted down, it might still be nullified. Two aldermen were understood to be planning an amendment to strike out the vacant land sites from the compromise, thus rendering it wholly unacceptable to the Authority and to PHA in Washington. To pass an amendment required only a majority of those present, whereas to pass an ordinance required a majority of the whole Council. Therefore, unless the Mayor and Duffy could maintain the most rigid discipline, the compromise would be defeated.

If all else failed, the opposition might be able to secure a referendum on the issue. To do that it would be necessary to get 520,000 signatures on a petition, but most of the 1,500 members of the Chicago Real Estate Board were willing to circulate petitions and so it was not altogether impossible to get the issue on the ballot the next November.[2] Other cities had rejected public housing in referenda, and Chicago might do so too.

When the time came to prepare for the second hearings, the Strategy Committee was determined to profit by the lessons of the first. Well in advance, it circularized the pro-public housing organizations with an "action bulletin" which gave directions for preventing the gallery from being filled by the anti-housing claque.

"A minimum quota of twenty-five persons per organization has been set in order to guarantee the desired result," the bulletin said.

Freifeld had now become a principal influence in the Public Housing Association. He objected strongly—as we have indicated —to an arrangement whereby a representative like himself, who he claimed could speak for an organization of 35,000 members, had no more weight in the affairs of the Association than others who could speak only for themselves. Unless the Association's board were reorganized to give 12 of 35 votes to B'nai B'rith and the organizations which were usually associated with it, the leaders of these groups warned they would set up a competing organization. "We were not seeking control," an official of one of these organizations explained later, "we were only trying to box in the more dangerous potentialities of some of the Association's leaders while making use of their talents."[3] To the Association's leaders, however, it seemed clear enough that Freifeld and his associates were seeking control. Nevertheless they agreed to this proposal for reorganizing the board, since these organizations could not be spared. The Association was under altered direction and its name was shortly changed to the Housing Conference of Chicago.

The public housing supporters, Freifeld thought, were now reasonably well organized. He himself was spending most of his time on housing and he had two office helpers working nearly full-time on housing. In addition A. Abbott Rosen, ADL's executive head, devoted much of his time to the issue. The CIO had a representative who spent more than one-third time for several months on housing. Public housing was one of the Congregational Union's major projects for the year and Adrian Robson, the representative of the Union, spent a large part of his time on it. Morris H. Hirsh, the executive director of the South Side Planning Board, and representatives of the Independent Voters of Illinois and other organizations spent smaller amounts of time.

But while the public housing supporters might have better success in bringing forth testifiers and spectators this time, it was not at all clear whether they should have them applaud or boo. Was this or that site a good one or a bad one? Was the program as a whole acceptable or not? On these questions there was no agreement. "It is the consensus of the pro-housers that the present program is inadequate," the Strategy Committee's Action Bulletin said. "An ideal housing program for Chicago would have larger vacant land sites, less concentration of units on slum sites, would include more sites in predominantly white slum areas and would make provisions for more humane relocation. Beyond this general statement, final policy and strategy has not been decided."[4]

On the day before the hearings, when the Strategy Committee met, Freifeld, following the lead of Aldermen Becker and Carey, argued that it would be good strategy to oppose the compromise in the hope of improving it. Although he knew that his organization would support almost any public housing program if the alternative was no program at all, he maintained that the City Council had been anti-semitic in locating the two sites in Becker's ward and that this justified at least partial opposition to the compromise. Shufro and Liveright agreed with this position; however they were for giving the compromise limited support (as well as criticism), not because they liked it, but because they were afraid that large-scale opposition by the public housing supporters would be used as an excuse for killing the program altogether and leaving responsibility for its death with the public housing group.

In a letter to Freifeld, Liveright (who had expected to be out of town when the Strategy Committee met) gave four reasons for supporting the compromise: "1. It would at least indicate that Chicago intends to move ahead on some public housing, 2. It establishes a principle of public housing on vacant land sites, 3. If present opponents to public housing defeat even this program I believe the chances for getting any decent future public housing program are almost non-existent, and 4. If this program is defeated the chances of the Real Estate Board moving ahead on a referendum will, I think, be greatly increased." The Strategy Committee adopted this position.[5]

Although they had no intention of sacrificing anything of practical value, Freifeld, Shufro and Liveright formulated their strategy with an eye to the instrumental-abstract significance of the issue. For Freifeld, a principal issue was anti-semitism; for all of them, a principal issue was the standing and bargaining position of the public housing movement at some future time. Neither side based its strategy solely on the intrinsic-concrete significance of the issue—of the satisfactions that would or would not accrue to particular consumers of housing. They were concerned, also, with what the public would think about public housing in general (or about Jews) at some future time.

Once the hearings began, it was obvious that the Strategy Committee had not prevented the opposition from packing the gallery once more. The housewives were there, angrier than ever, wearing badges reading "We Want No Public Housing," and ready to hoot, jeer, boo, hiss, and catcall whenever a public housing supporter spoke. Outside City Hall, the anti-public housing forces marched up and down, carrying banners inscribed with the slogans, "Don't Destroy Our Homes," "We Want No Public Housing Camps," and "We Are Against Public Housing."

There were present in the gallery many residents of Altgeld Gardens, a large all-Negro public housing project for which an extension was being proposed. The project residents, who testified, did so on that one site only, they were by no means as excited as were the white property owners, and, since they had come partly to show how respectable they were, they did not boo or hiss.

Alderman DuBois, in whose ward the Altgeld Gardens project was located, opened the testimony. "We are opposed to public housing out our way," he said. "We are against it as a people. We worked for what we got—we expect others to work for what they want. It's not a free ride for anyone."[6]

Cornelius Teninga, the banker and realtor who headed the Taxpayer's Action Committee, spoke later. He attacked the Authority. "They were authorized to give us slum clearance," he said, "and instead have created class hatreds and confusion by their policies which include the seizure of homes at a fraction of their cost and a fraction of the value to their owners.

"For their many high-handed activities injurious to private property and free enterprise this administration should be removed and a new one should replace it which has a sympathy for the institution of private property—

(Applause)

"And is qualified with experience pertaining to real estate.

"We do not understand the principle which places in the hands of social workers an authority which so vitally affects the value of all real estate in the city and influences the essential revenues for local governments which are derived from Real Estate taxes.

"Under a free enterprise, sympathetic administration the problems of Slum Clearance could long since have been solved. Get rid of this alien administration without further delay."

Six Altgeld Gardens tenants testified. All had some special claim to high status (one was a college graduate, another a minister, and a third had a reputation as an orator) and all were members of the project Tenants' Council. These witnesses did their best to justify public housing by the code of private home ownership, a code which they seemed to accept themselves.

Thus, William Chester Robinson, a minister, sought to show that project residents possessed the characteristic virtues—self-reliance, independence, thrift—which are supposed to come from providing for oneself and not from depending upon the government. Under the circumstances—a project built and managed by the government with subsidized rentals—this was not easy, but Robinson tried to make the old image fit the new facts. "We put in our sweat and labor to make Altgeld what it is today," he said. "There were no lawns when we came."

When their turn came to testify, the property owners evoked the same image of frontier self-sufficiency, and they, too, had difficulty making it fit the facts. Thus, in the next day's testimony, the owner of a "pill box" built by a contractor and financed by the Federal Housing Administration, said, "My blood and my wife's blood is in that soil." If it was incongruous for the residents of a government project who had no more than the normal responsibility of renters for the maintenance of grounds and general upkeep to claim the characterological benefits of the frontier, it was hardly less so for the owner of a heavily mortgaged and heavily subsidized pillbox to claim them.

That Altgeld was subsidized also seemed to weigh against it in the eyes of the residents who testified. (They did not perhaps realize that most urban housing since the thirties, whether public or private, benefitted from government subsidies.) "We don't want a free ride, Alderman DuBois," one of them said. "We have not had a park district and we have not had a playground. The only two public agencies operating in Altgeld are the Board of Education and the Board of Public Welfare."

In ideology, the project residents and the home owners had much in common; the main difference between them was that the home owners had a few hundred dollars "down." This was a point that one of them, Larry Eugene, who came from the middle-class community of Jeffrey Manor, stressed on the second day of the hearings. Because he and his neighbors owned their own homes, he said, some people seemed to think that they were so rich that they deserved no consideration at all. "There is nothing in our deeds that says for value received we withdraw from the group of animals known as people," he said. Nor, he went on, were he and his neighbors to be regarded as "real estate lobbyists." Nobody could buy out the leaders of his neighborhood association, he said, "and that goes for all of us fighting this project."

Eugene had four principal objections to the project planned for his area.

"1. We already have one. It is pretty large, and it was there before we came. Some of us who moved in did not know about it, but we didn't attempt to move it out of the neighborhood. It was there—O.K. but we don't need another project. There is no guarantee that Tenth Ward people would be able to live in it, and therefore it would not clear our slums.

"2. There is a terrible school shortage in Jeffrey Manor. I have a little girl who in 1952 will be entering grammar school, and at present it's operating on a double shift. CHA says that if we get a project we'll get all kinds of facilities, but there is absolutely no guarantee of this. If CHA built this project, they would have accomplished their purpose and we would be left holding the bag.

"3. CHA argues that property values have increased in the vicinity of their projects. Maybe in low-value areas, but ours is not such. Property in Jeffrey and Merrionette Manors reaches a value of $12,000,000. We are not forgotten when it comes to assessment of taxes. Taxes on my house are $214 per year.

"4. Another point is the attitude of CHA in this question. They recognize that whenever they want to put up a project on vacant land they are going to get opposition. Instead of conducting an open meeting in Trumbull Park and telling us, 'We are thinking about putting another project in here—we know you don't like it, and we are going to educate you'—they didn't do that. Not at any time were we approached. It seems to me, on the other hand, that the technique was to sneak the thing through. There has never been anything that looked more like a conspiracy. We came down here last time and gave them our opinions and they come right back here like the Politbureau and say, 'No, it must be done.'

"I'll tell you what has been going on in our neighborhood as a result of this stubborn attempt. We are very proud of the houses we have built. Aside from the actual building, every blade of grass and every piece of soil has been handled by us. I bought my home in 1947, and this is the first free summer that I have been able to sit out and enjoy the lawn. I could stay here all day long listing the things we have had to do. I am not going to let a bureaucratic group whose salaries we pay do anything to force me to surrender that.

"Gentlemen, the heart of American life is the home. It was the dream of every G.I. to have a home with a few square feet of lawn and a few kids. We sweated to landscape the place, paint it, and make it grow. Now that we have got that done, CHA insists upon putting in a project which has already done great damage to Jeffrey Manor. In the block where I live, we have already lost two people. These people began thinking about this. They found people accusing them of being this or that because they were against the project. They have moved away.

"Consider the cost at which we are going to provide housing for the ill-housed. Is it worthwhile to build 300 units and wreck the entire area? We are the majority and in America the majority rules. If you remember that we are the people and that we have problems, and if you remember the effect that this project is having on our homes—for example, it is creating unrest and arguments in my home because I am running around trying to do something about the project and my wife objects to so much activity.

"The issue to me is very clear. CHA is supposed to represent the interests of the people of the city of Chicago. City Council is an elected group—elected by the city of Chicago. There cannot be any other answer unless this is Nazi Germany or Soviet Russia or any other totalitarian state. The answer is that the 103rd and Oglesby project shall not go in."

Not all the opponents were white. Some Negroes, perhaps in some cases acting on advice of white strategists, made the same points that were made by the white property owners. One Negro testified:

"Why are we opposed to public housing on vacant land at Lake Park Avenue and Oakwood Boulevard?* First, because we are Chicagoans, and want only good things for our city. That land can and should be used for housing for middle income people. They need housing as badly as those who must go into public housing. Chicago Dwellings Housing would be a way to meet this need.

"Secondly, we recognize this proposal for what it is, the beginning of the destruction of yet another neighborhood where Negroes have bought property.

"Already we are told that there are sociological reasons why our neighborhood must become a slum. After all, the houses were not built yesterday, and Negroes live in them. Also, some Negro small property owner has dared to have a rental unit in the building where he lives. Even though he is operating according to law, he is a criminal, a scoundrel, a public enemy number 1. That neighborhood must be reclassified as blighted.

"All rental property on the South Side must be owned and operated by Draper & Kramer,† the New York Life Insurance Company, outfits like that. Condemn that Negro small owner's land and give it to the Illinois Institute of Technology or anybody, just so it is not another small owner or group of owners. Profit is not for him. We are told all this by some of those who pressure you to put public housing in our neighborhood.

---

* This site was a small vacant one on the Lake Front surrounded by areas which had been rapidly deteriorating.

† Draper & Kramer was the large real estate firm of which Ferd Kramer, head of the Metropolitan Housing and Planning Council, was president.

"In the third place, since we believe in public housing properly used, that is, put good housing where there is bad housing, we object to its misuse because it seems to be clear from all that has happened during the last few months of hearings that the people of Chicago do not like the kind of slum clearance and redevelopment program, including public housing, that has been offered them.

"We realize that misuse of public housing, putting it on land which is too expensive, using it to destroy small property owners, and other abuses, will result in the complete rejection of public housing by the people of Chicago."

The minister of the Grant Memorial African Methodist Episcopal Church brought the books of the church to the Council chamber so that he could show the aldermen that his congregation had invested $150,000 in the church property. "We have members in that community who have invested their life savings in homes," the minister said, "that they might bring their children up in a wholesome atmosphere. We are in favor of housing projects, as any good American citizen would be at this time, but we are opposed to this low rent housing situation being put in our community, for the reason that it will displace many of our members who are supporting not only the church, but supporting our aldermen and the city in making it a better place in which to live.

"As the pastor of the church, and representing a constituency of 3,000 members, I am here representing the church. I do not live in that community, it is true, but I am certainly interested in the people who have their life savings in that community. We feel that we have sufficient land around the City of Chicago, and in slum areas where they can be placed as low renters.

"If there is to be a housing location in that community, it should be for the middle class, who are going to pay taxes.

(Applause)

"Who are going to be supporters of our city and not on relief."

Other Negroes opposed the projects because they realized that the compromise program would increase congestion in the Negro slums. One of these was the Rev. James M. Howard, who lived across the street from one of the proposed sites:

"I am sorry I can't say that I am for Chicago housing for my people, because I am not. I am not for Chicago housing, I am persuaded that Chicago Housing Planning [sic] is against my people.

(Applause)

"And to me that is one of the real reasons for this whole confusion. I think the Negro is at the bottom. We had just as well to be frank and let you know how we feel. I could not afford to come up here and say I was against housing if I believed that housing would give one or two more dwelling places for my people. But I understand that when it is all over we will have less housing than we have now. I don't mean that as a race, but as a people.

"The housing plan, as I understand it, and as I read it, will not increase housing, but decrease housing. And that means we must still live in that ghetto and be penalized for living there. We are forced to live in a ghetto and penalized for living there.

"Just the other day someone said to me that we are overcrowded; that there is a great density. There will be more density when the housing plan is over.

"Therefore, I am against it. I would that those gentlemen of the cloth who appeared here could realize that they can't do it; what it means to be placed in an area where you can't have any let-up, and everywhere you go you are not wanted, and yet you are wanted to be American citizens."

Liveright, testifying for the Public Housing Association, which had decided eventually to accept the compromise, criticized the compromise at this time and blamed the Mayor for it, hoping to improve the housing program thereby.

". . . First of all," he said, "the Public Housing Association urges that the Mayor and the City Council come forth with a workable, well-balanced public housing program immediately, with vacant land sites to balance the slum clearance sites proposed. . . .

"Second, we believe that the responsibility for the inexcusable delay in the compromise housing program now being considered should be squarely placed where it belongs. Had Mayor Kennelly assumed any degree of leadership when the initial sites were presented to him by the Housing Authority almost a year ago, in October 1949 . . .

CHAIRMAN LANCASTER: Mr. Liveright, why don't you confine yourself to the subject before the Committee?

LIVERIGHT: Mr. Chairman, I believe . . .

CHAIRMAN LANCASTER: The report as submitted by the Chicago Housing Authority.

LIVERIGHT: This is a resolution adopted by the Chicago Public Housing Association.

CHAIRMAN LANCASTER: Confine your remarks to the program that is before the Council now.

LIVERIGHT: We believe it is relevant, Mr. Chairman. I will get to the relevant matter. The censored portion here deals with the people that we feel are responsible for the delay, mentioning the Mayor and certain city councilmen. Then, going on to say—no, I won't mention any names.

"The present program is inadequate because it provides no substantial addition to the net housing stockpile in Chicago.

"Second, we believe that it will tend to perpetuate the present pattern and segregation, and is basically discriminatory in nature.

"Third, it will create new slums by the pressure on the marginal areas now surrounding the slum clearance sites.

"Fourth, it makes inadequate provision for rehousing both the low income and middle income families that will be dislocated as a result of condemnation.

"We believe that the real estate interests combined with the improvement associations have misled the people of Chicago in a calculated effort to defeat any public housing.

"Well-built and well-maintained vacant land projects do not deteriorate land values. On the contrary, they add to it."

The representative of the *DuSable Worker,* a version of the *Daily Worker* directed to Negroes in Illinois, testified angrily:

"Had the leaders of the Chicago Housing Authority had the courage of their convictions, they would have come to the people of Chicago with the whole ugly story of how they have been bullied and threatened by persons in high places, who demanded that they either accept this Jim Crow Housing Program, or no program at all.

"The people would have rallied to the side of the Chicago Housing Authority, had they known the truth, and would have forced the retreat of those who opposed a democratic housing program.

"By accepting this program, the Chicago Housing Authority has betrayed its staunchest supporters, the Negro people, who face wholesale eviction from their homes if it should pass."

After four days of hearings, the housing committee went into executive session. Then it appeared that the compromise was in some danger of collapse. Aldermen Bowler and Sain, who had agreed to have a "white" site from their wards added to the program because they thought this might be a way to stop a certain transitional neighborhood from becoming wholly Negro (the Authority would probably have limited Negro occupancy to keep the project bi-racial), now insisted that the site be withdrawn. "A lot of small rooming houses would be torn down to make way for the project," Bowler explained. "That would put those landlords out of business."[7]

If this "white" site were dropped, the compromise would no longer be acceptable to CHA and PHA. The Mayor, Duffy, and Lancaster persuaded Bowler and Sain to agree to a different site a few blocks west. The Authority knew nothing of this change until it was announced by the aldermen. The commissioners accepted the new site, however, although they had almost no information about it. With this change, the housing committee approved the program.

Three aldermen—Becker, Carey and Merriam—signed minority reports. Becker and Carey, who signed a joint report, said that the number of vacant land units should be increased from 2,100 to 9,200. They urged that the compromise be voted down. "It is clearer than ever," their report said, "that the selection of any vacant site will arouse the opposition of the surrounding community. Nevertheless, the problem of slum clearance and providing decent housing for low-income families is ours. It is at times such as these that Aldermen must rise to their responsibility as City Fathers and place the interests of all the people above a group. The acceptance of this program will constitute a blow at the principles and practices of public housing and slum removal. It will permanently freeze a vicious pattern of segregation. *Not even the impelling need for housing justifies compromise with such basic principles.*"

In the Council, Becker's language was less restrained. He called for the aldermen to rebel against the Kennelly-Duffy "dictatorship" which, he said, had made "prostitutes" of the Authority and the Plan Commission.[8] Merriam, in his minority report, said 4,260 units should be built on vacant land. However, he did not urge rejection of the compromise. Merriam, some of his associates said later, had been told by Duffy that if he expected to continue to play any part in Chicago politics, he had better support the compromise.[9]

When the time came for the final vote, there was a last-minute flurry of excitement. It was whispered that the City Hall lacked votes to pass the compromise. Alderman Cullerton, one of the "Big Boys," took Becker aside and offered to switch 200 units from a site in his ward to a site in DuBois' ward (DuBois was certain to oppose the compromise anyway) in return for his support. Becker accepted this proposal. After Becker had won this concession, Carey allowed himself to be persuaded to support the compromise because it seemed clear that the alternative was no housing program at all.

But even with the votes of Becker, Carey, and Merriam, the Council leaders did not feel quite safe. They therefore called a recess and escorted several aldermen across the street to a hotel where the Mayor, Duffy, Arvey, Joseph L. Gill, Democratic chairman for Cook County, and John S. Boyle, state's attorney, reminded them of the facts of political power. One who was present later recalled the conversation between an alderman and a party leader:

"Are you going to vote for the program," the alderman was asked as he came into the room.

"No."

"Why not?"

"I can't. My people are against it. My people won't stand for it."

"Your people, Hell! Who put you in office, your people or the Party?"

"The Party. But . . ."

"Well, by God, if you ever want to get in office again, you'll do as the Party says now."[10]

Some of the "regulars"—Wagner, Corcoran, Murphy, and Sheridan (all of them of the South Side Bloc)—were permitted to vote against the compromise. These were Duffy's special friends or men who were known to be in especially precarious positions in their wards. Like Thomas Hobbes' ruler,[11] the Party expected submission to any penalty except the death penalty: if it were clear that an alderman might lose his seat by voting for the compromise, he might vote against it.

In the end, the machine had plenty of votes to spare. The compromise passed 35 to 12. Then a motion by DuBois to submit the question to a referendum was defeated 27 to 14. "Administration leaders," the *Tribune* said, "had the vote so well oiled they didn't even have to take the floor."[12]

Now that the Council had acted, the editors of the *Sun-Times* reflected with satisfaction on the significance of the struggle. "The enemies of public housing as a public policy took a licking in Chicago," they wrote. "The Chicago need is so distressing and acute that the tactics which have sabotaged projects in other cities failed here. There were occasions when the anti-housing lobby seemed to have a majority of the Council in its bag. That lobby never made any inroads on the fundamental thinking of Mayor Kennelly, however. When compromise had sliced the program to a minimum, the mayor's perseverance was the factor that made the victory for principle inevitable."[13]

Which specific principle was victorious was, of course, unclear. Surely, insofar as planning and politics can be separated from each other, the principle of decision by political power took precedence over decision by planning.

"In the early days of CHA, site selection was an informal rule-of-thumb process," the Public Housing Association's newsletter had declared during the site selection struggle. "Since 1945, however, a systematic and thoroughly developed program of site planning has been inaugurated. A Planning Department has become an integral part of CHA and is constantly working to keep the picture of housing possibilities in Chicago complete and up-to-the-minute. . . ."[14]

It was true that progress had been made along these lines. By the summer of 1950, when it was becoming clear that Chicago was not likely to have very much additional public housing in the remaining five years of its six-year program, the Planning Division was getting well started on the task that had been set for it. But it was still getting started, and it had not progressed as far as the newsletter implied. The planners were far from having made a long-term development plan for public housing in Chicago, but they had prepared procedures, data and criteria for such a plan and for the future selection of sites.

The circumstances under which the Planning Division labored had been far from ideal. Meyerson's time had been largely taken up by conferences at the Authority—conferences which usually had to do with problems of the day, not with long-range planning—and by meetings and discussions with aldermen and other interested parties. As crisis followed crisis, he found it was also necessary to put his staff to work on day-to-day problems. Long-range planning, it seemed, was something that would always have to wait until the crisis of the moment had passed. But with the next moment, there was always another crisis.

To a certain extent Meyerson had anticipated this and provided against it. He had organized the Planning Division in three sections — Program Planning, Technical Services, and Project Planning—in order to have one unit (Technical Services) which would handle drafting and other routine jobs, which other branches of the Authority were sure to impose on the Planning Division. By having Technical Services available for such jobs, he hoped to keep the other two sections free: Program Planning to make site recommendations and do long-range, comprehensive planning for current and future public housing, and Project Planning to plan the specific development of each of the sites and its integration into the surrounding community.

After the site selection struggle was over, McMillen indicated that Meyerson's intention to make a long-term plan for public housing for Chicago, hopefully in conjunction with the Plan Commission, was neither essential nor desirable. The proper role for the Planning Division, in his opinion, was to collect data on an *ad hoc* basis for the use of the commissioners. " 'Now study that,' we might say, 'get the low-down on that site,' and the Planning Division can be of real use," he explained.[15]

Miss Wood, although she was sympathetic to comprehensive planning, also wanted the Planning Division to occupy itself mainly with fact-gathering and fact-analysis. After the site selection struggle was over, she listed seven main functions which, she felt the CHA Planning Division should perform:

"1. Participate in a joint project to collect housing market data for the needs of the Land Clearance Commission and the Chicago Dwellings Association as well as CHA.

"2. Accumulate a body of working knowledge on industrial trends so that when the Executive Secretary is faced with a choice between sites, Planning can advise.

"3. Have a comprehensive knowledge of the plans of effectuating agencies like the Board of Education, transit, etc. Because there is no master plan, it is necessary for the Planning Division to keep in touch with these agencies and to do joint planning with them when feasible.

"4. Collect data on land use: present use and trends, areas of residential and industrial use. Be able to make the best possible case for the best possible site.

"5. As needed, make analysis of social structures (churches, settlements, etc.) on a proposed site and submit recommendations regarding the retention of some of these.

"6. Make detailed recommendations regarding street patterns, densities, etc., in connection with project plans. Recommend the average size of units in the project as a whole.

"7. Influence the effectuating agencies to serve CHA's ends as well as their own; for example, encourage the Plan Commission to make studies which will be of use to the Authority."[16]

This was Miss Wood's view of the proper role of a planning division in June 1952, after the site selection struggle was over. "I would have been more manic about planning two years ago," she remarked in the perspective of the political struggle. Even if planning technicians in an operating agency were given full opportunity they might not be able to justify all the pretense about "comprehensive planning." If the opportunity should occur to make decisions in the public interest they could best be made by those who took technical matters into consideration along with political ones.[17]

As for McMillen, he had not intended that the Planning Division should have any major function other than that of site planing and of gathering data on specific sites at the request of the commissioners and he was convinced that if the politicians should allow the Authority to make far-reaching decisions, the decisions should be made not by the staff, but by the commissioners. However, he thought there was little likelihood that the politicians would give the Authority much latitude to make decisions in matters which they regarded as important. "It would be silly to say that Planning applies criteria to sites," he observed after the struggle was over. "There is only one criterion: can we get it approved by the Council?"[18]

By the middle of November 1950, three months after the Council accepted the City Hall compromise, the final decisions on the housing program had still not been made, but the situation had changed in several important respects. Taylor resigned from the Board and was succeeded as chairman by McMillen. The term of Benjamin, the commissioner most friendly to the staff and the only one who had voted against the City Hall compromise, expired and the Mayor did not reappoint him. With the support of the *Sun-Times,* Duffy was elected to the County Board (although not to the presidency of it) and he was succeeded as boss of the Council by his friend Wagner, an irreconcilable foe of public housing. Merriam was made chairman of the housing committee in place of Lancaster, who had been moved to a more important post.

The November election also brought a change in the housing program that had been agreed upon. The voters of the 40th Ward returned Becker. But at the same time they helped elect a Republican Sanitary District Board which at once rescinded the action by which its Democratic predecessor had made a vacant land site in Becker's ward available for public housing. This action reduced the already small number of vacant land units in the program. Another vacant land site was subsequently dropped because a railroad was able to retain title to it.

Meanwhile, the Planning Division established that the so-called "white" slum site which had been substituted at the last moment for another in the wards of Aldermen Bowler and Sain was neither slum nor white. Most of the dwellings on this site needed only minor repairs, the technicians found, and in the normal course of events the area would be almost all Negro in a few years. This was a case where the aldermen probably were hoping to use the Authority to keep Negroes out.

At about the same time, the Public Housing Administration issued a new set of standards as part of an economy drive; virtually all of the site planning the Authority had so far done had now to be discarded, for the new standards necessitated increases in density of land use and reductions in the size of dwelling units and in room sizes.

If the City Council's program was bad to begin with, all of these developments had made it much worse. Meyerson (who was now returning to his duties at the University of Chicago) had opposed the City Hall compromise from the beginning; now he believed that the Public Housing Administration ought to disapprove the slum sites. Meyerson went to his colleague, Louis Wirth, a sociologist who was a member of the National Committee Against Discrimination in Housing and a race relations adviser to the Public Housing Administration in Washington. Wirth was easily persuaded that the Chicago program should be disapproved in Washington, and he said he would do what he could to bring that about.

By now the Public Housing Association also wanted the program killed or significantly altered and Alinksy, its president, wrote to the PHA administrator in Washington urging him to veto the slum sites.[19]

Meanwhile, the race relations adviser of PHA's Chicago field office publicly recommended to his superiors that the program be turned down because of the hardships that slum clearance without accompanying measures for relocation would inflict upon the Negro community. It was highly questionable, the race relations adviser said, whether any slum sites at all should have been included in the first year's program.

McMillen took sharp issue with this position. Admitting that the program was by no means perfect, he pointed out that the Authority could postpone demolition until the relocation problem ceased to be acute. That, he said, was exactly what the Authority would do. The worst that could happen, then, would be that new construction on some sites would be indefinitely delayed. "The Housing Authority faced two alternatives," he wrote the National Committee Against Discrimination in Housing, ". . . either to build no housing under the present law, or proceed with the program approved by the City Council. We have accepted the latter choice and believe that it was not only the best we could do, but also that it will have constructive results and will confer needed benefits upon thousands of Chicago families."[20]

This did not satisfy the race relations advisers of the Federal housing agencies. They were employed to represent the point of view of the agency to the Negro; to do this, they had also to represent the Negro to the agency, and, accordingly, to take a "race" position. It was not surprising, then, that they were unanimously agreed that the Chicago program should be rejected if it could not be improved. But whether they could succeed in having it rejected or not (they had very little hope of improving it), they intended to use it as a case in point in the discussion of which the issues of racial policy would be clarified.

The most influential of the racial advisers was Frank Horne of the Housing and Home Finance Agency. Horne had long been fearful that the vast powers and resources provided in the Act of 1949 would be used to worsen the position of the Negro unless there was a concerted effort to plan housing in such a manner as to protect the Negro. Horne's mission, as he once described it, was to "hold the program by the tail," i.e. to prevent its over-rapid expansion in a form inimical to the Negro.[21] The Chicago public housing program, which came to Washington for approval at about the same time as the Land Clearance Commission's "Lake Meadows" project, an undertaking which would displace 4,600 more persons than it could house, provided an illustration of the very situation against which Horne was trying to guard. Accordingly, he determined to use the Chicago program as a demonstration of the unrealized possibilities for coordinated planning and the dangers that lay in failure to coordinate public housing and private urban redevelopment.

Horne persuaded his superior, Foley, to write Mayor Kennelly pointing out that the Chicago program could be considered acceptable, if it could be considered so at all, only on the assumptions that in the remaining years of the six-year program more vacant land would be provided for relocation and that all future plans for housing in Chicago—not only plans for public housing, but for urban redevelopment and for private construction as well—would be coordinated so as to bring about an eventual solution of the relocation problem. In his letter, Foley listed the things which the Federal agencies might do to help bring about a coordinated program of this kind and he suggested some things the Mayor might do. One of these was to call a conference of private real estate and building interests to plan for increasing the supply of private rental and purchase housing for Negroes.

When he received this letter, Kennelly reportedly called Foley on the telephone to say that he felt Foley was applying in the Chicago case a procedure which had not been applied elsewhere. Kennelly said Foley should approve the program as it stood, without attaching a lot of ifs, ands, and buts. He added that he had no intention of calling a conference of real-estate men and builders.[22]

Foley, meanwhile, had heard from Ferd Kramer, the president of the Metropolitan Housing and Planning Council of Chicago, who saw no advantage in rejecting the program. "In view of the steadily deteriorating prestige of the Authority in the community and in the City Council," Kramer wrote, "and the fact that the Authority agreed to the compromise, we believe it highly unrealistic and a disservice to Chicago to attempt to knock out this program in the naive belief that either remorse or conscience will then impel the city fathers to produce a better one at this time. This is tantamount to saying, 'Let them eat cake.' "[23] This view of the matter was also pressed upon the Federal officials by Alderman Merriam and by the Mayor's Acting Housing and Redevelopment Coordinator who had come to Washington to persuade the Public Housing Administrator to approve the "white" slum site.

In November 1951, one year and three months after the Council approved the compromise and nearly two and one half years after the passage of the Housing Act, the Public Housing Administration approved all of the slum sites. The crucial decisions had at last been made.

Foley approved the program against the advice of the race relations advisers. Horne, for example, felt that the Chicago program was unjust and that its rejection would dramatize the larger issues. Nevertheless, he was satisfied that something had been gained from the extended discussion of the Chicago program. "A mounting number of people and organizations took positions and stiffened their positions because of the Chicago program," he said in an interview afterward. "Some of the organizations got themselves forged, so to speak, in the controversy on Chicago. The controversy caused them to take a stand on segregation in housing—and this included even Negro organizations like NAACP."[24]

The discussion also clarified opinion within the Federal housing agencies and some of the opinion was expressed in policy declarations. These were general statements of the agencies' intentions to do better next time, rather than formalizations of criteria which would be decisive in cases such as Chicago. The most important such statement was incorporated in the PHA manual early in 1952. It listed five policies for the guidance of local authorities in the selection of sites for public housing:

1. Sites should be such as to make possible racial equity in tenant selection.
2. The number of units developed for a racial minority should not be less than the number occupied by that minority which are destroyed.
3. Sites should not reduce the land area available to a minority.
4. Effort should be made to avoid sites which result in displacement of minority group populations.
5. Slum sites occupied by minority groups should be used only when relocation is feasible.[25]

Whatever their effect might be in other cities, these declarations would probably make little difference in Chicago. Most observers agreed that there could not be very much more public housing in that city until times had changed.

Whether or not the Chicago program was as bad as its critics said depended in a considerable measure on a question which only time could answer: would the displaced Negroes suffer great hardships for lack of relocation housing, or would they somehow manage to find other suitable housing?

The question had been answered in part by 1954, but no one knew for sure what the answer was. Despite McMillen's assurance that demolition would not take place except as dwellings could be found for people to move to, the Authority promptly cleared some of the slum sites; by the end of 1952, about one-fourth of the slum-dwellers had been displaced. This was not McMillen's decision only. Once the sites had been finally approved and little stood in the way of construction except the convenience of the slum-dwellers, the importance some of the staff members attached to the relocation problem declined somewhat. Construction-minded people were now dominant in the CHA Development Department.

At any rate, many of the slum-dwellers had moved from the sites by 1954 and no one knew for sure whether they had gone to better housing or to worse. Some had been assisted by the Authority to find places, and concerning these some information existed. But there were many others who, when they learned that their slum dwellings were to be torn down, simply moved away, no one knew how or where. The hardships of these people would have to be taken into account in making a satisfactory evaluation of the final program, but the extent of those hardships was unknowable. There was no way of comparing the sufferings of those displaced with the satisfactions of those to be housed or for that matter with the gratifications and deprivations of the many others who had, or thought they had, an interest in public housing.

Whether the long drawn out struggle had served any purpose was a matter for conjecture. Duffy believed that the Authority would have done better to make a deal in private. "If the commissioners had come to us for advice before the sites were submitted to the Council," he told an interviewer afterward, "I can't say they would have got a better housing program, but that way they would at least have done away with the delay and the possibility of losing the program altogether. The Mayor was on the spot. It wasn't easy to get the Council to vote for the program but they were sold [by the Council leadership] on the necessity of clearing slums and rebuilding. Fellows who didn't have any confidence in the Authority whatever were willing to vote for a program. While they [CHA] never submitted anything that was good, the Council would have tossed it over anyway because of the general attitude of the fellows. They were suspicious of everything the Authority came in with. They [CHA] are lying on the bed they made for themselves. Positively no public relations."[26]

The top staff of CHA and the Strategy Committee leaders, however, believed that they had been wise to fight or at least that the fight had done no harm. "The dividend from the fight," Miss Wood afterwards remarked, "was the fact that we got vacant land sites."[27] Liveright afterwards said, "We would have got zero by making a deal and we got zero anyway."[28]

The commissioners afterwards felt that it had been a mistake not to seek the advice of the leading aldermen before presenting the sites to the Council. When the time came to submit sites for the second year of the six-year program, McMillen, who was now chairman, asked the Mayor to arrange for the appointment of an advisory committee of aldermen to make selections from a large number of sites that the commissioners considered suitable. But the "Big Boys," the Mayor told McMillen after calling them into his office, were entirely unwilling to serve on such a committee. They may have come to the conclusion that they did not have to advise: they could dictate. Or they may have decided that it would be best for them not to take any responsibility for site selection.[29]

For his part, Meyerson in retrospect felt that the Authority would have done better to have attempted to engage in reasonable discussion with the "Big Boys" while its supporters pressured the aldermen as best they could. The "Big Boys" could have been shown, Meyerson believed, that in terms of *their* ends more housing on vacant land was needed: that without it Negroes displaced from the slums by public works and slum clearance projects would be pushed into the conservation areas, the very thing that the aldermen most wanted to avoid.* If the realities of the situation had been brought forcibly to Duffy's attention before the relocation sites were proposed and while the Housing Act of 1949 was still on the horizon, it might have been possible to get him to agree in advance that a certain number of units should be built on vacant land. With this commitment to go on, the Authority might have planned accordingly. It might have drawn up a list of acceptable sites and then have privately asked the "Big Boys" to indicate certain preferences among the sites.

That the "Big Boys" were unwilling to follow such a procedure when McMillen proposed it after the struggle does not mean that they would not have done so earlier when they were less confident of their ability to dictate to the Authority. Perhaps Duffy's confidence resulting from his easy victory over the commissioners in the relocation housing program (*supra,* pp. 129-136) may have made it too late to try this approach, however. If this was the case, the settlement that resulted from the fight was certainly better for the Authority than any that the commissioners were likely to have made with Duffy in private.

Whether or not the fight resulted in a better or a worse set of sites than might have been obtained otherwise, it had certain other advantages: it was, as one organization leader said, "good ideological education for the thought leaders."[31] As this quotation suggests, a few of the public housing supporters might have preferred a public fight to a private compromise even if they had expected the compromise to yield somewhat more and better housing than the fight. These few, like some of the opposition, were interested either primarily or incidentally in symbolic-ideological ends. There were ideological gains that could be made from a fight and only from a fight, and these gains may have been more valuable than any losses in terms of practical ends

* "If the aldermen really got smart," McMillen remarked afterward, "they would pick a place about a mile square and move all the Negroes there. 'You're the fall guy,' they'd tell the alderman of that ward. 'You take the punishment.' As to whether I would support such a proposal, I would have to think it through: a square mile of new housing is better than a square mile of old housing. It would be a brutal approach, but I don't expect anything but a brutal approach at present."[30]

that were likely to be incurred by fighting. They wanted to create a public opinion, one which could be brought to bear on the public housing issue and on other related issues as well, especially the issue of race relations. Housing was suitable for such a purpose, because it united people in political action along a broad range of interests. By bringing representatives of Negroes, Jews, Catholics, Protestants, labor unions, women's clubs, and businessmen together in a common effort, it created formal and informal systems of communication which could be used in the future in various ways.

A negotiated settlement of the kind that could have been looked for from the commissioners meeting in the privacy of Duffy's office would also have influenced public opinion, of course, but it would have influenced it in what these public housing supporters believed was the wrong direction. Such a negotiated settlement would have tended to minimize or obscure the important differences of program between the liberal-left and the conservative-reactionary ideologies. Not to fight would therefore have been a failure of leadership, for someone had to make clear to the public what was involved. As Archibald Carey, the Negro alderman who was a leader of the pro-public housing forces, explained after the struggle was over, "If your sole object was to get up some bricks and mortar, it would have been better to have asked the power boys, 'What will you give us?' And when they say 'Two,' you say 'Four.' However, the issue should have been *right* housing, and in that case there should have been no compromise." Carey himself was probably willing to sacrifice some bricks and mortar for the sake of airing the larger issue of segregation. "I don't think the public housing advocates necessarily felt that they were going to win," he said afterward in justifying their strategy.[32]

But if the fight had these advantages for the public housing supporters and the liberal-left, it had similar advantages for their opponents. If organizations on the liberal-left "got themselves forged" (as Horne, the race relations adviser, put it), so did organizations of the conservative-reaction. When the site selection struggle began, the local opposition to public housing was weak and unorganized, but at the end of the struggle it was strong and well financed. There were indications, too, that the effect upon public opinion had been as much to increase the affect of those sectors of opinion that were inclined to oppose public housing (or at any rate the particular program of sites) as to increase the affect of its potential supporters.

"YOO—HOO!"

CHAPTER NINE □ □ □ □ □ □

POLITICS

THE STRUGGLE over site selection was not altogether a struggle among opposing interests or groups; in part it was a struggle among conflicting tendencies within the same interest. There was a conflict of ends between the leadership of the City Council and heads of the Authority to be sure. But there was also a conflict within the end-system of the Council leadership itself.

On the one hand, the leaders of the Council wanted some public housing. On the other hand, they did not want to do anything which would encourage spread of Negroes into the outlying white neighborhoods. These two ends were clearly somewhat at odds (how seriously they conflicted was not generally realized at the time) and so it was up to the Council leaders to find the terms on which they could be harmonized or compromised. By trial and error these leaders hoped to find a package of sites which would not entail a painful sacrifice of either end, i.e., which would provide a housing program of reasonable scope without seriously disturbing the *status quo* of the white neighborhoods. Not until it had made many trials and errors—a process which might not have occurred except for the interaction with the Authority—did the Council leadership conclude that there was no "saddle-point" to be found: that any compromise it might make would entail painful sacrifices of one or both ends.

From one logical standpoint, the Authority could have been an innocent bystander while the policy-making Council leadership struggled to compromise its conflicting ends. Only when the Council had reached a settlement of this conflict within its own end-system (as it finally did after a fashion) would it have then been logically necessary for the Authority to become a party to the issue, and then, of course, the issue would be whether the City Hall settlement should be accepted, rejected, or modified. But although there were really two conflicts, one of which was logically prior, the two went on together as if they were a single issue and since contention between the Council and the Authority was more visible and dramatic than the conflict that went on within the minds of the Council leadership, there seemed on the surface to be only one conflict, that between the Council and the Authority.

The conflict within the ends of the leadership of the Council was of course a reflection of a similar conflict both among their constituents and within the end-systems of some constituents. There were, as we have shown, some forces which favored and some which opposed public housing. Both sides had votes, and Duffy, who was running for a County office and who also had to think of what was good for the Democratic machine, looked for a settlement which would appease both sides. But there was also a large and politically important sector of opinion which did not appear actively on either side. It was likely that many of the white people who just voted the way the Democratic Party advised, plus others who voted for the redevelopment bond issue in 1948, wanted both a certain amount of public housing and the maintenance of the *status quo* in the outlying white neighborhoods. In other words, a sector of the electorate probably had inconsistent ends—the voters in this sector wanted public housing, but they inconsistently wanted it under circumstances in which it could not be had. But the voters (since unlike the politicians they did not have to select or approve a program of sites) did not become aware of the conflict within their end-systems or try to work out an acceptable compromise. They went on expecting to clear slums *and* to maintain racial segregation, and it was quite possible that they would punish a politician who did not manage to do both at once. If he opposed slum clearance, Duffy, for example, might lose the votes of people who favored it, but who would vote against him if slum clearance brought Negroes (as it surely would!) into their neighborhoods.

The politicians might have attempted to point out the contradiction which existed within the end-systems of their constituents. This, no doubt, is what political leaders or statesmen would have done. But the "Big Boys" themselves did not see clearly that any slum clearance program was bound to disturb the *status quo* in the outlying neighborhoods (indeed, it was only *after* the site selection struggle was over that anyone could be perfectly sure that this had happened) and the institutions of government in Chicago were better suited to finding ways of avoiding an unpopular step than to putting issues before the public for reasonable discussion.

It was just as well for the cause of public housing, perhaps, that the politicians did not put the issue before the public in a clearcut way. If they had succeeded in making public opinion consistent, it would have been by splitting into two camps that sizeable sector of it which wanted ends which were empirically irreconcilable. And if such a split had occurred, opinion might have crystallized against slum clearance, not for it. It was because many passive supporters of public housing did not realize its implications for their other ends that any compromise at all was possible.

If, however, the politicians had been more aware of the inconsistency within their own end-system, a settlement more acceptable to both sides could probably have been reached—and reached with less delay and confusion. If they had realized that any public housing program, even one built in the Negro slums, would necessarily displace slum dwellers and so cause them to find their way into the outlying white neighborhoods, the politicians would have been no less anxious to find some sites for public housing, for however apparent the inconsistency might be to them, as long as the voters wanted both ends served (viz., to have public housing and to preserve the *status quo*), they would have to try to serve them both. Seeing the situation more clearly themselves, the politicians could probably have more expeditiously and effectively resolved the dilemma which faced them.

If the Authority had been in a position to talk frankly and privately to the "Big Boys," it might have shown them that from their standpoint (i.e., from the standpoint of people who wanted both housing and the preservation of the *status quo* in the white neighborhoods) the best possible solution would be large isolated projects on the outskirts of the city. Such projects (e.g., the one proposed for Duffy's ward) would keep many Negroes and other public housing tenants together in an area apart from the rest of the white community. This would probably have been more acceptable from the standpoint of the anti-Negro whites than a housing program (such as that actually settled upon) which by building in the slums would not only displace Negroes but leave them to find their way into the white areas in a random, unguided movement.

This was a case, in other words, where the same means (building chiefly on vacant land) would serve for the attainment of opposed ends (viz., from the standpoint of the Authority and its supporters, to make possible a large slum clearance program, and, from the standpoint of the Council leadership and the opponents of public housing, to minimize the inevitable disturbance to white neighborhoods).

The question, therefore, arises why the Council and the Authority engaged in a long struggle rather than in cooperation. We will limit our discussion to the choice of a strategy by the Authority. This strategy was, of course, to some extent a response to that adopted by the Council leadership or, more precisely, to what the heads of the Authority supposed was the strategy of the Council leadership.

The strategy of the Authority was to struggle rather than to bargain. Indeed, the Authority went somewhat out of its way to provoke the leaders of the Council; it did this by refusing to enter into even a *pro forma* discussion with the housing committee of the Council before the sites were formally submitted, by locating a large project in Duffy's ward without giving him any advance notice of it, and by taking a hostile tone in its public appearances before the Council.

It is quite possible that, given the situation that existed in 1949, this was a rational strategy. Certainly it would have been rational if the Authority's ends had been symbolic-ideological, i.e., if it had been interested chiefly in what one public housing supporter called "good ideological education for the thought leaders." But even though its ends were (as we believe) mainly intrinsic-concrete, struggling may nevertheless have been its best strategy under the circumstances. For in 1949 the "Big Boys" were sure they could dictate a settlement; their experience in the relocation program had probably convinced them that the commissioners could be bullied into accepting almost anything and so, although they seemingly were willing to discuss matters with the commissioners, they undoubtedly expected to do most of the talking themselves. If the alternative to a struggle was a dictated settlement, it was better for the Authority to struggle. And if it was necessary to struggle, it was possibly good strategy (although this seems to us very much open to question) to take a hostile posture.

But at an earlier time—say in 1947—the rational strategy might have been very different from that which the Authority actually followed. At that time the heads of the Authority, recognizing that despite the formal independence of their agency they would have to share power with those who controlled the city government, should have tried to reach an understanding on essentials with the new Mayor and with the leaders of the Council. This could not have been done simply on the basis of "good fellowship" of course (although this would have had its place), but it might have been done by making it clear to the politicians that the advantages to them of cooperating with the agency would be greater than the disadvantages. This, in fact, was what Shufro and others had done when they helped persuade Mayor Kelly to make public housing part of his appeal to the liberal, labor, and Negro votes. The Authority's strategy should have been to persuade the "Big Boys" to accept its ends and its view of the situation, of course, but, failing that, it should have made a general compromise which would have defined in broad terms the place that public housing was to occupy in Chicago.* Only

* If it could have been sure that the Authority would not go beyond certain agreed-upon bounds, the Council leadership might have been very glad to leave the whole unpleasant business of site selection to the Authority. In that case the Authority could have held its own public hearings on terms favorable to itself (as is done in other cities), and the aldermen could have had the satisfaction of being both for public housing and against disturbance of white neighborhoods without having to take any responsibility for compromising these two ends.

if it appeared that more could be gained by struggling than by making such a settlement should the Authority have ceased its efforts to negotiate.

A number of reasons can be pointed out why this strategy, which in our opinion was the optimum, was not adopted.

1. During Mayor Kelly's regime the Authority could be independent because Kelly paid its political bills. After Kelly's departure, it had to earn its own political living in a hostile world, but it did not become fully aware of this necessity or its implications for a long time. Until 1948, when the state law was changed to give the Council veto power over sites, the Authority had been free to put projects where it liked. That this freedom existed in part because of the backing of the head of the Democratic machine was lost sight of during the several years Kelly protected it. After his retirement the Authority had only the shell of independence but out of habit it acted as if it had real independence.

2. It was not until late in 1947 or early in 1948 that the heads of the Authority fully realized that Mayor Kennelly was not going to be a mayor in the same sense that Mayor Kelly had been or, indeed, in any significant sense at all. Until 1948 it was reasonable for them to suppose that the Mayor was the person with whom a general understanding would have to be reached. But when at last it became evident that the city government was to be run by the "Big Boys" of the Council, it would not have been easy for the heads of the Authority, even if they had tried, to reach an understanding with them. The "Big Boys" were not especially interested in public housing except when it was a "hot" issue; for the most part they were occupied with matters such as street lighting and garbage collection which had a more intimate connection with the interests of their wards. It would probably have been hard for the Authority to get the attention of the key aldermen when the housing issue was not especially "hot."

3. The heads of the Authority were, in our judgment, somewhat disposed to underrate the willingness of Duffy and Lancaster to take a reasonable view of things and to make concessions. At the same time they were somewhat disposed to

overrate the political power that they and their allies could bring to bear upon the aldermen. This disposition to overrate their power was perhaps, to some extent, an aspect of the "producers' bias" which, in our opinion, caused them to magnify the demand for public housing.

4. Because it interposed a group of part-time amateurs who had no real responsibility for the agency's program between them, the board form of organization made effective contact between the operating heads of the Authority and the political heads of the city government very difficult. Taylor was a conscientious and devoted chairman, but he did not have enough detailed knowledge of the agency's work or a strong enough commitment to its purposes to make him the most effective bargainer on its behalf. The staff could not negotiate with the politicians directly, of course, for the politicians, knowing that Taylor and the other commissioners would be easier to deal with, would have refused to talk with them. Thus, although the situation did not preclude fighting (it was not necessary to be recognized by the politicians in order to fight them of course) it did preclude both cooperation and bargaining, for negotiation could have been carried on only by the board.

5. The Authority was committed to its supporters. During the New Deal era, it was an advantage to be identified with the larger issues of reform and with the liberal-left. Shufro had labored to make the Authority and its leadership a symbol around which believers in good government and, to a lesser degree perhaps, the welfare state would rally. This was good strategy at the time; it was probably in order to have the advantage of such a symbol that Mayor Kelly gave the Authority his protection. But during and after the War the political climate changed so that affiliations which had formerly been an advantage became a decided disadvantage. Assuming as we do that its ends were principally concrete-intrinsic, it would opportunistically have been good strategy for the Authority to have made a break with its old associations and to have emphasized in its public relations line that its ends were purely "practical." However, if it turned its back on its old supporters it might have found no new ones to take their place.

6. The heads of the Authority were lacking in political knowledge (including information, insight, and judgment). Their knowledge may have been good compared to that of most municipal administrators, but, even so, it was not good enough to meet the demands of the situation. They would, we think, have chosen a different and more effective strategy if they had understood the political situation better: if they had realized, for example, how much they owed their independence to Mayor Kelly's protection and how necessary it would be to find some new source of power when that power was withdrawn; if they had seen earlier that it was Duffy, not Kennelly, with whom they had chiefly to deal; and if they had more correctly evaluated the amount of power their allies among the civic organizations could muster and how indifferent some of them—for example, the Negroes—would prove to the public housing site issue.

This lack of knowledge was not an "accidental" feature of the situation. The kind of knowledge that was needed—whether the Mayor would put pressure on Duffy or leave him to manage matters in his own way; how Duffy would evaluate the significance for his own position of pressure from the *Sun-Times* as against opposing pressure from the neighborhood improvement associations in his ward; at what point the residents of Jeffrey Manor would change their registrations from Democratic to Republican; how much importance the Mayor and Duffy would attach to the opinions of 89 pro-public housing Protestant ministers—could not be found in books and could not be obtained by the methods of fact gathering that bureaucracies usually employ. Indeed, some of the information that was most needed could not be obtained by any fact-gathering procedure; it had to be the product of judgment: somebody would have to try to look at matters through the eyes of the Mayor, Duffy, or the residents of Jeffrey Manor and make a guess.

Only people who were more or less constantly occupied with local politics were likely to have the bits and pieces of fact that were needed or to know where and how to get them. People who could think in somewhat the same terms as the Mayor, Duffy, and the residents of Jeffrey Manor—who "spoke their language" —might guess particularly well how they were likely to think.

The very fact that their outlook was fundamentally unsympathetic to that of the Mayor, Duffy, and the residents of Jeffrey Manor unfitted most of the supporters of public housing to judge how they would behave. But even if there had not been this difficulty in entering into the others' mental processes, there would still have been few who could have made sound judgments. For making sound judgments under conditions of uncertainty is an art; it cannot be reduced to a technique which one can learn from books.*

And, of course, even among people skilled in the art of making political judgments there would probably have been disagreement on some crucial questions. (It is possible, for example, that some astute politicians would have expected the Negro community to give the Authority much more support than it did.) Thus, even with the best information and the best judgment, the Authority might still have made the same mistakes (if mistakes they were); it is, of course, very common for astute politicians to make opposite judgments on the basis of the same facts.

Since there are few objective indicators of political competence except political success (even that is not a very good one, because it is possible to be successful in spite of poor judgment or to be unsuccessful in spite of good judgment), anyone may claim it and whether the claim is warranted or not there is no way to tell for sure.† In taking the advice of the Public Housing

---

* In his autobiography, *You're the Boss,* Edward J. Flynn has emphasized that a politician's skill lies largely in his ability to "guess right" (p. 228) and that this is something that can be learned only by experience. "It would be rather difficult to put your finger on one particular item or incident that would illustrate just what I learned from Mr. Murphy. It would be like trying to tell what you learned from your childhood nurse. My knowledge was mainly obtained by being with him and observing his political philosophy; by watching situations as they arose and seeing whether his handling of them resulted in success or failure." (p. 131.) Edward J. Flynn, *You're the Boss,* Viking, New York, 1947.

† J. S. Mill gives these criteria for distinguishing people of political wisdom: "Actual public services will naturally be the foremost indication: to have filled posts of magnitude, and done important things in them, of which the wisdom has been justified by the results; to have been the author of measures which appear from their effects to have been wisely planned; to have made predictions which have been often verified by the event, seldom or never falsified by it; to have given advice, which when taken has been followed by good consequences, which neglected, by bad. There is doubtless a portion of uncertainty in these signs of wisdom; but we are seeking for such as can be applied by persons of ordinary discernment. They will do well not to rely much on any one indication, unless corroborated by the rest; and, in their estimation of the success or merit

Association leaders, the heads of the Authority had to make a judgment of these leaders' political competence. And in doing so, they could not help judging their own political judgment.

Since political competence is so hard to gauge, it is easy for a political adviser to be disloyal to his principal. To protect himself against this possibility, the principal must discount the advice he gets from one whose loyalty cannot be counted on absolutely; only the advice of those whose motives are beyond question can be taken at face value. Thus, only the advice of dedicated supporters of public housing was given full weight by the leaders of the Public Housing Association. If someone whom they did not fully trust told them that the Negroes would not support public housing vigorously, this advice would probably have been disregarded. Since the people who were in close touch with the Mayor, Duffy, and the opposition were not dedicated public housing supporters, the advice of many politically well informed people was in general not sought or taken.

Dedicated public housing supporters tend to have what Mannheim termed a "utopian" thought-style: they are systematically biased by virtue of being generally oriented toward changing reality.* People who are not biased in this way are not likely to be leaders of such groups as the Public Housing Association or even, perhaps, to be dedicated supporters of public housing at all.

A political process which involves negotiation (cooperation or bargaining) necessitates fuller communication among the parties to the issue than does one which involves only struggling. Negotiation must take place through discussion, whereas a struggle, although it involves some exchange of meanings, is

---

of any practical effort, to lay great stress on the general opinion of disinterested persons conversant with the subject matter." *Utilitarianism, Liberty and Representative Government,* J. M. Dent, London, 1910, p. 320.

* "The concept of utopian thinking reflects the . . . discovery . . . that certain oppressed groups are intellectually so strongly interested in the destruction and transformation of a given condition of society that they unwittingly see only those elements in the situation which tend to negate it. Their thinking is incapable of correctly diagnosing an existing condition of society. They are not at all concerned with what really exists: rather in their thinking they already seek to change the situation that exists. Their thought is never a diagnosis of the situation; it can be used only as a direction for action." Karl Mannheim, *Ideology and Utopia,* Routledge and Kegan Paul, London, 1936, p. 36.

primarily a mutual endeavor to apply power. A discussion can be initiated and carried on only if all parties are able and willing to exchange meanings, whereas one party can force others into a struggle simply by attacking them. In our opinion, the choice of struggle rather than negotiation by the leaders of the public housing forces is to be explained in some part by these considerations. The board—and not the CHA staff or the Public Housing Association—was the one body with which the "Big Boys" were willing to negotiate; therefore, the only strategy open to the staff and the Association was struggle. Moreover, none of the public housing leaders—not even the commissioners—was able to communicate effectively with the aldermen, and this was another circumstance which may have inclined them toward struggling as a strategy.

The circumstances which impeded communication between the public housing leaders and the aldermen seem to have been mainly differences in social class, temperament, professional style, and ideology.

The importance as a barrier to communication of differences in social class (along with such empirically related characteristics as education and moral refinement) may be seen in Miss Wood's relations with most of the aldermen. How was she, who had taught English to the girls at Vassar, to do business with Paddy Bauler, a saloon-keeper from a river-ward whose way of dealing with a problem might sometimes be to say, "Hell, boys, let's go 'round and have a few drinks?" Even with Duffy, who kept a florist shop instead of a saloon, her communication was not much better. (This was so, although Miss Wood, apparently to overcome the handicap of her class origin, was in the habit of using the word "guy" in place of "person" and even though Duffy, apparently to overcome the handicap of *his* class origin, was in the habit of using the word "fellow" in place of "guy.") Even with Kelly, who was her strong supporter, she had not been able to communicate effectively. "Kelly respected and admired what I stood for," she once remarked, "but he hated to talk to me. We didn't talk the same language. But communication between us was excellent because Kelly liked to talk to Shufro and Shufro could talk the language of the street."[1]

That Miss Wood was a woman was a further barrier to communication. Some of the aldermen found it very difficult to express themselves in private conversation without resort to profanity.

Miss Wood's militant spirit prevented her from communicating effectively with some people. "She is not a person you can sit down and talk reasonably with," Teninga once complained. What was needed in her position, he went on, was someone who was not emotional and who had experience in the real estate business. This was the point of view of an opponent of public housing, but it was also held by some friends of public housing as well.

In part the difficulty in communication arose out of the difference between the "style" of the efficient professional administrator and that of the professional politician. Miss Wood apparently thought that it was becoming for an administrator to be brisk and businesslike and to give a prompt and highly articulate answer to any question that might be asked. This style seems to have irritated the politicians. They would probably have been more comfortable with someone who appeared ignorant at times, not only factually ignorant but morally ignorant as well. It would not be necessary for Miss Wood actually to be more ignorant—only to appear so. It was, in other words, more a matter of manners than anything else; the politicians seemed to think that to know all of the answers was a sign of arrogance in a bureaucrat—by knowing all of the answers he might mean to convey that he knew more than *they* did and perhaps that he was of higher social standing as well.*

Finally there were ideological differences, real or imagined,

---

* "The civil servant," Professor Shils has written, "particularly the civil servant of the level called before Congressional committees, tends to be considerably more educated and probably of a higher social and economic status as regards his origin than the legislator who is requesting a service of him or interrogating him. He is . . . not only more expert in the matter at hand but he usually, either wittingly or unwittingly, is also more the master of the situation than is the legislator. Resentment against those whose fortunate accidents of birth gave them educational opportunities which were not available to the legislator is heightened—it certainly was heightened during the Roosevelt administration—by an attitude of personal, social and intellectual superiority. This sense of superiority very often does not exist at all but is nonetheless assumed to exist." The animus of the legislator against the bureaucrat is fed, Professor Shils goes on to say, by another cleavage in American life, that between intellectuals and politicians. Edward A. Shils, "The Legislator and his Environment," *op. cit.*, pp. 577 and 579.

that stood in the way of communication between Miss Wood and most of the aldermen and opponents of public housing. Many of them supposed—wrongly, of course—that she was bent on overturning the social order and, in particular, on building a vast amount of public housing, taxing the middle and upper classes to support the lower classes in comfortable idleness, and all but forcibly mixing the races. For her part, Miss Wood was apt to think that her opponents comprised a vast conspiracy against good government and against any social reform whatever. Insofar as both sides distrusted each other profoundly, there was no basis for discussion.

Many of these same difficulties existed in varying degrees in the relations of the other representatives of the Authority, both the commissioners and staff, with the aldermen and with Finitzo, Stech, Teninga, Sachs, and other small property and neighborhood spokesmen. Taylor was able to talk to the aldermen more easily than was Miss Wood; they knew that he was a businessman who had some influence among Negroes and this won him some respect. The aldermen could see, too, that he was anxious to be a good fellow. But Taylor did not conform to the stereotype of the Negro as a jolly colored man or for that matter to any other stereotype, and he was too dignified, too much a gentleman in his bearing, for most of the aldermen to feel quite at ease with him.

Shufro, Liveright, Alinsky and the many other aggressive spokesmen for the liberal-left were intolerable to many of the aldermen; they were, Duffy once remarked contemptuously, "pinks."[2]

One man who could communicate with the opposition was Commissioner Kruse, the official of the Flat Janitors' Union. Kruse had the vocabulary—the vocabulary of words, intonation, gesture, dress, ethnicity—which made him understood by the aldermen. But Kruse, unfortunately, was not a strong believer in public housing and he could not communicate with Miss Wood or the staff.

Another who could communicate with the aldermen and the opponents of public housing was Sykes, the Australian-born engineer who had been chairman of the board of the Inland Steel Company. Sykes was not of the same social class as the aldermen, but he had cultivated the art of getting along with the people with whom he had to do business. Once he, Kruse, and McMillen met a group of anti-housing aldermen in the corridors of the City Hall. The aldermen began to attack the Authority. Sykes lifted his hat and pointed to the top of his head in a dramatic way. "Look," he said, "I haven't any horns. Why don't you fellows come over and talk to us?" As a result of this invitation, four aldermen did have an informal discussion with the commissioners, one of the first such discussions to take place.[3]

Miss Wood was aware of these problems. In making certain appointments she acknowledged the need to establish effective communication with the people with whom the agency had to deal: the comptroller, to cite one example, was a man who could talk the language of bankers, accountants, and businessmen. While Kelly was mayor she had used Shufro as a medium of communication with him. But Shufro, a man whom both she and Kelly liked, was a lucky accident, and when it was necessary for her to deal with Duffy and others of the South Side bloc who did not happen to like Shufro she made no effort to find some new intermediary. Although it was a well understood convention in Chicago that most public jobs went to Catholics (and especially to Irish Catholics) there were very few Catholics on the top policy staff. Many of the top staff were Jews.

One reason why Miss Wood and the public housing supporters did not give more attention to the problem of establishing communication with the City Hall was that they were convinced that nothing short of abject surrender by the Authority would satisfy the politicians. She noted that although Sykes had a friendly conversation with the agency's enemies, they remained its enemies and nothing was changed by the conversation. Communication was valuable only as there was the possibility of reaching agreement and that this possibility existed she very much doubted in 1950.

In our judgment her skepticism was justified then. But a year or two earlier there might have been a possibility of establishing a somewhat more successful relationship with the Council, although certainly not one which would have permitted the Authority to do all that its heads believed should be done.

When Mayor Kelly retired and it became evident that the predominant power lay with the South Side Bloc and especially with Duffy, Miss Wood might have done well, we think, to have appointed someone Duffy liked and trusted and for whose appointment to a high-paying job he would be grateful.* By making such an appointment, Miss Wood might have relieved herself of certain political tasks for which she was not particularly well qualified, thus freeing herself for long-range planning and for leadership, tasks for which she was preeminently well qualified.

---

* In the Spring of 1953 the board, on the initiative of Sykes, appointed as the Authority's general counsel a young man who was the second cousin of Richard J. Daley, the chairman of the Democratic County Central Committee. Miss Wood publicly protested the appointment, pointing out that a CHA regulation provided that a chief counsel must have eight years legal experience whereas the appointee had only five. The appointee, she told the newspapers, had stood 183rd in a class of 191 in law school and his assistant in the Authority would be a woman who had graduated from the same law school six months before he did standing fifth in a class of 203. "Up to now," Miss Wood said, "the commissioners have taken pride in the fact that the CHA has been untainted by politics. The commissioners do not set a very good example for the staff when they make a political appointment of this nature."

Miss Wood's protest was backed by local and national civic and church leaders. Finally the young man withdrew, hinting that he had been opposed because he was a Catholic. ("As a young American," he wrote, "I thought I would be entitled to the same fair play that any person, regardless of race, color, creed, religion, or nationalistic origin, is entitled to.")[4]

In our opinion, Miss Wood was wise to oppose this appointment, even though doing so must have created much ill-will. The appointee would have been the board's man, not hers. Moreover, the position of general counsel was too important to take any risks. But we think she would have been wise to have appointed such a man to a major position and to have done so on her own initiative, thus insuring the selection of someone whose loyalty would be to her.

Make No Little Plans

CHAPTER TEN □ □ □ □ □ □

PLANNING

THE PROCESS by which a housing program for Chicago was formulated resembled somewhat the parlor game in which each player adds a word to a sentence which is passed around the circle of players: the player acts *as if* the words that are handed to him express some intention (i.e., as if the sentence that comes to him were *planned*) and he does his part to sustain the illusion. In playing this game the staff of the Authority was bound by the previous moves. The sentence was already largely formed when it was handed to it; Congress had written the first words, the Public Housing Administration had written the next several, and then the Illinois Legislature, the State Housing Board, the Mayor and City Council, and the CHA Board of Commissioners had each in turn written a few. It was up to the staff to finish the sentence in a way that would seem to be rational, but this may have been an impossibility.

The comparison is a little far-fetched, of course, but it cannot be doubted that the many prior decisions of these other bodies —decisions which for the most part had to be taken as unalterable conditions by the staff—were made with reference to no common intention or to none more meaningful than the generality, "to improve the housing of low-income people." Indeed, although all of the decision-making bodies presumably shared this general purpose, each of them made some decisions on the basis of other ends which were *not* shared. The Public Housing Administration's regulation, which in the name of economy tended to prevent the Authority from building projects which would be attractive in the eyes of many of the people of the community, was based on such an unshared end. So was the

City Council's decision not to allow the building of many units on vacant land.

The end-system which was given to the Authority staff by these various actors was full of inconsistencies. The end of avoiding racial discrimination was incompatible with that of avoiding disturbance to the *status quo* in white areas. The end of providing low-rent housing for status-conscious whites was incompatible with that of building so cheaply that public housing would not compete with private developments. Obviously, some of these ends could be served only by sacrificing others. As long as it was required to serve inconsistent ends, the Authority would have to undo with one hand what it did with the other.

The opportunity area within which the staff could devise courses of action was thus circumscribed by decisions which did not arise out of a single clear and consistent intention and which were mostly made by actors who had little or no communication with each other. But these decisions were not the only limiting conditions. Public opinion was another of great importance: some courses of action which might have been allowed by laws and regulations were ruled out by the circumstance that some ideas could not be made to seem plausible to the man on the street. Thus, that unsegregated public projects on outlying vacant sites would bring Negroes into white areas was clear to the public, but that projects in slum areas would cause Negroes to move into white areas was not clear and perhaps could not have been made so.

There were many other limiting conditions: public housing had serious status disadvantages in the eyes of many of the people it was intended to house; it was hard to get whites to live in projects that were predominantly colored; Negroes were often unwelcome in white areas and in some lower class neighborhoods they would be met with violence; there were no large vacant tracts in the slum areas; the location of schools, transportation lines, places of employment, and other such facilities had to be treated as largely fixed in the short run; and the various branches and units of local government were not centrally coordinated by the Plan Commission or by any other body. This list of limiting conditions could be considerably extended, of course; it contains only a few of the more obvious and important conditions which the planners had to take as given.

Not only was the opportunity area small, but its boundaries were vague and shifting so that CHA could form only a very approximate and uncertain idea of what possibilities were open to it. The Authority thought it very likely, for example, that the City Council would permit some public housing to be built on vacant land sites. But this was not a basis on which planning could very well proceed, for the range of what it was plausible to expect extended all of the way from, perhaps, one project of 300 units to 10 projects amounting to 10,000 units or perhaps even more.

When he worked for the Authority, Meyerson, like the other members of the staff, took it for granted that whatever else it might do the Authority would built projects and that this would be its principal means of achieving its ends. From a formal standpoint there was no reason why it had to concentrate on building projects; as a practical matter, however, it was assumed on all sides that this was the principal reason for which the agency existed. Thus, while it might have other programs in addition to building projects (e.g., it might rehabilitate slum neighborhoods) and while it had some latitude within which to decide what size and type of projects it would build and in what manner it would manage them, the Authority probably could not have followed any course of action which did not have as one of its principal features the building of projects. This also was a condition which the planners had to take as given.

Finally, it must be noted that until the passage of the Housing Act of 1949 the Authority did not have and probably could not have obtained funds with which to do large-scale developmental planning.

It is with awareness of these and other limiting conditions that the planning accomplishments of the Authority must be appraised. These accomplishments may be described in three aspects:

1. In many public statements (one of which we have quoted, *supra,* pp. 156-159), Miss Wood presented the outlines of a clear

and consistent developmental plan for public housing and for slum clearance in general. She proposed an end-system, clarified its implications for the selection of means, and pointed out certain conditions (e.g., laws and regulations) which stood in the way of effective action for its attainment. In these public statements she showed how the "sentence" which had been handed to the Authority by Congress, the Public Housing Administration, the state legislature and the other bodies that had made key decisions would have to be edited to make it consistent and fully meaningful.

As contributions to the discussion of housing policy, however, these public statements by Miss Wood suffered from certain limitations. They were not based on extensive or systematic research, and no matter how great her experience and wisdom there were some essentials on which Miss Wood could not make significant judgments without much more information than she or anyone else possessed. Moreover, although they took a good deal into account, essentially Miss Wood's proposals involved only one course of action—large-scale projects; alternative ways of meeting the problem, e.g., conservation of older structures or the use of rental subsidies, she did not discuss at any length. And although the State law authorized and required the Authority to report annually to the mayor on the housing problems of Chicago and the CHA reports often did cover general housing conditions and problems, for the most part, Miss Wood's policy proposals were made informally in public speeches. She did not try to make the Authority a planning agency in the field of policy for all kinds of private as well as public housing.

2. Within the opportunity area which was given it, the Authority staff did plan for the attainment of the agency's corporate ends, but this was at a rudimentary level. Careful or systematic study was not given to the alternative courses of action which might have been developed within the opportunity area, although, as we have explained, some consideration was given to slum rehabilitation and some to the building of small projects. The choice of a preferred course of action—large projects—was based on the thoughtful and experienced judgment of Miss Wood and

some of the other staff and commissioners but not on any thorough-going analysis of that or other possibilities.* Moreover, this course of action was elaborated only as a strategy, i.e., a set of general rules for selecting sites and for securing their approval by the City Council. The criteria for site selection were, of course, very general.

3. The Authority also planned for the attainment of community ends. Until early in 1950, when the work of the reorganized Planning Division began to bear some fruit, this planning had also been of a rudimentary sort; the Plan Commission had hitherto done little comprehensive planning and so the Authority staff relied chiefly on common sense and on what was common knowledge about the intentions of other city departments and agencies. The Planning Division, however, was able to establish fairly effective liaison with other agencies, including the Plan Commission, and it began to develop a comprehensive public housing plan for Chicago.

The Planning Division believed that such a plan should be based on a comprehensive plan for the development of the city. But there existed no such comprehensive plan and the Planning Division was not in a position to make one. Even the Plan Commission could not readily have made one. For a comprehensive plan has to be the expression of some intention regarding the fundamentals of city development and, if it is to have any significance, the intention must be one which will actually govern the use of land in the future, i.e., to which the actions of public and private agencies will conform or be subordinated. In Chicago in 1949 there existed no common intention toward the funda-

---

* Some of the planning technicians were of the opinion that since there was some evidence that projects of about 800 units were cheapest to operate this was, therefore, the optimum size and any departure from it represented a concession to political forces. But, of course, comparative costs are significant only if the ends to be served are the same in all cases. Thus, if it is an end to promote class or racial integration and if this end is achieved by projects of only 20-30 units, it is irrelevant to point out that the per unit costs of small projects are greater than those of large. The significant question in such a case is: is the additional end attained (*viz.* class or racial integration) valuable enough to justify the increased cost? It is in reference to such calculations as this that we say above that Miss Wood's and the staff's judgment was thoughtful and experienced but not based on thoroughgointg analysis.

mentals of city development and there was no one body which could and would require public and private agencies to conform to its intentions.

There were good reasons why the Plan Commission could not readily make a comprehensive plan of the kind described in the ideology of the city planning movement. Power to make fundamental decisions affecting city development, although resting penultimately in the City Council and ultimately in the state legislature, was widely dispersed. How much industry would there be and where in Chicago it would seek locations, what would future transportation policies, habits and facilities be, would the Negro ghetto be preserved or liquidated, would the flight to the suburbs continue?—these were a few of the important questions to which at least approximate answers would have to be given before a meaningful plan could be made. Furthermore, there were other crucial questions which were perhaps even more difficult—e.g., what would be the national pattern of population magnitude and the national level of income and production? There was obviously no agency—even a city planning commission—which could answer such questions. In our pluralistic society power over such matters is widely scattered. Most decisions are not made by public bodies at all: whether industry will locate in Chicago will depend in part upon the management of the industries, probably also upon the leaders of union labor, and probably also upon the choices made by millions of consumers in markets all over the world. And even within the public sector itself, power is divided among hundreds of Federal, State, and local agencies; in Chicago there were, as we pointed out above, no less than six local governments with independent taxing powers. To make a comprehensive plan which would be achieved—if not achievable we would not term it a "plan"—would mean subordinating all of these decision-makers, public and private, to a single intention—an impossibility so long as power is widely dispersed and powerholders have conflicting ends. Should the city plan to maintain racial segregation or to end it? Any answer that might be given to this question would be opposed by some powerful interest, either white or Negro. The same was true of all of the other fundamental questions for which answers had to be given or assumed in a comprehensive city plan. (In Chicago, with its wide diffusion of and conflicts among power groups—see *supra,* pp. 115-117—the framing of a meaningful comprehensive plan was undoubtedly less readily attainable than in other communities.)

The best that such an agency as the Authority could do, then, was to gather up what information it could about the intentions of others, use this information to bring about as much voluntary coordination as possible, and then to choose its course of action in such a way as to achieve its ends without interfering with (perhaps even while complementing) the activity of the agencies and individuals whose ends it wished to further. This is what the CHA staff did with the help of the Housing Coordinator, the Plan Commission, the Land Clearance Commission and other agencies. The density "plan" which it developed described the actions that many people were likely to take; some of these actions were by agencies (e.g., the Land Clearance Commission) which shared some intentions with the Authority. But in the nature of the case the density "plan" was mainly a listing of what many people, seeking many different ends, were likely to do: it did not express some common intention to which all public and private action would have to conform.[1]

Although we have called the planning of the Authority rudimentary (by an "ideal" criterion of rational decision-making), it was, nevertheless, more highly developed than that of most—we would even say of all—other local housing authorities. Certainly there were few local housing executives who gave as much thought or as intelligent thought to the fundamentals of housing policy as did the CHA top staff; in many cities the housing authorities put projects wherever real estate and other special interest groups wanted them to go. In other cities, too, there was generally no effort at all to relate public low-rent housing to other publicly aided and private housing or to community facilities and services such as schools, transportation, and places of work. In many cities if such matters were taken into account, it was largely because the Public Housing Administration required that they be given at least perfunctory attention. General as they were to begin with, the Authority's criteria of site selection were an improvement over the usual practice, for in many cities no criteria were explicitly formulated. The creation of the Planning Division of the Authority was a pioneering step; not another housing authority anywhere in the country had a staff at all comparable in size and training. In New York, where much more public housing had been built and where the political situation was much more favorable to planning, no comparable effort had been made to take all things into account in locating projects. When Meyerson once said in hyperbole that "public housing can ruin a city"[2] it was New York that he had in mind: by establishing land densities too high for wholesome family life, by overloading transportation and community facilities, and, perhaps most important, by fixing unsuitable land uses for at least a half century to come, the New York Housing Authority had, in Meyerson's opinion, put a great many handicaps in the way of making New York a better place to live.

We have emphasized that the opportunity area of the Authority was limited and that its planning, although rudimentary, was more elaborate than that of housing authorities in most, or perhaps all, other cities. We turn now to a consideration of some of the circumstances which deterred the Authority from doing as much planning as it might have done before 1949.

That the commissioners did not themselves plan or urge the staff to plan does not require much explanation. They were amateurs serving part-time and their interest in the affairs of the agency was necessarily limited by their other activities. Moreover, even though they might try to avoid it, they had to depend upon the staff for information and direction to a large extent; probably none of them realized just how much latitude the law allowed in selecting a course of action. The commissioners tended to take the Authority's existing course of action for granted and to assume that their principal job was to supervise its administration.

Because the commissioners would not consider fundamental matters, it was hard for the staff to consider them. There was a danger that the commissioners would be resentful at any evidence that the staff was considering radical changes in policy without having had instructions from them to do so.

But in our opinion even if the board had not existed, to have done much more planning would have been very difficult. Planning is costly. If it is to amount to anything, it must be done by able people. Those who are good at planning are likely to be good at opportunistic decision-making as well, and an organization which is fighting for its life will not ordinarily be willing to sacrifice the use of men whose help may be decisive in the emergency for the putative value of maximizing the most valued substantive ends over the long run. After the site selection struggle began, it was clear that the all-important need was to persuade the Council to accept a reasonable number of vacant land sites; this and related problems occupied the attention of the top staff day and night for many months. But even before 1948, when the Authority was free to select sites without much attention to the politicians, day-to-day problems were always more important than the long-term ones. Even then, planning was never an emergency and the problems of the day were always emergencies. Try as they might, the top staff never managed to insulate themselves from the pressures of the day long enough to think systematically about fundamentals.*

Some people are temperamentally incapable of reflection, of dealing with the larger aspects of matters, of seeing the elements of a situation in their mutual relations, or of viewing affairs in a long perspective of time. Although they may be poorly qualified, temperamentally, for planning these people are sometimes in charge of planning agencies or staffs. There is, in fact, a natural selection which tends to fill top planning posts with such people. Engineers, whose bent is often toward detailed designing or the making of precise calculations, are one source from which the heads of planning bodies are drawn. Administrators and

---

* This was perhaps not altogether because of the pressure of external circumstance. Meyerson found that the excitement of the site selection struggle had many attractions: one enjoyed the secret sessions where strategy was mapped, the hurried trips to the City Hall and the seats of power and returning home a wounded warrior after standing up to the boos and hisses of the gallery hour after hour. To escape the more rigorous demands of routine work by taking flight into a world of intrigue where wonders could be accomplished by pulling the right string was an allurement which some people found irresistible.

politicians—people with a flair for dealing with crisis situations and for solving the problem of the moment on an expediental basis—are another. That these types may not be good planners (although they may excel in other aspects of top staff positions) would be of relatively little consequence if it were not for the fact that as the heads of planning bodies they are in a position to prevent others from doing effective planning. Unless the head of an agency wants comprehensive planning to be done it is hardly possible for it to be done. In the case of the Authority, the commissioners were on the whole concerned with minutiae and this, as we have pointed out, tended somewhat to discourage the staff from planning. The principal staff members, however, were temperamentally inclined toward planning. Certainly Miss Wood, although she was often in haste, thus creating turmoil among the lower levels of the staff, had an unusual capacity for sustained thought about fundamentals.

Even if administrators are willing to incur the cost of devoting a good part of their own time and that of their most able associates to planning, they are often reluctant to make other sacrifices that may be required. They may, for example, in a housing agency prefer to employ an additional race relations adviser rather than an additional planner. Or they may prefer to use their limited stock of influence to get raises in pay for the typists rather than to defend budget requests for planning. The immediate and visible returns from these other uses of means are generally greater than from planning, and, whether or not they actually are greater, the organization can usually survive and prosper without planning, whereas without certain other services (e.g., typing) it cannot continue even a day.*

Finally, the Authority did not systematically explore the alternatives that existed within its opportunity area because—so it

---

* "This then," wrote Sir Henry Taylor in 1832, "is the great evil and want—that there is not within the pale of our government any adequately numerous body of efficient statesmen, some to be more externally active and answer to the demands of the day, others to be somewhat more retired and meditative in order that they may take thought for the morrow." But Taylor added, "I hardly know if that minister has existed in the present generation, who, if such a mind were casually presented to him, would not forego the use of it rather than hazard a debate in the House of Commons upon an additional item in his expenses." *The Statesman*, Cambridge, 1927, pp. 115-19.

seemed—common sense was enough to reveal that one alternative (*viz.* large projects) was obviously better than the others. Thus at one time the Authority gave the idea of small decentralized projects, for example, no serious consideration because the staff thought it obvious that small projects would soon be swallowed up by the surrounding slum, that they would surely be segregated, and that in most cases they would lack adequate community facilities. If common sense was enough to reveal these disadvantages—disadvantages that were certainly decisive, what need was there of an elaborate planning process that would only describe them more precisely and systematically?

To drop from consideration all alternatives which would have decisively undesirable consequences was, of course, the reasonable thing to do. But there was some danger that if only common sense were relied upon, alternatives might be dropped from consideration prematurely, i.e., that the anticipated consequences might not really be associated with the course of action, or that, even if they were, they might not be conclusive against it. Moreover, systematic research might show that such courses of action had advantages which were not apparent to common sense but which nevertheless more than outweighed the disadvantages. And, of course, eliminating all obviously objectionable alternatives until only one remained might obscure the disadvantages of the one remaining. Thus, although it was certainly a serious disadvantage of slum rehabilitation as a course of action that the rehabilitated areas might soon decay into slums again, it might be an even greater disadvantage of the alternative—large new projects—that it might destroy social organization in the neighborhoods that were to be rebuilt.

As the case study shows, the Authority made little use of social science or of any technical knowledge regarding social phenomena. Not only in Chicago but everywhere else housing authorities (and probably most agencies and organizations) made decisions on the basis of scanty and impressionistic data or of no data at all. No one, for example, had precise or systematic knowledge of the ends that people entertained regarding public housing. There had always been a sizeable fraction of the slum dwellers who did not move into public projects when they had the chance, but no one knew very clearly why they did not or exactly what became of them when they were displaced from their old neighborhoods. It might be that the clearance of slums in one place created new slums or worsened old ones somewhere else. No one knew. That Negroes who were displaced by projects would find their way into white areas seemed certain to the staff in 1949, but no one could say with assurance which areas would be most affected or to what extent. That the presence of Negroes would reduce property values in the outlying neighborhoods seemed certain to the anti-public housing property owners, but there was no real evidence bearing on the question one way or the other. And it was not clear that the opposition to Negroes rested altogether on race prejudice; as we have pointed out above, there were other possible explanations which would have quite a different practical significance. From a practical standpoint all of these questions were vital, but on none of them was there much of any information.

To have assembled a useful amount of information on even these few matters would have required a large staff of highly trained researchers (Meyerson found that most of the time of the 20 staff members who at one point were in the Development Department's Statistics and Research Division had to be devoted to operating statistics)—more of a staff certainly than it would be reasonable to expect the Authority to employ. If it had tried to get all the information it needed, the Authority would have been in danger of becoming a research rather than an action agency. And even if it confined its research to matters of pressing practical importance, it might for various reasons find it impossible to use the results effectively—for example, the results might come too late to be taken into account, the decision might have to be based on grounds to which the results were largely or wholly irrelevant, or there might not happen to be anyone on the staff who had the interest, skill, or more likely the time to interpret and apply the results.*

* As Miss Wood once explained: ". . . I have been very skeptical of the ability of research to help a housing operator solve the problems that confront him. At times I have been anti-research. . . . we did try to solicit the aid of research people. By the time the researchers had defined the problem, debated about proper methodology, taken their observations using the most precise techniques, made a highly refined and scientific analysis, and prepared their report, the emergencies which had given rise to the research had already

The knowledge the Authority most needed was not the kind that social scientists as such could supply. There was no reason to believe that a social scientist, or a planning technician using social science, would be better equipped, or even as well equipped, as an administrator like Miss Wood or a lawyer like Fruchtman to chart the agency's opportunity area, to clarify and order its end-system, to delineate the alternative courses of action that were open to it, or to identify and evaluate the consequences that would probably attend each course of action. Social science, when it could be used at all, could probably be best used to support and make more definite some general conclusions to which the administrators had already come.*

The Authority's most important decisions had to rest mainly

---

reached a climax several months earlier, been handled in the best way possible by the operators, and the housing program had passed on to other problems. Not only was this research too late, but most of it was phrased in a language which was difficult to understand and apply to practical situations.

"Many of the pieces of research which have proved most useful to public housing operators, such as myself, have been beaten out hastily, using the evidence that could be accumulated quickly, in order to help formulate a policy or make a decision that could not be delayed.

"Even when available, research findings can be only one of the elements entering into a decision. For example, we once sponsored a very successful study of the relationship between income and the ability to pay rent. The question was, 'Can a family pay 1/3 of its income for rent and yet have enough left to nourish the family?' Our study showed that under such conditions fathers and children were sufficiently well nourished, but mothers tended to be undernourished. With this conclusion, we were still confronted with the perplexing problem of whether to leave low-income families in health-destroying, overcrowded slum houses or to permit undernourished mothers to starve in greater comfort! The point I want to make clear here is this: a single piece of operation cannot be implemented with a single piece of research. Implementation involves many considerations to which research can only make a modest contribution." Elizabeth Wood in D. J. Bogue (ed.), *Needed Urban and Metropolitan Research, op. cit.*

* According to E. A. Shils, the vast majority of the social scientists in power-exercising bodies perform "intelligence functions." "This means that social scientists are not drawn upon for their wisdom as counsellors in the delineation of fundamental alternatives nor as guides in the choice from among these alternatives once discovered. Neither in the main are they looked to for basic truths about human behavior derived either from rigorous scientific research or from the slow accretion of wisdom. Social scientists are rather viewed as instruments for the reporting of descriptive data about particular and concrete situations. For the most part they provide estimates, more or less accurate, of the magnitude of the different variables." E. A. Shils, "Social Science and Social Policy," *Philosophy of Science*, Vol. 16, No. 3, July 1949, p. 223.

For a comprehensive discussion of the contribution that social science research might make to housing policy see Robert K. Merton, "The Social Psychology of Housing" in *Current Trends in Social Psychology*, University of Pittsburgh Press. Pittsburgh, 1948.

on value judgments (especially as to whose ends, among conflicting ends, should be made the basis of action) and on probability judgments (especially as to how actors would respond to situations that might arise or to incentives or sanctions that the Authority might offer). Social science research could do little to improve either kind of decision. How much, if any, weight the Authority ought to attach to the wishes of white property owners, for example, was not a question which research could help to answer. Neither was the question of how the City Council would respond to the pressure of an aroused Negro community. But even with such questions as research might help to answer (would whites be more apt to live harmoniously with Negroes in large projects or in small?) the "scientific" component of the answer was likely to be a small part of the whole: i.e., when a "technical" element existed, the decision-maker had to combine it with a vastly larger element of judgment. Whether factual knowledge that had to be so greatly diluted by judgment was worth what it cost might ordinarily be doubtful.

What was needed was not research, but experiment or, better yet, "pilot" operation of various alternatives. The Authority needed not so much to know the magnitudes of particular variables as to know what all of the relevant variables were and how they influenced each other: it needed to know the *set* of consequences which a characteristic *combination* of factors would bring into being. The way to discover and evaluate the advantages and disadvantages of slum rehabilitation as an alternative to slum clearance, for example, was actually to rehabilitate a few blocks and to appraise the results with care. Similarly, a way to find out whether publicly owned but privately managed projects would have fewer status disadvantages in the eyes of white tenants and neighboring property owners was to turn one or two projects over to private management and to study the results.

The Chicago Authority was more inclined toward experiment than most other housing authorities, but, even so, it did not do as much in this direction as it might have done and it did not systematically evaluate the results of such new undertakings as it did try.*

* In 1954 the Authority was actually developing a rehabilitation project.

The best opportunities for research and experiment lay not with any local authority but with the Public Housing Administration. That agency was in a position to serve hundreds of local authorities as a central research bureau and as a clearing-house through which the results of local studies and experience could be exchanged. The Housing and Home Finance Agency (the "parent" agency of PHA) did carry on research on construction technology and it did some economic and other fact-gathering and analyses. But these undertakings were far from sufficient to meet the needs of local authorities. How poorly informed the Chicago Authority was of experience elsewhere can be seen from the fact that it was necessary for the staff and the commissioners to work out a set of general site selection criteria on the basis of little information even though thousands of projects had already been built by some 900 local authorities. In our opinion, the experience of all these cities should have been continuously studied by PHA and the results of the studies should have been summarized and interpreted by it and made available to the cities in a form that would be serviceable to planning technicians and to policy-makers.

A nation can try out only one fiscal policy at a time, but housing is a different matter; since there were hundreds of cities and thousands of projects it was possible for PHA to have tested in pilot programs a wide variety of courses of action. It was entirely practical for one city to try out rent certificates and a rigid enforcement of the housing code while a second tried decentralized, privately-managed, publicly-owned housing and a third tried rehabilitation of slum structures, the creation in the interstices of the slum of facilities like parks and playgrounds, and the improvement of schools. In our opinion, PHA should have sponsored a systematic program of such pilot operations, underwriting any special financial burdens it might place upon the cities and making certain that the results of each operation were carefully appraised and made available in useful form to all local authorities.[3]

Whether this could be called a pilot operation was not clear, however. The site was one which the Authority had acquired as a slum fit only for clearance. Later it developed that most of the buildings were too good to be destroyed. No special arrangements were made for the systematic evaluation of the results of this undertaking.

Out of the Cocoon

CHAPTER ELEVEN ☐ ☐ ☐ ☐ ☐ ☐

THE PUBLIC INTEREST

AT THE HEIGHT of the site selection struggle, the editors of the *Sun-Times* pointed to it as evidence that the city government was in need of drastic reorganization.

"Chicago needs a city government which can govern," the editorial began. "Chicago needs a city government which will provide a just and workable balance between the local interests of its many neighborhoods and the general interests of the city as a whole. Chicago needs a city government which can plan, legislate, and administer public services for the common good of all of its two million citizens, rather than for the special interests of special groups."

With a city council consisting of 50 delegates from 50 localities, each elected by a small constituency, each owing nothing to the city at large, and with only the mayor elected by the citizens at large, it was inevitable, the editorial said, that local interests, narrow interests, sectional interests, factional interests should often prevail over the interest of the city as a whole. Chicago should have a council of 15 or 20 members. In order that local interests have fair representation, half of the council, perhaps, should be elected by districts. The rest of the members, together with the mayor, should be elected by and represent the city at large. "Such a city government," the editorial concluded, "would not always act wisely. But at least it could come to some decision on the vital problems of a vital metropolis. And when it acted unwisely, its members could be held responsible at the polls."[1]

This view was widely accepted among students of municipal government in Chicago and elsewhere. Indeed, not many important cities still had governments like Chicago's. For many years the trend all over the country had been to reduce the number and powers of aldermen and to increase the powers of the executive. In several hundred cities (although not in any of the 20 largest) a small elected council hired a professional manager who administered the affairs of the city as unpolitically as if it were a business or a factory.*

That Chicago's government was behind the times was unquestionable. But it was probably exaggerated to say, as the *Sun-Times* did, and as many liberals concerned with reform in Chicago did, that the struggle over public housing showed that the city could not act effectively because it was broken into 50 wards, each represented by an alderman. In fact, there rarely was a moment during the long struggle when Duffy and the other "Big Boys" could not have made a decision for the Council and for the city. Power was not divided among the 50 aldermen or even, as the *Sun-Times* suggested it should be, among 15 or 20 aldermen and a mayor: it was amply concentrated in the hands of two or three aldermen. These two or three, moreover, although particularly concerned with the interests of their wards and with the interest of the South Side, were also concerned very actively, if not with the interests of the city as a whole, at least with the maintenance of the Democratic organization in the city as a whole. In addition, Duffy, the most powerful of the "Big Boys,"

* The National Municipal League's first charter, published in 1900, was intended to make city government less susceptible to government by party machinery; it concentrated executive powers in the mayor, gave him authority to appoint his principal subordinates without approval by the legislative branch, and put legislative powers in a unicameral council elected at large. See H. A. Stone, D. K. Price, and K. A. Stone, *City Manager Government in the United States,* Public Administration Service, Chicago, 1940, pp. 4-5. The fifth edition of the model city charter called for a strong city manager. "For the accomplishment of its democratic purpose," the authors wrote, "the Charter concentrates all the powers of the municipality in a compact council of elected representatives with full responsibility for determinations of policy. In order to obtain administrative efficiency, the Charter concentrates the actual administration in a single administrative officer who is appointed by and is at all times responsible to the council. Under this plan, there can be no avoidance of responsibility either by the people's representatives for the determinations of policy, or by the administrative appointee for the actual administration. The plan of the Charter is based on the concept of entrusting administration to men trained in municipal management, which concept in turn assumes the building up of a profession of management. This assumption has already been realized." National Municipal League, *Model City Charter,* Fifth Ed., 1941, p. xv.

was running for a county office and so of course had to take account of the wishes of voters throughout the city.

Concentrated as it was, power was less concentrated in 1949 and 1950 than it had been for many years past. Mayor Kelly had ruled the city almost despotically. That Chicago had a weak mayor in 1949 and 1950 and that there were two factions within the Council was an unusual circumstance, one to be explained, perhaps, by the fact that some time would have to elapse before the power-vacuum created by Kelly's retirement could be filled. Certainly under Kelly's administration no one had ever complained that the city could not reach decisions regarding public housing or other matters. "Under Kelly," as Duffy once remarked, "the Housing Authority submitted a proposal and that was it."[2]

In Chicago, political power was highly decentralized *formally* but highly centralized *informally*. The city had what textbooks in municipal government called a "weak-mayor" form of government to be sure, but it also had a powerful mayor, or, if not a powerful mayor, a powerful leader of the Council. This paradox of a "weak" government that was strong was to be explained by the presence of the Democratic machine, an organization parallel to the city government but outside of it, in which power sufficient to run the city was centralized. The weakness of the city government was offset by the strength of the party.

The "Big Boys" could get and keep power enough to run the city only by giving the favors, protection, and patronage which were essential for the maintenance of the machine. It is quite possible, of course, that they preferred to operate the city government in this way. But whether they preferred it or not, the "spoils system" and even to some extent the alliance between crime and politics were the price that had to be paid to overcome the extreme decentralization of formal power. If overnight the bosses became model administrators—if they put all of the city jobs on the merit system, destroyed the syndicate, and put an end to petty grafting, then the city government would really be as weak and ineffective as the *Sun-Times* said. Indeed, under Kennelly the government of Chicago became both a great deal cleaner and a great deal weaker than it had been for many years.

The people of Chicago probably did not fully realize the price that was being paid to assemble power enough to govern the city. But although it had never calculated the costs in deliberate ways, the public, it seems safe to say, had some awareness both that these costs were there and that there were some benefits in return—in fact, the disadvantages of a formal centralization of power, although different in kind, might possibly be even greater.

As they actually worked (but not as they were formally designed to work), Chicago's governmental institutions achieved a high degree of centralization *and* a high degree of decentralization: they put a great deal of power over some matters in the hands of the city administration while leaving a great deal of power over other matters in the hands of the neighborhood and ward leaders. The politically active people in the wards had their way in all matters which were not of first importance to the city administration. The voter who stood well with his precinct captain (and most voters could) could expect prompt action if he complained that the street in front of his house needed repairs, if he wanted a change in the zoning law so that his son-in-law could go in the pants-pressing business, or if the traffic cop was too free with his tickets. Having power like this close at hand was of great importance to many people: street repairs, zoning changes, traffic tickets and the like were the main business of city government from the standpoint of most citizens. Government so close to many people and so responsive to them was "grassroots democracy," although perhaps not the kind that those who most use the term would recognize as such.

Most of the matters that were decided locally were of local interest. Whether a street was to be repaved, the zoning law for a block changed, and the traffic cop transferred were questions which had direct and clearly ascertainable consequences mainly for the locality. It was true that they might have even more important indirect consequences for the city as a whole (for example, an exception to the zoning law may set in motion a series of changes which cause the decay of the neighborhood and ultimately affect the ecology of the whole city) but these consequences were usually so obscure and so involved in detail that a central authority would rarely have staff or time to take them into account. Some matters were on the border between being of local and of city-wide interest or were of both local and city-wide interest. In these matters there would be friction because of overlapping jurisdictions of the local and central powerholders, but this was not a very strong argument for eliminating local autonomy altogether.

Whether an issue is to be regarded as primarily of local or primarily of city-wide interest may depend upon the observer's value premises and especially upon whether his model of the public interest is individualistic or unitary. One who takes what we call an organismic view of the view of the public interest subordinates all other interests to that of the social "organism." At the other extreme, the Utilitarian, granting that matters like housing have more than contingent or constructive importance to the whole population of the city, tries to compare utilities so as to arrive at the "greatest happiness."

Machine government (which, as its opponents have always recognized, depends for its existence upon ward organization and a formally weak executive) and its opposite, "honest and efficient administration in the public interest" (which implies a small council elected at large, often by proportional representation, and a strong mayor or city manager), are suitable to separate and distinct social and economic class interests.

Lower and lower-middle class people, especially members of ethnic minorities, have often favored machine government rather than its opposite, and not, we think, chiefly because, as Lord Bryce and many others have supposed, they have been ignorant of democratic traditions. Many of these people have found the ward and precinct organization an almost indispensable intermediary between them and the formal organs of government, especially the courts, and they have known that the machines, however corrupt they might be, are run by people of economic and ethnic origins similar to their own. The interests these people usually regard as most important are local, not city-wide, and their outlook is generally self- or family-regarding rather than community-regarding. Machine government seems to serve them best.

It is mainly upper and middle class people who have fought the machines and sought to establish a cleaner, more businesslike, and more respectable government. As a general rule people of these classes have little need of petty favors; many of them have business or other interests which are city-wide and which are facilitated by progressive, impartial, and low-cost administration; many of them act in representative rather than in personal roles (e.g., as officers of voluntary associations) and these roles are commonly community-regarding,* and, of course, upper and middle class people, too, like to be ruled by their own kind.

In communities where middle and upper class people have an overwhelming preponderance of political power—despite their sizeable numbers, these groups, except for some businessmen, were typically bypassed by the Chicago machine—this model of local government, the apogee of which is the council-manager system, is likely to succeed very well. But where control is not firmly in the hands of the middle and upper classes or where there is an important ethnic or class minority—and therefore in all of the great polyglot metropolises of the United States—"honest, impartial, businesslike" government is not likely to be tolerated for long because it runs counter to the ends and to the class feeling of many citizens.†

It was, we think, an advantage of the Chicago system of gov-

* ". . . the Gold Coast is the only element in the city's life that sees the city as a whole, dreams for it as a whole," Zorbaugh remarked in *The Gold Coast and the Slum, op. cit.*, p. 274. In the public discussion of sites for public housing it was notable, of course, that the proponents of public housing, most of whom were upper-middle class, viewed the problem in its city-wide aspects whereas the opponents, most of whom were lower-middle class, viewed it almost entirely from a neighborhood standpoint.

† Almost without exception, studies of the adoptions and abandonments of the city-manager form of government show that it is opposed by lower class and supported by upper class people. The following passages from a report on city manager government in Jackson, Michigan, can be paralleled by passages from almost all of the many similar reports: "The first thing that the council did threw light upon the motives which had brought about the change in the form of government. It discharged most of the Catholic municipal employees and replaced them mostly by Protestants. The religious difference between the new and the old governments was clearly drawn; it is significant that the new council celebrated the establishment of the new form of government with a reception in the Masonic Temple.

"Next, the council proceeded to take away the licenses of a number of saloons and to give some of them by preference to hotels, on the theory (according to

ernment that it conformed to the tastes and interests of the most numerous social group (no government which did not do this reasonably well could survive, of course, but foolish and costly and less successful attempts might have been made and might have persisted long enough to do great damage). But it was also an advantage of the Chicago system that, while keeping control over local matters within the voters' reach, it interposed the party between the voters and the most important city-wide (as well as state- and nation-wide) decisions. The heads of the machine could not ignore the voters on all issues, but they could ignore them on many issues and on almost any particular issue. The advantages of this were great. Chicago was not governed, as are some cities in which strong machines do not stand between the voter and the issue, by the pull and haul of a few irresponsible pressure groups which get the voter's ear at election time;* instead, there were only two important political organizations, the Democratic and the Republican parties, both of which had to accept some responsibility for not one or a few interests but for all of the many conflicting interests that were important in the life of the city. And since they depended upon a highly disciplined organization built upon a system of material incentives, the leaders of the machine did not have to rely mainly upon ideological

the newspapers) that it was both more moral and more profitable to sell liquor to non-residents." (pp. 221-22.)

The small taxpayers were not satisfied with the impartial administration of the city manager. "It did not comfort them to know that even the mayor himself was not exempt from arrest for speeding when the scale of fines had been increased and that the manager was proclaiming that 'the citizen arrested can make all the fuss he wants to but the manager will give him no satisfaction.' They were not interested in a mechanical, impartial system of administration, and the *Saturday Evening Star* voiced their feeling in 1922 when it said that 'a majority of the voters are sick and tired of the aristocratic, highbrow, unrepresentative administration by the five commissioners.'" (pp. 225-26.) From H. A. Stone, D. K. Price, and K. H. Stone, *City Manager Government in Nine Cities,* Public Administration Service, Chicago, 1940, and Edwin O. Stene and G. K. Floro, *Abandonments of the Manager Plan,* University of Kansas Governmental Research Center, 1953.

* In Minneapolis, for example, nonpartisanship in local elections "has resulted in government by pressure groups—labor unions, business associations, etc.—rather than by parties at the city level." The aldermen in Minneapolis "consider themselves more dependent upon the support of powerful pressure groups and party organization has suffered as a consequence." Robert L. Morlan, "City Politics: Free Style," *National Municipal Review,* Vol. XXXVIII, No. 10, November 1949, pp. 485-490.

appeals to the voter. This meant that, although issues were often decided upon non-ideological grounds, they were not settled upon the basis of an anti-democratic ideology. The South Side of Chicago, it should be remembered, was Studs Lonigan's stamping ground, and Studs and his friends would have been happy to vote for a man like Senator McCarthy (who was a product of ideological, not of machine, politics); instead, they voted for Governor Adlai Stevenson and Senator Paul Douglas because Jacob Arvey, the man who ran the Democratic machine, could afford on behalf of its liberal wing the luxury of some "high class" candidates.

In our opinion, believers in traditional democracy, both the conservatives and the liberals among them, in their criticism have neglected the advantages of effective machines in Chicago. The machines not only give the mass of the people, with their limited interest in politics (what some would call their "apathy") the kind of government they seem to want—or least object to—but they also insulate traditional democratic values and institutions from the forces which unscrupulous demagogues using mass communications media can so easily unloose in a society deeply divided by ethnic, economic and other conflicts.* Naively to

---

* Mannheim observes that the destruction of certain social structures which mediate between the elites and the masses "heightens the significance of the completely fluid mass." The political machine may be regarded as one such structure and its disappearance as an incident in a process which is occurring in many social realms. See Karl Mannheim, *Man and Society in an Age of Reconstruction,* Harcourt, Brace, New York, 1948, pp. 96-98.

Robert K. Merton has pointed out that large sectors of the American population make moral evaluations of the political machine in terms of the manifest consequences of a practice or code: bossism violates the code that votes should be based on individual appraisal of political issues, etc. However, Merton says, the machine satisfies basic latent functions, including the following: 1. It is an antidote to the constitutional dispersion of power, 2. It humanizes and personalizes all manner of assistance to those in need, 3. It provides business (including illegal business) those political privileges which entail immediate economic gains, and 4. It provides alternative channels of social mobility for those otherwise excluded from the more conventional avenues for personal "advancement." The importance of these and other latent functions of the machine explains why efforts at reform are typically short-lived and ineffective; "*any attempt to eliminate an existing social structure without providing adequate alternative structures for fulfilling the functions previously fulfilled by the abolished organization is doomed to failure.*" *Social Theory and Social Structure,* The Free Press, Glencoe, Illinois, 1949, pp. 72-79.

David Riesman has mentioned another latent function of the machine and one especially pertinent to this study. ". . . It is important to study those institutions in our society which allow society to function precisely in the face of profound disagreements on fundamentals. One of these institutions, I suggest, is the city

destroy the political machines and to undertake to govern the city in the way its "best elements" think is impartial, businesslike, and in the public interest is to run the risk of deepening the conflicts which already exist while at the same time discarding a social structure by which conflicts may be confined and managed.*

If, as some of the reformers had suggested for years, the size of the Council were to be reduced to 15 or 20 members, half of them elected at large, and if the power of the machine were also reduced (as we suppose they intended), the result in our opinion would be to eliminate both the regulated local autonomy which many people so prize and the concentration of power in the hands of the city's leaders which makes effective city-wide action possible. Instead of

---

bosses and their machines: these act as brokers among competing urban values, based as they are on religious, ethnic, occupational and other identifications. These bosses can trade a park in a middle-class section for a symbolically important Italian judgeship, and otherwise keep a tolerable peace by appropriate pay-offs from the spoils of American productivity. The current attempt to unify the country against municipal patronage and bossism seems to me dangerous, because by enforcing an ideological unity on politics we threaten with extinction a few men, soaked in gravy we can well spare, who protect our ideological pluralism." *Individualism Reconsidered,* The Free Press, Glencoe, Illinois, 1954, pp. 17-18.

* This is not the place to discuss at length what should be done about civic corruption or the alliance between crime and politics in Chicago. In our opinion, a great deal of reform can and should be expected, although a machine probably cannot exist without some kind of patronage or favors (what some people will call graft). The main reason why the machine leaders—even in the face of adverse public opinion—do not reform it is, in our opinion, that most of them do not have sufficient power; i.e., they cannot afford to sacrifice the support of certain corrupt powerholders, much as they might wish to do so.

The reader should be cautioned also that since our focus is on how certain decisions were made in a recent period we concentrate on static or short term concerns. Speculating on the longer term prospects of the local political machines, a parallel to Joseph Schumpeter's analysis of capitalism occurs to us. (*Capitalism, Socialism and Democracy,* Harper, New York, 1950 ed.) Both capitalism and the political machine have a logical structure capable of effectively allocating rewards and punishments in a way to maintain and develop an ongoing system. However, as Schumpeter indicates for capitalism, and as we suggest for the political machine, in actuality the successes of both kinds of systems breed men and conditions which are not conducive to their long-term effectiveness. In both systems the bold entrepreneur gives way to the official without "nerve." Tammany Hall's De Sapio in New York and the present leaders of the machine in Chicago are "genteel" compared to their predecessors. (See Robert L. Heilbroner, "De Sapio: The Smile on the Face of the Tiger," *Harper's,* Volume 209, No. 1250, July 1954, pp. 23-33.) Situationally, a high level of economic opportunities, the assimilation of ethnic groups, the substitution of Federal welfare and public works programs for local ones, and the adoption of certain machine tactics by labor and citizen organizations are leading to major transformation of the machines as they have been known.

making the government of the city stronger, such a change would make it weaker; while making it impossible to decide anything on a neighborhood basis, it would also make it impossible to decide anything centrally.

In order to centralize formally as much power as is now centralized informally, a governing body of not more than six persons, all elected for long, overlapping terms from a city-wide constituency and a mayor whose power is preponderant within the governing body might be required. Little short of such extreme centralization would yield power enough to govern the city in the absence of some kind—not necessarily the present kind—of a strong machine. The dangers of such a government we have already pointed to, but the more probable danger—the danger associated with a half-way proposal such as that proposed by the *Sun-Times* and the liberal reform groups—is of a government which would not have enough power, formal and informal, to enable it to rule effectively.

Since 1938, New York has had the kind of a governmental structure that students of municipal administration generally approve.* New York, therefore, offers an instructive contrast to Chicago, the institutions of which are often taken as an example of the worst that can be found.

In New York, power is highly centralized both formally and informally. The city is governed by the Board of Estimate, a body consisting of the five borough presidents, the comptroller, the president of the almost vestigial City Council, and the mayor. The mayor has three votes in the Board and he is the chief ad-

* It is of interest, however, that Robert Moses once said (in 1939) that the charter of 1938 "has done little more than complicate our city government, and make it more expensive, longwinded, cumbersome, and discouraging to first-rate talent than it was before." "There were," according to Moses, "too many aldermen and too many districts under the old system, but the district plan of representation based on one man getting more votes than any other among the people who knew him best was a useful safety valve in our polyglot city. Personally I got an immense amount of sound advice and help from the old aldermen, and I devoutly hope we shall return to some kind of district representation. . . ." Robert Moses, *Theory and Practice in Politics*, Harvard University Press, Cambridge, 1939, pp. 38 and 40.

New York, it should be noted, differs decidedly from Chicago in having much less inter-racial antagonism and, in fact, a widespread acceptance of the principles of non-discrimination and non-segregation.

ministrative officer of the city: the major city departments are directly responsible to him. Within this formally-centralized structure, moreover, there has arisen a further, informal centralization. Since 1934, a gifted man named Robert Moses has come to be the undisputed head of what is virtually a parallel government of matters concerning public works and related activities. Moses' only salaried job is Park Commissioner, but he has managed to get formal or informal control of several key agencies and, by placing his engineers, architects and other followers in strategic positions and by rewarding his friends and punishing his enemies among the host of contractors, consultants, and politicians who depend in one way or another on the operations he controls, he has managed to build what Chicago politicians would call an "organization," albeit one which is generally supposed to be "clean." City administrations come and go, but Moses keeps his tight grip on countless committees, boards, authorities, and commissions, and Moses is an exceedingly highhanded man.*

New York City has built a great deal of public housing and it has built it without graft. Unlike the Chicago ones, the New York projects are not racially segregated, but this is owing not so much to the centralization of municipal government in New York or to Moses as to the circumstance that the city has about 2,500,000 Jews, 600,000 Negroes, 250,000 Puerto Ricans, and 1,000,000 Italo-Americans. Moses himself has never been especially concerned about racial issues: indeed, he has been outspokenly contemptuous of "long-haired" efforts to achieve "social" objectives of any kind.

The Board of Estimate and Moses have had enough power between them to prevent the New York City Planning Commission

---

* In addition to his salaried job as Park Commissioner, Moses is City Construction Coordinator, chairman of the Triborough Bridge and Tunnel Authority, a member of the City Planning Commission, chairman of the Long Island State Park Commission and of several related authorities, chairman of the State Council of Parks, and chairman of the City Emergency Housing Committee and of a successor committee on slum clearance. In 1954 he became chairman of the State Power Authority as well. These, however, are only the organizations with which he has a formal connection; others, including the New York City Housing Authority, he greatly influences, by informal means. For an account of the way Moses functions, see the case-history "Gotham in the Air Age," in Harold Stein (ed.), *Public Administration and Policy Development*, Harcourt, Brace, New York, 1952.

from functioning effectively, and this although the Commission has extraordinary legal powers. The City Charter directs the Commission to prepare a master plan for city development and it provides that all proposals for capital improvements must either conform to the master plan, be approved by the City Planning Commission or be approved by a three-quarters vote of the Board of Estimate. Despite these requirements, the Commission, the budget of which is passed upon by the Board of Estimate, has never been given staff sufficient to prepare a comprehensive or master plan.[3] As a basis for decisions regarding public housing, the work of the New York City Planning Commission was no more derived from a comprehensive plan than that of its counterpart in Chicago.

Ordinarily in New York it is possible to protest the location of a public housing project only *after* the decision has been virtually made. Such preliminary planning as is done is usually completed before a project proposal is submitted to the City Planning Commission and the Board of Estimate and the groundwork for the project's acceptance by the Board is laid in advance behind the scenes by the Moses organization. Thus the Citizens' Housing and Planning Council of New York is occupied not so much appealing for new projects as getting an opportunity to be heard before the Board of Estimate on projects already planned. Sometimes the Council is unable to get any information about a project until the planning is almost done. Recently, when the City Planning Commission held hearings on a housing and redevelopment plan, the proposal was criticized by the Council, the Citizens' Union, the New York Chapter of the American Institute of Planners, and the Metropolitan Committee on Planning. The areas selected for housing and redevelopment, the Citizens' Council said, "have been spotted without any consideration of their relationship to the larger areas of which they are a part, or to the existence of basic utilities, schools, transportation, and other facilities which are necessary for the proper development of entire areas in the city as a whole."

Judging from this, these sites were not particularly superior to the "bus-window" selections made by the Chicago aldermen. But the parallel between New York and Chicago is even closer. According to the Citizens' Housing and Planning Council, Moses in 1952 by-passed the Federal regulations requiring equitable provision of public housing for all minority groups. According to a Council spokesman, one of Moses' committees said that 20 per cent of the persons living on certain proposed public housing sites would find places in the new projects, whereas in fact, because of income and other requirements, only four per cent were eligible.[4]

These indications are perhaps enough to suggest that, even if ample power is centralized in the hands of an able administrator (in this case, of course, one opposed to planning), site selection for public housing may not be done much better, if indeed any better, than it was done in Chicago. But even if this was not the case—even if the public housing program in New York was all that Moses would claim—we do not think that it would necessarily follow that the New York way of making decisions is altogether preferable to the Chicago way. In even the biggest cities the local community remains an important agency of social control. To be sure, in metropolitan areas it is not possible for the local community, as such, to take much part in deciding the "big" issues of the day; nevertheless, it is politically important, for identification with a local community or neighborhood seems to encourage some people to acquire the interests and skills that make for political competence.* But this identification and this encouragement to political competence can only occur if some real power remains in the local community. If all power is in the hands of a hierarchy with a high-handed and "efficient" administrator like Moses at the top, then a local community leader like Stech, the truck driver who led a crusade against public housing in Chicago in order to get into politics, would not have a path to political action or power. However, unless there is real power—not merely the shadow of it—to be exercised locally, "grassroots democracy" is meaningless. Even in New York, of

* This thesis is developed by Morris Janowitz, *op. cit.*, pp. 216-222.

J. S. Mill stressed the view that local administrative institutions are the chief instrument by which the public education of the citizens, an object the importance of which, he said, could hardly be overemphasized, was to be attained. ". . . these local functions, not being in general sought by the higher ranks, carry down the important political education which they are the means of conferring to a much lower grade in society." *Op. cit.*, p. 348.

course, political and other organizations do offer local community leaders some scope; these opportunities, though, seem to be fewer and more limited there than in Chicago.

That the "Big Boys" had power enough to make decisions in the public interest did not mean that they would do so. The very fact that most of their power was held informally was an encouragement to *sub rosa* deals by which they might personally profit at the expense of the public interest; "insiders" who "knew the ropes" might have undue influence on them, perhaps even by bribery. Unquestionably there have been times when some leaders of the machine have taken bribes. (It was said that Samuel Insull was more responsible for the corruption of Chicago government than any one man.) In the case of the public housing issue, however, it seems that the "Big Boys" were not bribed or otherwise "captured" by the powerful interests which opposed public housing or, for that matter, by the Authority itself.*

Our conjecture is that in the housing struggle the "Big Boys" were trying to do what they thought would be best for the party. What was best for the party, they probably thought, would also be best for the city as a whole.†

---

* In 1952, however, a prominent real estate broker told an interviewer that a group of private developers was thinking of building housing for Negroes on the site in Duffy's ward which had been proposed by the Authority and rejected by the Council in 1949. "Mr. ——— feels," the interviewer recorded, "that the site could be made available through the efforts of Alderman [sic] Duffy. He admits that Duffy would probably lose his job and that another would have to be provided for him, but this would be a small price to pay for the new housing. He stated that a group of 'public spirited citizens' was going to make the money available."[5] Whether or not Duffy would have listened to such a proposition we do not know. But it seems fair to say that the real estate broker was not proposing to "bribe" Duffy, but only to offer him a reasonable recompense for losses he might suffer from allowing the "public interest" to prevail over the interest of his ward. We suspect that the real estate broker would not have dared to offer Duffy a bribe and that even if he had dared, he would have refrained from doing so out of principle. The Authority, of course, was even higher principled: it would not offer Duffy any favors—not even deference—in return for the sacrifices it expected him to make.

† That organizational maintenance and the public interest are closely related if not quite identical, that organizational maintenance is more important to the head of the machine than is the public interest, and that it is considered good public relations to assert the paramountcy of the public interest can all be seen from the following quotation from the Bronx boss, Edward J. Flynn: ". . . any action I take must be one which will benefit the people of the Bronx first and enhance the prestige of the organization second. I mention the people first, because it is one of our political legends that bosses never pay any attention to

This, of course, was a rather simple-minded view of the matter. The public on which the machine depended for maintenance—despite our stress on the machine's broad base—was by no means the whole public of Chicago: and so what might be very good for the machine might be very bad for large sectors of the public. Moreover, the leaders and mainstays of the machine all represented individual, neighborhood, and class interests and, except when some compelling necessity arose (in the case of public housing, conflict among local and special interests), it was to the interest of the machine to sacrifice the interest of the city as a whole to these special interests. Insofar as it coincided with it at all, the interest of the machine coincided with only one conception of the public interest among many possible ones and not, perhaps, with the one which was most appropriate. The machine took as the ultimately relevant data those ends, whatever they might be, the satisfaction of which would tend to make the party an effective vote-getting organization and those ends, whatever they might be, that the voters happened to have uppermost on election day. Organizational maintenance was best served by doing what was least likely to antagonize any group or faction within the party and by devoting attention to the economy of incentives which held the principal figures in the party together. Issues were secondary or even altogether unimportant. In order to win an election, it was not necessary to take a far-sighted and comprehensive view of the city's fundamental problems, to point out in clear terms the alternatives that were before it, or through leadership to resolve fundamental conflicts by appeals to reason and to the most comprehensive and morally significant ends. To win an election it was necessary to be stronger than the other party on election day. This did not mean that it was necessary to please the voter. It was only necessary to be in the eyes of the voter the lesser of two evils.

And yet, after these qualifications are made, there was an important element of truth in the politicians' belief that what was

---

the public. Of course the legend will not stand up against any logical analysis, for it must be rather obvious that a political boss can survive only so long as he wins elections, and equally obvious that the only way to win elections year after year is to know what the voters want and give it to them. . . . always the primary purpose is to win an election." Edward J. Flynn, *op. cit.*, p. 221.

good for the party was in the public interest. The party was a mechanism through which a vast number of more or less conflicting interests arrived at terms on which they could work together, and over the long run the party could not survive and prosper if it deeply offended any large sector of its public. The Democratic machine, for example, could not survive if it outraged the Negroes or the whites in the conservation areas. The survival and prosperity of the machine depended upon its ability to find settlements which both sides would agree represented the public interest or something approaching it.

The staff of the Authority self-consciously sought to determine the content of the public interest, and the conceptions it employed were characteristically different from those of the politicians.

From the standpoint of the Authority, the public interest was an amalgam of ends of various types. Its corporate ends were of course assumed to be consistent with the public interest and a part of it: just as the machine leaders supposed that in trying to win elections they were serving the public interest, so the staff of the Authority supposed that in strengthening their organization and in furthering the cause of public housing they were serving the public interest. They also assumed that, when doing so would not entail large sacrifices in terms of the ends of their own organization, they ought also to serve the ends of other official and semi-official agencies. Thus, the Authority took into account the ends of the Board of Education, the Mayor's Commission on Human Relations, the Land Clearance Commission and other agencies which had some legal or other claim to represent the community. The ends of these agencies were often vague, inconsistent, and unstable, and sometimes they conflicted with other ends which had some claim to be considered in the public interest. These were practical difficulties; the staff took it for granted that to be in the public interest a housing program ought to harmonize "as far as possible" with the ends of these agencies.

In addition to its own corporate ends and to the ends of other public agencies, the Authority took account of certain ends which it imputed to the community as a body politic. These were ends which the staff of the Authority assumed that the people of Chicago entertained as a group or entity. Some of the staff may have thought of the city as a "body politic" which had ends apart from those of the individuals who comprised it; some may have thought that there were certain ends which were statistically frequent when Chicago people, taking community-regarding roles, thought about their city; and some probably entertained both ideas. At any rate, the staff seemed to assume that there existed a "creed" or "code" that was widely held, and that actions which ran counter to this code were not in the public interest. The code specified that racial amity and integration were very much to be desired, that waste was to be avoided, and that all citizens should be treated with rigorous impartiality, that the values of family, home, and good citizenship should be furthered by public effort, and that public officials should subordinate neighborhood and private interests (particularly, personal ones) to the public interest.

Most important, the code specified that the ends contained in it were to be regarded as more important than any conflicting ends that individuals might have. That most whites in conservation areas might be opposed to anything that would cause Negroes to move into their neighborhoods was irrelevant from the standpoint of this conception of the public interest since the code specified that racial prejudice should not be a relevant motive or end. Similarly, if it would cost more to locate a project on one site than on another (e.g., because it would be necessary to reroute a planned superhighway and to build an extra bridge) and if the only ends to be served by so doing were the self-regarding ones of a few hundred property owners, the change ought not to be made, for the code specified that the self-regarding ends of a small minority ought not to be served at any substantial cost to the community. The Authority paid little attention to individualistic preferences: even if a majority of the people of Chicago had favored racially segregated public housing, that would not have meant that segregation was in the public interest according to the conception that the Authority had.

The code which the Authority imputed to the body politic of Chicago was, of course, more nearly the code of the upper social classes in America (or at least the professional-intellectual groups among them) than of the lower and of people who acted in representative (and hence group- or community-regarding) roles than of people who acted in private (and hence self-regarding) roles. As Miss Wood once told 350 civic leaders who were gathered at a testimonial dinner in her honor, the Authority always tried to express "the wish and the will, the ideal, the objectives, the moral code of you, the good people of the City."[6] But this is only to say, perhaps, that there was less ambivalence in the acceptance of the code by some members of the upper classes than by the lower: the lower classes no doubt favored racial justice, impartial administration, economy and the rest; the difference was that most of them also favored keeping the Negroes out of the conservation neighborhoods at all costs.

The Authority also may sometimes have put its corporate interest ahead of what by its own conception was the public interest, and its conception of the public interest was not the only defensible one that was or that might have been put forward: possibly there were other lines of action, diametrically opposed to those followed by the Authority, which had at least as good a claim to being called in the public interest.* But the Authority framed one view of the public interest and made it a basis for decisions in the spheres of politics and planning. This we think was a considerable achievement.

---

* It could be argued, as Morton Bodfish, head of the Savings and Loan League, did argue, that the public interest would be served by allowing the market to allocate housing as it does other consumers' goods. Taking a thorough-going individualist point of view, one might say that consumer satisfaction or utility is the only relevant criterion and that there are no communal ends (e.g., the promotion of wholesome family life) which justify interfering with the operation of the market. According to this theory, if a free market distributes goods (chewing gum and automobiles no less than housing) "unfairly," the remedy lies in improving the income distribution. But given an income distribution which is in the public interest, the public interest is best served by letting every consumer decide for himself how he wants to spend his income; i.e., by not interfering if he chooses to live in a slum in order that he may have an automobile. This libertarian conception of the public interest assumes that the individual is capable of making a morally meaningful choice among his ends, whereas in fact many slum-dwellers never having lived in decent housing and in some cases being culturally incapable of significant choices in such a matter, cannot be assumed to use their income in a way to maximize their satisfaction or welfare. And as a practical matter, this view takes it for granted that the housing market works fairly well or could be made to work fairly well. Even if there were not a serious structural defect in the housing market due to race prejudice, this would be a dubious assumption.

SUPPLEMENT □ □ □ □ □ □

NOTE ON CONCEPTUAL SCHEME*

OUR PURPOSE in this note is to explain the three conceptions—"politics," "planning," and "the public interest"—in the light of which the case-material was largely selected, organized, and interpreted. The explanations given here do not by any means encompass all of the concepts that were used in the case-study. Concepts that are familiar to social scientists (e.g., organization, public opinion, representation, identification, class, role, etc.) are not described or elaborated here; it is enough for our purposes to clarify the logical structures of those leading ideas which may not be familiar to the reader.

The reader should be warned that in this note we do not use the terms "politics," "planning," and "the public interest" in their ordinary senses; politics, as we define it, has only a very rough correspondence to what people ordinarily called politicians actually do; similarly planning, by our definition, is not necessarily what people who are called planners actually do. The reasons why our definitions of these terms do not correspond to common usage is that we are trying to establish analytically significant formulations of these ideas. We want a conception of politics which will apply as well to office politics as to national politics and a conception of planning which will apply as well to planning in industry as to city planning. In order to achieve analytical significance we have had to sacrifice conformity with common usage. We have also had to focus rather narrowly on some aspects of the case-study to the exclusion of others which

* This supplement is the work of Banfield. He wishes to acknowledge suggestions from Meyerson and the stimulation of work on related matters with Professor Edward A. Shils.

from the standpoint of common sense notions about politics and planning would be of equal significance. It follows that there is much in the case-study which is not explained by the ideas elaborated here.

Our frame of reference involves actors (both persons and formal organizations) who are oriented toward the attainment of ends. An *end* is an image of a state of affairs which is the object or goal of activity. It may be the end of a housing authority (an actor), for example, to improve the housing of low-income people; this means that the housing authority, a corporate body, is viewed as having an idea or imaginary picture of a situation which it would like to bring about and toward the realization of which its activity will be directed.

POLITICS

When there is a conflict, real or apparent, between the ends of different actors (or within the end-system of a single actor)* and not all of the conflicting ends can be realized, an *issue* exists and the actors whose ends conflict are parties to the issue. If, for example, a housing authority has the end of locating projects on vacant land sites and a city council has the end of locating them on slum sites, an issue exists between two parties, the authority and the council. The ends which are made the basis of action ending a conflict form the *settlement* of an issue. Thus, when it is finally decided to locate projects on slum sites, the city council's end has been made the settlement of the issue between it and the authority.

Politics is the activity (negotiation, argument, discussion, application of force, persuasion, etc.) by which an issue is agitated or settled. By this definition, if a housing authority and a city

* A political incident may arise in part or even wholly out of conflicts not between the ends of different actors but within the end-systems of actors. The members of a public may agree upon an issue and yet all be "of two minds"—and opposed minds—about it. To the extent that this is the case, a political process is not contention between groups or factions, but interaction in which the members of the public seek to reconcile their ends (intra-individually, not inter-individually), to order them, and to discover their implications for action. Such a process may take the guise of a conflict between actors and in doing so it may give rise to an actual conflict between them. In such a case, the settlement of the inter-individual conflict is likely to await the resolution of the prior conflict within the end-systems of the actors.

council are parties to an issue their activity is political insofar as it affects the manner in which the issue is agitated or the terms on which it is settled.

It will be seen that a description of the simplest conceivable unit of politics (*viz.* two actors who face a single issue) must consist essentially of an account of those ends of each party which are relevant to the issue, of the respects in which the ends of the two parties are in conflict, of the nature of the activity by which the issue is agitated and a settlement reached, and of the terms of the settlement. These are the most fundamental categories into which the data bearing upon politics in the foregoing chapters can be organized. The remainder of our discussion in this section on politics is intended to elaborate these categories somewhat.

The activity by which the parties to an issue agitate it or bring it to a settlement may be described broadly as one or more of the following types: A. Cooperation, B. Contention, C. Accommodation, and D. Dictation.*

A. *Cooperation.* In this mode of activity the parties make a shared end (or ends), or some procedural principle which is mutually agreed upon, the basis of the choice among the ends which are at issue, i.e., they engage in a cooperative search for that settlement which is implied by ends or principles which they agree ought to be decisive. Thus, for example, a housing authority and a city council which are at odds over whether projects are to be located on vacant or on slum sites may agree to do whatever will provide the largest amount of housing. If they make this common end decisive of the issue, they may engage in a cooperative effort to discover that allocation as between

* In all of these modes of activity the parties either take each other into account (i.e., they interact) or one party takes the others into account (i.e., acts unilaterally with respect to them). Two other modes of reaching a settlement may be mentioned in which no party to the issue takes the others into account: these are *competition,* a process in which the settlement is the outcome or resultant of unconcerted activity by parties who are not oriented either as cooperators or adversaries to other parties and who may even be unaware that an issue exists or that they are parties to it (competition in this sense does not imply emulation of course) and *arbitration,* a process in which an actor who is not a party to the issue fixes the terms of the settlement. Since these two types of process do not involve either interaction or the taking account by one party of others, we do not class them as political.

slum and vacant sites which will maximize the number of units. In a cooperative choice process the relative power of the parties does not affect the settlement of the issue since this depends entirely upon the implication of the common ends or procedural principles.

In a cooperative political process the parties may look for a settlement:

1) which is implied by common substantive ends (such as, for example, that of maximizing the number of housing units).

2) which is implied by common procedural principles or "rules of the game,"

a) in our society one procedural principle which is widely held is that one party should make a small sacrifice of his ends when doing so will enable the other party to make a large gain or to avoid a large loss. Thus, for example, if there was only a very slight advantage from the point of view of the city council in locating projects on slum sites and if there were crucial advantages from the standpoint of the authority in locating them on vacant sites, the council might accept vacant sites.

b) according to another widely held procedural principle the cooperating parties should look for a settlement which will empirically reconcile ends which are logically opposed. Such a settlement may sometimes be found if the parties, although having incompatible "motives," nevertheless have compatible "intents." Thus, for example, although they have opposite motives, proponents and opponents of racial equality sometimes agree that there should be a quota on Negro occupants of bi-racial housing projects; the proponents agree because they want to prevent the projects from becoming entirely Negro and the opponents agree because they want as few Negroes in the projects as possible.

B. *Contention.* In this mode, the parties mutually endeavor to make their ends prevail over those of the other parties, their adversaries, by the exercise of power. Each party seeks to bring the contention to a close (i.e., to reach a settlement) on the terms most favorable to him; the contention accordingly continues as long as a critical number of parties think that they may reach a more favorable settlement by continuing it. How long this will be and what will be the terms of the eventual settlement depend upon the various contenders' estimates of their power and that of their adversaries.

Two forms of contention may be distinguished:

1) *Struggle.* In a struggle each contender (or coalition) seeks to emerge supreme, i.e., to acquire enough power to dictate a settlement. A struggle may be either: i) a *fight,* in which the few means the contenders are allowed to employ are specifically cally stated as "rules of the game," or ii) a *contest,* in which the few means the contenders are allowed to employ are specifically stated.

2) *Bargaining.* A contender who bargains seeks not to emerge supreme, but to emerge on terms which are relatively favorable. At the conclusion of a bargain all parties retain some power—perhaps each retains as much as he had to begin with; the settlement is reached by arriving at terms which are viewed as mutually advantageous. The bargainer, therefore, expects to give up something in order to get something.

C. *Accommodation.* In a settlement reached by accommodation one party freely chooses to make the ends of the other his own (if he exacts a *quid pro quo* it is bargaining, not accommodation), thus ending the conflict.

D. *Dictation.* A settlement is reached by dictation when one party, the dictator, compels the other to accept a settlement on his terms.

A concrete political process often exhibits more than one of these modes of action. Cooperation and struggle may even occur as a "mixture," and if one party cannot dictate a settlement, the parties often turn to bargaining or, perhaps, one accommodates the others.

When the parties to an issue engage in contention, each employs a *strategy,* i.e., each decides what he will do to influence or counter his adversary. A description of a political process involving contention should therefore include an account of the strategies of the various parties.

If the contention takes the form of bargaining, the strategy of each party is directed toward reaching a *compromise* (i.e., a settlement involving mutual concessions on a *quid pro quo* basis) on most favorable terms. The compromise is a system of incentives (the concessions made by one party serving as inducements to another) by which all parties are brought to agree to the settlement. A compromise is therefore the expression in concrete terms of the equilibrium of power which exists among the parties at the time it is made. Each contender, having done what he can to impose on the other contenders the action possibilities most acceptable to him, makes what concessions he must. These concessions, when made and accepted mutually, constitute the compromise.

From the standpoint of any one party to a bargaining process, an increase of political knowledge (the cost of which is not greater than the return that can be expected from it) is obviously to be desired. From the standpoint of *all* parties to the issue, an increase in knowledge—either in the knowledge of all players or in that of one party whose knowledge is considerably less than the others—may also be desirable. This is the case if the parties are anxious to reach a settlement by cooperation or through a compromise which is based on the existing distribution of power. The advantage of an increase in the general level of knowledge in such a case is obvious. The advantage of an increase in the knowledge of one party whose knowledge is much less than the others is that, lacking knowledge, this one party may prevent a settlement by cooperation and may insist upon a struggle—a struggle which cannot improve his own position (if it could, he would be acting not out of ignorance but out of knowledge, of course) and might worsen it.

We suspect that such cases may be empirically important—that the politically ignorant often provoke conflicts which are of no advantage—and may be of great disadvantage—to them and to all other parties. If this be true, a good deal of waste may be avoided by improving the political knowledge of such parties.

What has been said of investment in improved knowledge may also be said of investment in improved communication. The ability to reach a negotiated settlement on the most mutually advantageous terms—and especially to reach a settlement by cooperation—is largely a function of the ability of the parties to communicate.

An issue is settled *on its merits* if the settlement is logically implied by some standards of equity which are deemed relevant to it. Issues sometimes cannot be settled on their merits because no standards are agreed to be relevant, because relevant standards cannot be applied so as to yield an appropriate result, or because one or more of the parties will not agree to make them decisive of the issue. Any issue which can be settled on its merits can, in principle, be settled by the method of cooperation, for (by definition) cooperation is a way of discovering the implications for action of common ends.

An issue cannot at the same time be compromised *and* settled on its merits. A compromise may be equitable or inequitable, but its terms are not (by definition) implied by a standard relevant to the issue. Thus, for example, King Solomon, when he threatened to cut the infant in half, was proposing what may have been an equitable compromise of the claims of the two mothers, but he was not settling the issue on its merits, for the only relevant standard was that the true mother should have the child.

Similarly, while it may lead to concessions by some or all of the parties, a cooperative choice process cannot of itself lead to a compromise: the terms of a settlement reached by cooperation depend (by definition) solely upon their being logically implied by common ends and not at all upon their acceptability to some or all of the parties on other grounds.

Arranging a compromise, like arranging any system of incentives, is essentially an entrepreneurial function: i.e., it is a matter of getting people to agree to the terms on which they will act in relation to each other.

Empirically, an actor is seldom solely concerned with the all-or-none gratification of specific ends in relation to a single issue; ordinarily he is concerned with the gratification-deprivation balance of his end-system as a whole and with this over time and with respect to many issues. Accordingly, the terms of a compromise may involve concessions or incentives which are logically unrelated to the particular issue. Thus, for example, if the issue concerns the location of a housing project, the mayor may induce the head of a housing authority to compromise by promising him something in exchange for accepting an unpopular racial policy.

When a party to an issue accepts an incentive which is logically unrelated to the issue *in lieu* of the gratification of the end which he has at issue (e.g., when he accepts support for a bi-racial policy *in lieu* of having the project located as he would wish) a *substitution* takes place. Substitutions may be of two types: a) they are *transfers* if an end of a different substantive kind is substituted for the end at issue (e.g., bi-racialism for proper location), and b) they are *postponements* if an end of the same substantive kind is to be gratified at some later time (e.g., if the authority concedes regarding the location of a particular project on the understanding that it will be permitted to locate others as it pleases some other time). An account of a compromise should, of course, show what transfers and postponements, if any, are involved.

In a continuing political process issues are not generally settled each by itself without relation to others. Some issues are settled on their merits or are compromised without any substitutions being made, to be sure, but to a large extent settlements are made by arranging compromises involving transfers and postponements which cut across several or many issues. In order for this to occur, it is essential that there be a certain amount of continuity in the exercise of the entrepreneurial "compromising" function: certain persons—"politicians" usually—must be in a position to arrange settlements of various issues which arise over a period of time and so to accumulate a stockpile of incentives or "favors" which can be used in "trades" from one issue to another. By having such a stockpile (and it could not be had, of course, if all issues were settled on their merits or compromised without substitutions), it is possible to settle certain issues through compromise. Among these issues may be some vital to the life of the society which are in principle not susceptible to being settled either on their merits or without substitutions. Because both parties to a trade may gain, it is possible, too, that the aggregate of satisfaction accruing to the parties may be greater if a large number of issues are treated as a stockpile from which compromises involving substitutions may be made than if each is settled on its merits or by compromises not involving substitutions.

It is necessary to distinguish between a *particular issue* and the *larger issue* (or issues) to which it relates. Issue A is particular and issue B is larger in relation to it if the terms on which B is settled are likely to be affected by the manner in which A is agitated or settled and if B is deemed of wider or more lasting significance than A. Thus, for example, one of the several larger issues involved in the struggle over sites in Chicago was race relations reform. An actor who deems one issue larger than another does not necessarily deem it more important however: he does not necessarily believe that in those situations where something must be sacrificed the larger issue should be served at the expense of the particular one.

All of the parties to a particular issue may be mainly concerned with a larger issue (or issues) and for each of them the larger issue (or issues) may be somewhat or entirely different. In an account of a political process it is therefore important to show what, from the standpoint of each party to the particular issue, are the larger issues and what is their relative importance in comparison to it (i.e., what in terms of the particular issue would the party be willing to sacrifice in order to gain what in terms of the larger issues?).

Ordinarily, of course, it is bad strategy for a bargainer to reveal his end-system or, especially, to admit that he is much or mainly interested in some larger issue: usually he has to pretend that he is seeking to settle the particular issue on its merits and almost always he has to conceal the fact that he is trying to use the particular issue to improve his position with respect to some larger issue. Therefore in describing a political process it is often necessary to distinguish between the ends a party professes (his *nominal* ends) and those he actually seeks (his *real* ones) and between what he professes is the relative importance of his ends and what is actually their relative importance.

A particular issue may be said to have *intrinsic-concrete, in-*

strumental-abstract, or *symbolic-ideological* significance (or some combination of these) from the standpoint of a party to it. It has intrinsic-concrete significance if the party is interested in the issue for its "practical" outcome without relation to larger issues or larger ends. It has instrumental-abstract significance if the party is interested in the particular issue because of the effect that it may have on some larger issue (or issues) or larger ends. It has symbolic-ideological significance if the party thinks the particular issue is important as a sign of a complex of diffuse ends or issues. Thus, a man who favors building a particular housing project may do so because he wants to see certain individuals sheltered (intrinsic-concrete), because he feels that by supporting this particular project he will advance the cause of public housing in general (instrumental-abstract), or because he feels that the particular project is a symbol of democracy or the welfare state (symbolic-ideological).

A description of a political choice should, of course, show what significance the issue has for each of the parties, how each party's view of its significance effects his strategy, and how the difference in the significance the parties attach to the issue affects the manner of their interaction.

PLANNING

A *course of action* is a sequence of prospective acts which are viewed as a unit of action; the acts which comprise the sequence are mutually related as means to the attainment of ends. A *plan* is a course of action which can be carried into effect, which can be expected to lead to the attainment of the ends sought, and which someone (an effectuating organization) intends to carry into effect. (By contrast, a course of action which could not be carried out, which would not have the consequences intended, or which no one intends to carry out is a "utopian scheme" rather than a plan.) If a housing authority, for example, decides to clear slums and to build low-rent projects, these prospective acts which are related to each other as a "chain" of means for the attainment of the end "to improve the housing of low-income people" constitute a plan, providing, of course, that the authority has the necessary legal authority, funds, etc., to build projects and that building them will serve to improve the housing of low-income people. As distinct from planned ones, *opportunistic* decisions are made as the event unfolds and they are, therefore, not mutually related as a unit having a single design. The execution of any planned course of action involves the making of opportunistic decisions as well as planned ones.

Any concrete planning process may be described in terms of the following distinctions: a plan is *comprehensive* if it indicates the principal acts by which all of the most important ends are to be attained; it is *partial* if it indicates how some but not all of the most important ends are to be attained or only how ends of subordinate importance are to be attained.

The single set of ends sought in a planning process may be substantively a directive to attain (or maximize the attainment of) the ends of the individuals who comprise some plurality or public. Thus, one of the ends of a housing authority may be to build projects that will be as comfortable and convenient as possible (given certain limitations) for tenants. In this case, the tenants are a "public" of the authority. *Public* planning is planning to attain those ends of an organization which are substantively directives to attain the ends of some public. An organization may, of course, seek to attain the ends of the individuals who comprise more than one public. By contrast to public planning, *corporate* planning seeks to attain ends which pertain to the organization as such and are not substantively directives to attain the ends of some public.

Community planning is that special case of public planning in which the public is the whole community. A city planning commission, for example, is generally supposed to engage in comprehensive community planning, i.e., to make a plan which takes into account all of the important ends of the whole community (the community being considered as a plurality of individuals, a body politic, or both). An agency such as a housing authority which is primarily engaged in corporate planning (i.e., the principal task of which is to attain such organizational ends as "to improve the housing of low-income families") may, however, do community planning as well; i.e., in planning for the attainment of its corporate ends it may, for example, seek also to attain the ends of the individuals who comprise the community (e.g., taxpayers, commuters, etc.) or of the body politic (e.g., ends defined by the mayor as pertaining to the community as an entity).

Since planning is designing a course of action to achieve ends, "efficient" planning is that which under given conditions leads to the maximization of the attainment of the relevant ends. We will assume that a planned course of action which is selected rationally is most likely to maximize the attainment of the relevant ends and that therefore "rational" planning and "efficient" planning are the same. As a practical matter, of course, this assumption may be in many cases unwarranted: sometimes the most careful deliberation will result in a worse selection than might be made by flipping a coin. Even so, it will be useful for our present purposes to assume that rational planning leads to the maximization of the attainment of ends while capricious or "non-rational" planning does not.

By a *rational* decision, we mean one made in the following manner: 1. the decision-maker considers all of the alternatives (courses of action) open to him; i.e., he considers what courses of action are possible within the conditions of the situation and in the light of the ends he seeks to attain; 2. he identifies and evaluates all of the consequences which would follow from the adoption of each alternative; i.e., he predicts how the total situation would be changed by each course of action he might adopt; and 3. he selects that alternative the probable consequences of which would be preferable in terms of his most valued ends.* Obviously no decision can be perfectly rational since no one can

---

* This definition of rationality is adapted from Herbert Simon, *Administrative Behavior,* Macmillan, New York, 1947, p. 67 and from Talcott Parsons, *The Structure of Social Action,* The Free Press, Glencoe, Illinois, 2nd ed., 1949, p. 58. "Action is rational," Parsons writes, "in so far as it pursues ends possible within the conditions of the situation, and by means which, among those available to the actor, are intrinsically best adapted to the end for reasons understandable and verifiable by positive empirical science. . . . The starting point is that of conceiving the actor as coming to know the facts of the situation in which he acts and thus the conditions necessary and the means available for the realization of his ends. As applied to the means-end relationship, this is essentially a matter of the accurate prediction of the probable effects of various possible ways of altering the situation (employment of alternative means) and the resultant choice among them."

ever know all of the alternatives open to him at any moment or all the consequences which would follow from any action. Nevertheless, decisions may be made with more or less knowledge of alternatives, consequences, and relevant ends, and so we may describe some decisions and some decision-making processes as more nearly rational that others.

This conception of planning as the rational selection of a course of action provides a framework within which in the foregoing chapters we selected, organized and evaluated the data regarding planning by the Chicago Housing Authority. We were led by this conception to examine particularly the ends of the Authority; the conditions of the situation as these affected the courses of action which were open to the Authority; the ability or inability of the Authority to predict the consequences of various courses of action that were open to it; and finally its ability or inability to know by the methods of positive empirical science which means were intrinsically best adapted to its ends.

If we were interested only in describing how the Authority did make decisions (i.e., in what may be called the sociology of decision-making) this framework would not be the most useful one, for organizations, even ones that are considered efficient, do not ordinarily approximate the kind of behavior described above as rational. However, we are ultimately interested not in how plans are actually made but in how they would have to be made in order to be most effective (the very idea of planning, as we have pointed out above, presumes that there are ends to be attained or maximized) and for this purpose the model of rational planning, unreal as it may be, is useful as a guide.

In the remainder of this section we will elaborate somewhat the model of rational planning. The purpose of this elaboration is to put the reader more fully in possession of the standards we have used in selecting and interpreting that part of the case-study data bearing on planning.

1. *Analysis of the Situation.* As we have said, the selection of a rational plan presupposes consideration of all of the action alternatives that are open to the actor and thus of the conditions which characterize the situation, including, of course, the means that are available to the actor. A *condition* is a feature of the

situation which the planner must treat as fixed either because he does not choose to use his scarce means to change it or because he absolutely lacks means to do so. Thus, for example, the existence of race prejudice is a condition which the planner may have to accept as an unalterable feature of the situation at least in the short run. Conditions may, of course, be either favorable or unfavorable in terms of the relevant ends. A *limiting condition* is one which restricts the range of action open to the planner.

The *opportunity area* consists of all of those acts or courses of action which the effectuating organization is not precluded from taking because of some limiting conditions. Thus, the design of a course of action leading to the attainment of the end "interracial housing" may be rendered impossible by any one of the following conditions: white people cannot be persuaded to live among Negroes, the mayor will not permit an interracial project, the Authority lacks funds to build a project, materials for building one are not available, etc. Under these conditions, certain actions essential to the desired course of action lie outside the planner's opportunity area.

2. *End Reduction and Elaboration.* If only one end were relevant in the making of a plan, it would be a simple matter for the planner to choose a course of action. Almost always, however, there are numerous ends to be served and no one course of action will maximize the attainment of (or perhaps even attain) all of them. The planner must, therefore, make a choice among the relevant ends, either as to those that are to be served at all or as to the relative importance of those that are to be served. Thus, a housing authority with the ends, "to clear slums" and "to preserve neighborhood social organization," might find the two ends utterly incompatible and it would certainly find that a gain in terms of one end would necessarily involve some loss in terms of the other.

In order to make a choice the planner must know the relative value to be attached to each of the ends. He must know not only that end A is more valuable than end B, but also how much more valuable A is than B, i.e., how much of B should be sacrificed to increase the attainment of A by a certain amount. He has a complete ordering of ends when he knows how much should be sacrificed of each end in order to increase by a certain amount the attainment of all possible combinations of all other relevant ends.

We have defined an end as an image of a situation which is the object or goal of activity. The end may be thought of as having active and contextual elements. The *active* elements are those which occupy the fore-ground of the image so to speak: they are the features of the desired situation which have been singled out and made the focus of interest and activity. *Contextual* elements lie in the background: they are value conditions which ought to be realized or ought not to be violated in the attainment of the active elements. The explicit formulation of an end is usually elliptical: the active elements are set forth, but the contextual elements are described incompletely or not at all. Thus, if a housing authority declares that its end is "to clear slums," it is giving an account only of the active element of its end; if the desired situation is described fully, i.e., if an account is given of contextual elements as well, it will be seen that the end "to clear slums" exists in the context of other value elements: "to avoid racial discrimination," "to avoid waste," "to avoid inflicting undue hardship on people who must be relocated," "to avoid over-burdening school and transportation facilities," etc.

In designing a course of action the planner must find a way to attain the active elements of the end. But although this is a necessary condition of a course of action, it is not a sufficient one. For if the end is fully stated, the desired situation is seen to consist not of a single element (the active one) but of several or many elements, and it is, of course, all elements—the desired situation as a whole—which the course of action should attain.

When the content of an end is fully elaborated, it may appear that its active elements cannot be attained without sacrifice of certain contextual elements. In such a case, if the contextual elements are valued more highly than the active ones, the end may be rejected altogether. Thus, if a housing authority discovers that it cannot clear a slum (active element) without at the same time creating great hardship for the slum dwellers who must vacate (contextual element), it may drop the undertaking altogether.

A distinction may also be made between incidental and principal ends. An *incidental* end is one which is relevant only if it can be attained without additional cost or at trivial additional cost. If a housing authority wants to promote consumer education among its tenants and, therefore, encourages its project managers, whose salaries will have to be paid anyway, to give occasional talks on the subject, it makes consumer education an incidental end. If, however, the authority is willing to make more than a trivial sacrifice of other ends to attain a certain end (if, for example, it is willing to hire specialists to promote consumer education), that end is one of its *principal* ends.

3. *The Design of Courses of Action.* The decisions which constitute a course of action are commitments. A *commitment* is an action which obliges the effectuating organization to take certain other acts or which limits its choice of acts in the future by foreclosing certain action possibilities which would otherwise exist. Thus, for example, when it demolishes a slum, a housing authority makes a commitment both negatively in that it is no longer possible for it to decide to rehabilitate the structures and positively in that after tearing down the old buildings, it is obliged to put up new ones and to provide for their management and maintenance.

Courses of action may be described at various levels of generality. If only the most important or far-reaching commitments are described in it, a plan (or a course of action) is at the *developmental* level of generality; if commitments of lesser importance are also described, it is at the *program* level; and if the actions to be taken are described in great detail, it is at the *operational* level.

It will be seen that a plan at a lower level of generality is a relatively detailed account of the means to be employed in carrying out one at a higher level of generality and that, accordingly, it represents a selection from among the alternatives not foreclosed by decisions at the higher level. Thus, if a housing authority, after considering such other developmental courses of action as the granting of consumer subsidies or the repair of dilapidated structures, decides upon projects as a way of achieving the end "the elimination of slums," this decision constitutes a development plan. A program plan results from a further consideration of remaining alternatives: whether to build high-rise or row-house projects, large ones or small ones, and the like. Thus, if the program plan is to build large high-rise projects, it is necessary to decide whether to build them of concrete or steel and whether to design them for large families or small. The operational plan includes decisions regarding these matters and, necessarily, the prior decisions as well. Thus, the operational plan may be to build large high-rise projects of reinforced concrete for occupancy by large families.

It may be noted in passing that a plan at a lower level of generality may be a highly rational eleboration of a plan which at a higher level of generality is quite irrational. Thus, a housing authority may decide capriciously to build projects rather than to rehabilitate dilapidated buildings and then, having made this crucial decision, choose with great care among the various ways of building projects. We will say that an operational program plan made in this way is *functionally rational* but *substantively irrational.*

4. *The Comparative Evaluation of Consequences.* A *consequence* is a change in the situation which is caused by an act or number of acts, i.e., which follows the act and would not occur without it. Consequences may be *anticipated* or *unanticipated,* and anticipated consequences may be either *sought* or *unsought* depending upon whether the planner positively wants to bring them about or merely accepts them as part of a set which is wanted. Of course, all unanticipated consequences are also unsought.

The situation consists only of those objects which have relevance in terms of the end-system of the organization: therefore, consequences (i.e., changes in the situation) exist only in relation to ends. Thus, an act would have no consequences at all (i.e., would not change the situation at all) if the organization had no relevant ends, even though from the standpoint of another actor with different ends (and therefore concerned with a different situation) the consequences of the act might be manifold and of the greatest importance. Thus, for example, if life in a housing project tended to enrich religious life, this would be a consequence of great importance from certain standpoints, but it would not be a consequence at all from the standpoint of an authority whose end-system had no implications for religious life.

Consequences which are positively valued in terms of a relevant end are *advantages;* those which are negatively valued are *disadvantages.* Unanticipated and unsought consequences may, of course, prove to be either advantages or disadvantages. It often happens, of course, that consequences which are advantageous in terms of some of the relevant ends are disadvantageous in terms of the others. Thus, before one can say that a given consequence is advantageous or disadvantageous from the standpoint of the end-system as a whole, it is necessary to calculate whether or not the gains in terms of some ends outweigh the losses in terms of others.

Consequences the value of which can be expressed in terms of numbers (usually prices) are *benefits* or *costs.* Consequences the value of which cannot be so expressed are *intangible.*

The greater the number of ends sought, the more difficult it becomes to design a course of action which will attain *all* of them. There are at least three reasons for this: 1. the organization's means are usually limited and as the demands upon the means increase, the probability that all can be satisfied decreases; 2. the number and stringency of the limiting conditions within which the planner must work increases with the number of ends he is seeking to attain, since additional limiting conditions are likely to be associated with additional ends; and 3. as the number of ends increases, the probability increases that some of them will be negated or violated by the unanticipated consequences of action taken in pursuance of other ends.

Of course, if an elaborate end-system makes it less likely that the organization will attain all ends, it also makes it more likely that it will attain *some* ends. Commonly an organization fails to attain its principal ends and yet succeds in attaining some incidental end. So also an organization may discover unanticipated consequences of its activity which are extremely valuable in terms of some contextual element of an end. In such cases, it is to be expected that the organization will "rationalize" its activity by assimilating these incidental ends and contextual elements into its system of principal active ends and by declaring that it "intended" to attain them all along. To a considerable extent, this is the dynamic of the process by which organizations acquire new ends and discard old ones.*

A private organization is generally free to seek the attainment of a few principal ends which have few contextual elements. A public agency, on the other hand, is expected to take into account a very wide range of contextual elements along with the active element of its ends and it is expected to serve many incidental ends and discard old ones.†

Thus, a housing authority may be expected not only to "improve the housing of low-income families" (the active element of a principal end) but also to: a) restore purchasing power to the central business district (the active element of another principal end), b) to reduce or eliminate residential racial segregation (the active element of still another principal end), c) to broaden the tax base (the active element of an incidental end), d) to avoid measures which would decrease the birth rate (contextual element), e) to avoid measures which would cause people to rely unduly upon the government for assistance (another contextual element), and so on almost *ad infinitum.* A private agency, on the other hand, is ordinarily free to seek only a few principal ends which have few contextual elements.

The significance of this for planning by public agencies is four-fold: a) end reduction is likely to be immensely more complicated in public than in private agencies, b) the ramification of consequences (including unsought and indirect ones) which must be taken into account, i.e., which have significance for some end, is likely to be far greater in planning by a public agency; c) the number of courses of action which can be devised that will attain all principal ends decreases as the number and stringency of the contextual elements increases, so that it becomes

* This happens even in the planning of physical structures. Chester Barnard quotes an engineer: "You know, we often make plans which eventuate into achievements quite different from, and much better than, those we contemplated. Then we are apt to credit ourselves in all seriousness and sincerity with accomplishments that are really fortuitous. We put in our thumbs and pull out the plums and cry: 'What great engineers are we!'" *Organization and Management,* Harvard University Press, Cambridge, 1949.

† Simon remarks on this, *op. cit.,* p. 69.

more probable that there will be no course of action at all which will attain the relevant ends of the public agency, and d) the hazard of unanticipated consequences of radical importance in terms of some of the ends increases; in seeking to attain an incidental end like "consumer education," for example, a housing authority may unexpectedly provoke the ire of a politician who may destroy the agency altogether.*

Very often the "incidental" ends that a public agency is expected to serve are not really incidental at all: the visible additional expenditures to attain the ends may indeed be trivial but the cost in terms of loss of achievement of principal ends (e.g., because a relatively undesirable course of action has to be adopted in order to serve the "incidental" ends) may be very great.

It is also characteristic of planning by a public agency that the agency is expected to attain ends which include a large number of contextual elements *at no more cost* than would be necessary to attain ends consisting only of a few active elements. Thus, an authority may be expected to clear slums without undue hardships to relocatees, without destroying neighborhood social organization, and without racial discrimination and to do so at no more cost than would be required merely to clear slums.

THE PUBLIC INTEREST

A decision is said to serve special interests if it furthers the ends of some part of the public at the expense of the ends of the larger public. It is said to be in the *public interest* if it serves the ends of the whole public rather than those of some sector of the public.

Within this very general framework, a variety of conceptions

---

* Probably if the hazard of incurring unanticipated consequences were counted as a cost, as it should be, no end could rightly be considered incidental.

George Cornewall Lewis argued that an act of legislation should take account of contextual elements but not of incidental ends. "Assuming," he wrote, "that the primary and intended effect of a law is good, it ought further to satisfy this condition—that its incidental effects, so far as they can be calculated beforehand, are innocent; that they are *not bad;* and if they comply with this negative condition, the legislator need not in general trouble himself further. . . . Hence, in estimating the effects of a law, our attention should be steadily fixed on its primary purpose; and its worth ought not to depend, to any great extent, on consequences which are not part of its direct and legitimate policy." *Op. cit.,* Volume I, Chapter 12, Section 10.

are held of the logical structure of the public interest—varying conceptions which significantly influence the kinds of political and planning decisions made. The differences among the views as to the nature of the public interest seem to turn on what is meant by "the ends of the whole public." We will distinguish five differing conceptions:

A. *Unitary Conceptions.* The "whole" may be conceived as a single set of ends which pertain equally to all members of the public. Two contrasting unitary conceptions may be distinguished:

1. *Organismic.* According to this conception, the plurality is an entity or body politic which entertains ends in a corporate capacity; these ends may be different from those entertained by any of the individuals who comprise the public. A person who thinks of Chicago as a "social organism" having certain ends, such as the viability of the organism, which should have precedence over the ends of individuals entertains this conception of the public interest.

2. *Communalist.* According to this conception, the ends which the plurality entertains "as a whole" are ends which its individual members universally or almost universally share: they are in this sense "common."* Ends which many people share are, according to the communalist conception, more valuable than others simply by virtue of being shared. Thus, the communalist attaches more weight to common ends than to unshared ones even though the individuals who entertain the ends may themselves attach more weight to the unshared ones. Thus, for example, a person who takes this view of the public interest would maintain that the end of "providing decent housing for all" (presumably a common or at least a widely shared end) should take precedence over such ends as "to maintain property values in Fernwood," "to retain a slum structure from which Messrs. A and B make large profits," and "to prevent Negroes from moving into our block" (all presumably ends that are not common or widely shared).

* "The public interest," Professor Schattschneider has written, "may be described as the aggregate of common interests, including the common interest in seeing that there is fair play among private interests." E. E. Schattschneider, "Political Parties and the Public Interest," *Annals of the American Academy of Political and Social Science,* Volume No. 280, March 1952, p. 23.

In the nature of the case, of course, common ends are likely to be very general or vague in their formulation. The communalist tends to feel that a concrete proposal (e.g., to build a certain project in a certain place) should be evaluated in terms of the general (common) end (e.g., "to improve the housing of low-income people") rather than in terms of the more particularized (and less widely shared) ends which become relevant in the concrete case (e.g., to avoid the destruction of some units of good housing in this particular neighborhood).

B. *Individualistic Conceptions.* According to these conceptions, the ends of the plurality do not comprise a single system, either one which pertains to the plurality as an entity or one which is common to individuals. The relevant ends are those of individuals, whether shared or unshared. The ends of the plurality "as a whole" are simply the aggregate of ends entertained by individuals, and that decision is in the public interest which is consistent with as large a part of the "whole" as possible.* This view implies the possibility of making meaningful comparisons not only as to the amount of satisfaction to be had from various classes of ends but also as to the worth of that satisfaction.

Three sub-types may be distinguished:

1. *Utilitarian.* The distinguishing feature of this conception is that the ends of the individual, as selected and ordered by himself, are taken as the relevant quantity: the public interest is "the greatest happiness of the greatest number" of those who constitute the public. According to this view, if there are common ends, there is no reason to attach special value to them simply because they are common; the relevant ends are whatever ends the individual happens to have uppermost—his utility—be they idiosyncratic, widely shared, or common.

According to this conception, one discovers whether or not a decision is in the public interest by identifying all of the gains

---

* "The interest of the community," Jeremy Bentham wrote, "is one of the most general expression that can occur in phraseology of morals: no wonder that the meaning of it is often lost. When it has a meaning, it is this. The community is a fictitious *body*, composed of the individual persons who are considered as constituting as it were its *members*. The interest of the community then is—what? The sum of the interests of the various members who compose it." *Principles of Morals and Legislation*, Clarendon Press, Oxford, 1876 reprint, p. 3.

and losses in utility that are likely to be caused by it and, treating everyone's utility as of equal worth (for to do otherwise would be to introduce a standard other than the utilitarian one), by estimating whether or not there has been a gain in "total utility" or, to put it more properly, whether or not the magnitude of the gains in utility is greater than that of the losses.*

Thus, according to this view, the dissatisfaction a pillbox dweller feels from having what he considers an unsightly project located near him and the dissatisfaction of a white property owner at having Negroes move into his neighborhood are as worthy of being taken into account (since one man's utility is as good as another's and since utility is the indiscriminate satisfaction of ends) as the dissatisfaction of a Negro at having to live in a slum or of a civic booster at having to admit that his city contains vast slums. To determine the public interest, the loss of satisfaction of the pillbox dweller and of the white property owner must somehow be measured against the gain in satisfaction to the Negro and the booster.

2. *Quasi-Utilitarian.* According to this conception, the utility of the individual is the relevant quantity, but a greater value is attached to some men's utility than to others: i.e., along with utility, a second standard is introduced. Thus, the ends of the "whole" are whatever ends the individuals who comprise it may happen to have uppermost, but with those of some individuals being given more weight than those of others. Thus, for example, one decision-maker might attach more weight to the utility of white property owners than to that of Negroes while another might make the opposite valuation; both decision-makers, however, would have the same conception of the logical structure of the public interest.

---

* Whether or not inter-personal comparisons of utilities can meaningfully be made has been the subject of elaborate discussion among welfare economists. See, Charles Kennedy, "Concerning Utility," *Economica,* February 1954. Kennedy concludes that we cannot speak of "greater or less total utility" or of "maximizing the utility of the community" (p. 18), but that "the difference between any pair of magnitudes of utility—which, for one interpretation of utility, may be identified as a 'preference'—is a quantity of a kind to which a special type of addition and subtraction can be applied." (p. 15). Thus, the difference between the magnitude of a Negro's happiness before and after the elimination of segregation may be similarly compared. But the happiness of the whites and of the Negroes cannot be added or subtracted to yield a "total utility."

3. *Qualified Individualistic.* According to this conception, the ends of the "whole" are the aggregate of those selected by individuals, but only of those selected by them *from among certain classes of ends* that are deemed appropriate. In other words, in considering the ends of the plurality the person who employs this conception of the public interest excludes from account altogether certain classes of ends which he deems inappropriate or irrelevant.

Various principles may be employed to include or to exclude certain classes of ends. Perhaps the most familiar pattern in our society admits into account ends which: a) are community-regarding rather than self-regarding; b) are stable rather than transitory; c) are general rather than particular in reference; d) pertain to the role of citizen rather than to some private role; e) are common or statistically frequent rather than idiosyncratic or infrequent; f) are logically or morally justified rather than (as with mere whims) expressively justified or not justified at all.* Thus, for example, an official trying to decide whether to locate a housing project in a particular neighborhood may ignore the arguments of all those persons who view the question not from the standpoint of citizens concerned with the welfare of the city as a whole but from the standpoint of some private and personal interest.

It will be seen that since either the same or different decision-makers may employ opposed conceptions of the public interest, the question of which conception is to be regarded as *the* public interest, either in a specific situation or in general, may itself become a matter of controversy. Moreover, given agreement on any one conception of the formal nature of the public interest, there may be controversy as to its concrete content. Indeed, the

---

* Thus, for example, J. S. Mill observes that electors will often "have two sets of preferences—those on private and those on public grounds." Private preferences, however, however, ought to be altogether excluded from account: the elector's vote "has no more to do with his personal wishes than the verdict of a juryman." *Op. cit.*, pp. 306 and 299. Mill would also give more weight to one's "real ultimate interest" than to his "immediate and apparent interest" (p. 251) and to "higher motives and more comprehensive and distant views." (p. 256.)

A classification of types of ends which may be useful in analyzing such conceptions has been worked out by E. A. Shils and E. C. Banfield in an unpublished paper, "Individual Ends and the Structure of Social Choice."

agreed upon conception may imply equally any one of a wide range of outcomes.

A somewhat different decision-making mechanism is implied by each of these conceptions of the public interest. A unitary conception implies a cooperative choice process, i.e., one in which the outcome or settlement is derived from a single set of ends. Any individualistic conception, on the other hand, implies a mechanism through which competing ends are compromised.

Thus, a unitary conception implies central decision-makers who are specially well qualified to know the ends of the body politic or the common ends, who can perform the largely technical function of adapting means most efficiently for the attainment of these ends, and who have power to assert the unitary interest of the "whole" over any competing lesser interests. The decision-maker whose task it is to spell out the implications for action of the body politic or of the *ethos* ought, of course, to be free to take account of the "real" rather than the "apparent" interest of the members of the society and to ignore their preferences in the immediate situation if these are inconsistent with the most general and fundamental ends of the society.*

A mechanism which is to assert an individualistic conception of the public interest, on the other hand, must select from among or must compromise individual interests in such a way as to create the greatest "total" of end-satisfaction. The utilitarian and quasi-utilitarian conceptions are most nearly realized in a free market (assuming in the one case that the income distribution is such as to give everyone's utility the same weight and in the other case that it gives more weight to the utility of some than of others), for in a market each individual expresses whatever ends he has uppermost (within the range of expression allowed by the market) and the ends expressed are brought into an equilibrium which is the mutually most satisfactory compromise among

---

* "Parliament," Edmund Burke said, "is not a *congress* of ambassadors from different and hostile interests, which interests each must maintain as an agent advocate, against other agents and advocates, but Parliament is a *deliberative* assembly of one nation, with *one* interest, that of the whole; where not local purposes, not local prejudices ought to guide, but the general good. . . ." Quoted by C. J. Friedrich, *Constitutional Government and Politics,* Harper, New York, 1937, p. 230.

them. The utilitarian conceptions of the public interest may also be asserted through mechanisms other than the market, of course, but non-market (i.e., political or administrative) mechanisms, if they are to serve the utilitarian conception of the public interest, must perform compromising and equilibrating functions analagous to those performed by the market.* To the extent that legislators or other representatives are able to perform the functions of the market, i.e., to arrange that compromise which is mutually most satisfactory in terms of the preferences of the constituents as ordered by the constituents themselves, they function as a utilitarian choice mechanism.

Non-market mechanisms intended to exemplify this conception of the public interest must make use of representatives, but they should employ representatives who represent the smallest possible number of constituents (the more numerous the constituents, the more the representatives must make selections among the ends to be served), and the representatives should be under the necessity of acting only as their constituents specifically instruct (for otherwise the constituents' preferences would be imperfectly represented).

The qualified individualist conception of the public interest implies a mechanism which takes into account the appropriate classes of ends and excludes from account those which are not appropriate. The market will not do this, of course: it makes no distinction between self-regarding ends and community-regarding ones, for example. What is indicated is a political process in which an equilibrium is reached among those ends which are appropriate. A representative process in which the representative gives more weight to his constituents' "real ultimate interest" than to their "immediate and apparent interest" and special weight to "higher motives and more comprehensive and distant views"

---

* Of liberalism Professor Knight has written, ". . . the end of action is whatever the individual wants and strives to do, or to get, or to be. . . ." "Thus ideally all political decisions in a liberal state represent the best possible compromise between the (more or less conflicting) interests of individuals—a composite, or center of gravity, or 'equilibrium of forces,' force being the form under which interests are conceived as operating." *Freedom and Reform*, Harper, New York, 1947, pp. 53 and 78.

is implied."* This is likely to be a system in which the representative can be called to account only infrequently and then by a relatively large constituency, an arrangement which permits him to ignore all inappropriate ends and to bring into equilibrium with others only those ends which, by the standards deemed relevant, ought to be taken into account in determining the greatest satisfaction "of the whole."

An institution may function as a mechanism which asserts at the same time different, and perhaps logically opposed, conceptions of the structure of the public interest. The members of a citizen board, for example, may endeavor to explicate the meaning of some very general ends which pertain to the body politic or *ethos* while at the same time—and perhaps inconsistently—seeking to find that compromise among the ends of individuals which will represent the greatest "total" satisfaction. Thus, the outcome of a process in which various conceptions of the public interest are asserted is likely to be an analgam.

Since the nature of the choice mechanism employed determines in part the content of the public interest, the question of which conception of the structure of the public interest is appropriate, in particular circumstances or in general, is suitably discussed in terms of which *mechanism* of choice is preferable—or whether, for example, representatives should have long terms or short, large constituencies or small, or whether the market or another mechanism should be employed.

* The quoted phrases are from J. S. Mill, *op. cit.*, pp. 251 and 256. The structure of the choice process ought to be such as to encourage the representative to make the appropriate selection from among his constituents' ends. He should, for example, "have such a term of office to look forward to as will enable him to be judged, not by a single act, but by his course of action." *Ibid*, p. 313.

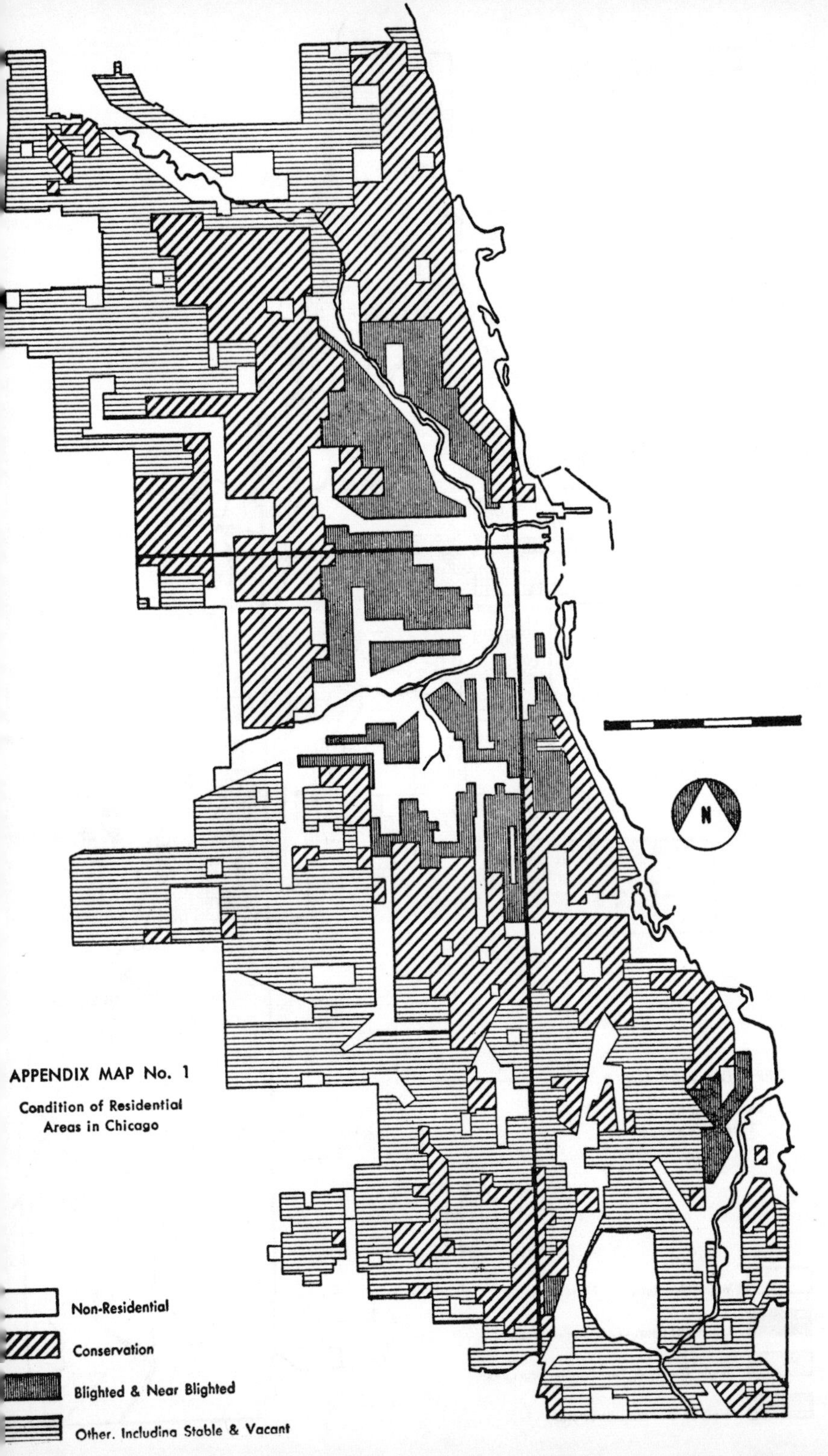

APPENDIX MAP No. 1

Condition of Residential Areas in Chicago

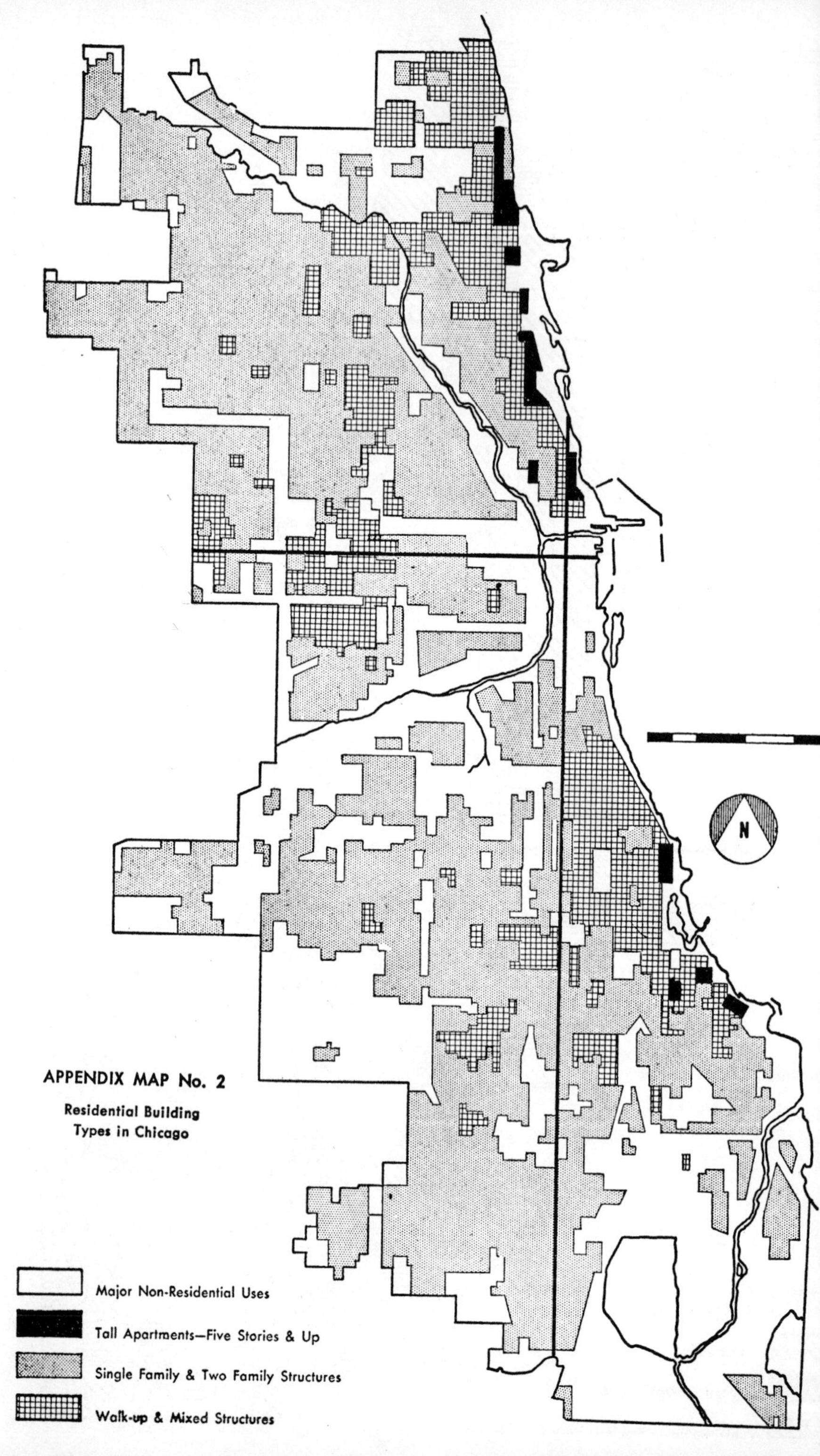

APPENDIX MAP No. 2

Residential Building Types in Chicago

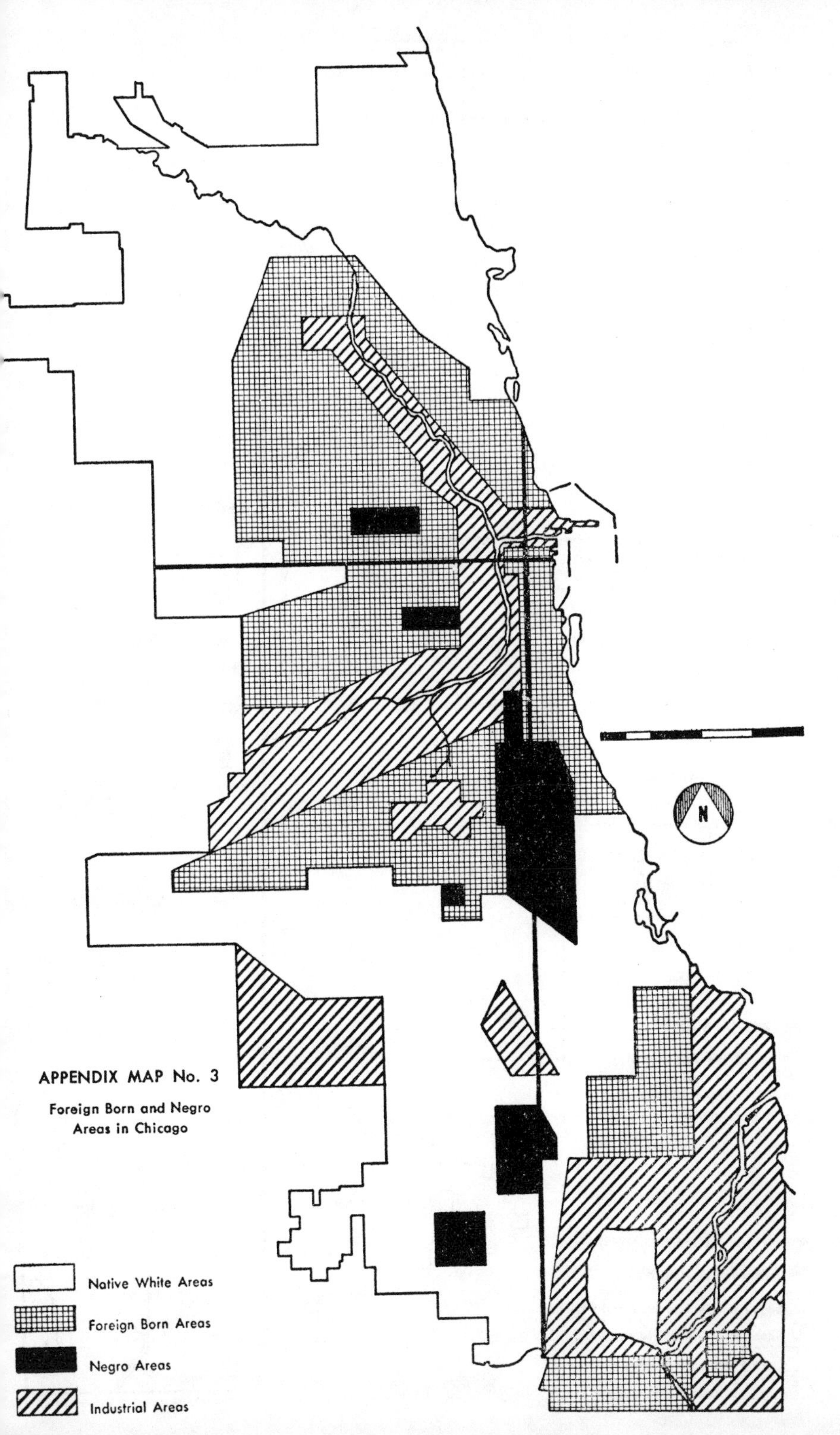

APPENDIX MAP No. 3

Foreign Born and Negro Areas in Chicago

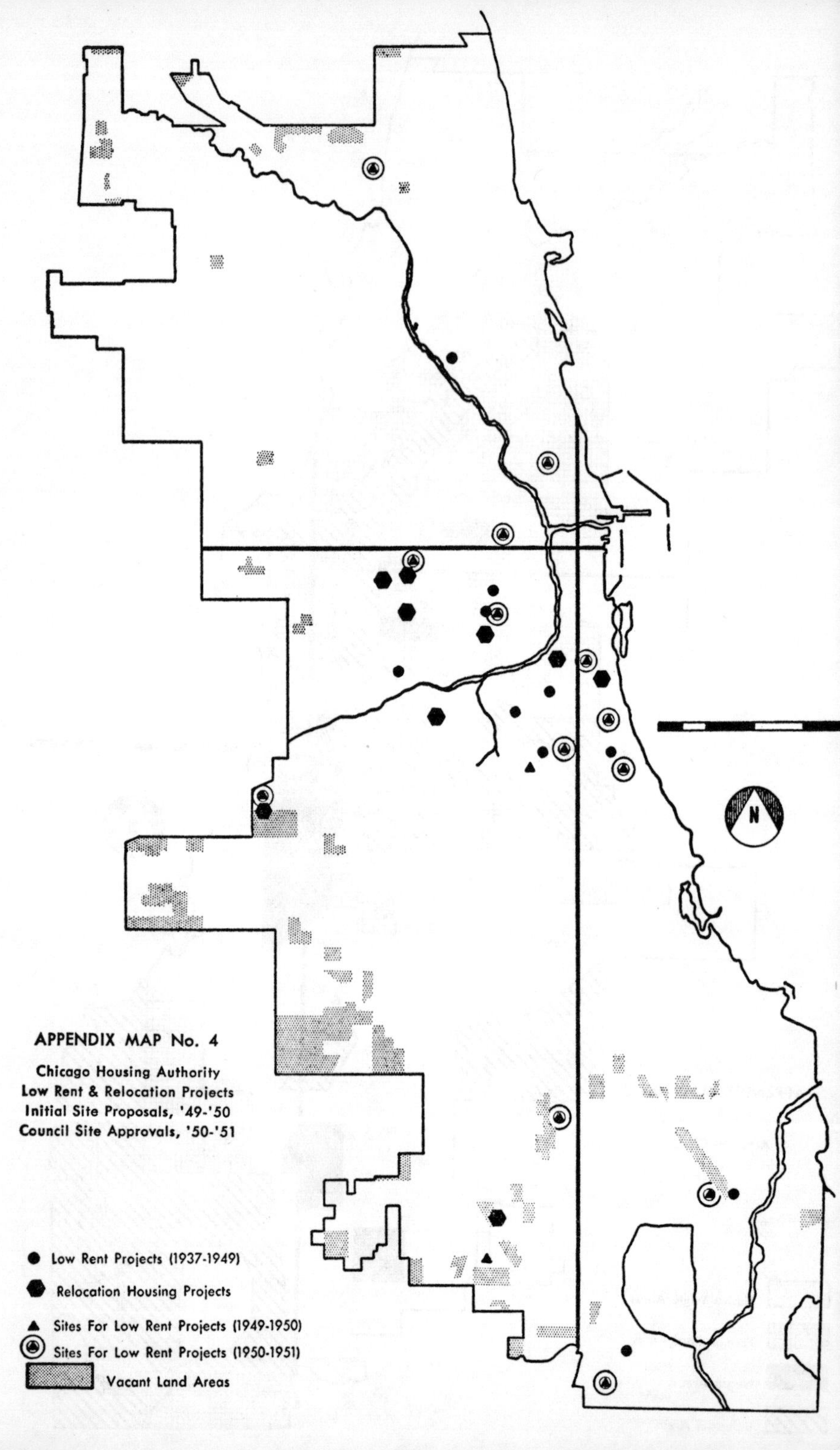
APPENDIX MAP No. 4
Chicago Housing Authority
Low Rent & Relocation Projects
Initial Site Proposals, '49-'50
Council Site Approvals, '50-'51
Low Rent Projects (1937-1949)
Relocation Housing Projects
Sites For Low Rent Projects (1949-1950)
Sites For Low Rent Projects (1950-1951)
Vacant Land Areas
N

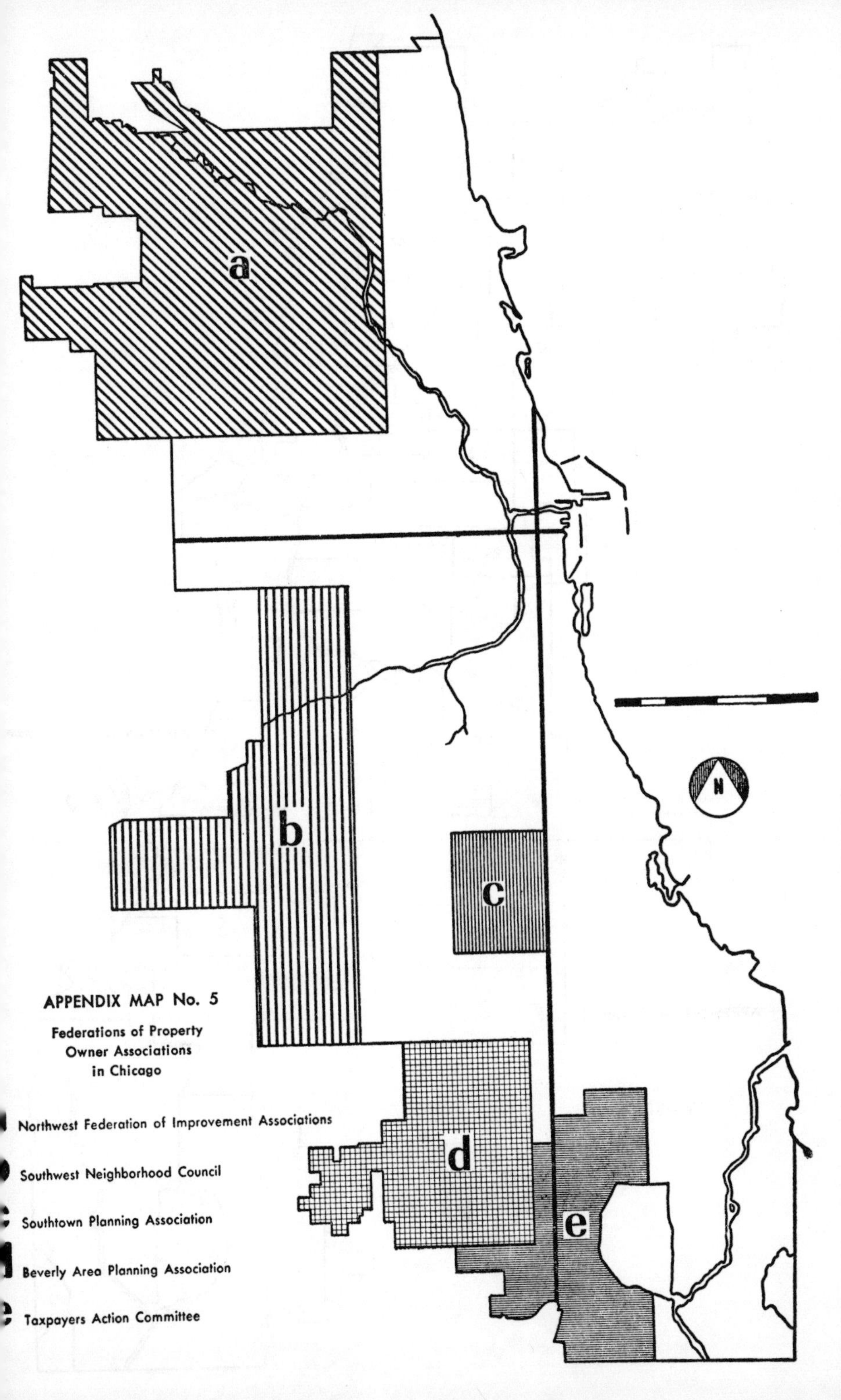

a
b
c
d
e
N
APPENDIX MAP No. 5
Federations of Property Owner Associations in Chicago
Northwest Federation of Improvement Associations
Southwest Neighborhood Council
Southtown Planning Association
Beverly Area Planning Association
Taxpayers Action Committee

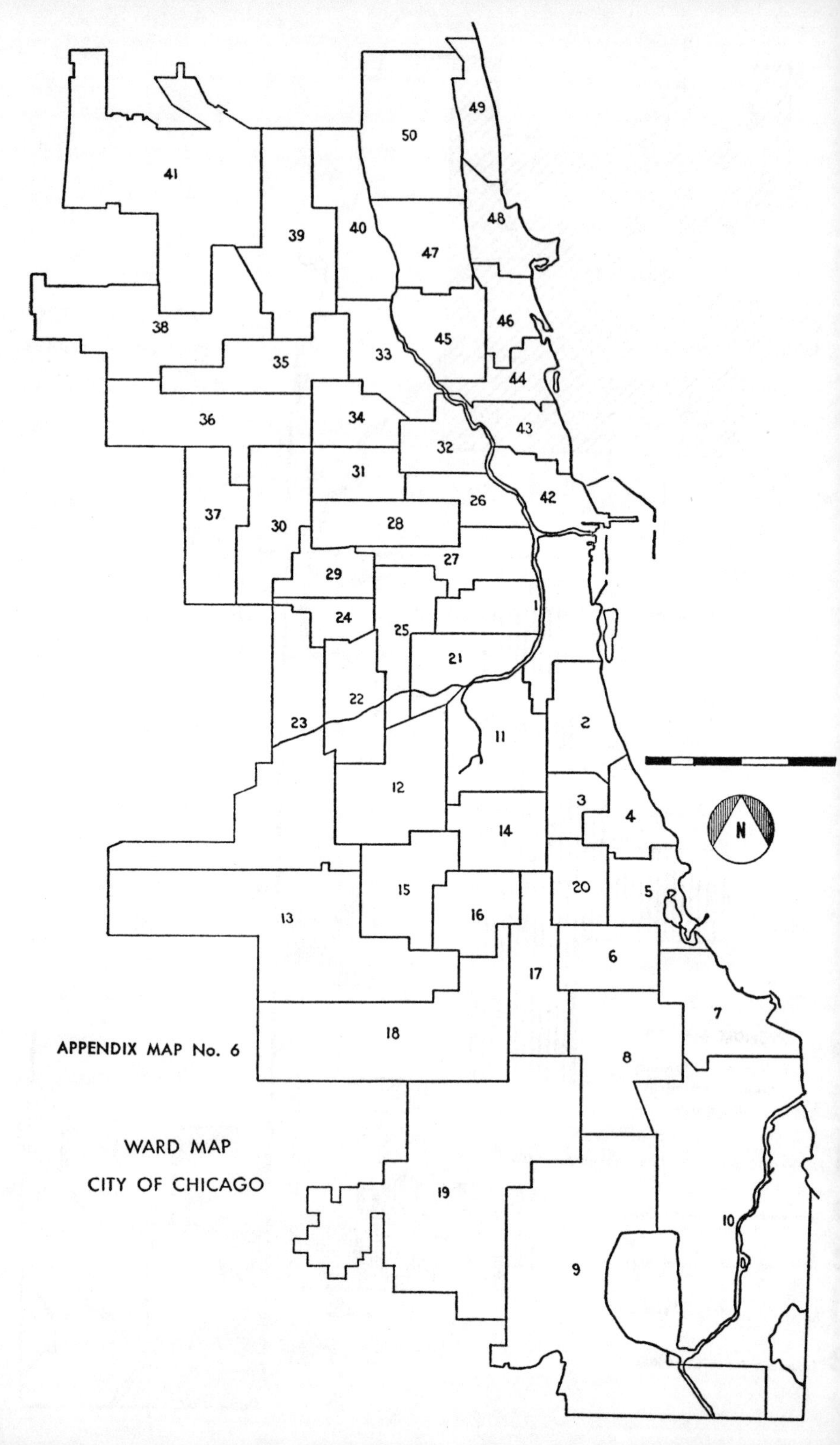

APPENDIX MAP No. 6

WARD MAP
CITY OF CHICAGO

Anticipated and Final Aldermanic Site Votes

Ward	*Alderman*	*Anticipated Vote on CHA Sites**	*Final Vote on CHA Sites†*
1.	J. Budinger	Yes	Yes
2.	W. H. Harvey	No	Yes
3.	A. J. Carey, Jr.	Yes	Yes
4.	A. H. Cohen	Yes	Yes
5.	R. E. Merriam	Yes	Yes
6.	F. J. Hogan	Doubtful	Yes
7.	N. J. Bohling	Yes	No
8.	R. E. Olin	Doubtful	No
9.	R. DuBois	No	No
10.	E. V. Pacini	No	No
11.	J. F. Wall	No	Yes
12.	E. J. Kucharski	No	Yes
13.	J. E. Egan	No	No
14.	C. P. Wagner	No	Yes
15.	E. F. Vyzral	No	Yes
16.	P. M. Sheridan	No	No
17.	W. T. Murphy	No	No
18.	T. J. Corcoran	No	No
19.	J. J. Duffy	Doubtful	Yes
20.	A. Pistilli	Yes	Yes
21.	J. F. Ropa	Yes	Yes
22.	O. F. Janousek	Yes	Yes
23.	G. J. Tourek	No	No
24.	L. London	Yes	Yes
25.	J. B. Bowler	Doubtful	Yes
26.	M. W. Bieszczat	Yes	No Vote
27.	H. L. Sain	Yes	Yes
28.	G. D. Kells	Yes	Yes
29.	J. S. Gillespie	Yes	Yes
30.	E. J. Hughes	Doubtful	Yes
31.	T. E. Keane	Doubtful	Yes
32.	J. P. Rostenkowski	No	Yes
33.	J. B. Brandt	No	Yes
34.	H. F. Geisler	Yes	Yes
35.	W. J. Orlikoski	No	Yes
36.	F. R. Ringa	No	Yes
37.	W. J. Lancaster	Doubtful	Yes
38.	P. J. Cullerton	Yes	Yes
39.	H. L. Brody	Yes	Yes
40.	B. M. Becker	Yes	Yes
41.	J. P. Immel	Doubtful	No
42.	D. R. Crowe	Yes	No Vote
43.	M. Bauler	Yes	Yes
44.	J. C. Burmeister, Jr.	Doubtful	Yes
45.	T. W. Merryman	Doubtful	Yes
46.	J. F. Young	Doubtful	Yes
47.	J. J. Hoellen	Doubtful	No
48.	A. A. Freeman	Yes	Yes
49.	F. Keenan	Yes	No Vote
50.	A. Weber	Doubtful	No

* As projected by Public Housing Association at beginning of site controversy, January 1950.

† Aug 4, 1950.

ACKNOWLEDGMENTS AND REFERENCE NOTES

THE AUTHORS wish to acknowledge the kindness of the many people who permitted themselves to be interviewed or who supplied information in other ways. We are especially grateful to those who read and commented upon the manuscript. These included: (among the participants in the events we describe) Alderman Archibald Carey Jr., Walter H. Blucher, Robert R. Taylor, David A. Wallace, John G. Vaughn, and Miss Elizabeth Wood; (among our colleagues) Charles Abrams, John W. Dyckman, Herbert J. Gans, Robert B. Mitchell, and William L. C. Wheaten of the University of Pennsylvania and Isaac Green, Richard L. Meier, Harvey S. Perloff, and Edward A. Shils of the University of Chicago; and Catherine Bauer, Dorothy Gazzolo, Margy Ellin Meyerson, and Harold Orlans. Mr. Wallace generously permitted us to use interview materials he obtained as background for a doctoral dissertation at Harvard University. Mrs. Janet Abu-Lughod and Miss Joyce Whitley gave us the results of research done by them.

We wish also to acknowledge the courtesy of the *Chicago Sun-Times*, which permitted the reproduction of the cartoons by Jacob Burck and of long quotations from its political columnist, Thomas Drennan, and of the *Reporter* magazine, which also permitted a quotation. The maps were adapted from materials prepared by the Chicago Plan Commission, the Chicago Housing Authority, and the University of Chicago Community Inventory.

The notes which follow include a few background references to supplement those in the footnotes. For additional references to the literature of housing, city planning and related subjects see, U.S. Housing and Home Finance Agency, *A Reading List on Housing in the United States*, Government Printing Office, Washington, Rev. ed., January 1953.

To avoid revealing the identity of some of our informants, all references to interview materials appear below as "interview document." These documents are on file at the Institute for Urban Studies, University of Pennsylvania.

CHAPTER 1

Background to the Case Study

1. For a brief review of governmental activities in housing, *cf.* National Association of Housing Officials, *Handbook for Housing Commissioners,* The Association, Chicago, 1950, pp. 10-53.

2. Formally referred to as the United States Housing Act, Public Law 412, 75th Cong., 50 Stat. 888.

3. Myres S. McDougal and Addison A. Mueller, "Public Purpose in Public Housing; An Anachronism Reburied," *Yale Law Journal,* Volume 52, No. 1, December 1942, p. 48.

4. Charles Abrams, "Slums, Ghettos, and the G.O.P.'s 'Remedy,'" *The Reporter,* Volume 10, No. 10, May 11, 1954, p. 28.

5. For a recent statement of this viewpoint, *cf.* U.S. Housing and Home Finance Agency, *The Relationship Between Slum Clearance and Urban Redevelopment and Low-Rent Public Housing,* Government Printing Office, Washington, 1950, p. 15.

6. Charles Abrams, *op. cit.*, pp. 28-29.

7. For a current survey of race relations and housing, *cf.* Charles Abrams, *Forbidden Neighbors: A Study of Prejudice in Housing,* Harper, New York, 1955.

8. For the four cases against racial covenants, *cf.* Miriam Abbell Rosenblum, "The Legal Status of the Negro as Affected by Supreme Court Decisions," Unpublished dissertation, University of Chicago, Chicago, 1953, p. 77.

9. U.S. Bureau of the Census, *County and City Data Book 1952,* Government Printing Office, Washington, 1953.

10. U.S. Public Housing Administration, *Monthly Progress Report,* November 30, 1953, The Administration, Washington.

11. Unpublished, undated notes, National Association of Housing Officials, Chicago.

12. *Journal of Housing,* Volume 9, Number 6, June 1952, p. 195.

13. *Journal of Housing,* Volume 7, No. 3, March 1950, p. 80.

14. For a review of main factors influencing public housing location, *cf.* M. T. Cooke, Jr. "Housing Site Problems: A review of the Site Selection Experience of 12 Cities Since 1949," *Journal of Housing,* Volume 9, No. 2, February 1952, pp. 48-50, 61, 64, 66, 67.

15. For comments on the relation between city planners and public housers, *cf.* Warren Jay Vinton, "A New Look at the Role of Public Housing in Urban Redevelopment," in *Planning 1949,* the American Society of Planning Officials, Chicago, pp. 24-34.

CHAPTER 2

The Organization and Its Tasks

1. Chicago Housing Authority, *Chicago's Housing Need: An Interim Measurement,* The Authority, Chicago, 1949, p. 1.

2. Chicago Plan Commission, *Master Plan of Residential Land Use of Chicago,* The Commission, Chicago, 1943, p. 73.

3. *Ibid.*, p. 73 and pp. 91, 103.

4. Metropolitan Housing and Planning Council of Chicago, *Areas of Negro Residence in the City of Chicago 1950,* The Council, Chicago, 1952, unpaged.

5. Maurice R. Davie, *Negroes in American Society,* Whittlesey House, New York, 1949, p. 221.

6. George A. Nesbitt, "Break Up

the Black Ghetto," *Crisis,* January 1949, p. 49.

7. Chicago Housing Authority, *op. cit.*, p. 17.

8. Interview document.

9. Chicago Plan Commission, *Housing Goals for Chicago,* The Commission, Chicago, 1946, p. 236.

10. Public Law 171, 81st Cong., 63 Stat. 413, Sec. 2.

11. The most important of these laws were the Housing Authorities Act (1934), the State Housing Act (1933), and the Housing Corporations Law (1937). These and other relevant laws are to be found in Illinois State Housing Board, *Illinois Housing Laws.*

12. Illinois Associated Statutes, Biennial Code, Sec. 128K.

13. An Act in Relation to Housing Authorities, Ill. Rev. Stat. 1949, Ch. 67½, Sec. 9 as amended.

14. Public Law 171, 81st Cong., *op. cit.*, Sec. 305 (b).

15. United States Public Housing Administration, *The Low-Rent Public Housing Program,* The Administration, Washington, p. 10.

16. *The Sunday Star,* Washington, D.C., December 11, 1949.

17. Interview document.

18. Chicago Housing Authority minutes, Book 19, 1950, pp. 26-27.

19. Also, *cf. Chicago Sun-Times,* June 28, 1950.

20. Chicago Housing Authority, *Monthly Report,* October 1949, The Authority, Chicago, p. 10.

21. Interview document.

22. "Community Planning: Therapeutic and Utopian," Manuscript of lecture, University of Chicago.

23. Chicago Plan Commission, *Proceedings,* February 17, 1944.

24. *Chicago Daily News,* June 17, 1949.

CHAPTER 3

The Politicians

1. H. W. Morris, "The Chicago Negro and the Major Political Parties, 1940-48," Unpublished dissertation, Department of History, University of Chicago, March 1950, p. 73.

2. *Journal of Housing,* Volume 4, No. 5, May 1947, p. 30.

3. Chicago Plan Commission, *Housing Goals for Chicago, op. cit.*, p. 125.

4. For a critique of the filtering down process in the housing market, *cf.* Richard U. Ratcliff, *Urban Land Economics,* McGraw-Hill, New York, 1949, pp. 321-334.

5. Chicago Plan Commission, *Housing Goals for Chicago, op. cit.*, p. 127.

6. William R. Gable, "The Chicago City Council: A Study of Urban Politics and Legislation," Unpublished dissertation, Department of Political Science, University of Chicago, Chicago, 1953, p. 13.

7. John P. White, "Lithuanians and the Democratic Party, A Case Study of Nationality Politics in Chicago and Cook County," Unpublished Ph.D. dissertation, Political Science Department, University of Chicago, Chicago, 1953, p. 25.

8. *Ibid.*, p. 28.

9. *Ibid.*, p. 64.

10. Interview document.

11. Interview document.

12. Harvey W. Zorbaugh, *The Gold Coast and the Slum,* University of Chicago Press, Chicago, 1929, p. 287.

13. Leonardo Neher, "The Political Parties in Chicago's 42nd Ward," Unpublished dissertation, Department of Political Science, University of Chicago, Chicago, 1952, pp. 65-66.

14. W. R. Gable, *op. cit.*, p. 74.

15. James A. Rust, "The Ward Committeeman in Chicago," Unpublished dissertation, Department of Political Science, University of Chicago, Chicago, 1953, p. 56.

16. Chester I. Barnard, *The Functions of the Executive,* Harvard University Press, Cambridge, 1938, Ch. XI. Barnard discusses the special case of the political organization on pp. 156-57.

17. H. Dicken Cherry, "Effective

Precinct Organization," Unpublished dissertation, Department of Political Science, University of Chicago, Chicago, 1952.

18. Leonardo Neher, *op. cit.*, p. 76.
19. *Chicago Daily News*, August 27, 1949.
20. Quoted in Fay Calkins, *The CIO and The Democratic Party*, University of Chicago Press, Chicago, 1952, pp. 67-68.
21. H. D. Cherry, *op. cit.*, pp. 67-68.
22. Neher, *op. cit.*, p. 92.
23. Independent Voters of Illinois, *The Kohn Report; Crime and Politics in Chicago*, Chicago, 1953, p. 10.
24. Interview document.
25. *Chicago Daily News*, December 7, 1950.
26. Interview document.
27. Interview document.
28. Interview document.
29. W. R. Gable, *op. cit.*, p. 121.
30. Interview document.
31. Quoted by Gable, *op. cit.*, p. 121.
32. Interview document.
33. *Chicago Sun-Times*, April 4, 1950.
34. Interview document.
35. Interview document.
36. Interview document.
37. Interview document.
38. Interview document.
39. Interview document.
40. W. R. Gable, *op. cit.*, p. 227.
41. Interview document.
42. *Chicago Sun-Times*, June 28, 1950.
43. Public Housing Association, *Newsletter*, February 10, 1950.
44. *Chicago Sun-Times*, February 18, 1947.
45. *Southtown Economist*, July 24, 1949.

CHAPTER 4

The Climate of Neighborhood Opinion

1. Chicago Housing Authority, *Chicago's Housing Need: An Interim Measurement*, *op. cit.*, 1949, p. 8.
2. *Ibid.*, p. 9.
3. For a detailed critique of housing market analysis, *cf.* Chester Rapkin, Louis Winnick, David M. Blank, *Housing Market Analysis: A Study of Theory and Methods*, U.S. Housing and Home Finance Agency, Washington, Government Printing Office, 1953, p. 92.
4. U.S. Public Housing Administration, *Low-Rent Housing Manual*, Sec. 207.2, "Promoting Economy and Avoiding Extravagance in the Design and Specifications for Public Low-Rent Housing," mimeo.
5. Interview document.
6. Chicago Housing Authority, *Manual for Architects*, The Authority, Chicago, prelim. ed., 1950, p. 12 *et seq.*
7. *Chicago Sun-Times*, December 20, 1953.
8. Interview document.
9. George A. Nesbitt, "Break Up the Black Ghetto," *op. cit.*, p. 49.
10. *Chicago Defender*, January 17, 1948.
11. George A. Nesbitt, "Break Up the Black Ghetto," *op. cit.*, pp. 49-50.
12. *Ibid.*, p. 52.
13. *Ibid.*, p. 50.
14. *Chicago Defender*, February 28, 1948.
15. Interview document.
16. For documentation on these activities of the Chicago improvement associations, *cf.* Herman H. Long and Charles S. Johnson, *People vs. Property: Race Restrictive Covenants in Housing*, Fisk University Press, Nashville, 1947.
17. Interview document.
18. Interview document.
19. Interview document.
20. Interview document.
21. Interview document.
22. Interview document.
23. Zorita Mikva, "The Neighborhood Improvement Association: A Counter-Force to the Expansion of Chicago's Negro Population," Unpublished dissertation, Department of Sociology, University of Chicago, Chicago, 1951, p. 100.

24. *Journal of Housing,* Volume 7, No. 1, January 1950, p. 8.
25. *Hearings Before the House Select Committee on Lobbying Activities,* 1950, Part 2, p. 553.
26. For example of use of such "kit" material, *cf. Journal of Housing,* Volume 8, No. 2, February 1951, p. 49.
27. Interview document.

CHAPTER 5

The Development of Policy

1. Chicago Housing Authority minutes, October 4, 1937.
2. Chicago Housing Authority minutes, January 17, 1938.
3. For this and other background on Chicago and major cities, *cf.* Robert C. Weaver, *The Negro Ghetto,* Harcourt, Brace and Company, New York, 1948, p. 404.
4. Interview document.
5. For a summary of race relations in Chicago for the period, 1947-51, *cf.* The Chicago Commission on Human Relations, *The People of Chicago,* The Commission, Chicago, undated, 61 pp.
6. *Chicago Times,* December 5, 1946, and *Chicago Tribune,* December 6, 1946.
7. *Calumet Index,* May 19, 1947.
8. *Ibid.*
9. For the impact of the ideology of the American creed on institutional structures, *cf.* Gunnar Myrdal, *et al., An American Dilemma: The Negro Problem and Modern Democracy,* Harper, New York, 2 vols., 1944, p. 80.
10. For material on the opposition of Alderman DuBois to the Chicago Housing Authority, *cf. A Digest of the Hearings Held for the Study of the Chicago Housing Authority, Nov. 20-21, 24-25, 1947,* mimeo, unpaged.
11. Statement of November 20, 1946, reported in *Human Relations in Chicago,* Report for 1946, Mayor's Commission on Human Relations, Chicago, p. 124.
12. August 16, 1947.
13. Wilford G. Winholtz, "Public Statement on Relocation Sites for the City of Chicago," South Side Planning Board, Chicago, mimeo., unpaged, July 1, 1948.
14. Quoted in Homer A. Jack, "Homes for Chicago's D.P.'s," *The Nation,* September 11, 1948.
15. *Southtown Economist,* August 25, 1948.
16. Interview document.
17. Interview document.
18. Also *cf.* Chicago Council Against Racial and Religious Discrimination, *Summary of the Policy of the Commission on Human Relations Relative to Living Space,* mimeo., 1948.
19. For current social science analysis of racial prejudice, *cf.* Gerhart Saenger, *The Social Psychology of Prejudice,* Harper, New York, 1953, and Gordon W. Allport, *The Nature of Prejudice,* Beacon Press, Boston, 1954.
20. Interview document.
21. Interview document.
22. July 8, 1949.
23. Public Housing Association, *Newsletter,* July 15, 1949.
24. Interview document.
25. *The Southtown Economist,* February 13, 1949.
26. *Chicago Sun-Times,* October 15, 1949.
27. Interview document.
28. Interview document.
29. Samuel D. Freifeld, Guest Columnist for Stella Counselbaum, *The Pittsburgh Courier,* May 27, 1950.
30. Interview document.
31. Interview document.
32. Robert C. Weaver, *op. cit.,* p. 95.
33. Interview document.
34. Interview document.
35. Interview document.
36. Interview document.
37. Interview document.
38. March 17, 1949.
39. Interview document.
40. Interview document.
41. *Chicago Sun-Times,* July 18, 1949.

CHAPTER 6

The Struggle Begins

1. Address before the American Public Works Association printed in *The Journal of Housing,* Volume 3, No. 1, December 1945-January 1946, pp. 12-14.
2. Interview document.
3. Interview document.
4. Memorandum, September 2, 1949.
5. Memorandum to Commissioners, "Criteria for Site Selection," September 2, 1949.
6. Memorandum, October 3, 1949.
7. *Chicago Sun-Times,* March 27, 1950.
8. Interview document.
9. Interview document.
10. Interview document.
11. January 16, 1950.
12. *Chicago Sun-Times,* October 15, 1949.
13. Interview document.
14. Interview document.
15. Interview document.
16. Interview document.
17. *Chicago Sun-Times,* December 21, 1949.
18. *Chicago Sun-Times,* December 16, 1949.
19. *Chicago Sun-Times,* December 27, 1949.
20. *Chicago Sun-Times,* December 30, 1949.
21. Interview document.
22. *Chicago Sun-Times,* December 10, 1951.
23. January 25, 1950, p. 3.
24. Interview document.
25. Interview document.
26. Zorita Mikva, *op. cit.*, p. 86.
27. From the observations of Donna Myers, "The Community and Public Housing," Unpublished manuscript, University of Chicago, 1950.
28. Interview document.
29. Notes prepared by Mayor's Commission on Human Relations, Chicago, undated.
30. *Ibid.*
31. March 8, 1950.

CHAPTER 7

Climax

1. *Chicago Daily News,* March 13, 1950.
2. *Chicago Sun-Times,* March 29, 1950.
3. Public letter from Robert R. Taylor to Ald. William J. Lancaster covering second submittal of sites, March 31, 1950.
4. *Chicago Sun-Times,* April 4, 1950.
5. *Chicago Sun-Times,* April 11, 1950.
6. *Chicago Sun-Times,* April 11, 1950.
7. *Chicago Sun-Times,* April 11, 1950.
8. Interview document.
9. Interview document.
10. Interview document.
11. Interview document.
12. Interview document.
13. Interview document.
14. *Chicago Tribune,* April 30, 1950.
15. *Chicago Sun-Times,* April 27, 1950.
16. *Chicago Tribune,* April 27, 1950.
17. Superintendent Hunt, speech, mimeo.
18. *Chicago Sun-Times,* May 16, 1950.
19. Ralph H. Burke, "Report to Hon. Martin H. Kennelly, Mayor on Redevelopment of Certain Slum Sites in the City of Chicago," May 1950, mimeo, pp. 8-9.
20. "Site Principles," Technical

Staffs, Chicago Plan Commission, Chicago Housing Authority, May 12, 1950.

21. *Ibid.*
22. *Chicago Sun-Times,* April 25, 1950.
23. Interview document.
24. Interview document.
25. Interview document.
26. Interview document.
27. Interview document.
28. *Chicago Defender,* December 17, 1949.
29. June 16, 1950.
30. Interview document.
31. Interview document.
32. Public letter from Robert R. Taylor to Ald. William J. Lancaster covering transmission of ordinance draft on the compromise sites, June 21, 1950.

CHAPTER 8

Settlement

1. Interview document.
2. Zorita Mikva, *op. cit.*, p. 106.
3. Interview document.
4. July 1950.
5. July 7, 1950.
6. This quotation and the subsequent quotations of the second hearing testimony come from the stenographic transcript of those hearings, Metropolitan Housing and Planning Council, Chicago.
7. *Chicago Daily News,* July 7, 1950.
8. *Chicago Daily News,* July 17, 1950.
9. Interview document.
10. Interview document.
11. Thomas Hobbes, *Leviathan,* in *Selections,* Scribner's, New York, 1930, p. 292.
12. *Chicago Tribune,* August 5, 1950.
13. *Chicago Sun-Times,* August 9, 1950.
14. Public Housing Association, *Newsletter,* May 17, 1950.
15. Interview document.
16. Interview document.
17. Interview document.
18. Interview document.
19. December 20, 1950.
20. Records, National Committee Against Discrimination in Housing, New York, New York.
21. Interview document.
22. Interview document.
23. January 23, 1951.
24. Interview document.
25. U.S. Public Housing Administration, *Manual,* Sec. 208-8, The Administration, Washington, March 27, 1952.
26. Interview document.
27. Interview document.
28. Interview document.
29. Interview document.
30. Interview document.
31. Interview document.
32. Interview document.

CHAPTER 9

Politics

1. Interview document.
2. Interview document.
3. Interview document.
4. *Chicago Sun-Times,* April 15 and 17, 1953.

CHAPTER 10

Planning

1. *Cf.* the discussion of this kind of "planning" by Michael Polanyi in *The Logic of Liberty,* The University of Chicago Press, Chicago, 1951, pp. 134-35.
2. Speech before dinner meeting of CHA employees, 1950.
3. The President's Advisory Commit-

tee on Government Housing Policies and Programs has, to a limited extent, advocated experimental or pilot developments; *cf.* the Committee's *Report,* December 1953, U.S. Government Printing Office, Washington, p. 377.

CHAPTER 11

The Public Interest

1. *Chicago Sun-Times,* April 11, 1950.
2. Interview document.
3. Robert A. Walker, *The Planning Function in Urban Government,* University of Chicago Press, Chicago, 2nd ed., 1950, p. 356.
4. *New York Herald Tribune,* May 21, 1952.
5. Interview document.
6. October 9, 1952.

INDEX TO PARTICULAR CONCEPTS

NOTE: We have indexed here some (but not all) of the concepts elaborated in the Supplement. The reader of the narrative may look here to find his way to definitions of the few pieces of jargon we have introduced into the text and the reader of the Supplement may look here to discover where in the text some of the concepts are applicable. It should be remembered that the application of the concepts is not always explicit in the text, that some concepts (e.g. "politics") are implicit on almost every page, and that others are developed in the Supplement for the sake of logical completeness and not because they are relevant to the present study. These last are not listed in this index. In the case of concepts (like "politics") which have very general applicability throughout the present study, the only indexed reference is to the definition of the term. In all cases, the first reference is to the definition.

Advantage, 320, 155, 279
Anticipated consequence, 319, 279

Bargaining, 307, 148, 250, 262
Benefit, 320, 166

Community planning, 313, 54, 273, 300
Communalist (conception of public interest), 323, 300-01
Comprehensive (plan), 313, 273-74
Compromise, 307, 142, 257
Condition, 315-16, 40, 270, 272
Consequence, 319, 154, 281
Contention, 306, 148-49
Contextual (element of end), 317, 161
Cooperation, 305, 248, 256, 262
Corporate (planning), 313, 272, 300, 302
Cost, 320, 166
Course of action, 312, 153, 156, 270, 272, 279

Development (planning), 318, 271, 272
Dictation, 307, 257
Disadvantage, 320, 155, 279

End, 304, 35, 39-40, 41, 49, 51, 253-54, 255, 269-70, 272, 281, 300-01
End reduction, 316, 162-63, 164-65

Fight, 307, 45, 148-49, 249

Incidental end, 317, 156
Individualist (conception of public interest), 324, 289
Instrumental-abstract (significance of issue), 312, 139-41
Intrinsic-concrete (significance of is-

sue), 311-12, 118, 136, 139-41, 142, 146, 147, 250
Issue, 304, 253-54

Larger issue, 311, 139, 141, 144
Limiting condition, 316, 270

Opportunistic (decision), 313, 277
Opportunity area, 316, 270, 271, 272, 278
Organismic (conception of public interest), 323, 300-01

Particular issue, 311, 140
Planning, 312
Politics, 304-05

Public interest, 322-23, 51, 54, 289

Quasi-Utilitarian (conception of public interest), 325, 299, 301

Settlement, 304, 250
Strategy, 307, 141, 148-49, 248, 256, 257, 258, 259
Struggle, 307, 249, 253, 256
Symbolic-ideological (significance of issue), 312, 86, 115, 118, 136, 139-41, 142, 145, 147-48, 249, 250

Unitary (conception of public interest), 323, 289, 300-01
Utilitarian (conception of public interest), 324, 289

GENERAL INDEX

ADL; See Anti-Defamation League
Airport Homes, 125-26, 128
Alderman (office of), 64-66, 69
Alinsky, Saul D., 139, 142, 143, 175, 179, 243
American Jewish Committee, 181, 218
American Veterans Committee, 130, 181, 184
Anderson, David, 149, 172, 177, 178, 215, 216
Anti-Defamation League, 143, 144, 180-81, 217-18, 227
Anti-semitic, See Jews
Architecture (of projects), 94-5, 165
Arvey, Col. Jacob, 79, 82, 87, 176, 238, 291
Assimilation, 104
Austin, Rev. J. C., 101, 102
Authority (form of organization), 38; See also Chicago Housing Authority

Becker, Ald. B. M., n75, 97, 169, 190, 199, 202, 205, 217-18, 225, 228, 237, 238
Benjamin, Claude A., 43, 47, 193, 194, 203, 219, 221, 242
Bieszczat, Ald. M. W., 190
"Big Boys" (of Chicago City Council), 67, 129, 159, 190, 191, 193, 196, 202, 216, 218, 248-49, 255, 257, 258, 263, 286-87, 298
Big business, 116
Bi-racial (projects), 122-31, 167, 170
Black Belt, 31, 32, 100
Blucher, Walter, 45, 208
B'nai B'rith, 139, 143, 180, 181, 227
Board of Education, See Chicago Board of Education
Bodfish, Morton, 116, 117-18, 302
Booster spirit, 61, 106
Boyle, John S., 238
Burke, Ralph H., 204, 206, 207, 208-11 212, 213, 214, 221

Carey, Ald. Archibald J. Jr., 76, 77, 100, 102, 137, 169, 194-95, 228, 237, 238, 250
Catholics, 49, 50, 65, 102, 266
Catholic Labor Alliance, 181
Catholic Youth Organization, 139
Chicago; importance, for public housing study, 11-12; similarity of public housing experience to other cities, 13, 26; reasons for studying, 14; increase in home ownership in, 22; nature of housing problem in, 29-34; organization of, 54; political structure of, 64-82, 274, 285-94
Chicago Board of Amalgamated Clothing Workers, 184
Chicago Board of Education, 52, 54, 124, 162, 163, 165, 168, 202-03, 241, 300
Chicago City Council: site selection powers, 36; committees concerned with housing, 54; relations with Plan Commission, 56; membership and functioning of, 64-81; attitude toward Authority, 86-88; approves relocation housing program, 131; acts to curb authority, 136-37; acts on Carey resolution, 137; receives site proposals, 173-75; receives committee report, 186; accepts sites, 239; conflicting ends of, 253; organization of criticized, 285; organization of, defended, 286-88
Chicago Council Against Racial and Religious Discrimination, 139, 184
Chicago Daily News, 59, 179, 191, 215
Chicago Daily Sun-Times, 59, 62-63, 82, 137, 149, 150, 169, 177, 178,

179, 191, 200, 215, 216, 220, 239, 242, 285-86
Chicago Defender, 219
Chicago Dwellings Association, 56, 162, 165, 168, 241
Chicago Housing Authority: estimates housing need, 32; proposes program under Act of 1949, 33; legal basis and powers of, 36, 39-40; ends of, 41; internal organization of, for planning, 42, 52; relations with Plan Commission, 58; relations with politicians, 82-86; estimates of housing demand, 92; view of opposition, 115; racial policy of, 121-38; investigates alternatives, 152-54; selects site criteria, 164-65; chooses particular sites, 167-71; criticized, 237; strategy of, 256; view of public interest, 301-02
Chicago Metropolitan Home Builders' Association, 111, 116
Chicago Mortgage Bankers Association, 116, 117
Chicago Park District, 52, 54, 124, 162, 163, 165, 168, 202
Chicago Plan Commission, 30, 35, 52, 53, 56-58, 59, 63, 83, 107, 116, 132, 160, 165, 170, 189, 192, 198, 200, 201, 202, 207, 211, 212, 213, 214, 220, 238, 241, 270, 273, 274
Chicago Real Estate Board, 62, 113, 116, 117, 182, 226, 228
Chicago Tribune, 200
Church Federation of Greater Chicago, 182
CIO, See Congress of Industrial Organizations
City Council, See Chicago City Council
City planning movement, 53, 274
Civic Federation of Chicago, 62, 116
Class, See Social class
Commission on Human Relations; See Mayor's Commission on Human Relations
Commissioners (of Chicago Housing Authority): appointment of, 37; powers, 39, 41; brief biographies of, 38-44; views on policy re segregation, 38-45; relations with staff, 47-48; as "legislators," 49; relations with interest groups, 49-50; attitude toward research, 93; unaware of alternatives, 155; views uncertain, 159; accept principles of site selection, 164; select sites, 167-71; make new proposal, 193; scolded by Mayor, 194; vote to accept compromise, 221; change strategy, 248; amateurs, 259, 276
Committee for Housing Action, 62, 64
Comprehensive plan, 25, 52-54, 56-58, 153, 273-75
Competence (political), 261-62, 297
Congestion, 13
Connors, William J., 68-69, 71
Conservation areas: defined, 31; appeals of political machines in, 73; hostility toward public housing, 87; as opinion-interest group, 102; identifications with, 105-06; improvement associations in, 106-114
Conservative-reaction, 22, 142, 250
Consumer preferences, 93, 302n
Coordination, 55-56; See also Mayor's Housing and Redevelopment Coordinator
Communication, 262-66
Community identification, 99, 105, 297
Congregational Union, 181, 227
Congress of Industrial Organizations, 99, 130, 181, 227
Cook County League of Women Voters, 182
Corruption, 74-75, 287
Council-manager (form of government), 290
Crime syndicate, 74, 287
Criteria (for site selection), 161-63, 164-65, 170-71, 196, 242, 246, 275-76
Cullerton, Ald. P. J., 81, 190, 238

Dawson, Congressman William L., 76-79, 221
Decentralization of power, 288, 291
Decision-making, 13
Democratic Party, 62, 169, 176, 207, 254, 286
Density (of population), 57, 211, 275
Depression, 17, 21, 94
Detroit, 24
Development Department (of CHA), 42, 52
Discrimination, 22, 32, 36, 73, 107, 135-36, 144, 206, 221, 246
DuBois, Ald. Reginald, 126, 128, 174, 193, 199, 229, 238, 239
Ducey, John M., 131-32, 184
Duffy, Ald. John J., 62, 80, 86, 87, 131, 139, 141, 169, 170, 173, 174, 176-77, 178, 179, 184, 192, 193, 194, 195-99, 200, 201, 202, 204, 214,

216, 219-20, 225, 226, 237, 238, 239, 242, 247-48, 249, 254, 258, 260, 263, 286-87
DuSable Worker, 236

Economy, 166
Economy of incentives, 70
Egan, Ald. J. E., 195
Egan, John Taylor, 206, 207, 221
Eugene, Larry, 231-32
Experiment, 282-83

Federal regulations, 37
Federal Housing Administration, 20, 113
Fernwood project, 127-28
Field, Marshall, Jr., 215
Field, Marshall, Sr., 139, 149, 179, 220
Filtering down process, 63
Financing (of projects), 37-38
Finitzo, Ralph J., 111-12, 114, 183, 195, 225, 265
Fisher, Bernice, 181
Foley, Raymond, 208, 245
Freeman, Ald. A. A., 97
Freifeld, Samuel D., 143-45, 180-81, 217, 218, 227, 228
Fruchtman, Edward, 46, 173

Gardner, Carl, 201, 203-04
Geisler, Ald. H. F., 97
Gertz, Elmer, 139, 140, 141, 143, 148
Gill, Joseph L., 238

Harvey, Ald. William, 76, 178, 179, 221
Hearings, 182-87, 229-37
Himmel, Harry S., 107
Hirsh, Morris H., 227
Hoellen, Ald. J. J., 97
Horne, Frank, 244-45, 246
Housing: problem in Chicago, 29-34; recomendations of Plan Commission, 56-58, 63; politicians' views regarding, 61; supply of and demand for, 91-92
Housing Act: of 1937, 17, 19, 23; of 1949, 22, 23, 29, 35-36
Housing and Home Finance Agency, 208, 244, 283
Housing Committee (of City Council), 172, 173, 186, 189, 191, 194, 237, 242
Housing Conference of Chicago, 227; See also Public Housing Association
Housing Goals for Chicago, 35, 63
Housing policy (development of), 17-26
Howard, Rev. James M., 234-35
Ickes, Harold, 121
Ideology, 231, 259
Illinois Housing Authorities Act, 36
Illinois State Housing Board, 108
Improvement associations, 106-114
Income (of potential tenants), 98
Independent Voters of Illinois, 130, 205, 227
Informal controls, 66-67
Interest groups, 50, 96-118, 138-50

Jack, Rev. Homer, 131
Jewish Labor Committee, 218
Jews, 49, 65, 73, 143, 190, 199, 217-18, 229, 266
Journal of Housing, 25, 93

Keane, Ald. T. E., 190, 193
Kelly, Mayor Edward J., 61, 79, 80, 83-86, 124-25, 128, 173, 257, 258, 263, 266, 267, 287
Kellstadt, Charles, 44
Kennelly, Mayor Martin H., receives housing proposal, 29; his stand on housing, 61-63; political background, 79-80; relations with Party and Council, 80-82, 87; criticizes appearance of projects, 93; his views on racial policy, 128-29; role in relocation housing program, 129-31; opposes Carey resolution, 137; refuses to negotiate, 150; receives site proposals, 111-12; contrasted with former Mayor Kelly, 173; receives Strategy Committee, 176; protests press criticism, 177-78; not criticized by *Sun-Times,* 179; sympathizes with opposition, 184-85; addresses Council, 187; urges agreement on sites, 192; refuses to take position, 193; scolds commissioners, 194; urges compromise, 200, 204; urges settlement, 220; urges Federal approval, 245; not understood, 258
Knowledge, need of, 259, 281, 308
Kramer, Ferd, 145-46, 147, 219, 245
Kruse, Henry A., 44, 47, 50, 220, 221, 265, 266

Lake Meadows (redevelopment project), 78, 101, 244
Labor unions, 99
Lancaster, Ald. William J., 71, 88, 136,

172, 173, 174, 175, 183, 184, 185, 186, 192, 193, 195, 196, 200, 202, 204, 219-20, 226, 236, 237, 242, 258
Land Clearance Commission, 53, 55, 64, 114, 137, 162, 165, 167, 192, 210, 212, 241, 244, 275, 300
Liberal-left, 22, 142, 250, 259
Liveright, A. A., 139, 176, 228, 235-36, 248
Los Angeles, 24

Machine (political), 65-79, 289, 290, 291, 299
Market analysis, 91, 92, 160
Master plan, See Comprehensive Plan
Master Plan of Residential Land Use of Chicago, 56
Mayor of Chicago: powers re CHA, 37, 39; relation to City Council, 66; See also Kennelly, Martin H.
Mayor's Commission on Human Relations, 125, 127, 128, 130, 132-33, 300
Mayor's Housing and Redevelopment Coordinator, 56, 62, 64, 129, 245, 275
McDonnell, William, 107
McMillen, Wayne, 43, 47, 51, 84, 85, 130, 148, 193, 200, 203, 215, 240, 242, 243, 247, 248-49
Merit system, 80
Merriam, Ald. Robert, 169, 190, 205, 225, 237, 238, 242, 245
Metropolitan Housing and Planning Council, 145-47, 219, 245
Meyerson, Martin, 46, 52-53, 58, 159, 163, 168, 170, 171, 173, 184, 189, 191, 192, 203-04, 206-08, 211, 214, 216, 219, 240, 243, 248
Minorities, 20-21, 25, 31, 49, 65, 103-05
Morgan Park Association, 198
Moses, Robert, 294, 295-97

NAM (National Manufacturers Association), 44, 117
Nash, Patrick A., 79
Nash, Thomas D., 80
National Association for the Advancement of Colored People, 100, 205, 246
National Association of Home Builders, 116
National Association of Real Estate Boards, 20, 116
National Negro Congress, 184
National real estate lobby, 116-18
Negroes: in development of national housing policy, 20-21; and Chicago housing problem, 31-32, 34-35; Taylor's views on, 43; represented by Taylor, 50; vote for Kennelly, 61; politicians, 76-79; press, 78, 215; object of CHA public relations, 85; disliked in conservation areas, 87; their need and demand for housing, 92; their opinion of projects, 95; affected by redevelopment plans, 96; opinion of public housing, 100-102; attitudes toward them, 103-05; opposition to, 113; CHA policy toward, 121-38; oppose projects, 198; not to be displaced, 201; propose criteria for sites, 205; affected by stage development plan, 208, 211; attitude of Jews toward, 218; leaders do not support public housing proposal, 218-19; testify against sites, 233-35; site becoming Negro-occupied, 243; sites opposed by, 243-45
Neighborhood conformity (policy of), 21, 121-22
Nelson, Herbert U., 116
Newspaper wards, 75, 97
New York City, 23, 276, 294-97
North Side, 75, 97

Opinion: trends of, in development of national housing policy, 22, 24, 25; of politicians, 75; of housing projects, 93-94; held by business, 96; by North Side, 97; by slum dwellers, 98-99; by labor unions, 99; by Negroes, 100-02; by conservation areas, 102-05; by improvement associations, 106-14; favoring public housing, 138-50; changes in, 214-17
Opposition (to public housing or to sites), 24, 25, 26, 58, 93-118, 178-79, 182-87, 204, 225-26, 229, 231-35
Owings, Nathaniel, 56, 201

Pacini, Ald. Emil V., 174, 178, 189
Packinghouse Workers Union, 139, 205
Park District, See Chicago Park District
Patronage, 76-77
Pistilli, Ald. A., 201
Plan Commission, See Chicago Plan Commission
Planning Division (of CHA), 52-54,

159-60, 168, 191-92, 211, 239-42, 273, 276,
Policy (racket), 77
Political competence; See Competence
Politicians, 61-88
Power structure, n115
Powers of local authorities, 36
Precinct organization, 68-69, 70, 72
Preliminary Comprehensive Plan, 58
Program reservation, 58
Progressive Party, 181, 184
Public Housing: similarity of political history in Chicago and other cities, 12; significance of site selection issue, 13; development of national policy with respect to, 17-26; legal basis of, 18, 23, 35-36; myths of, 18-19; connection with race relations, 22; opposition to, 24; financing of, 37-38; administration of, 38; need and demand for, 91-92; appearance of projects, 94-95; opposition to, 93-118; support for, 85, 138-50; criticized by Ald. Duffy, 196-98
Public Relations, 83, 84-85, 259
Public Housing Administration; See U.S. Public Housing Administration
Public Housing Association, 138-43, 145, 146, 147, 148-50, 172, 175, 177, 179, 181, 183, 184, 187, 193, 205, 219, 227, 235, 236, 239, 262

Quasi-legislative (powers), 41, 49

Race man, 43
Race prejudice, 103, 112, 114, 217-18; See also Negroes
Race relations, 21-22, 35, 102-04, 141
Racial policy, 121-38, 132-33
Rathje, Frank C., 107
Real Estate Board, See Chicago Real Estate Board
Real estate lobby, See National real estate lobby
Rehabilitation of slums, 154, 271, 282
Relocation projects, 129-30, 148
Rent control, 31, 114
Republican Party, 97
Research, 92, 93, 133, 154, 272, 279-83
Restrictive Covenants, 20, 21, 22, 107
River wards, 74
Robbins, 108
Robinson, William Chester, 230
Robson, Adrian, 181, 227
Role conception, 47n
Rosen, A. Abbot, 180, 217, 227
Rubel, Mrs. Dorothy, 146

Slum Clearance: legal basis of, 18; sentimental importance of, 33-34; Negro views of, 100-02; emphasis on, 162, 164; by stage development, 208-11
Slums: changing character of, 20; location and extent of in Chicago, 30-31; preferences for, 92; functions of, 98
Slum dwellers, 92, 97-98, 247
Slum rehabilitation, 154
Small Builders' Council, 111
Social absenteeism, 74
Social class, 13, 95, 104, 263, 289, 290, 301-02
Social science, 279, 281, 282
South Side, 32, 34, 82, 87, 193, 292
South Side Bloc, 70, 80, 82, 86, 88, 239, 266, 267, 286
South Side Planning Board, 130, 184, 227
Southtown Economist, 107
Southwest Neighborhood Council, 107, 109, 111, 112, 113, 114, 180, 182, 183
Southtown Planning Association, 107, 108
Southtown Realty and Development Corporation, 108
Staff (of CHA): personnel of, 45-46, 84-86; relations with commissioners, 47-48, 259; not apolitical, 148n; leaks to press, 172; under pressure, 277; seeks to determine public interest, 300
Stage demolition, 209-11
State Street Council, 62, 96, 115, 182
Stech, George, 109, 183, 265
Strategy Committee, 139, 176, 177, 181, 226, 228, 229, 248
Sun-Times, See *Chicago Daily Sun-Times*
Support (of public housing or sites), 85, 95, 138-50, 175-77, 180-81, 205-06, 226-28, 230-31, 259
Sykes, Wilfred, 44, 47, 48, 221, 265, 266
Syndicate, See Crime syndicate
Sachs, Arthur, 112, 113, 114, 180-81, 183, 265
Sack, Bernard, 107
Sain, Ald. Harry, 71, 81, 237, 243
San Francisco, 12
Sanitary District, 124, 242

Sears Roebuck Co., 44, 108
Secrecy, 51, 136
Segregation: recent history of, 20-21; in Chicago, 31-32; relation to slum clearance, 34; ignored by Plan Commission, 35, 57; PHA takes no stand on, 40; commissioners' views on, 43-45, 51; Negro views on, 100-01; effect on property values, 106; support of, 113; CHA policy toward, 121-38; reinforced by public housing, 238; issue agitated, 246
Sharp, Rev. Waitstill, 180
Shufro, Milton, 84-86, 142, 228, 257, 263, 266
Sites: described, 167-71; criticized, 183; supported, 184; approved by Council committee, 186; "bus window" selections, 190; compromise proposal, 199-200; stage development of, 208-11; criticized by Planning Division, 214; opposed and supported, 228-36; "white" site dropped, 237; accepted by City Council, 239; changed, 242-43; finally approved, 246; evaluated, 247
Site selection: significance of issue, 12-13; opposition to vacant sites, 25; chronology of events summarized, 26; authority over, 36 ;for veteran housing, 124; for relocation housing, 129-31; racial policy regarding, 133; City Council gets veto over, 136-37; study of sites, 160; memo on, 161-63; criteria for, 164-65; consideration of particular sites, 167-171; by aldermen, 189-91; long range plan for, 192; by "Big Boys," 195-99; standards for, 212-13; function of Planning Division in, 241-42; sole criteria political, 242; national policy created, 246

Talman Federal Savings and Loan Association, 113
Taylor, Robert R., brief biography, 42-43; acts for Board, 47; favors businessman, 86; part in relocation program, 130-31, 135; distrusted, 148; chooses strategy, 149-50, 153; asks Mayor's help, 150; presents sites to Mayor, 171-72; presents sites to Council, 173-75; influenced by hearings, 186; favors new proposal, 192; urged to compromise, 200; uninfluenced by Negro leaders, 205; favors bargain, 216-17; seeks settlement, 220-21; votes for compromise, 221; resigns, 242
Taxpayers Action Committee, 107, 113, 114, 182, 229
Teninga, Cornelius, 113-14, 229
Thompson, Mayor William H., 61
Touhy, John J., 71
Tourek, Ald. G. J., 178
Truman, President Harry, 23, 59, 205, 220

U.S. Public Housing Administration, 26, 27, 33, 38, 40, 94, 154, 166, 174, 175, 206, 243, 246, 269, 275
U.S. Savings and Loan League, 116
Urban League, 100
Urban redevelopment, 19, 20, 27, 55, 101, 133
Utopian thought-style, 262

Vacant land, 25, 32, 33-34, 115, 129, 160, 162, 164, 169, 207
Vaughn, John G., 46, 52, 58, 159, 160, 168, 173
Veterans' housing, 124-29
Vinton, Warren Jay, 206, 207, 208, 220

Wagner, Ald. Clarence, 81, 86, 87, 193, 194, 242
Ward committeemen, 67-68
Weber, Ald. A., 97
West Lawn Women's Club, 182
West Side, 70, 74, 82
White Circle League, 116
Wiebolt's Department Store, 108
Willis, N. M., 205
Wirth, Louis, 180, 243
Wood, Miss Elizabeth: brief biography, 45-46; support of planning, 52, 58, 241; pride in "clean" agency, 83, 87; public relations, 85; influenced by Shufro, 86; opinion of racial quotas, 134; her advisers, 147; unable to employ planners, 153; favors large projects, 155-59; discourages discussion, 160-61; memo on site selection, 161-63; participates in site selection, 168; confers with PHA, 206-08; lists planning functions, 241; defends strategy, 248; difficulty of communication with, 263-64; as planner, 278

FREE PRESS PAPERBACKS

A NEW SERIES OF PAPERBOUND BOOKS
IN THE SOCIAL AND NATURAL SCIENCES, PHILOSOPHY, AND THE HUMANITIES